Philipp Casula and Jeronim Perovic (Eds)
in collaboration with Ivo Mijnssen

IDENTITIES AND POLITICS DURING THE PUTIN PRESIDENCY

The Discursive Foundations of Russia's Stability

With a foreword by Heiko Haumann

ibidem-Verlag
Stuttgart

Bibliografische Information der Deutschen Nationalbibliothek
Die Deutsche Nationalbibliothek verzeichnet diese Publikation in der
Deutschen Nationalbibliografie; detaillierte bibliografische Daten sind im
Internet über http://dnb.d-nb.de abrufbar.

Bibliographic information published by the Deutsche Nationalbibliothek
Die Deutsche Nationalbibliothek lists this publication in the Deutsche Nationalbibliografie;
detailed bibliographic data are available in the Internet at http://dnb.d-nb.de.

Frontcover Picture: Monument "To the Conquerors of Space", Moscow. Photograph by © Philipp Casula 2009.

∞

Gedruckt auf alterungsbeständigem, säurefreien Papier
Printed on acid-free paper

ISSN: 1614-3515

ISBN-10: 3-8382-0015-2
ISBN-13: 978-3-8382-0015-6

© *ibidem*-Verlag
Stuttgart 2009

Alle Rechte vorbehalten

Das Werk einschließlich aller seiner Teile ist urheberrechtlich geschützt. Jede Verwertung
außerhalb der engen Grenzen des Urheberrechtsgesetzes ist ohne Zustimmung des Verlages
unzulässig und strafbar. Dies gilt insbesondere für Vervielfältigungen,
Übersetzungen, Mikroverfilmungen und elektronische Speicherformen sowie die
Einspeicherung und Verarbeitung in elektronischen Systemen.

All rights reserved. No part of this publication may be reproduced, stored in or introduced into a retrieval
system, or transmitted, in any form, or by any means (electronic, mechanical, photocopying, recording or
otherwise) without the prior written permission of the publisher. Any person who does any unauthorized act
in relation to this publication may be liable to criminal prosecution and civil claims for damages.

Printed in Germany

Soviet and Post-Soviet Politics and Society (SPPS)   Vol. 92
ISSN 1614-3515

General Editor: Andreas Umland, *The Catholic University of Eichstaett-Ingolstadt*, umland@stanfordalumni.org

Editorial Assistant: Olena Sivuda, *Dragomanov Pedagogical University of Kyiv*, SLS6255@ku-eichstaett.de

EDITORIAL COMMITTEE*

DOMESTIC & COMPARATIVE POLITICS
Prof. **Ellen Bos**, *Andrássy University of Budapest*
Dr. **Ingmar Bredies**, *University of Regensburg*
Dr. **Andrey Kazantsev**, *MGIMO (U) MID RF, Moscow*
Dr. **Heiko Pleines**, *University of Bremen*
Prof. **Richard Sakwa**, *University of Kent at Canterbury*
Dr. **Sarah Whitmore**, *Oxford Brookes University*
Dr. **Harald Wydra**, *University of Cambridge*
SOCIETY, CLASS & ETHNICITY
Col. **David Glantz**, *"Journal of Slavic Military Studies"*
Dr. **Rashid Kaplanov**, *Russian Academy of Sciences*
Dr. **Marlène Laruelle**, *EHESS, Paris*
Dr. **Stephen Shulman**, *Southern Illinois University*
Prof. **Stefan Troebst**, *University of Leipzig*
POLITICAL ECONOMY & PUBLIC POLICY
Prof. em. **Marshall Goldman**, *Wellesley College, Mass.*
Dr. **Andreas Goldthau**, *Central European University*
Dr. **Robert Kravchuk**, *University of North Carolina*
Dr. **David Lane**, *University of Cambridge*
Dr. **Carol Leonard**, *University of Oxford*

Dr. **Maria Popova**, *McGill University, Montreal*
FOREIGN POLICY & INTERNATIONAL AFFAIRS
Dr. **Peter Duncan**, *University College London*
Dr. **Taras Kuzio**, *Carleton University, Ottawa*
Prof. **Gerhard Mangott**, *University of Innsbruck*
Dr. **Diana Schmidt-Pfister**, *University of Konstanz*
Dr. **Lisbeth Tarlow**, *Harvard University, Cambridge*
Dr. **Christian Wipperfürth**, *N-Ost Network, Berlin*
Dr. **William Zimmerman**, *University of Michigan*
HISTORY, CULTURE & THOUGHT
Dr. **Catherine Andreyev**, *University of Oxford*
Prof. **Mark Bassin**, *University of Birmingham*
Dr. **Alexander Etkind**, *University of Cambridge*
Dr. **Gasan Gusejnov**, *Moscow State University*
Prof. em. **Walter Laqueur**, *Georgetown University*
Prof. **Leonid Luks**, *Catholic University of Eichstaett*
Dr. **Olga Malinova**, *Russian Academy of Sciences*
Dr. **Andrei Rogatchevski**, *University of Glasgow*
Dr. **Mark Tauger**, *West Virginia University*
Dr. **Stefan Wiederkehr**, *German Historical Institute*

ADVISORY BOARD*

Prof. **Dominique Arel**, *University of Ottawa*
Prof. **Jörg Baberowski**, *Humboldt University of Berlin*
Prof. **Margarita Balmaceda**, *Seton Hall University*
Dr. **John Barber**, *University of Cambridge*
Prof. **Timm Beichelt**, *European University Viadrina*
Prof. em. **Archie Brown**, *University of Oxford*
Dr. **Vyacheslav Bryukhovetsky**, *Kyiv-Mohyla Academy*
Prof. **Timothy Colton**, *Harvard University, Cambridge*
Prof. **Paul D'Anieri**, *University of Florida*
Dr. **Heike Dörrenbächer**, *Naumann Foundation Kyiv*
Dr. **John Dunlop**, *Hoover Institution, Stanford, California*
Dr. **Sabine Fischer**, *EU Institute for Security Studies*
Dr. **Geir Flikke**, *NUPI, Oslo*
Dr. **David Galbreath**, *University of Aberdeen*
Prof. **Alexander Galkin**, *Russian Academy of Sciences*
Prof. **Frank Golczewski**, *University of Hamburg*
Dr. **Nikolas Gvosdev**, *Naval War College, Newport, RI*
Prof. **Mark von Hagen**, *Arizona State University*
Dr. **Guido Hausmann**, *University of Freiburg i.Br.*
Prof. **Dale Herspring**, *Kansas State University*
Dr. **Stefani Hoffman**, *Hebrew University of Jerusalem*
Prof. **Mikhail Ilyin**, *MGIMO (U) MID RF, Moscow*
Prof. **Vladimir Kantor**, *Higher School of Economics*
Dr. **Ivan Katchanovski**, *State University of New York*
Prof. em. **Andrzej Korbonski**, *University of California*
Dr. **Iris Kempe**, *Heinrich Boell Foundation Tbilisi*
Prof. **Herbert Küpper**, *Institut für Ostrecht München*
Dr. **Rainer Lindner**, *University of Konstanz*
Dr. **Vladimir Malakhov**, *Russian Academy of Sciences*
Dr. **Luke March**, *University of Edinburgh*

Prof. **Michael McFaul**, *US National Security Council*
Prof. **Birgit Menzel**, *University of Mainz-Germersheim*
Prof. **Valery Mikhailenko**, *The Urals State University*
Prof. **Emil Pain**, *Higher School of Economics, Moscow*
Dr. **Oleg Podvintsev**, *Russian Academy of Sciences*
Prof. **Olga Popova**, *St. Petersburg State University*
Dr. **Alex Pravda**, *University of Oxford*
Dr. **Erik van Ree**, *University of Amsterdam*
Dr. **Joachim Rogall**, *Robert Bosch Foundation Stuttgart*
Prof. **Peter Rutland**, *Wesleyan University, Middletown*
Dr. **Sergei Ryabov**, *Kyiv-Mohyla Academy*
Prof. **Marat Salikov**, *The Urals State Law Academy*
Dr. **Gwendolyn Sasse**, *University of Oxford*
Prof. **Jutta Scherrer**, *EHESS, Paris*
Prof. **Robert Service**, *University of Oxford*
Mr. **James Sherr**, *RIIA Chatham House London*
Dr. **Oxana Shevel**, *Tufts University, Medford*
Prof. **Eberhard Schneider**, *University of Siegen*
Prof. **Olexander Shnyrkov**, *Shevchenko University, Kyiv*
Prof. **Hans-Henning Schröder**, *University of Bremen*
Prof. **Yuri Shapoval**, *Ukrainian Academy of Sciences*
Prof. **Viktor Shnirelman**, *Russian Academy of Sciences*
Dr. **Lisa Sundstrom**, *University of British Columbia*
Dr. **Philip Walters**, *"Religion, State and Society," Oxford*
Prof. **Zenon Wasyliw**, *Ithaca College, New York State*
Dr. **Lucan Way**, *University of Toronto*
Dr. **Markus Wehner**, *"Frankfurter Allgemeine Zeitung"*
Dr. **Andrew Wilson**, *University College London*
Prof. **Jan Zielonka**, *University of Oxford*
Prof. **Andrei Zorin**, *University of Oxford*

* While the Editorial Committee and Advisory Board support the General Editor in the choice and improvement of manuscripts for publication, responsibility for remaining errors and misinterpretations in the series' volumes lies with the books' authors.

Soviet and Post-Soviet Politics and Society (SPPS)
ISSN 1614-3515

Founded in 2004 and refereed since 2007, SPPS makes available affordable English-, German- and Russian-language studies on the history of the countries of the former Soviet bloc from the late Tsarist period to today. It publishes approximately 15 volumes per year, and focuses on issues in transitions to and from democracy such as economic crisis, identity formation, civil society development, and constitutional reform in CEE and the NIS. SPPS also aims to highlight so far understudied themes in East European studies such as right-wing radicalism, religious life, higher education, or human rights protection. The authors and titles of all previously published manuscripts are listed at the end of this book. For a full description of the series and reviews of its books, see www.ibidem-verlag.de/red/spps.

Note for authors (as of 2009): After successful review, fully formatted and carefully edited electronic master copies of up to 250 pages will be published as b/w A5 paperbacks and marketed in Germany (e.g. vlb.de, buchkatalog.de, amazon.de) and internationally (e.g. amazon. com). For longer books, formatting/editorial assistance, different binding, oversize maps, coloured illustrations and other special arrangements, authors' fees between €100 and €1500 apply. Publication of German doctoral dissertations follows a separate procedure. Authors are asked to provide a high-quality electronic picture on the object of their study for the book's front-cover. Younger authors may add a foreword from an established scholar. Monograph authors and collected volume editors receive two free as well as further copies for a reduced authors' price, and will be asked to contribute to marketing their book as well as finding reviewers and review journals for them. These conditions are subject to yearly review, and to be modified, in the future. Further details at www.ibidem-verlag.de/red/spps-authors.

Editorial correspondence & manuscripts should, until 2011, be sent to: Dr. Andreas Umland, ZIMOS, Ostenstr. 27, 85072 Eichstätt, Germany; e-mail: umland@stanfordalumni.org

Business correspondence & review copy requests should be sent to: *ibidem*-Verlag, Julius-Leber-Weg 11, D-30457 Hannover, Germany; tel.: +49(0)511-2622200; fax: +49(0)511-2622201; spps@ibidem-verlag.de.

Book orders & payments should be made via the publisher's electronic book shop at: www.ibidem-verlag.de/red/SPPS_EN/

Authors, reviewers, referees, and editors for (as well as all other persons sympathetic to) SPPS are invited to join its networks at www.facebook.com/group.php?gid=52638198614 and www.linkedin.com/groups?about=&gid=103012

Recent Volumes

83 *Natalya Shevchik Ketenci*
Kazakhstani Enterprises in Transition
The Role of Historical Regional Development in Kazakhstan's Post-Soviet Economic Transformation
ISBN 978-3-89821-831-3

84 *Martin Malek, Anna Schor-Tschudnowskaja (Hrsg.)*
Europa im Tschetschenienkrieg
Zwischen politischer Ohnmacht und Gleichgültigkeit
Mit einem Vorwort von Lipchan Basajewa
ISBN 978-3-89821-676-0

85 *Stefan Meister*
Das postsowjetische Universitätswesen zwischen nationalem und internationalem Wandel
Die Entwicklung der regionalen Hochschule in Russland als Gradmesser der Systemtransformation
Mit einem Vorwort von Joan DeBardeleben
ISBN 978-3-89821-891-7

86 *Konstantin Sheiko in collaboration with Stephen Brown*
Nationalist Imaginings of the Russian Past
Anatolii Fomenko and the Rise of Alternative History in Post-Communist Russia
With a foreword by Donald Ostrowski
ISBN 978-3-89821-915-0

87 *Sabine Jenni*
Wie stark ist das „Einige Russland"?
Zur Parteibindung der Eliten und zum Wahlerfolg der Machtpartei im Dezember 2007
Mit einem Vorwort von Klaus Armingeon
ISBN 978-3-89821-961-7

88 *Thomas Borén*
Meeting-Places of Transformation
Urban Identity, Spatial Representations and Local Politics in Post-Soviet St Petersburg
ISBN 978-3-89821-739-2

89 *Aygul Ashirova*
Stalinismus und Stalin-Kult in Zentralasien
Turkmenistan 1924-1953
Mit einem Vorwort von Leonid Luks
ISBN 978-3-89821-987-7

90 *Leonid Luks*
Freiheit oder imperiale Größe?
Essays zu einem russischen Dilemma
ISBN 978-3-8382-0011-8

91 *Christopher Gilley*
The 'Change of Signposts' in the Ukrainian Emigration
A Contribution to the History of Sovietophilism in the 1920s
With a foreword by Frank Golczewski
ISBN 978-3-89821-965-5

Contents

About the Authors	9
Acknowledgments	15
Foreword by *H. Haumann*	17

Introduction

The Stabilisation of Russia during the Putin Presidency:
Critical Reflections
J. Perovic, P. Casula — 19

I   Discourses in Russian Politics

Populism in Context
D. Howarth — 31

Dislocation in Context
A. Norval, I. Mijnssen — 39

Political and National Identity in Russia: Developments
in Russian Political Thought in the 1990s
P. Casula — 47

II   Regime Type and National Identity

What Kind of Political Regime Does Russia Have?
H.-H. Schröder — 67

The Specific Features and Future of Post-Soviet Transitions
A. Ryabov — 94

Russian Political Discourse in the 1990s: Crisis of
Identity and Conflicting Pluralism of Ideas
O. Malinova — 107

Russian "Sovereign Democracy": A Powerful Ideological
Discourse in a Quasi-Authoritarian Regime
N. Hayoz — 125

Varieties of Post-Communist Nationalisms in Eastern Europe
K. Müller, A. Pickel — 148

Russian Nationalism and Xenophobia
L. Gudkov — 171

III Sovereign Democracy and its Competitors

Sovereign Democracy as a Discourse of Russian Identity
V. Hudson — 189

Sovereignty and Democracy in Contemporary Russia:
A Modern Subject Faces the Post-Modern World
V. Morozov — 211

Ordering Chaos: Russian Neo-Fascist Articulation
Z. Bowden — 248

IV Symbols and the Past

The Symbolic Politics of the Putin Administration
I. Kurilla — 269

An Old Myth for a New Society
I. Mijnssen — 284

Russia in Plural: (Re)Constructing Otherness, (De)Constructing Power
A. Makarychev — 306

Rethinking Identification With the Hegemonic Discourse of a "Strong Russia" Through Laclau and Mouffe
M. Müller — 327

V Outside Perspectives

The View from Elsewhere: Western Mediation of Potential Sources of Russian Dislocation in the 1990s
F. Macgilchrist — 348

"Europe" and "Russia" in Ukraine's Narratives on National Identity: Historical and Cultural Myths
S. Kobzar — 369

Constructing or Deconstructing Democracy? The Geopolitical Context of Ukraine's Democratic Choice
S. Glebov — 390

Index — 404

About the Authors

Zachary Bowden received his PhD in Politics from the University of California, Santa Cruz in June 2007. His dissertation was titled *Tomatoes and T-n-T: Neo-Fascism in Contemporary Russian Politics and Culture*. His research interests are centred around discourse and politics (broadly defined), the intersections of music and politics, and post-Soviet Russian politics, particularly questions of youth, extremism, and social movements. His latest publications include "*Poriadok* and *Bardak* (Order and Chaos): The neo-fascist project of articulating a Russian 'People'" (2008) in the *Journal of Language and Politics*.

Philipp P. Casula is a research fellow and PhD candidate at the University of Basel. After completing his studies in political sociology at the Free University of Berlin, he further specialised in Russian transformation processes and in theories of hegemony and discourse. His PhD research adopts discourse theory to the analysis of how national and political identities changed in Russia after the collapse of the USSR. Among his latest publications are "Interpreting the 'Democratic Revolutions': Culture, Hegemony, Discourse" (published in Stopinska et al.: *Revolutions: reframed, revisited, revised*, 2006) and "Political and National Identity in Russian Political Discourse" (with Olga Malinova, published in Lecours/Moreno: *Nationalism and Democracy*, Routledge 2009).

Sergii V. Glebov is an associate professor at the Department of International Relations and the chief research fellow at the Centre for International Studies, Odessa Mechnikov National University. His research and teaching interests are in the field of foreign and security policy of Ukraine, European and Euro-Atlantic security, international relations in the Black Sea-Caspian region, and Russian foreign policy. He was a visiting scholar at the Centre for European Studies at the University of Exeter in 2000/2001, and at the Harriman Institute at Columbia University in 2003. He has received several fellowships from the HESP/AFP Open Society Institute, the Carnegie Foundation, and the Jean Monnet Program.

He wrote more than 30 scientific articles and chapters that were published in national and international editions.

Lev D. Gudkov was born in Moscow in 1946. He is a sociologist and director of the *Levada Center*, editor-in-chief of the journal *The Russian Public Opinion Herald*, and a professor at the Russian State University of Humanities (RGGU) and at the State University "High School of Economy" (HSE). He is the author of books and articles about the problems of a post-Communist society, the sociology of culture and literature, and the methodology of sociology.

Nicolas Hayoz is an associate professor of political science and the director of the Interdisciplinary Institute of Central and Eastern Europe at the University of Fribourg (Switzerland). Since 2007, he has also served as programme director of the Regional Research Promotion Program (RRPP) on the Western Balkans. In 2009, he started directing a research promotion program in the Southern Caucasus. He has published articles on politics and state reform in Eastern Europe and has conducted research projects in Russia and in Georgia. His research interests include transition studies in Eastern Europe, particularly the transformation process in Russia, and political theory. One of his latest publications is *Tax Evasion, State Capacity and Trust* (together with Simon Hug; Peter Lang, 2007).

David Howarth is a reader in Political Theory in the Department of Government at the University of Essex, where he is co-director of the Centre for Theoretical Studies and director of the Masters Programme in Political Theory. He is the author of *Discourse* (Open University Press, 2000) and *Logics of Critical Explanation in Social and Political Theory* (Routledge, 2007 co-authored with Jason Glynos). He is also the co-editor of *South Africa in Transition* (Macmillan, 1998); *Discourse Theory and Political Analysis* (Manchester University Press, 2000), and *Discourse Theory in European Politics* (Palgrave, 2005). He is currently working on a book entitled *After Poststructuralism* (Palgrave) and *The Politics of Sustainable Aviation* (Manchester University Press).

Victoria Hudson is a doctoral candidate under the CEELBAS programme at the Centre for Russian and East European Studies (CREES) at the University of Birmingham. Her PhD focuses on Russia's exploration of non-coercive means of achieving its foreign policy goals, with particular emphasis on cultural, linguistic, and ideational initiatives in the former Soviet Union and Europe as a way to improve Russia's image and position in those areas. Her research interests lie in the fields of identity, security, foreign policy, and political philosophy.

Svitlana Kobzar is a Gates Scholar at the University of Cambridge. She specialises in the European Neighbourhood Policy, Ukraine's foreign policy, and issues pertaining to national identity. Her doctoral research adopts discourse theory to the analysis of how Ukraine's ruling elite articulated the concept of "Europe" during the presidency of Leonid Kuchma (1994-2004). She has conducted additional research projects with several think-tanks and academic institutions, including the German Council on Foreign Relations, the Institute for International Relations in Prague, the Italian Institute for International Political Studies, and the Harvard Ukrainian Research Institute.

Ivan Kurilla is a professor of History and International Relations, and a department head at Volgograd State University, Russia. His fields of interest include the history of Russian-US relations, especially image construction of the two countries, civil society in Russia, and the use of history in the post-Soviet political space. He is the author of three monographs and the editor of several collections of articles. He has received several research grants and fellowships, including from the Fulbright Program and the Kennan Institute of the Woodrow Wilson International Center for Scholars.

Felicitas Macgilchrist is a research fellow at the Georg Eckert Institute in Braunschweig, Germany. Her doctoral thesis, *Imagining Russia*, investigated the discursive imaginings of Russia and Chechnya in the international news media. Central research interests include discourse theory, (new) media, positive discourse analysis, and issues of representation, especially in relation to Russia, political conflict, and diversity.

Andrey S. Makarychev is the head of the Academic Department at the Civil Service Academy in Nizhny Novgorod, Russia. His teaching courses include Theories of International Relations, International Integration, International Organisation, Regionalism in World Politics, Gender Studies, and Globalisation in Eastern Europe. He specialises in issues of regional identities and security, and participates in a number of research projects with the Centre for European Policy Studies, the Friedrich Ebert Stiftung, the Free University of Berlin, the Danish Institute for International Studies, Odessa National University, and other institutions. Andrey Makarychev is a member of PONARS and the Kennan Institute Alumni Association.

Olga Malinova is a chief research fellow of the Institute of Scientific Information for Social Sciences at the Russian Academy of Sciences and a professor at the Moscow State Institute of International Relations. She is the author of a number of books and articles about political ideologies, political discourse, and the study of identities in post-Soviet Russia. Her most recent Russian-language publication is *Russia and 'the West' in the Twentieth Century: Transformation of the Discourse about Collective Identity* (Rosspen, 2009).

Ivo Mijnssen is a research assistant for the project "Discourses on Democracy and National Identity in Russia", funded by the Swiss National Science Foundation. He received a BA from Brown University and is currently obtaining his MA in Eastern European History and Sociology from the University of Basel. His research focuses on national identity and the role of history in Russian politics, especially the commemoration of the Great Patriotic War. His MA thesis analyses the discourse of the "patriotic" youth organisation "Nashi".

Viatcheslav Morozov is an associate professor at the School of International Relations of St. Petersburg State University, and the head of the academic program on International Relations and Political Science of Smolny College. His research focuses on Russian national identity and foreign policy, poststructuralist IR theory, and discourse analysis. He has worked as a visiting researcher and/or lecturer at the Copenhagen Peace Research Institute, the University of Denver, and the University of Tartu, among others. Apart from a number of articles and book chapters in both Russian and English, he has published the Russian-language monograph *Russia and the Others: Identity and Boundaries of a Political Community* (Novoe literaturnoe obozrenie, 2009).

Klaus Müller is a professor at the Faculty of Humanities at the AGH University of Science & Technology, Cracow, and a lecturer at the Free University of Berlin. He published *Allgemeine Systemtheorie* (1996) and *Globalisierung* (2002), edited *Postkommunistische Krisen* (1998), and co-edited *Postcommunist Transformation and the Social Sciences* (2002).

Martin Müller is an assistant professor in the School of Humanities and Social Sciences at the University of St. Gallen. He read for an M.Phil. in Development Studies at the University of Cambridge and holds a PhD in Human Geography from the University of Frankfurt. His doctoral research combined ethnography and poststructuralist discourse theory to analyse the situated production of Russian geopolitical identity at the Moscow State Institute of International Relations. Papers of his have appeared in *Political Geography, Millennium: Journal of International Studies, Geopolitics,* and *Area*.

Aletta J. Norval is a reader in the University of Essex, Department of Government, where she is also director of the Doctoral Programme in Ideology and Discourse Analysis. She is a co-director of the Centre for Theoretical Studies in the Humanities and the Social Sciences. She has published widely in the field of political theory and discourse analysis, including *Deconstructing Apartheid Discourse* (Verso, 1996). Her most recent book – *Aversive Democracy: Inheritance and Originality in the Democratic Tradition* (Cambridge) – investigates the relation between deliberative and poststructuralist approaches to democracy.

Jeronim Perovic is senior researcher at the Institute of History at the University of Basel and a visiting scholar at the Center for Security Studies at ETH Zurich. He studied History, Political Science, and Russian Literature at the University in Zurich, where he received his PhD in 2000. He worked as a senior researcher at the Center for Security Studies, ETH Zurich. He is the author of, inter alia, *Die Regionen Russlands als neue politische Kraft* [Russia's Regions as a New Political Force] (Peter Lang, 2001) and co-editor of *Energy and the Transformation of International Relations* (Oxford University Press, 2009), *Russian Energy*

Power (Routledge, 2009), and *Russian Business Power* (Routledge, 2006, 2nd ed. paperback 2009).

Andreas Pickel is a professor in the Faculty of Social Sciences at Trent University, CA. He is the author of *Radical Transitions* (1992) and *The Grand Experiment* (1997, co-authored with Helmut Wiesenthal). He is the editor of *Postcommunist Transformation and the Social Sciences* (2002, co-edited with Frank Boenker and Klaus Mueller) and *Economic Nationalism in a Globalizing World* (2005, co-edited with Eric Helleiner).

Andrey Ryabov is scholar-in-residence at the Carnegie Moscow Center and the editor-in-chief of the academic journal *World Economy and International Relations*. His scientific and analytical interests include such issues as the evolution of the Russian political system in the post-Communist era, political ideology in contemporary Russia, and political institutions in the transitional period. For the last five years, he has conducted comparative research on political transformations in post-Soviet states, Russian foreign policy, and international relations in the CIS. He also works as an expert on current political processes for the Gorbachev Foundation.

Hans-Henning Schröder is the head of the Russia/CIS Division at the German Institute for International and Security Affairs and a professor for East European History at the University of Bremen. He was an assistant professor for East European history at the Ruhr Universität Bochum (1981 to 1986) and a senior analyst at the Bundesinstitut für osteuropäische und internationale Studien, Cologne (1986 to 2000). His main fields of research are the role of elites in the Russian transition process after 1991 and Soviet/Russian defence and security policy. He is a board member of the "Deutsche Gesellschaft für Osteuropakunde" and of the "Bertelsmann Transformation Index" (BTI), and editor of *Russlandanalysen*.

Acknowledgments

The research for this book was originally undertaken for a workshop entitled "New Stability, Democracy and Nationalism in Contemporary Russia", which took place on 26–27 September 2008 at the University of Basel, Institute of Sociology. It was co-hosted by the Chair of Eastern European History of the University of Basel and sponsored by the Swiss National Science Foundation and the Freiwillige Akademische Gesellschaft (FAG) Basel. After the event, the editors focused on the conceptualisation of a book and selected the most appropriate papers from the contributions prepared for the workshop. The editors would particularly like to thank the FAG Basel for financially supporting the publication of this volume. We are also indebted to Urs Stäheli, Heiko Haumann, Andreas Umland, and all the workshop participants. Finally, we would like to express our gratitude to Christopher Findlay, Kerstin Pietzonka Findlay, and Valerie Lange for their editorial help. Despite the support of colleagues, the editors remain solely responsible for any errors in the text.

Philipp Casula, Jeronim Perovic
Basel, Switzerland

Foreword

As scholars of Russian history and politics, we are following developments in Russia with great interest. In the Western media, reports on this country often focus on human rights abuses, social inequality, rising nationalism, and tendencies toward more authoritarian power structures. Historians observe that access to archives is being limited again. Debates within Russia on Stalinism have become less frequent. A more assertive state limits the scope and the activity of civil society. "Sovereign Democracy" is criticised as a mere "veil" that covers up the above-mentioned tendencies.

Are these assessments correct? Or do they reflect a stereotypical way of thinking that applies Western models of democracy to Russia, without recognising that the country is attempting to develop its own political path? Is this the continuation of a tradition of Western arrogance that is biased by ideas of a backward, barbaric "East" incapable of developing democracy and dependent on authoritarian rule?

In September of 2008, a workshop in Basel looked at these issues from a very specific perspective. Philipp Casula designed the workshop as part of his doctoral project. It was organised by Basel's Institute of Sociology in collaboration with the Chair of East European and Contemporary History. Its goal was to merge theoretical approaches – namely discourse theory – with an empirical analysis of Russian politics. The thought-provoking presentations and discussions showed that this combination is a promising approach towards an analysis of contemporary Russia. Occasionally, the subject gave rise to controversial discussions; at times, one got a sense that some theoreticians were reluctant to become involved in empirical research. Conversely, some political scientists and historians seemed sceptical as to which tangible benefits theory had to offer.

Philipp Casula and Jeronim Perovic decided to publish contributions to the workshop, along with essays that could not be presented there. The aim of this collection is to document the current level of discussion and stimulate further development of theory-informed discussion, thus establishing a new foundation for the analysis of events in Russia. The volume provides us with fascinating insights into contemporary Russia: We catch a glimpse of discourses there and of the struggles for hegemony; we can follow conflicts over national identities, symbols, and political myths. Last but not least, the essays presented here can serve as valuable contributions to our "analytical toolbox": Discourse theory is a promising method for the analysis of political systems.

The editors deserve thanks for this stimulating collection of essays. I hope that it will meet with favourable reception.

Heiko Haumann
Basel, Switzerland

Introduction

The Stabilisation of Russia During the Putin Presidency: Critical Reflections

Jeronim Perovic and Philipp P. Casula

The advent of Vladimir Putin to power in 2000 marked the start of the stabilisation of Russia's political system and economic recovery. Already during his first term in office, Putin set out to re-establish what he referred to as the "power vertical". As a result of the Kremlin's re-centralisation attempts, opposition parties, the free media, or regional governors were increasingly brought under control of the centre. At the same time, the state managed to recapture strategic sectors of the economy and tamed Russia's powerful oligarchs. Backed by strong economic growth and a massive inflow of petro-dollars, Russia also demonstrated a new assertiveness in international affairs.

Under Putin, Russia moved further away from Western conceptions of democracy, stressing the country's "special" path with regard to domestic trajectories and its international orientation. In the economic sphere, the principles of the liberal market were still upheld, yet the state re-established itself as its main regulator, arbiter, or owner – especially in strategically important sectors.

The question this book addresses is not so much why Russia during the Putin era did not follow the trajectory initially expected, but to understand the *kind of stability* that was established during these years. In essence, rather than attempting to understand to what extent exactly Russia has approached the Western type of liberal democracy, we aim to attain a deeper understanding of the essence of stability that emerged during Putin's time in the presidential office. Proceeding from the assumption that the stability under Putin can only be fully appreciated if the Russian discourses on political and national identity are taken into account, we will analyse the trajectories during the past years mainly, but not exclusively, through the lens of discourse theory.

This introductory chapter provides a brief overview on some of the key notions and theoretical approaches that figure prominently throughout the book. We will first present a short description of Russia's trajectory from the time of Boris Yeltsin and assess the stabilisation achievements during Putin. In a second section, we will discuss the Russian democracy debate and establish the link to the issue of identity and the Russian state's role in identity construction. In the third section, we give a brief introduction into discourse theory, especially drawing on the works of Laclau and Mouffe; we will also frame key theoretical questions that we deduct from this theory. Finally, we provide an overview of the book by explaining the different parts and the individual chapters.

Russia's triple transformation

In Russia, stability has long been a central demand in both official and public discourse. "Stability" is, however, a relational term, as it refers to a previous situation that is not considered stable. In Russia's case, the point of reference lies in the 1990s, which are widely perceived as a time of chaos. During this time, Russia underwent a triple transformation. In the economic sphere, the therapy of privatisation was meant to heal the ailing Soviet economy, but was badly planned and poorly executed, bringing hardship to millions of people – while only a few managed to enrich themselves.

In the political realm, democratisation did not lead to a system of checks and balances between the different political players, but was fought as a diehard "winner-takes-all" struggle. Russia was poorly ruled during a time when all of the central government's energy was absorbed by the fight over political control and dominance – in the Duma, among the Russian governors, or among the powerful oligarchs. Russia's attempts at democratisation amounted in essence to the emergence of a polycentric system where various political and economic actors competed with each other. If hopeful Western observers saw this polycentrism as the starting basis for Russia's nascent democracy, the mass of the Russian people perceived it as a system producing disorder, a rise in crime, corruption, poverty, and insecurity. It is little wonder that most Russians showed a total lack of trust in the state institutions that emerged under Yeltsin.

Finally, the 1990s were also accompanied by a deep crisis of political identity as the regime officially rejected the former Communist ideology. Communism was brought down as the hegemonic ideological narrative, but was replaced only by a vague pledge to "democracy" that was founded on anti-

THE STABILISATION OF RUSSIA 21

Communism. The official rejection of established ideological norms was also reflected in the search for a new Russian "national idea". The confused discussions surrounding this notion mirrored Russia's ideological void and disorientation during the 1990s.

Against this background, the time seemed ripe for a change at the top of political power. Putin, the man whom Yeltsin installed as his successor, was a largely unknown figure. This, however, was precisely what made it possible for the public to ascribe all those qualities to him that they found lacking in his predecessor. Putin did not come up with a new comprehensive programme of his own and did not attempt to reverse the essentials of Yeltsin's economic reforms. It did not even seem to matter that he was an appointee of Yeltsin; the public accepted him largely because he was not associated with Russia's troubled 1990s.

In the eyes of the public, Putin passed his first test as prime minister when he demonstrated his resolution to fight off the Chechen incursion of Dagestan in August 1999. In October of that same year, he ordered Russia's federal troops to invade Chechnya for a second time. This invasion followed a series of bombings of apartments in Moscow, Buinaksk, and Volgodonsk, all of which Russia blamed on "Chechen terrorists". While the first Chechen war had not won the approval of the Russian population, the second invasion war was highly popular. Against the background of terrorism hysteria, Putin's actions were highly acclaimed, as many seemed to believe that Russia was finally succeeding in bringing order to this troubled part of the country. Moreover, many within Russia's political and military establishment supported the invasion, as they sought to undo the perceived humiliating defeat that Russian federal troops had suffered when leaving Chechnya after the end of the first war in 1996.

Nevertheless, it is highly unlikely that Putin or any other new president would have survived long had it not been for important structural changes that helped Russia back on her feet. Putin's rise to power coincided with the start of unprecedented growth of Russia's economy at rates of, on average, six percent during 2000-08. Economic growth was possibly due to the after-effects of the August 1998 financial crisis and the increase in oil prices after 2000, which brought a massive inflow of petro-dollars filling the state coffers. Signs of recovery had already appeared in the late Yeltsin years, yet they were felt only later, and economic success was thus never attributed to Yeltsin, but to Putin only.

The combination of structural changes in terms of economic growth accompanied by a more assertive political course to re-centralise state power were necessary factors that helped to create the stability of what in the West was sometimes referred to as the "Putin system": A highly centralised organisation of power based on a combination of rent distribution to various elite factions, the curtailing of political liberties, and the extension of state control over the economy.

During Putin's presidential terms, the discussions on Russia's identity also calmed down. To be sure, the process of Russia's search of a post-Communist identity has not come to any definitive conclusion, if only because the formation of any political identity (or rather identities) can never be fixed. It is an ongoing process subjected to constant social construction and reconstruction. However, unlike during the early 1990s, the discourse on Russian political identity seems to have at least temporarily consolidated around a narrative that stresses not anti-Communism, as during Yeltsin's time, but Russia's "uniqueness" and "special way".

Already towards the end of Putin's first term in office, it had thus become increasingly clear that Russia's triple transformation would not follow the path that Western observers of Russia expected or hoped for.

The discourse on democracy and identity, and the role of the state

Transformation theory – at least in its more traditional version – suggests that a situation of stability is reached once the "endpoint" of the transformation (free market and democracy) is achieved. Thus, many observers of Russia would hesitate to call Russia (or any authoritarian ruled states) "stable" as long as this stability is seen as being largely held together by a system of rent distribution – backed largely by the inflow of oil money – and authoritarian governance.

Nevertheless, the analytical shortcomings of attempting to measure stability through Western standards of democracy are precisely that this is an *outside* perspective that does not consider the *inside* (Russian) view. Thus, in order to complement our (Western) understanding of Russia's domestic trajectories, it is necessary to comprehend this transformation *sui generis* and look at the essentials of what we have referred to as the stabilisation process under Putin. These essentials can only be fully grasped if analysed against the background of how Russians – and in particular Russia's political elite – viewed this process, or in other words, how stability was framed at the level of political and official *discourses*.

The kind of stability created under Putin is connected to a certain type of political identity. To be sure, Russians are by no means ignorant of the key features of a functioning Western-style democracy such as freedom of speech or the right to free and fair elections, as opinion polls have shown (see McFaul and Colton 2001). Polls also show, though, that for many Russians, "democracy" also means order, justice, equity, and a certain level of prosperity. A majority of Russians were especially appreciative of the personal freedoms they gained after the dramatic changes of 1991, yet they rejected "democracy" as it manifested itself in the political, economic, and social spheres.

Also, official Russia never rejected democracy as such; on the contrary, the Putin regime embraced it as an essential part of Russia's political identity. Nevertheless, Putin's rise to power coincided with a reading of Russian identity that abandoned formerly Western-oriented narratives and focused on a "special way" for Russia of dealing with modern political and socioeconomic challenges. As Putin put it in his state of the union address on 25 April 2005:

> "The democratic road we have chosen is independent in nature, a road along which we move ahead, all the while taking into account our own specific internal circumstances" (Putin 2005).

At the same tame, the regime's understanding of democracy needs to be contextualised through the notion of Russia as a *strong power,* which has figured prominently in political rhetoric. In his 2003 address to the nation, for example, Putin declared that "Russia must become and will become a country with a flourishing civil society and stable democracy." Later in his speech he stated that: "A strong and responsible government based on the consolidation of society is vital to preserve the country. Without strong power, it will also be impossible to move forward into the future" (Putin 2003).

The idea of a strong state and of Russia as a strong power certainly appealed to many Russians in the face of the disorder and chaos of the 1990s. Then again, these and other official statements also implied that the values of "democracy" and "strength" needed to be combined in order for the state to be able to "guide" society in the right direction. Thus, from a Western point of view, Putin's statement could be interpreted as an indirect way to justify the empowering of the state at the expense of societal and political liberties. Conceptually, this idea was elaborated further and formed the basis of ideological constructions such as the one developed by presidential aide Vladislav Surkov, who in 2005 introduced the notion of Russia as a "sovereign democracy" (Surkov 2007).

Even though the contents of Russia's version of democracy remain vague in Surkov's notion, the kind of language applied here seemed sufficient to strike a positive chord with Russia's *class politique*, which saw this as an expression of Russia's right to follow its "sovereign" path to democracy in opposition to Western-prescribed directions. The kind of official rhetoric around democracy must also have resonated well with parts of the population. At least from opinion polls, we learn that a majority of Russians was clearly in favour of Russia following an "own path of development", which also coincided with high popularity rates for Putin throughout his presidency (Levada Center 2007).

If the 1990s can be aptly summarised as a period when various non-state actors captured the state, the years following Putin's ascendancy to the presidency saw the re-emergence of the state as the main player in Russian domestic political and economic life. To be sure, the state under Putin was never a unified actor and never able to control all the discursive realms. However, if we attempt to analyse how a certain discourse became the dominant or *hegemonic* discourse, it is essential that we take into account the role of the state in Russia's stabilisation process.

With the state at the centre of social development, stability in Russia was very much subjected to "what the State makes of it" (paraphrasing Wendt 1992). In constructing "stability", the state drew on and eventually transformed already existing discourses, with a concrete political purpose in mind. For example, the decision of Putin to abandon the right of the Russian population to elect its own governors – which was an important element in the government's re-centralisation attempt – was enacted after the Beslan tragedy in 2004 and portrayed as a means of fighting terrorism more effectively. While transformation theory would tend to see a loss of democracy in this action, a more constructivist approach would stress the aspect of inscribing political action in the discourse of anti-terrorism and frame it as Putin's attempt to "securitise" a political decision (Buzan et al. 1998) for the sake of stability.

Introducing a poststructuralist approach

Unlike other books on Russia's stabilisation process under Putin, this work considers Russia's developments mainly (but not exclusively) against the background of poststructuralist discourse theoretical approaches. Discourse theory and analysis, here, are meant to complement, not to replace, transformation theory. Especially helpful in this regard are Laclau and Mouffe's works (Laclau and Mouffe 2001; Laclau 2005), which propose a theory of discourse and hegemony that allows us to grasp the processes of transformation (the guiding theoretical lens of most of the literature on post-Soviet Russia) and to understand the kind of stability created during this process.

If we shift the focus of research to political and national identities, at least three questions deducted from poststructuralist theories need to be addressed: How do these collective identities emerge? How do they change? How do they achieve stability?

How do identities emerge? Identities are seen as being bound to discourses. Different discourses[1] offer different ways of fixing or articulating identities and thus compete with each other to integrate them. Each discourse offers specific subject positions to identify with. The aspects of competition and negotiation make the construction of identities a deeply political process.

How do identities change? This competition of discourses for creating meaning and significance makes all stability in society and all stability of identity precarious. Identity change is thus the result of a shift in the prevalence of a certain discourse, the floating of signifiers between discourses. On a larger scale, identity change can mean the success of a counter-hegemonic discourse to disarticulate hegemonic discourses, to disorganise a certain consensus, and to create an alternative one.

How do they achieve stability? The prevalence of a discourse, its hegemony, is the point at which it becomes the leading ideological horizon in society. It successfully incorporates different discursive elements, establishes an empty signifier, which represents the whole discourse, and excludes certain other elements by drawing a clear line of separation, dividing the social into two camps, and thus constituting an "outside" and an "inside". This shows that while threatening each other, hegemonic and counter-hegemonic discourses need each other to define themselves: They depend on each other to make clear what they

---

1   A discourse is defined as "a differential ensemble of signifying sequences in which meaning is constantly renegotiated" (Torfing 1999: 85).

do not represent (constitutive outside), keeping a demarcation line that provides stability. Identities are therefore always relational:[2] They embrace what they oppose.[3]

These three questions make the basic theoretical assumption of this discourse theory clear: collective (and personal) identities are never completely stable or fixed. They are subject to change, negotiation, and reshaping. With this strong focus on identity formation, dissolution, and fixation, we believe that Laclau and Mouffe's approach leaves us well equipped to analyse Russian identity formation – and also get a better sense of what we have referred to as the essence of Russia's stability.

In our attempt to deal with issues of political construction and identity politics, this book places itself in a wider theoretical tradition. International Relations studies have been more inclined than transformation theories to translate the *Cultural Turn* into their theories, adopting constructivist (Wendt 1992; Campbell 1992; Katzenstein 1996) and sometimes poststructuralist perspectives (Connolly 1991; Edkins 1999; Hansen 2006). At least since the 1990s, a rapprochement between rationalists and reflectivists has emerged, with "[m]ore philosophical issues [being] increasingly welcome in the mainstream" (Wæver 1997: 168).

The poststructuralists' basic claim is that it is not possible to step outside the world and observe it impartially. However, this does not mean that there is no world "out there". Instead, what we can observe are networks of (verbal and non-verbal) interactions (i.e., discourses) that construct different realities around one and the same "objective" issue. Similarly, identities are seen as constructs, and International Relations theory has been quick to recognise their importance for the formation of international relations (Connolly 1991; Kassianova 2001; Tsygankov 2006; cf. also Knutsen 1996: 278f.). Hence, introducing poststructuralist and constructivist elements into transformation theory also means releasing it from the grip of a normative and largely Western-centred transitology.

---

2 As Connolly (1991: 64) succinctly puts it: "Identity requires difference in order to be, and it converts difference into otherness in order to secure its own self-certainty. Identity is thus a slippery, insecure experience, dependent on its ability to define difference and vulnerable to the tendency of entities it would so define to counter, resist, overturn, or subvert definitions applied to them." It is precisely the task of hegemonic discourses to offer opportunities for fixing identities and clearly defining otherness.

3 "A hegemonic formation also embraces what opposes it, insofar as the opposing force accepts the system of basic articulations of the formation as something it negates, but the place of the negation is defined by the internal parameters of the formation itself" (Laclau and Mouffe 2001: 139).

THE STABILISATION OF RUSSIA 27

Organisation of this book
This volume is structured into five parts. In the first part, titled "Discourses and Russian Politics", the book will introduce some key theoretical terms of discourse theory that seem especially useful when analysing the Russian case. The first chapter in this part is devoted to *populism*. David Howarth analyses how this notion, although not often used by authors, implicitly describes the basic operation of the political. The primary way in which populism establishes a discursive hegemony is by incorporating as many demands as possible into a discourse that it counterposes against a constitutive outside. *Aletta Norval and Ivo Mijnssen* describe the meaning of *dislocation*. The term is essential for understanding how Soviet discourse was increasingly incapable of incorporating the massive changes that were underway in the late 1980s. It was unable to explain economic decline and failed to articulate rising democratic demands. The signifier "Perestroika" was an attempt to provide a new vision for progress and democratic participation within the Soviet discourse. The "democratic" official discourse started with very similar promises. Here again, the economic and political decline represented *dislocations* that made it impossible to uphold "democracy" as a key signifier in official discourse. In a third chapter, *Philipp Casula* then describes the processes of discursive shifts in more detail against the background of these terms, elaborating how different discourses articulated national and political identity in post-Soviet Russia.

The second part of the book deals with "Regime Type and National Identity". "Managed democracy", "sovereign democracy", and similar terms have been used to describe the Russian regime. The chapters in this part investigate what these terms actually mean for Russia's everyday practice. More specifically, this part of the book tries to link this aspect, which is *prima facie* merely a political one, to the aspect of national identity that it conveys. The guiding idea is that any political vision for Russia entails a specific imagination of national identity. Thus, this part includes analyses of the political regime that emerged in post-Soviet Russia (*Hans-Henning Schröder* focuses, *inter alia*, on the importance of trust, while *Andrey Ryabov* examines the type of transition), on the articulations in official discourse (*Olga Malinova*), on the ideology of the Putin regime (*Nicolas Hayoz*), as well as on nationalism (*Klaus Müller* and *Andreas Pickel*) and xenophobia (*Lev Gudkov*).

In the third part, the authors of the book will take a closer look at "Sovereign Democracy and its Competitors". Sovereign democracy as a concept arose in 2005 and was extremely prominent within the elites' discourse. However, it was more of a description of past policies than a vision for future political action. After the electoral cycle of 2007/08, the importance of the term was diminished, although policies remained unchanged. The authors recognise the importance of the term as an attempt to construct something resembling an ideology at least at the level of the ruling elites ("sovereign democracy" as an ideology of *Edinaia Rossiia* and *Nashi*, for instance). *Victoria Hudson* discusses the connection between the term "sovereign democracy" and the messages it conveys about political and national identity, while *Viatcheslav Morozov* frames it in an international context. *Zachary Bowden*, on the other hand, explores the resistance to this discursive mainstream. "Fascism" traditionally played the role of the *constitutive other* in Russian discourse. Hence, he focuses on Russian neo-Fascism as an attempt to disrupt official discourse.

The fourth part, "Symbols and the Past", deals with specific symbols and signifiers that are important in Russian public and official discourse. Putin's Russia was full of symbolic politics. In the first chapter of this part, *Ivan Kurilla* analyses how the successes of the two presidential terms were linked to a fortuitous combination of economic growth and a skilled use of Russia's symbolic universe. The author shows this by drawing on the case of Volgograd. Under Putin, 9 May and the victory over Fascism in general became a particularly strong symbol: *Ivo Mijnssen* discusses 9 May as an example of a "myth" and demonstrates how this myth of the Great Patriotic War became a nodal point within the official Russian "statist" discourse. *Andrey Makarychev* shows how culture and politics intersect by analysing a wide array of fiction and movies. He demonstrates how such representations add to a variety of political articulations that are deemed to be the basis for identity construction in today's Russia. *Martin Müller* underscores the importance of a "strong Russia" combining ethnographic and poststructuralist approaches at a major Russian university.

In the fifth part, the book offers room for "Outside Perspectives". *Felicitas Macgilchrist* traces Western mediation of potential sources of Russian dislocation and argues that Western media exhibited a lacuna in their reporting on Russia in the 1990s. Many key signifiers of the 2000s had already been articulated in the 1990s, but this went unnoticed in Western media coverage. *Svitlana Kobzar* deals with the role of intellectuals and government officials in trying to fix the meaning of the Soviet past shared by Ukraine and Russia, and with the consequences resulting from the divergent historical narratives. The final chapter in this part is *Sergii Glebov's* analysis of Ukraine's democratisation as a choice between the West and Russia as two poles competing for geopolitical influence.

Bibliography

Buzan, B., O. Wæver, and J. de Wilde. 1998. *Security: A New Framework for Analysis*. Boulder: Lynne Rienner.

Campbell, D. 1992. *Writing Security: United States Foreign Policy and the Politics of Identity*. Manchester: Manchester University Press.

Edkins, J. 1999. *Poststructuralism & International Relations: Bringing the Political Back in*. Boulder: Lynne Rienner.

Hansen, L. 2006. *Security as Practice*. London: Routledge.

Kassianova, A. 2001. "Russia: Still Open to the West? Evolution of the State Identity in the Foreign Policy and Security Discourse". *Europe-Asia-Studies* 53, 6. 821-839.

Katzenstein, P.J. 1996. *The Culture of National Security: Norms and Identity in World Politics*. New York: Columbia University Press.

Knutsen, T.L. 1996. *A History of International Relations Theory*. Manchester: Manchester University Press.

Laclau, E. 2005. *On Populist Reason*. London & New York: Verso.

Laclau, E. and C. Mouffe. 2001 [1985]. *Hegemony and Socialist Strategy: Towards a Radical Democratic Politics*. London & New York: Verso.

Levada Center. 2007. "Rossiia i mir". http://www.levada.ru/press/2007 081001.html [accessed 30 August 2009].

McFaul, M. and T. Colton. 2001. "Are Russians Undemocratic?". *Working Papers of the Carnegie Endowment for International Peace*, No. 20. Washington, D.C.: Carnegie Endowment for International Peace http://www.carnegieendowment.org/files/20ColtonMcFaul.pdf [accessed 1 September 2009].

Putin, V. 2003. "Annual Address to the Federal Assembly of the Russian Federation". Moscow. 16 May. http://www.kremlin.ru/eng/speeches/2003/05/16/0000_type70029type82912_44692.shtml [accessed 1 September 2009].

―――― 2005. "Annual Address to the Federal Assembly of the Russian Federation". Moscow. 25 April. http://www.kremlin.ru/eng/speeches/2005/04/25/2031_type70029type82912_87086.shtml [accessed 1 September 2009].

Surkov, V. 2007 (2006). "Suverenitet – eto politicheskii sinonim konkurentnosposobnosti". In *PRO Suverennuiu demokratiiu*, edited by L.V. Poliakov, 33-61. Moskva: Evropa.

Tsygankov, A.P. 2006. *Russia's Foreign Policy: Change and continuity in national identity*. Lanham: Rowman & Littlefield Publishers.

Wæver, O. 1997. "The rise and fall of the inter-paradigm debate". In *International Theory: Positivism and Beyond*, edited by S. Smith, K. Booth, and M. Zalewski, 149-185. Cambridge: Cambridge University Press.

Wendt, A. 1992. "Anarchy is what States Make of it: The Social Construction of Power Politics". *International Organization* 46, 2. 391-425.

I Discourses in Russian Politics

Populism in Context

David Howarth

In the years since the breakdown of the USSR, Russia has undergone dramatic political changes. While the 1990s were marked by institutional, political, and economic upheavals, the years of Putin's presidencies seem to be associated with a higher degree of political stability and economic growth. Many argue, however, that this stabilisation has come at the expense of democratic freedoms. Poststructuralist discourse theory seems in many way destined to help to grasp this development. Ernesto Laclau's concept of populism seems particularly suitable to describe the abovementioned movement toward consolidation of the political spectrum and overall stabilisation.

Populist reason or populist peril?

We often speak of a populist stance, gesture, action, or movement when it is seen to appeal to the interests of the ordinary people, or is perceived to be popular by a large majority of a country's population. A politician's populist gesture – a call to "crack down on welfare scroungers", for example, or a policy designed to "get tough on criminals" – is frequently taken as a pejorative description of a politician's speech or decision, which allegedly appeals to the baser instincts of the mass of a country's *populus*. However, even a cursory acquaintance with everyday discourses makes it clear that the term *populism* can be used to describe a wide and diffuse range of locutions, actions, and groups.

Theoretical misnomers

The academic discourse on populism displays a similarly chaotic and confusing mixture of theories and usages.[1] Consider, for instance, Gerry Stoker's recent critique of populism in *Why Politics Matters*. He begins by admitting that populism is a "fragile ideology built on the axis of 'us' against 'them'", which can take a variety of diverse positions and political platforms, and he goes on to enumerate a diverse set of movements, parties, and ideologies that can encompass both right-wing and left-wing positions (Stoker 2006: 135ff.). Nevertheless, he is confident that he can stipulate clear criteria with which to identify populist politics: Populism taps into a "sense of resentment" about "normal politics" by mobilising "outsiders" who have previously "not been engaged in the political process"; populists articulate a "simple direct" rhetoric that seeks to divide "the people" from "the establishment", though in practice distinctions are usually drawn between "the people" and a series of "others", be they racial, national, or class enemies (Stoker 2006: 136ff.). Stoker is also confident in making definitive evaluative pronouncements about its character: Populism is an essentially "*reactive* form of politics" that is "often aggressive, antagonistic and intolerant"; it is "the *politics of anti-politics*", which is "illiberal" and exhibits a tendency to "demonize its opponents"; it constitutes, in short, an "uneasy element in democratic politics" (Stoker 2006: 139, 144).

It is, of course, possible to employ the notion of populism simply to denote the kinds of politics that one opposes or is suspicious of: Nazism, Chavezism in Venezuela, the *Front National* in France, Luiz Inácio Lula da Silva's Brazilian Worker's Party, the Freedom Party in Austria; in fact, all those forces and movements that do not play by the existing rules of the political game – what Stoker calls "mainstream politics" – and thus challenge the status quo (Stoker 2006: 137). However, the critical question is *how* precisely one distinguishes these phenomena from other movements and political forms that, even though one might find them more morally and politically congenial, are structurally similar: "United Russia" in Russia, the United Democratic Front (UDF) in South Af-

---

[1] The literature on populism is, of course, vast and growing. It would be impossible to provide a survey of its various currents here. Stoker's work is analyzed here because it exemplifies some of the prejudices about populism in the existing academic literature, and it highlights some of the latter's difficulties in providing an appropriate theoretical language for dealing with populist movements and ideologies. For an interesting critique of the literature that is broadly in keeping with my arguments here, see Laclau 2005b: 3-20. For overviews, see Canovan (1981) and Taggart (2000).

rica, Solidarity in Poland, Néstor Kirchner's Justicialist Party in Argentina, Jesse Jackson's "Rainbow Coalition", Chartism in 19th-century Britain, Václav Havel's Civic Forum, the Movement for Democratic Change in Zimbabwe – the list could go on and on. The crucial theoretical point in this regard is that it is unclear what Stoker means by the concept of "populism".[2] In short, while there is much theoretical confusion about the concept of populism, as well as a good deal of slippage between ethnographic and theoretical usages of the term, it is important not to confuse our commonsensical views and prejudices about certain political practices and forms with a theory of populism.

The logic of populist reason

By contrast, Laclau seeks to construct a theory of populism that focuses on the construction of equivalential linkages between dispersed social and political demands, in which the latter requires the production of specific means of representation – what Laclau calls *floating* and *empty signifiers* – that can serve as points of subjective identification (Laclau and Mouffe 1985; Laclau 2005a). For example, the figure or signifier of "president Putin" (Prozorov 2005: 121) served the function of holding together a diverse set of social demands – demands for political stability, economic welfare, and an efficient state domestically and in international relations – that were put forward by a number of different social actors in various social sites.

In this conception, then, populism is not a specific ideological *content* – for instance, a set of rhetorical appeals to "stop illegal immigration" or "withdraw from the EU" – or a certain *type* of movement, political party, or leader who is against the system, for example.[3] Instead, it speaks directly to the political *dimension* of social relations. That is, if the political refers to the contestation and institution of various social relations, then the logic of populism captures the practices through which society is divided into opposed camps in the endless struggle for hegemony (Laclau and Mouffe 1985; Glynos and Howarth 2007). A populist politics thus involves the construction of a collective agency or project –

---

2   In fact, the only theoretical discussion in Stoker's book consists of a somewhat bizarre detour on William Riker, where he actually argues against Riker's sceptical claims about populist democracy (in which the latter draws upon Arrow's "impossibility theorem"), and ultimately in favour of the idea that populist ambitions are possible and achievable, if not desirable (Stoker 2006: 140ff.).

3   This is not to argue that rhetoric is not an important element of populist discourse; on the contrary, rhetoric is constitutive of all political practice.

e.g., "the people" – through the drawing of a political boundary between a *we* and a *they* within a social formation; and the latter presupposes a set of antagonisms and the availability of indeterminate ideological elements (or floating signifiers) that can be articulated into a particular ideological formation.

Thus, simplifying Laclau's more formal and structural logic of populism consists of five basic features. First, the articulators of a populist discourse appeal to a collective subject such as "the people" or "the community" as the privileged subject of interpellation. They seek to construct and naturalise a certain meaning of "the people" or its functional equivalent, using such appeals to forge political identities and thus recruit differently positioned subjects. Secondly, the articulation of populist discourse involves the drawing of political dividing lines, which, if successful, pit "the people" against a defined enemy or adversary, whether the latter take the form of a power elite, the government, or vested interests. Thirdly, the establishment of this political boundary, which divides the people from its *other*, is grounded on the creation of equivalential relations between particular social demands, which are linked together in a more universalistic, populist discourse. This presupposes that demands are internally split between their particular content – the particular thing that is demanded (such as "higher wages" or "better hospitals") – and the fact that a particular demand also expresses a more universal opposition to the system as a whole. Thus, populist discourses invariably speak in the name of "the people", "the nation", or "the community", and their rhetoric seeks to galvanise a common set of values, beliefs, and symbols that can advance the interests of such collective subjects. The identity of the demands that constitute a populist movement thus depends upon the hegemonic practices that confer meaning in a particular historical context (Howarth 2005). Fourthly, the construction of a people requires the production of *empty signifiers* – symbols that can unite heterogeneous elements into a singular identity by standing in for a community's "absent fullness" – which in populist discourses tends to be invested in the name and body of particular political leaders (Laclau 2005a: 99f.).

The first four elements of Laclau's approach go some way towards accounting for the form and structuring of popular identities. But, in adding a final element to his approach, Laclau goes on to stress the force of our subjective attachments to particular signifiers by referring to the role of what he calls "radical investment" (or *affect*) in social life (Laclau 2005a: 110). Drawing parallels between his neo-Gramscian theory of hegemony and psychoanalysis, especially the logic of the *object petit a*, which has been developed by Lacan, Zizek, and Copjec, Laclau stresses the way in which "a certain particularity [...] assumes the role of an impossible universality" (Laclau 2005a: 115). In other words, a certain partial object assumes the dignity of "a Thing" – thereby embodying the whole – which serves as an (impossible) point of "passionate attachment". Moreover, whilst this radical investment in a cathected object is radically contingent – nothing predetermines the fact that one signifier performs this role – "once a certain part has assumed such a function", it retains a grip that "cannot be changed at will"; indeed, "it is its very materiality as a part which becomes a source of enjoyment", thus "making an object the embodiment of a mythical fullness" (Laclau 2005a: 115). This means, in short, that the logic of populist hegemony is "nothing more than the investment, in a partial object, of a fullness which will always evade us because it is purely mythical" (Laclau 2005a: 116).

An important implication of this approach is the distinction between populist and non-populist forms of politics. In Laclau's terms, populism refers to the *degree* of division and contestation brought about by a particular project or practice (Laclau 2005b: 45). To put it in quantitative terms, the greater the number of demands articulated into an equivalential chain across a greater number of social spaces, the greater the degree of populism. On the other hand, the failure to articulate different demands across a multiple range of contested sites – or indeed the struggle to disarticulate equivalential demands – is a feature of a more non-populist, or what might be termed an "institutional" form of politics. Instead of an equivalentially-based politics, the latter is characterised by the primacy of a differential logic, in which demands are articulated and negotiated in a piecemeal fashion, rather than as part and parcel of a wider set of struggles. Furthermore, while populist politics serves to split different social spaces into opposed camps, more institutionally bound politics tends to operate within the existing rules of the political game. More formally, populist and non-populist politics are best viewed as two poles of a spectrum – both of which are no more than regulative ideals – where non-populism involves no equivalence or the disarticulation of equivalence, and populism the precise inverse (see Griggs and Howarth 2007).

Three further aspects are worth noting in this regard. First, it is important to stress that the logic of populism is not conceded a normative or explanatory priority in this theoretical approach; populism is not necessarily more radical or progressive than a more institutional form of politics. Nor does the logic of populism partake of an either/or logic, in which populism and a more institutional politics are separated by an unbridgeable chasm. Instead, the construction and deconstruction of social relations always involves a continuous interplay between the two logics. In this regard, Margaret Canovan's idea of two styles of democratic politics – the *pragmatic* and the *redemptive* – where the former refers to a form of managing antagonisms, while the latter is a "politics of faith" in which *the people* believe they can build a better world by taking control of their lives, displays some resonances with Laclau's model (Canovan 1999; see also 2005). In Laclau's terms, the pragmatic style is akin to the institutional, while the redemptive shares a strong resemblance with the logic of populism. For Laclau, then, the logic of populism does not exhaust democratic politics: While it is an important aspect of political life and democratic politics must be attentive to it, new projects are always institutionalised and sedimented in various contingent and precarious ways, and they are always vulnerable to new (populist) challenges.

Secondly, in developing his model, Laclau elaborates a more complicated notion of political representation. Representation in this view is not just confined to the practices of liberal democracies, such as voting in elections and assemblies, or participating in various forms of democratic consultation or deliberation, but involves a complex process of constructing identities and interests. In this conception, the articulation of a hegemonic project requires constant mediation between leaders/representatives, on the one hand, and those they seek to represent on the other. Rather than transparently transmitting pre-existing interests and identities, or simply constituting such interests or identities in a top-down fashion, the practices of representation comprise a to-and-fro movement between the leader and the led – those that represent and those that are represented – during which interests and identities are constantly modified and adapted as they are iterated in different institutional contexts (Laclau 2005a: 167-174).

Finally, as against aggregative, deliberative, and agonistic models of democratic politics, Laclau fleshes out his commitment to radical democracy in terms of hegemony and populism, rather than reasoning, sensibility, or ethos. He thus relies upon a form of weak transcendence – a "failed unicity" – to constitute a progressive coalition of forces. Today's official discourse in Russia, for example, seeks to construct a series of equivalential linkages between disparate identities around the signifier "Russia as a great power": In it are articulated demands for a clearly defined national identity, a just political system, and a strong state. However, the great power identity is denied or blocked by internal and external foes such as "the West" or "oligarchs" (cf. also Martin Müller in this volume). It is this production of a more universal notion of Russia, coupled with its shared negation, that may enable the official discourse to build a discursive unity amongst different ethnic and social particularities. Laclau thus insinuates a dialectical interplay between particularity and universality in the very constitution of any political identity. The latter involves the elaboration of an empty signifier and a common discourse that can challenge and ultimately restructure and transform a practice or regime.

Laclau offers a highly complex and multifaceted account of populism, where notions like the "act of naming", the role of radical investment, and the forging of *collective wills* all play a vital part in the political construction of popular identities. This is on top of the view that his conception of political subjectivity – in which a "subject of lack" (to use Lacan's terms) identifies with new objects in conditions of dislocation – stresses the role of active agency in the constitution of identity. At the same time, Laclau makes it clear that his category of "the people" is a theoretical rather than ethnographic notion, and must not therefore be conflated with particular historical usages of the term "populism". In short, the constitution of collective popular wills and identities in Laclau's approach are the complicated outcome of equivalential and differential logics in which demands are linked together and decoupled by particular agents and forces in particular contexts.

Bibliography

Canovan, M. 1981. *Populism.* New York: Harcourt Brace Jovanovich.

––––––– 1999. "Trust the People! Populism and the Two Faces of Democracy". *Political Studies* 47, 1. 2–16.

––––––– 2005. *The People.* Cambridge: Polity.

Glynos, J. and D. Howarth. 2007. *Logics of Critical Explanation in Social and Political Theory.* London: Routledge.

Griggs, S. and D. Howarth. 2007. "Protest Movements, Environmental Activism and Environmentalism in the United Kingdom". In *Handbook on Environment and Society*, edited by J. Pretty et al. 314-324. London: Sage.

Howarth, D. 2005. "Populism or Popular Democracy?". In *Populism and the Mirror of Democracy*, edited by F. Panizza. 202-223. London: Verso.

Laclau, E. 2005a. *On Populist Reason*. London: Verso.

―――― 2005b. "Populism: What's in a Name?". In *Populism and the Mirror of Democracy*, edited by F. Panizza. 32-49. London: Verso.

Laclau, E. and C. Mouffe. 1985. *Hegemony and Socialist Strategy*. London: Verso.

Prozorov, S. 2005. "Russian Conservatism in the Putin Presidency: The dispersion of a hegemonic discourse". *Journal of Political Ideologies* 10, 2. 121-143.

Stoker, G. 2006. *Why Politics Matters*. London: Palgrave.

Taggart, P. 2000. *Populism*. Buckingham: Open University Press.

Dislocation in Context

Aletta Norval and Ivo Mijnssen

"Dislocation" is a central term in Ernesto Laclau's theory of discourse. However, the term raises the following questions: To what extent is dislocation part of any identity? What is the relation between dislocation and antagonism? What role does an outside without access to representation play? How do discourses act as compensation for dislocations? These questions will be answered in the context of Russian politics and identity. The main Interest here lies in establishing how the category of dislocation can be put to work in relation to a concrete political analysis. Although Laclau situates the category at an ontological level, it can only really come to life, and the complexities associated with it become visible, once it is deployed ontically, in the analysis of a specific political conjuncture. This requires a political analysis of available discourses and counter-discourses that is historically sensitive and informed, and is able to place events and dislocations into the context of larger trajectories of political imaginaries and their associated forms of subjective identification.

Crisis and dislocation

There is general agreement that by the late 1980s, the Communist system in Russia was in deep crisis. Its signs included a proliferation and deepening of antagonisms and divisions in society in the wake of Gorbachev's *perestroika* and *glasnost'* as well as a deepening economic crisis.

Although this list gives one some sense of the seriousness of the situation, a mere enumeration of the symptoms and effects of the crisis is not sufficient. Rather, reflection on the character of the crisis is needed. There were not merely eruptions of antagonisms but also efforts by forces opposed to the Soviet system – mainly "liberals" advocating for free markets – to turn events in their favour. These responses, in turn, were accompanied by persistent efforts to conserve and defend the Soviet system. The perestroika discourse was stuck somewhere between these poles, trying to reform the system without abolishing it. However, while its opponents on one side demanded changes that reached further, the other side argued that the reforms had already gone too far. Together, these challenges and the responses to them resulted in a generalised sense of crisis, culminating in an organic crisis in the Gramscian sense. Its fault lines ran through the domains of politics and that of economics, as traditionally conceived. The very principles ordering society were thrown into question through a proliferation of events that could no longer be contained within it. The old was dying, and the new could not yet be born (Gramsci 1971: 276).

It is precisely in characterising these sorts of conditions that Laclau's account of dislocation provides a set of theoretical insights that are of great use. In the following, we will outline the main features of Laclau's account of *dislocation*, returning to the Russian example where appropriate. In so doing, we will seek to highlight what we think are the key issues that we need to be sensitive to when analysing such conditions, as well as the range of possible *responses* to dislocations.

Definitions

Although the term "dislocation" appears earlier in Laclau's writings, most notably in *Hegemony and Socialist Strategy*, it only receives a fuller theoretical expression with the publication of *New Reflections*. There, Laclau introduces the term with the claim that:

> "every identity is dislocated insofar as it depends upon an outside which both denies that identity and provides its conditions of possibility at the same time. [...] If on the one hand, [...] [the effects of dislocation] threaten identities, on the other, they are the foundation on which new identities are constituted." (Laclau 1990: 39)

This already provides us with an initial outline of an answer to two central questions of this chapter concerning the relation between dislocation and identity. Every identity, for Laclau, is *ontologically* dislocated, that is, it depends upon an *outside* that, in principle, acts as its condition of possibility and impossibility. In this sense, Laclau argues, "dislocation is the primary ontological level of the constitution of the social. To understand social reality, then, is not to understand what society *is*, but what *prevents it from being*." (Laclau 1990: 44)

It is interesting that Laclau sets this discussion of the ontological character of dislocation in the (ontic) context of what he calls the "dislocatory rhythm of capitalism". Laclau suggests that the dislocatory rhythm of capitalism heightens our sense of historicity. Drawing out the more general features of this discussion for the relation between subject and structure, Laclau offers further reflections on the question of dislocation and its relation, on the one hand, to the *social structure* and, on the other, to the *subject*. He argues that the more dislocated a structure is, the more the field of decisions/the role of the subject expands; and that, as a consequence, a decentring of the structure is coterminous with the construction of a plurality of power centres (Laclau 1990: 39f.).

Let us consider the first claim. With regard to *structure*, the suggestion here is simply that new possibilities for historical action arise out of conditions of structural dislocation ("The situation of dislocation is that of a lack which involves a structural reference"). There is a widening of the field of the possible, but this takes place in a *determinate* situation: that is, one in which there is always a relative structuration (Laclau 1990: 43).

Hence, a condition of total or complete dislocation is very rare or even non-existent (it would imply a complete lack of structure, which is nearly inconceivable). In concrete terms, this means that one always needs to be attentive both to the *degree* of de-structuring, since "the more points of dislocation a structure has, the greater the expansion of the field of politics will be" (Laclau 1990: 50),[1] and to *what* precisely is subject to such de-structuring or dislocation. It is in this sense that the general insights offered by this account of dislocation can only come to life once it is deployed to help make sense of a particular dislocation or context of dislocation. Methodologically, it requires attention to the terrain *prior to* dislocation, including (1) a thorough understanding and analysis of the political imaginaries shaping a particular terrain; (2) an understanding of the relations of force in this terrain and, hence, of the forces and terms in which existing political imaginaries are contested, so that one has a clear sense of the available discourses of contestation; (3) an understanding of the specific areas and issues under contestation, which are thus potentially available for articulation into political projects.

With regard to the question of the *subject*, the new possibilities for historical action opened up by dislocation suggest not only that there is more space available for action by subjects, but also that the very identities of the actors

---

1   Laclau makes a similar point elsewhere: "the greater the dislocation of a structure is, the more indeterminate the political construction emerging from it will be" (Laclau 1990: 51).

themselves stand in need of reconstruction. If, as Laclau argues, the subject is the "space between the dislocated structure and the decision", then a dislocated structure suggests that if the world itself is dislocated, so are the identities of the actors therein (Laclau 1990: 42f.).

Dislocation and the reworking of identities

Returning for a moment to the case of Russia, there is no doubt that the dislocations of the 1980s forced the members of the regime/dominant bloc to rework their political identities. The "bleeding wound" in Afghanistan, the Eastern European satellites that were in the process of becoming independent, the proliferation of informal organisations (*neformaly*) in the USSR, and many other phenomena made it increasingly clear that the existing order of things could not continue (Chafetz 1996). The aborted coup attempt in August 1991 discredited the forces of the status quo and eroded the power of the Communist reformers. It brought to power the market liberals around Boris Yeltsin.

However, the collapse of the Communist discourse, the *other* against which its opponents had defined themselves, forced the latter to rework their identities as well. If, indeed, every identity is relationally defined, then the dislocation of one side of a set of identities that were defined in an antagonistic relation to one another would also force a reworking of its counterparts. As a result, their identity could not remain unchanged as they prepared to "become state".

Now, the space that dislocation opens up for new historical action and for the (re-) formation of political identities results from the fact that the structure cannot fully determine identity (Laclau 1990: 44). Therefore, Laclau argues that dislocation is "the very form of freedom". However, in contrast to the liberal tradition, the freedom won in relation to the structure is initially a *traumatic* fact (and not a cause for celebration), and it calls forth the need to construct new hegemonic articulations and new forms of identification. This is why, analytically and methodologically, a genealogical analysis of the available discourses and sites of contestation is necessary. Such an analysis would highlight two further issues, namely, the relation between antagonism and dislocation, and the question of the role of "an outside without access to representation" in the appearance of dislocation. Let us deal with each in turn.

Regarding the latter, Laclau argues explicitly that "the subjects constructing hegemonic articulations on the basis of dislocation are not internal but external to the dislocated structure" (Laclau 1990: 50). This means, quite simply, that insofar as the structure is dislocated, the emergence of "new" articulations can arise only from somewhere "outside" of the dislocated structure; that is, from a position that previously had not managed to find a place of representation in the dominant political imaginary of the day. In this sense, we would not argue that such positions are in a complete and radical *outside*, but rather that they have not managed to break through the "threshold of visibility". Much can be said about this.[2] From an analytical point of view, it means that one needs to map out the (subterranean) terrain of contestation in order to be in a position to analyse why and how certain discourses – but not others – succeed in breaking through that threshold. The latter part of the analysis picks up another important point that Laclau makes with regard to the success or failure of discursive articulations. As he puts it, it is not the case that

> "any discourse putting itself forward as the embodiment of fullness will be accepted. The acceptance of a discourse depends on its credibility, and this will not be granted if its proposals clash with the basic principles informing the organization of a group." (Laclau 1990: 66)

Hence, the re-articulation of a dislocated space must be able to speak to the particular conditions that are dislocated if it is to be successful. Not everything is possible.

The second question – whether or not such a re-articulation takes the form of an antagonism – is a matter to be determined by contextual research. A dislocation, by its very nature, is a disruptive moment (an *event* in the Foucauldian sense) that does not predetermine the range and possible responses to it. Dislocations may be sutured politically, or they may facilitate the development of new and multiple antagonisms. That is, an existing dominant political imaginary may re-absorb them into what we characterise as an institutionalist discourse (see below), or a dominant imaginary may fail to do so. In the latter case, the conditions are ripe for a set of equivalential demands to be articulated together in a discourse that may challenge the existing order of things. However, either case must be the result of particular processes of political articulation, which need to be analysed carefully and with great attention to detailed historico-political conditions.

---

2 One could, for instance, turn to Ranciere's analysis of the framing of spaces of representation in order to supplement the discussion of dislocation in Laclau's work.

This brings us to a fourth issue, namely, that of the process of "compensating" for dislocation in the context of populism as a cornerstone of hegemonic politics. The issue pertains to the question of "responses to" dislocations. Since David Howarth deals extensively with populism, it will not be discussed in detail here. We will rather concentrate *tout court* on the conditions for it to do its work. The issue here concerns that of *identification*. If the subject's identity is dislocated – insofar as the structure has failed to constitute identity fully – identity can only be reconstituted through a process of identification (a category that receives a fuller discussion in Laclau's most recent work). Such identification will always be more or less partial, but never fully achieved. Any attempt to respond to a condition of dislocation will have to be able both to respond to existing conditions and to offer something by way of novel forms/terms of identification.

This combination of the new and the old in the process of identification is one that, we would suggest, could be understood and accounted for as a matter of aspect change in the Wittgensteinian sense (see also: Norval 2007). Aspect change, according to Wittgenstein, occurs where our established ways of doing and acting have run out, and a new set of connections is established between things not previously belonging together. This moment, characterised by Wittgenstein as that in which the subject exclaims "Now we see!", "Now it all makes sense to me!", is crucial to account for shifts in identification, and has the distinct advantage of highlighting several features that are helpful in thinking about this process methodologically. First, it maintains a nuanced and complex interplay between old and new identifications, avoiding assumptions both of simple continuity and of radical, revolutionary breaks. This, once again, leads us to focus on the detail and nuances of what is dislocated, what is under contestation, and which new myths are articulated to respond to those precise issues. Second, it places an important emphasis on subjective responses. Wittgenstein shows us how pictures may hold us captive, enabling us to see certain things while failing to notice other aspects of a phenomenon; how the identification with a picture depends upon it speaking and relating to us; but also how such identification requires acknowledgment (*Anerkennung*) and responsiveness. Indeed, the emphasis on acknowledgment runs through his account, not only in terms of how we come to see and experience the grip of pictures, but also in his account of a therapeutic method.

This is particularly pertinent to thinking about re-identification after dislocation. It is only when we *acknowledge* the grip of a previous picture, or the ways in which a new picture or expression may make sense to us, that we either understand the limitations of a previous way of seeing or doing, or the new alternatives that have opened up to us. Hence, the requirement of acknowledging the ways in which one's thinking and acting has been dominated by this or that picture or analogy is a precondition both for successful therapy and a criterion of the correctness of the diagnosis. Such acknowledgment is free (we cannot be coerced to acknowledge something against our will); it is specific to the case; and it emphasises responsiveness (and the fact of the responsibility to respond).

These insights, drawn from Wittgenstein, flesh out important aspects of the subjective side of the process of identification, giving particular attention to the question of responses and responsiveness to claim-making. It also challenges any suggestion that dislocation can ever be an entirely "objective" affair. There is no dislocation without reference to the subject and to the need to reconstitute forms of identification. Laclau's account of populism presumes a developed conception of identification and builds on it to highlight what is considered to be a dimension of all political imaginaries. A further emphasis on responsiveness in the context of claim-making begins to develop an account of the demands of a democratic process of claim-making, or a democratic populism.

Further questions

In conclusion, we would like to raise some issues relating both to the characterisation and delimitation of dislocation, which stand in need of further discussion.

First, attention needs to be given to what is dislocated, because one needs to make a judgment about the centrality of the feature of a society that is subject to dislocation. This is not, however, something that can be decided in an a priori fashion. We no longer have the certainties of a Marxist theory that situates issues of class and economic relations at the centre of societal organisation. Economic crises may or may not be decisive; crises of a more cultural character[3] may be decisive, even in situations of economic dislocation.

Second, the depth and extent of the dislocation depends to a large extent upon responses, both from a dominant bloc and from subaltern forces to a particular dislocation. A response that addresses relevant issues, that resonates

---

3   This is not to suggest that the way in which one conceives of the economy is not also cultural; indeed, the economy is an object that is meaningful in different ways in different contexts.

with demands, may serve to alleviate a set of issues that could very well have resulted in a deeper, more widespread crisis had it not been addressed. Hence, it is crucial to be attentive to the range of the demands that arise out of the conditions of dislocation: As Laclau argues, the more dislocated a structure is, the more possibilities there will be for political (re-) articulation.

Third, this is also why we have emphasised the importance of understanding both the resources available to the dominant bloc (or the dominant political imaginary), and those articulated by resistance movements or subaltern forces. Knowledge of the potentially available resources puts one methodologically in a position to investigate why certain responses are adequate to a situation, or why others might fail to address demands and concerns.

Bibliography

Chafetz, G. 1996. "National Identity in Post-Soviet Russia". *Political Science Quarterly* 111, 4. 661-687.

Gramsci, A. 1971. *Selections from the Prison Notebooks of Antonio Gramsci.* New York: International Publishers.

Laclau, E. 1990. *New Reflections on the Revolution of Our Time.* London: Verso.

Norval, A. 2007. *Aversive Democracy: inheritance and originality in the democratic tradition.* Cambridge: Cambridge University Press.

Political and National Identity in Russia: Developments in Russian Political Thought in the 1990s

Philipp P. Casula

The present chapter traces the developments in Russia's political and national identity during the 1990s. Political and national identity are understood as intertwined discourses: Each discourse of political identity entails specific demands concerning national ideas, and each discourse on national identity has distinctive ideas about the political community. The chapter first introduces some key concepts of discourse theory, and then proceeds to adopt them to the Russian case, tracing the ups and downs of political thought and the connected ideas of national identity. In doing so, it describes how at the end of the 1990s the Statists' position emerged as hegemonic in official discourse and paved the way for a more elaborated ideological stance during Vladimir Putin's terms in office as president.

Introduction – transformation theory and identities

Since the late 1980s and early 1990s, transition and transformation theories have played a central role in the understanding of post-Communist societies, their politics, and their economies. The seminal article by Thomas Carothers (2002), however, uncovered the weaknesses of that approach, especially when it comes to those countries that seem to have got stuck in the course of their transformation. According to this interpretation, Russia finds itself in a "grey zone", caught "Between Dictatorship and Democracy" (McFaul et al. 2004). Russia under Yeltsin did not develop a full-fledged democracy and market economy. Under Putin it has developed and successfully stabilised its political system within such a "grey zone". Hence, a first observation to be made is that there is no linear or quasi-linear development to democracy and capitalism. Rather, we have to take into account the possibility of this grey zone constituting a form of stability *sui generis*.[1] This observation has to be taken further: While admitting the possibility "of getting stuck in the process", we would still commit another of the mistakes Carothers pointed out – namely, that even *deviations* from the theory are reframed in the same theoretical terms. Hence, if we acknowledge that Russia or, for that matter, Belarus, Uzbekistan, or Kazakhstan have become trapped during transition, we still do not depart from our original assumption – namely, that these are countries *in transition*. This would be the second observation. Both of these together elucidate that while transformation theory continues to be a central tool of analysis, it is often hard pressed to grasp the unique nature of the "grey zone" cases, such as Russia.

One possible reason is that transformation theory has always been very concerned with "hard factors" such as institutional set-up, economic development, and previous regime type. "Soft factors" such as identity politics or cultural issues have been left mostly aside, as they are deemed to be dependent on the hard ones.

One of these soft factors is the impact of national identity and nationalism. In the transformation literature dealing with the issue of national identity, the assertion that Russia underwent a severe identity crisis after 1991 became commonplace (Malinova 2007; 2008). Still, most accounts either fail to provide detailed evidence for this claim and/or fall short of embedding it into a theoretical framework. All in all, transformation theory, the less teleological version of transitology, has been sluggish in picking up the issue.

A particularly promising approach that could shed a new light on Russia's identity crisis is Laclau and Mouffe's (2001) theory of discourse and hegemony. It is well suited to complement transformation theory, as it can specifically deal with identity change and formation. It is also suitable for investigating the underpinnings of any form of economic or political stability in the discursive realm.

With this explicit focus on identity formation, dissolution, and fixation, Laclau and Mouffe's approach is predestined to be used to analyse the Russian case. The focus of such an effort should be on *demands* as the smallest unit of analysis (Laclau 2005). The following sections will hence highlight three dis-

---

[1] Thus, stability without democracy is possible. This was typically denied both by political scientists and politicians who believed in a smooth and linear transition. A typical statement in this vein of thinking is the following by Yegor Gaidar: "I do not believe in the stability of non-democratic regimes in a highly urbanised and well-educated society. The problem is how and when the regime will be dismantled, rather than whether it could be dismantled in principle." (Gaidar 2005: 225)

courses that emerged to tackle the Russian identity crisis in different ways. They will analyse how demands shifted, were seized by the discourses, were released from their grip, and were reshuffled again.

The "democratic" discourse evolved in the late Soviet Union and had many facets until a specific subset of "democrats" took power; the "national-patriotic" discourse persists until today; and the Statist discourse, which emerged in the mid-1990s, gained more and more influence, eventually becoming the leading political horizon in Russia.[2] All of the aforementioned discourses entail specific visions of national identity and of the political system to be established. In the following, we will show that both visions, the strictly political and the national, are closely interwoven.

The "democratic" discourse on democracy

Studies of democratisation processes often depict a bipolar view of the actors involved. On one side stands the old regime, trying to defend the old order, clinging to old values and ideologies. Its antagonist is the "opposition" composed of young idealists, dissidents, and civil society representatives who strive for Western-type democracy. This view, however, is too simple and reminiscent of Antonio Gramsci's discussion about "fundamental classes" – as if only very specific social agents can lead to social change, and as if identities were predefined. In the late Soviet Union, neither the regime nor the democratic opposition were monolithic. Neither was the latter's understanding of democracy consensual: Different views of democracy, i.e., of the political system to be installed, competed with each other (Lukin 2000).

"Democracy" was already an element of the Soviet discourse. The USSR claimed to be "democratic", though not in the bourgeois sense. Thus, support for "democracy" was neither illegal nor subversive, in principle. However, "democracy" was not a *constitutive* element of the Soviet discourse, so it would have been odd to highlight this aspect. It was at this point that being "democratic" began to be tantamount to subverting the system: As this discursive element became isolated from the Soviet discourse, dislocating effects ensued. The democratic identity became detached from the Soviet one and started to threaten it.

---

2   There are many different terms to denote these ideological camps. In some cases, the same author may even adopt different labels over time (Tsygankov 1997; 2005; 2006). Here, we will restrict ourselves to the most convenient terms and to how the groups in part refer to themselves.

Interestingly, some Marxist and Communist axioms, such as materialism and belief in progress, were still present in the subversive democratic discourse. The democrats believed in the deviating character of the USSR: Andrei Kozyrev, minister of foreign affairs under Yeltsin, for example, reiterates at various points (e.g., Kozyrev 1995: 16) that Russia should become a "normal" democratic state, stressing the universality of democracy.[3] Democratisation was, thus, also seen as a process of normalisation, a process of adaptation to the "most developed democratic powers" (ibid.: 25).[4]

Alexander Lukin (2000) identifies the following dimensions of democracy: The first dimension is democracy as "freedom from state control", i.e., as the antithesis to the totalitarian control of the Soviet state, as negative freedom, secured by majority rule. The Soviet state was seen as being in the hand of an oppressive class of bureaucrats.[5] The democrats started to conceive of the Soviet state as "totalitarian", not necessarily in the Western sense of the term (ibid.: 171ff.; Gleason 1995: 211ff.), but still with a meaning strongly implying political opposition (Lukin 2000: 192).

The second dimension was the dimension of democracy as "social justice" (Lukin 2000: 204ff.), i.e., the elimination of the privileges of the leading party officials and social equality. "Privileges" referred not only to material benefits, but also to the legal impunity of many party officials. However, this view of legal equality and legality was only second to the wish for a just society. Therefore, some "democrats" argued that undemocratic laws could be broken. Khasbulatov (1993: 103) even phrases the problem in terms of *equality*.

Thirdly, democracy was a way of achieving "prosperity" – better living standards and higher levels of consumption. The West was idealised as being rich and prosperous. This view was fostered both by rejection of the Soviet propaganda ("prosperous Socialism at home and "unjust capitalism in the West") and by (second-hand) travel experiences. Andrei Kozyrev underscores that the

---

3   "Democracy and market economy are not a foreign cloak that somebody tries to put over Russia, but rather the best path taken by different countries in East and West, with which they achieved progress and prosperity as never seen before. And on this very path they managed to preserve their national character" (Kozyrev 1995: 23).

4   The main idea of this democratic ideology was the deviant character of the Soviet "totalitarian" system that differed fundamentally from "normal" societies (Malinova 2007: 11).

5   A position which can be found today as well.

POLITICAL AND NATIONAL IDENTITY   51

"Russian anomaly" specifically consists in the poverty of the country, despite its wealth in terms of resources and technology (Kozyrev 1995: 16).

These positions on democracy were highly interwoven. The most successful strand of democrats, however, were the market-liberalisers, who put less emphasis on social justice and more on prosperity. Sogrin (1997) summarises this strand under the term "liberal radicals" or just "radicals",[6] which he understands to include former dissidents, representatives of the artistic and academic intelligentsia (including the *shestidesiatniki*, or 1960s generation), as well as a part of the old Soviet party establishment. This latter group in particular played a pivotal role in shaping Russian politics in the 1990s.[7]

Among the well-known representatives of this type of liberals are Yegor Gaidar and Gennady Burbulis. Gaidar's generation took over from the so-called *shestidesiatniki*, who had counselled Gorbachev on economic matters. The difference was significant: While the *shestidesiatniki* were building on the ideas of Veblen or Myrdal, the key thinkers for the *"vosmidesiatniki"* (or 1980s generation) were Friedman and Hayek (Zweynert 2006: 6f.). The ideas of the *vosmidesiatniki* were the leading ones between 1991 and 1993 and remained influential until 1998 (partly even beyond).

From the perspective of discourse theory, it is obvious that democratic thought in Russia had various sources and encompassed a number of demands that were initially merged under the empty signifier of "democracy". But with the central demand fulfilled ("abolish Soviet power") and the vanishing of the constitutive outside ("Communism"), the early democratic discourse experienced destabilisation. The other attached demands had to be reshuffled. Other discourses attempted to seize them (the demand for social justice, for instance, was partly incorporated into the national-patriotic discourse). Hence they turned into floating signifiers. Since the democracy discourse had lost its clear profile and consisted of unfulfilled or challenged demands, it lost importance in public and official discourse. Later, especially in the late 1990s, "stabilisation" became a main concern, leading to a re-evaluation of national identity as a stabilising

---

6   In contrast to Lukin (2000), Sogrin focuses less on the role of the signifier of "democracy" and analyses the development of political thought as structured around "liberalism". However, he concedes that until summer 1990, the term "liberalism" was "practically not used: Instead, among these intellectuals, there was a firm belief in "democratic Socialism". Later, the reference to Socialism was abandoned (Sogrin 1997: 14).

7   They became the so-called "democrats in power", a term which sometimes is used in a derogatory sense.

factor. At the same time, the chaos of the 1990s was associated with "democracy", creating a need to reassess political identity.

The "democratic" discourse on national identity

In the late 1980s and early 1990s, many democrats who had advocated a preservation of the USSR ended up in the nationalist camp. Being "democratic" increasingly meant putting less emphasis on the preservation of the USSR and supporting the break-up of the Union.

Other democrats, such as Gaidar and Burbulis, were first and foremost concerned with the economy and did not perceive the national identity issue to be problematic. However, they had some clear ideas about Russia's role in the world and thus also about its identity. Kozyrev and other democrats from the Yeltsin camp took over elements of Gorbachev's foreign-policy doctrine and refined them. More than Gorbachev, who stressed the integration into the "common European house", they demanded integration into the *international* community in general.[8] Kozyrev is emblematic of the democrats' positions and of the school of thought labelled "International Institutionalists" (Tsygankov 1997).

These International Institutionalists believed that a maximal opening of Russia towards the West would provide the country with the "efficiency, wealth, and power associated with the liberal states of the North and West" (Richter 1996: 77).[9] The national security concept of 1993 perceives the real threats as residing not in the Western states, but rather within Russia itself, in the former Soviet Union, and in general in all non-democratic states. These threats are best countered through negotiations. NATO is mentioned only in the context of possible cooperation (Kassianova 2001: 830f.; Tsygankov 2006: 61). These guidelines led to a kind of isolationism within the former USSR and vis-à-vis Asian countries that went so far as to disregard even the interests of ethnic Russians living in the Russian "Near Abroad".

However, the International Institutionalists lost momentum. From 1993 on, they realised that the drift towards the West was not appreciated there to the extent they had expected. The establishment of a partnership on equal footing proved to be difficult. Kozyrev and others who had underlined common (democ-

---

8   Although Gaidar stressed his European aspirations: "For years, I was keen to make Russia a candidate for Europe [...] Europeans have never considered this a serious political option" (Gaidar 2005: 218).

9   Morozov (2003: 241) points out that Andrei Kozyrev firmly believed that regaining a great power status could be best achieved by integrating with the West.

ratic) *values* in the beginning, deeming them to be sufficient for the establishment of such a partnership, consequently started to identify common *interests*, as well. Thus, when describing the "Lagging Partnership", Kozyrev (1994) not only stressed the "natural friendship" between Russia and the West, but also pointed out possibilities for a "variable geometry" for and a "pragmatic approach" to the relationship (Kozyrev 1994: 59ff.). An additional element that actually comes from another political, more "national-patriotic", camp is introduced into this discourse: "Russia is predestined to be a great power" (ibid. 62), and as such deserves respect. According to Kozyrev, it is up to the West to decide whether this superpower will fall into the hands of the ultranationalists or whether it will stay on the path to democracy.[10]

This slight shift in the position of one of the most ardent proponents of a Western integration hints at the pressure this discourse was under, especially from the national-patriotic camp. The latter grew stronger as the partnership with the West failed to materialise and as the West declined to honour the principle of *do ut des* as rooted in international institutions. The OSCE did not become the primary security instrument in Europe, as hoped by the International Institutionalists. Instead, NATO kept this role and was even expanded into Central and Eastern Europe, leaving Russia out while trying to appease it with the NATO-Russia-Council. The expansion of NATO, decided upon in 1995, was a setback to the cause of the International Institutionalists. A further, severe blow came in 1999, when NATO forces intervened in Kosovo and bombed Serbia without a UN resolution and against Russia's will:[11] This meant a devaluation of institutions, of negotiations and of cooperation with Russia on equal footing.[12]

Domestically, the International Institutionalists accelerated their decline by their lack of cultural sensitivity and unconditional embrace of the West. In Lukin's

---

10 This line of argument became a mantra of the Yeltsin administration to secure Western support, as if Yeltsin was the only alternative to Communist or nationalist rule in Russia.
11 Ted Hopf points out three other events that dominated Russian political discourse in 1999: recovery from the 1998 financial crisis, the war in Chechnya, and the reshuffling of the political elite (Hopf 2002: 154). Furthermore, when it came to NATO's intervention in Serbia, "there was a discursive consensus: NATO's war against Yugoslavia was [seen as] a greater threat to Russian security than either the U.S. deployment of Ballistic Missile Defense (BMD) or the consequences of NATO expansion." (Hopf 2002: 213).
12 This development also reflects the shift in Western positions: from the "End of History" triumphalism (Fukuyama in 1989) and a happy "New World Order" (G.H.W. Bush in 1991) to a more antagonistic worldview (exemplified by the "Clash of Civilizations" thesis of Huntington, 1996) including the fear of and, paradoxically, the need for new wars.

view, even Gorbachev had more credentials on this issue than the "democrats". Tsygankov points out:

> "[U]nlike Gorbachev, who had offered his country a culturally distinct perspective and an opportunity to reformulate its sense of national pride, the new Russian leaders were astonishingly unimaginative in their vision of national identity. [...] At the time when Russian society was desperately searching for self-definition [...], Westernizers gave little consideration for the country's past experience and, by offering it the 'solution' of becoming a part of the West, they denied it the very legitimacy of a search for its own post-Soviet identity." (Tsygankov 2006: 86)

The "national-patriotic" discourse on democracy

The "national-patriotic" camp encompasses myriad different demands that are subsumed under the label "national-patriotic" for the sake of simplicity.[13] Again, this discourse shows how strongly foreign policy and national identity are linked: "The authoritarians' use of anti-Semitism, racism, and xenophobia domestically conforms to their desire for a new Russian imperialism based on pan-Slavism, racism, and fear of the West" (Chafetz 1996: 679). Hence, they see the West, and especially the US, as an enemy trying to surround and besiege Russia. International relations are, accordingly, a struggle against the threat of US domination (ibid. 678). In face of this risk, they demand a return to an authoritarian system that could counter this threat more effectively.

This grouping turned into one of Yeltsin's most important enemies: on the one hand, its members actually described themselves as opponents of reforms, and on the other hand, Yeltsin was able to use their existence, and the threat they posed, as a justification for his own rule. Within a discourse theoretical perspective, this could be seen as a typically populist move, as an attempt to divide the political space into two camps. Therefore, they continued to play an important role throughout the 1990s.

All in all, it is difficult to isolate the national-patriotic discourse. The *displacements* in Russian literature, however, offer a good proxy for enquiring as to the demands of the national-patriotic discourse: Literature had always been politicised in the USSR, and *perestroika* increased the competition between writers,

---

13   Other names for this group are "Civilisationalist" (Tsygankov 2006), "Expansionists" or "National Communists" (Tsygankov 2005), "Revolutionary Expansionists" (Tsygankov 1997), "Authoritarians" (Chafetz 1996), and "Left-Right Coalition" (Richter 1996).

since many previously forbidden authors resurfaced. Indeed, with the break-up of the USSR, a "civil war of writers" (Mey 2001) erupted.

Although he was not a direct participant in this dispute, and while he subsequently lost popularity in the 1990s, Alexander Solzhenitsyn can be considered as a prime exponent of the national-patriotic discourse and a "godfather" of many authors writing in this vein.[14] Solzhenitsyn's *Kak nam obustroit' Rossiiu?*, published on 18 September 1990 (in English 1991 as *Rebuilding Russia*) in the renowned *Literaturnaia Gazeta*, was widely read, since it openly demanded the dissolution of the USSR and advanced an outline of a new Russian identity.

Though it is primarily concerned with Russia's spiritual salvation, Solzhenitsyn's text also proposes new ideas for the political reorganisation of the country. The cornerstone of his political programme is the combination of a rural lifestyle and "healthy" private initiative. Traditional family structures and education should be fostered. He also demands that the provinces be strengthened vis-à-vis the political centre (Solzhenitsyn 1990: 27ff.).

Essentially, he demands more self-administration: As a new state grows from below, it has to be built from the bottom up (ibid. 35). Politicians should be elected locally and live where they are elected. As long as there is no class of professional politicians, there will be no corruption. Thus, democracy is accepted, but it should be a means and not a "cult", and it should be exercised in small territories. This is Solzhenitsyn's *Semstvo* system (ibid. 35ff.). On the national level, on the other hand, Solzhenitsyn advocates a strong president whose competencies are clearly delimited by law (ibid. 65ff.). In Solzhenitsyn's text, the political discourse is conflated with the discourse on national identity. A feature that can be found also with other authors.[15]

---

14 So while his direct influence may have decreased during and after the 1990s, Solzhenitsyn's ideas are considered to be emblematic for this discourse.

15 Alexandra Mey (2001) takes a closer look at four writers: Vladimir Souloukhin, Valentin Rasputin, Alexander Prokhanov, and Eduard Limonov. Souloukhin has a clear political system in mind for Russia, namely monarchy. Like Solzhenitsyn, Rasputin evokes the community of the village, but in contrast to Solzhenitsyn, he sees the Soviet collective farms as its logical extension. Prokhanov, in contrast, was faithful to the Soviet Union until its end. He always advocated a left-right coalition to return to the USSR. He praised both the USSR and Czarist Russia for their high degrees of centralism. Limonov, finally, is sceptical about the Western political system, although he is certainly more explicit in voicing this criticism than Solzhenitsyn himself (ibid. 338). His positions are most clearly expressed in the programme of the National Bolshevik Party. The party is strictly opposed to liberalism, capitalism, and democracy.

The "national-patriotic" discourse on national identity

Regarding national identity, Solzhenitsyn's work is also indicative of national-patriotic views.[16] His demand for the disbandment of the USSR means, of course, that he has to deal with Russia's new frontiers: He argues that, since the ethnic clashes in various parts of the country have proven that living together within the borders of the USSR was impossible, Russia had to consolidate a "Russian Union" comprising Russia, Ukraine, and Belarus. Since the times of the Kievan Rus', these nations have formed a single entity. Accordingly, Solzhenitsyn condemns the nationalist movement in Ukraine.

Solzhenitsyn does not openly break with the equation of the Russian and Soviet identities.[17] Other nationalist authors argued similarly. Apart from the question of the political system, they dealt with the following set of issues (Mey 2001: 12): The relation between the two Russian identities – *russkii* (ethnic Russian) and *rossiiskii* (civic Russian); sources of national identity; "typical" Russian features; and the relationship between the "near" and "far" abroad, especially including the West.

Despite their different backgrounds and biographies, some of the authors give surprisingly similar replies to these issues (Mey 2001). Concerning the first point, all of the four authors take pre-revolutionary Russia as their point of reference, which is praised for its allegedly excellent interethnic relationships. In this context, the Russians are the benevolent ruling national group. It is this role that the authors would like to see Russians play again. Only Prokhanov adheres to the idea of a community of peoples under both Russian *and* Soviet auspices.

The authors' ideas on the second issue are surprisingly individualistic. According to them, Russian identity depends on a personal declaration of allegiance to Russian culture and history (Limonov) or just on a subjective "Russian feeling" (Soloukhin). Rasputin proposes both subjective and "objective" criteria, such as intrinsic patriotism and loyalty to Russian traditions. While he dismisses

---

16 "Given its huge readership, the brochure inevitably served as a catalyst for ethnic Russians to begin thinking about the future of the Soviet empire" (Dunlop 1994: 620f.).

17 Despite the affirmative action policies carried out at various times to different degrees, Russians acquired a special status in the USSR that was supported by structural policies and resulted in a high degree of identification between "Russian" and "Soviet": "This identification had been reinforced structurally: unlike the other fourteen union republics, the Russian Soviet Federated Socialist Republic [...] had deliberately not been given many of the institutions enjoyed by the other republics [...]. The obvious aim behind this denial of structural parity to the Russian Republic was to bind Russians [...] as closely as possible to the USSR as a whole" (Dunlop 1994: 603).

a rationale based on *ius sanguinis* as the only or main criterion, he regards it as a further asset when it comes to identifying one's affiliation with the Russian nation (ibid. 217). Rasputin regards Russian (ethnic) identity (*russkii*) as being sufficiently open and inclusive already and rejects the notion of a civic identity (*rossiiskii*).[18] All authors, however, advance anti-Semitic positions.

The "typical Russian features" are hard to identify. It is easier for the authors to identify which features are *not* Russian. Especially Limonov, who lived in the US for several years, strongly condemns the "wrong" values of the West, its materialism, and its inclination to consumption, which, according to him, make a dialogue with Russia impossible. Prokhanov, too, condemns the West for similar reasons, although Mey (2001) suspects that he also admires the West, specifically for its technological achievements. Rasputin expresses a particular fear of modernisation in general. Finally, many national-patriots – Prokhanov being a notable exception – share a pronounced anti-Communism. This in turn, was a major feature of the course advocated by Yeltsin, as described above.

The Statist discourse on democracy

The Statists emerged as the influence of the "democratic" International Institutionalists waned.[19] Although this meant that domestic policies changed as well, the first sign of the Statist discourse having gained ground was the change at the head of the Foreign Ministry. Andrey Kozyrev – who in his late days in office declared himself to be a "democratic Statist" (Kozyrev 1995: 38) as well – was replaced by Evgenii Primakov. All in all, the Statists displayed a pragmatic approach to both foreign and domestic politics, apparently lacking any ideological foundation. However, it is precisely this lack of an explicit *Weltanschauung* that hints at their ideological underpinning.

This is apparent when it comes to describing the development of Russia in the 1990s. Primakov expresses his "indignation" about Russia's loss of influence, and especially about the decline of the state's capacities. His major concerns appear to be the rule of law, efficiency, order, and discipline. All of the

---

18   Nowadays, Edinaia Rossiia advocates a mixture of these positions, declaring that it is impossible to reject on "cultural grounds" a personal claim to be "Russian". Hence, being Russian is a matter of personal allegiance. However, Isaev (2006) also prefers the concept "russkii" over "rossiiskii".
19   Again, the homogeneity of the Statists should not be overestimated. Tsygankov (1997: 211) calls them "Realists" and differentiates between an "aggressive" and a "defensive" branch.

above, according to Primakov, were lacking in the 1990s.[20] The cure that the "Pseudoliberals" (Primakov) adopted led to corruption, crime, and unpredictable behaviour on the part of state bodies. Billions of dollars were acquired illegally and transferred abroad – the country's financial default in 1998 was the logical consequence (ibid. 212). At various points of his memoirs, Primakov denounces the effects of privatisation as it was carried out.[21]

Primakov changed posts and became prime minister after the financial crash in 1998. A Statist thus had an opportunity to influence domestic policies directly. He regarded the fight against the oligarchs and the *stabilisation* of the country as the major tasks at hand (ibid. 216). Because Primakov could not afford a direct confrontation with the oligarchs, he focused on *strengthening the state* in order to establish a "reasonable order". This entailed a higher degree of state intervention in the economy: "State intervention was propelled by the fact that Russia needed to find a way out of a very serious crisis. The market could not do the job alone" (ibid. 218).

In short: "Democracy" does not play a central role in the view of Primakov and of the Statists. Stability, efficiency, and order are their main goals. How they are to be achieved, and by which means, Primakov fails to explain – in fact, the "how" was less important to him. In many regards, therefore, starting with articulating demands for stabilisation and for the strengthening of the state, Primakov's conduct as prime minister foreshadowed and set the tone for Putin's presidency. At least on the level of political identity, both Primakov and Putin seem to be representatives of the same Statist discourse.

---

20   "What caused me the most concern and even indignation at that time was the lack of progress in strengthening the power of law. With public discontent rising over the inertia of the state bodies and the lack of order and discipline, voices were increasingly clamouring for an end of the 'democratic game' and a return to a 'strong hand' at the helm. [...T]hose voices were not solely those of nostalgic conservatives; they came from those who were disappointed by the inability of the powers to organise things and achieve results during the transition to democracy" (Primakov 2004: 72).

21   "I want to make it clear that I was never against honest entrepreneurs and business people, and gave them all sorts of support. [...] But along with honest entrepreneurs and business people, there are enterprising thieves and economic criminals, who I always thought had to be fought, and fought as hard as possible" (Primakov 2004: 228).

The Statist discourse on national identity

While the Statists have more pronounced opinions on national identity than on domestic policies, they remain vague when it comes to presenting a coherent view on this topic. They particularly stress Russian "uniqueness", but "they do not define this uniqueness except to say that Russia is different from Europe and the United States because of its religion, its history, its geopolitical position, and its underdevelopment" (Chafetz 1996: 677).

Hence – confirming the theoretical premises of the present chapter – their view on national identity is highly relational and antagonistic. It is this vagueness that makes the Statist discourse so inclusive and compatible with other positions, enabling it to take a hegemonic position. It can thus bind demands from different political camps and social segments. Two moments, especially, characterise the Statists view and can be seen as nodal points that bind other discursive elements:

- Russia as a great power, on par with the US
- Russia as a Eurasian nation with its own path of development

By advancing these claims, they found allies in the "national-patriotic" camp. However, in the mid- and late 1990s, their position was still not anti-Western, as many Statists had been followers of Gorbachev's *New Thinking* beforehand (Tsygankov 2006: 93). In one point, however, they distanced themselves from Gorbachev and the International Institutionalists. As mentioned above, while Gorbachev had at least provided some vision for the nation's identity, the International Institutionalists only offered the idea that Russia should integrate with the West (ibid.).[22]

Primakov, in turn, did not want Russia to be a follower of the West, but pushed for it to be treated as a truly equal state. Whether by following the West or by confronting it, Primakov believed in a third way. At the first meeting with his

---

22 Primakov believed that his predecessor had thought of Russia as belonging to the "trash part" of the world "Naturally, not everyone in the Foreign Ministry […] was of the opinion that the world should be divided into the 'civilized' and 'trash' and that the new Russia's most urgent goal should be to attain a strategic union with the 'civilized' […] at any cost. At the same time, the implied format had Russia as the follower and the West as the leader." (Primakov 2004: 126)

US counterpart, Warren Christopher, in 1996, Primakov presented a catalogue of demands that stress "parity".[23]

All this underlines the Statists' claim for a Russian great power status and their perception of Russia as great power (*velikaia derzhava*). This self-perception is also reflected in the National Security Concept of 1997. The country that it describes seems to be completely different from the one in the 1993 version of the concept (Kassianova 2001: 831). At various points, its parity with other great powers is stressed. NATO is not regarded as a possible partner anymore, but portrayed as a possible antagonist. Its expansion is considered to be extremely dangerous.

Here, the Statists are in full agreement with the national-patriotic camp. The same applies to the Statists' view of Russia as a Eurasian country:

"To many Statists, the notion of Eurasia became symbolic in describing Russia's special geopolitical location and multiethnic nature. [...] Statists insisted that [...] Russia was destined to act as a political bridge between Western and non-Western civilizations." (Tsygankov 2006: 93)

The 1997 National Security Concept describes Russia as an influential European *and* Asian power (Kassianova 2001: 831). Therefore, Sergei Stankevich argues, Russia can play an important role as a bridge and thus as a mediator between East and West (Richter 1996: 81).

Quite in contrast to the policies of Kozyrev, which were directed toward the West only, the Statists' approach focused much more on the former Soviet republics. It was there that, in the Statists' view, Russia had to defend and expand its primacy (cf. Richter 1996: 80f.; Tsygankov 1997: 252). The rapprochement with the former republics of the USSR also concerned the Russian minorities in their territories. While Kozyrev had previously denied any responsibility for them, Primakov actively addressed this issue: "Primakov felt that Russia had an obligation to respond to the political and cultural feelings of twenty-five million Rus-

---

23 "First, regular consultations; second, exchange of information on matters of concern to the other side; third, no surprises; fourth, implementation of the agreements reached; fifth, finding solutions to issues in which our interests do not coincide. [...B]ut frankly speaking, I said, it looked as though the American side was not paying enough attention to maintaining the parity of the two members of this relationship" (Primakov 2004: 134, emphasis added).

sians who had found themselves outside their homeland and continued to identify with it." (Tsygankov 2006: 116)

In this context, it is interesting to note how the Russian political discourse differentiates between the "Near Abroad" and the other countries. Being "near" implies not only geographical proximity, but also political, economic, and cultural interest based on a long common history. From the perspective of the countries so dubbed, the question arises whether their sovereignty is fully recognised.[24] In any case, the term shows that the lines between "outside" and "inside" are still blurred in Russia.[25]

All in all, the Statist discourse includes elements of the "national-patriotic" discourse, though in a more moderate form. The Statists seem to have a more "rational" perception of Russia as a great power. This leads to an antagonistic position vis-à-vis the West – a position that is, however, conducive to stabilising Russian national (and political) identity. A key factor for the failure of the International Institutionalists and thus for the appearance of the Statists was, simply put, the lack of reciprocity in the degree of goodwill demonstrated by Russia and the West. As mentioned above, NATO's expansion was a key issue for Russian politics in the late 1990s, and opposition against this expansion became one of the central issues of Primakov's foreign policy (Tsygankov 2006: 100ff.). With the former "enemy at the gates", the "West" and Russia were easily antagonised:

> "Primakov and the larger Statist community drew some tough lessons from Russia's engagement with the West. This engagement widened the gap between the two sides and reinforced the sense of Russia's identity as distinctive from that of the West. Russia's inability to stop NATO's expansion and Western military strikes on Iraq and Yugoslavia [...] reinforced the already-existing sense of isolation, at times even desperation, among the political class." (Tsygankov 2006: 106)

---

24 Certainly, the stress of the Statist discourse on great power politics as well as the orientation to Asia and to the former Soviet republics plays a role in Russia's behavior during and after the 2008 conflict over South Ossetia.

25 A good example is the renewed importance of 9 May as national holiday. When state officials refer to our victory in the Great Patriotic War, that we encompasses all former nations of the Soviet Union. Hence, the community referred to as victorious is not only "Russian".

Conclusion

This article has shown that the late Soviet and early independent Russian periods were marked by contestations of the political system in general and of political identity and democracy in particular, as well as of national identity. Different discursive strands with distinctive views on both issues developed. While the "democratic" discourse has either almost vanished or has been partly absorbed into other discourses, two others are still in place: the "national-patriotic" discourse and the "Statist" discourse. The Statist position undoubtedly consolidated an almost hegemonic position in the sense of Laclau and Mouffe (2001) in official discourse during the Putin presidencies. In many ways, it was already the Primakov government that reflected the growing consensus on Statist positions and its ability to integrate demands from the "democratic" and also from the "national-patriotic" discourses.

Thus, parts of the other discourses' demands have been integrated into the Statist discourse; the remaining demands or discursive elements survived as counter-hegemonic discourses. Further research is needed to see how the hegemonic discourse stabilised and grew stronger during the Putin administration. This apparently took place *inter alia* through a new integration of – interestingly enough – liberal and democratic demands (at least economically). Even while pursuing policies that were at least dubious by democratic standards, these were always framed in democratic language. The term "sovereign democracy" may be the climax of this development. But in the end, this is only a catchword that summarised Putin's policies *ex post*. The main point is that the Statist discourse picked up demands from very different sides and integrated them into a single discourse allowing for identification from a wide range of political camps. All sides could find pieces of what they demanded, desired, or wished.

A look at the party programmes of the new party of power, Edinaia Rossiia confirms this: It pleases the liberals and "democrats", demanding liberal economic policies or civil society development; it pleases the national-patriots, making claims for a (militarily) strong and independent Russia; and it pleases the Communists, picking up demands for social justice and social security. The formation and predominance of Edinaia Rossiia may be the best example of the institutionalisation of a hegemonic discourse. Furthermore, the centrality of Putin, or rather: Putin's *name*, as a symbol or empty signifier of stability, progress, and security, is striking, justifying the use of the term "populism" as defined by Laclau (2005). It is not a coincidence that Putin was called to stay the "national leader" before giving up his post as president and that he became chairman of Edinaia Rossiia – while not gaining membership of the party, and thus remaining a somehow *super partes* figure.

Additional research is also needed to explore how those "democratic" and "national-patriotic" demands that have *not* been articulated into the hegemonic discourse have formed alliances in order to oppose the predominance of the Statist discourse. One instance of such a *prima facie* unlikely alliance is Drugaia Rossiia, the "Other Russia" movement headed by Garri Kasparov, which unites the "democratic" and "right-wing" parties Yabloko ("the former Perestroika Intelligentsia") and the National Bolsheviks (the left-right coalition).

Bibliography

Campbell, D. 1992. *Writing Security: United States Foreign Policy and the Politics of Identity*. Manchester: Manchester University Press.

Carothers, T. 2002. "The End of the Transition Paradigm".In *Journal of Democracy* 13, 1. 5-21.

Chafetz, G. 1996. "The Struggle for a National Identity in Post-Soviet Russia". *Political Science Quarterly* 111, 4. 663f.

Dunlop, J.B. 1994. "Russia: Confronting a Loss of Empire, 1987-1991". *Political Science Quarterly* 108, 4. 603-634.

───── 2007. "Poststructuralism". In *International Relations Theory for the Twenty-First Century*, edited by M. Griffiths, 88-98. London: Routledge.

Gaidar, Y. 2005. "Russia as Europe's Neighbour: Strategic Challenges of Economic and Political Development.". In *The New Frontiers of Europe. The Enlargement of the European Union: Implications and Consequences,* edited by Daniel S. Hamilton, 217-226. Lisbon: Gulbenkian Foundation.

Gleason, A. 1995. *Totalitarianism. The inner history of the Cold War.* New York & Oxford: Oxford University Press.

Hansen, L. 2006. *Security as Practice.* London: Routledge.

Hopf, T. 2002. *Social Construction of International Politics. Identities & foreign policies, 1955 & 1999.* Ithaca & London: Cornell University Press.

Isaev, A. 2006. Edinaia Rossiia. Partiia russkoi politicheskoi kultury. Moscow: Evropa.

Kapustin, B.G. 2001. "Konets 'tranzitologii'? O teoreticheskom osmyslenii pervogo postkommunisticheskogo desiatiletiia". *Polis* 4.

Kassianova, A. 2001. "Russia: Still Open to the West? Evolution of the state identity in the foreign policy and security discourse". Europe-Asia-Studies 53, 6. 821-839.

Katzenstein, P.J. 1996. *The Culture of National Security: Norms and identity in world politics.* New York: Columbia University Press.

Khasbulatov, R. 1993. *The Struggle for Russia. Power and change in the democratic revolution.* London & New York: Routledge.

Kozyrev, A. 1994. "The Lagging Partnership". *Foreign Affairs* 73, 3. 59-71.

——— 1995. *Preobrazhenie.* Moscow: Mezhdunarodnye otnosheniia.

Laclau, E. 2005. *On Populist Reason.* London & New York: Verso.

Laclau, E. and C. Mouffe. 2001 [1985]. *Hegemony and Socialist Strategy: Towards a Radical Democratic Politics.* London & New York: Verso.

Lukin, A. 2000. *The Political Culture of the Russian "Democrats".* Oxford: Oxford University Press.

Makarychev, A.S. 2005. Russia's Discursive Construction of Europe and Herself: Towards new spatial imaginary. Unpublished paper presented at the conference on "Post-Soviet In/Securities: Theory and Practice", October 7-8, The Mershon Center of the Ohio State University.

Malinova, O. 2007. "Ideologicheskii pluralizm i transformatsiia publichnoi sfery v post-sovetskoi Rossii". *Polis* 1. 6-21.

―――― 2008. "Obrazy Rossii i 'Zapada' v diskurse vlasti (2000-2007): popytki pereopredelediia kollektivnoi identichnosti". In *Obraz Rossii v mire: stanovlenie, vospriiatie, transformatsiia*, edited by I.S. Semenenko, 86-106. Moscow: IMEO RAN.

McFaul, M., N. Petrov, and A. Ryabov. 2004. *Between Dictatorship and Democracy: Russian Post-Communist Political Reform*. Washington: Carnegie.

Mey, A. 2004. *Russische Schriftsteller und Nationalismus, 1986-1995: Vladimir Solouchin, Valentin Rasputin, Aleksandr Prochanov, Eduard Limonov*. Bochum: Projekt.

Morozov, V.E. 2003. "The Baltic States in Russian Foreign Policy Discourse: Can Russia Become a Baltic Country?" In: Lehti, Marko & Smith, David J. eds. *Post-Cold War Identity Politics: Northern and Baltic Experiences*. London: Frank Cass, pp. 219-252.

―――― 2005. "Sovereignty and Democracy in Contemporary Russia: a modern subject faces the post-modern world". *Journal of International Relations and Development* 11. 152–180.

Primakov, E. 2004. *Russian Crossroads. Toward the New Millennium*. New Haven: Yale University Press.

Prozorov, S. 2005. "Russian Conservatism in the Putin Presidency: The dispersion of a hegemonic discourse". *Journal of Political Ideologies* 10, 2. 121-143.

Richter, J. 1996. "Russian Foreign Policy and the Politics of Identity". In *The Sources of Russian Foreign Policy after the Cold War*, edited by C.A. Wallander, 69-93. Boulder: Westview Press.

Sogrin, V.V. 1997. *Liberalizm v Rossii*. Moscow: Magistr.

Solzhenitsyn, A. 1990. *Russlands Weg aus der Krise: ein Manifest*. München: Piper.

Torfing, J. 1999. *New Theories of Discourse: Laclau, Mouffe and Žižek*. Oxford: Blackwell.

Tsygankov, A.P. 1997. "From International Institutionalism to Revolutionary Expansionism: The foreign policy discourse of contemporary Russia". *Mershon International Studies Review* 41, 2. 247-268.

—— 2005. *Whose World Order? Russia's perception of American ideas after the Cold War*. Notre Dame: University of Indiana Press.

—— 2006. *Russia's Foreign Policy: Change and Continuity in National Identity*. Lanham: Rowman & Littlefield Publishers.

Wæver, O. 1997. "The Rise and Fall of the Inter-Paradigm Debate". In *International Theory: Positivism and Beyond*, edited by S. Smith, K. Booth, and M. Zalewski, 149-185. Cambridge: Cambridge University Press.

Wendt, A. 1992. "Anarchy is What States Make of it: The social construction of power politics". *International Organization* 46, 2. 391-425.

Zweynert, J. 2006. *Conflicting Patterns of Thought in the Russian Debate on Transition: 1992-2002*. HWWA Discussion Paper 345. Hamburg: HWWA.

II Regime Type and National Identity

What Kind of Political Regime Does Russia Have?[1]

Hans-Henning Schröder

A decade and a half after the disintegration of the USSR, a change of system has taken place, but this has not led to the establishment of democracy. In view of this situation, an analysis of the new systems should not be focused on the question of democratisation, but on the general model of political authority. Therefore, this article analyses the public acceptance of the state and the effectiveness of Russian policymaking during Putin's period in office. The assessment of the empirical data shows that the Russian state in the form of its constitutional organs has little support among the population; acceptance is only created through the person of the president. This difference between high personal trust and low institutional trust is characteristic of the political system as a whole, which achieves a certain degree of legitimacy solely through the plebiscitary approval of the person of the president. This instrument creates a fragile balance in a potentially unstable situation.

As the Soviet Union collapsed at the end of 1991 and the new Russian government proclaimed its programme of reform, it seemed that the new state was on track towards joining the democratic world. For, after the fall of the USSR and the clear failure of the Soviet political and economic model, most contemporaries could not see an alternative to democracy and the market economy. The governments of Western states accepted the Yeltsin administration as democratic without equivocation. In the discourse among social scientists, a swift transition to a functioning democracy was expected. The theory of *transformation* – the

---
1 This chapter was first published in: S. White (ed.) 2008. *Politics and the Ruling Group in Putin's Russia*. Basingstoke: Palgrave Macmillan. Reproduced in a revised and updated version with permission of Palgrave Macmillan.

dominant interpretative concept of these years – seemed to prescribe the processes of the implementation of democracy and the market economy.

Today, a decade and a half after the disintegration of the Eastern Bloc and the fall of the USSR, it is clear that though in many states (including Russia and most of the member countries of the Commonwealth of Independent States) a change of system has taken place, this has not led to the establishment of consolidated democracies. Alexander Solzhenitsyn even stated with great bitterness in a television interview that democracy has never existed in Russia – not even the facade of democracy.[2]

This observation expresses in radical form something many commentators have now established: that the process of democratisation in Russia has become exhausted and has not been completed. This in turn obliges researchers who have always placed the transition to democracy at the centre of their understanding of transformation theory to revise their thinking. This is not a total surprise: it would be unjust to suggest that the proponents of transformation theory were blind to actual developments in the countries in question (Gans-Morse 2004: 320-349). Many of them, on the contrary, have always insisted that the process of transformation need not necessarily result in a stable democracy, and that it is perfectly feasible to imagine a number of possible paths of development. As early as 1994, Guillermo O'Donnell stressed that – depending on historical conditions and the specific socio-economic problems – different paths of democratisation were conceivable and required a "typology of democracies":

> "Scholars who have worked on democratic transitions and consolidation have repeatedly said that, since it would be wrong to assume that these processes all culminate in the same result, we need a 'typology of democracies. Some interesting efforts have been made, focused on the consequences, in terms of types of democracy and policy patterns, of various paths to democratization.' My own ongoing research suggests, however, that the more decisive factors for generating various kinds of democracy are not related to the characteristics of the preceding authoritarian regime or to the process of transition. Instead, I believe that we must focus upon various long-term historical fac-

---

2 "Is our democracy under threat? After everything I have said, what sort of democracy is under threat? The power of the people? It is non-existent. It hasn't existed for a second. You can only take away what you have but if we don't have anything, there is nothing to take away from us. We have deprived the people of everything, absolutely everything. Starting from the first day of the Gorbachev era, and onward and onward. We have never had democracy. I have repeated many times, we don't have even a semblance of democracy." From a TV interview with Alexander Solzhenitsyn, TV RUSSIA, 5 June (Solzhenitsyn 2005).

tors, as well as the degree of severity of the socio-economic problems that newly installed democratic governments inherit." (O'Donnell 1994: 55)

As it became clear in the course of the 1990s that in many countries of Eastern Europe – and in particular the successor states to the Soviet Union – political change had taken a direction that did not follow the intended course of the transformation process and was in no way aimed at a consolidation of democracy, concepts like "deficient democracy" (Merkel 1999: 361-381; Merkel and Croissant 2000: 3-30; Merkel et al. 2003), and then later "hybrid system" (Rüb 2002: 93-118) or a "grey zone" (Carothers 2002a: 5-21; Carothers 2002b: 33-38), became increasingly prominent.

As useful as these terms were for the categorisation of political states, they still possess a weakness in that they are descriptions of a state *ex negativo*. They describe regimes that are not democracies or are neither democracies nor authoritarian systems. The choice of terms such as "hybrid system" or "grey zone" in itself betrays the fact that the research on transformation does not have an adequate terminological apparatus at its disposal. Consequently, it must make do with a makeshift solution.

In this respect, the concept of "competitive authoritarianism" represents a step forward. Lucan Way and Steven Lewitsky define this as a special case of the "hybrid system" and apply it to regimes in which democratic institutions exist, but in which the rules are so often broken that democratic standards cannot be met (Lewitsky and Way 2002: 54; Way 2004: 143-161). The juxtaposition of an authoritarian government and working democratic institutions creates a situation full of inherent contradictions that is highly unstable. They describe in this way a model that allows one to understand political procedures in the process of transformation. The approach is not limited to the categorisation of regimes; it does not place the question of whether a democracy is successful in the foreground, but rather concentrates on the political process itself. Thus, they approach the conclusion that Gel'man has recently formulated in a study of developments in Volgograd: "democratization", he writes, "is just a by-product of the political process" (2000: 112).[3] At the start of 2005, Richard Sakwa put this more cynically (2005: 391): "Lenin's slogan that 'democracy is expendable, development

---

3 Using Przeworski's argument, to be found in: Przeworski 1988; Gel'man has repeatedly criticised the thoughtless use by Western concepts of democratic theory; for example, see Gel'man 2001: 6-17; Gel'man 2001: 55-69; for an early discussion of the limits of the transformation theory approach, see Bunce 1995a and Bunce 1995b.

is not' appeared to have been resurrected in a type of Thermidorean postrevolutionary consolidation of the political regime."

The defining factors of politics in transition: state building and social change

If one places the analysis of political processes at the centre of the investigation or inquires about the structural elements, actors, attitudes, and behavioural patterns that influence it, one cannot limit the study to the political system and the form of economy. Certainly these are both important. After 1991, a change in the political system took place in Russia. This was enshrined in 1993 in a new constitution, which is still in force today. This constitution and the powerful position of the president within it have been described often enough. It is the expression of socio-political power relations following the violent dissolution of the first Russian parliament and the Supreme Soviet, which created a legal framework that is hardly suitable for the development of democracy. Meanwhile, the market economy system, which was progressively introduced from late 1991, created a new framework through the restoration of the right of property and the liberalisation of the circulation of goods and capital alongside the political upheaval of the period.

Changes in the political and economic system were only part of a broader pattern of historical events. Two further processes had a lasting influence on the unfolding of a new order after 1991 – processes that are not given priority in transformation theory: the rebuilding of statehood in the context of a reduced Russia, and the reconstitution of society. It was above all the latter that through a deep division of society created the conditions by which changing cartels of elites could exercise power and shape politics free of control from society. The reconstruction of Russian statehood has granted this cartel of elites increasing legitimacy since the end of the 1990s.

The building of a new state was at first an organisational problem that had to be solved in parallel to the reorganisation of the political and economic system. The new sovereign states that appeared on the territory of the former Soviet Union had to divide up the Soviet inheritance – land and natural resources, governmental institutions, infrastructure, armed forces (including their nuclear potential), international duties, and not least citizens – and to consolidate a new state structure. This procedure was made easier in that Russia had already constituted itself as an independent state system during the later years of the Soviet era and had an executive and a legislature that were legitimated by competitive election. The Russian leadership solved the most important problems in foreign policy that had arisen out of the fall of the USSR through co-operation, occasionally charged with tension, with the other successor states and in dialogue with the international community. Internally, the Yeltsin leadership possessed enough authority to bind the newly self-confident regions in a federally organised state through protracted bargaining (Shlapentokh et al. 1997; Hanson 1997: 35-44; Stoner-Weiss 1997; Kirkow 1998; Heinemann-Grüder 2000; Perovic 2001). Only in the case of Chechnya was it impossible to work out a political solution, and the attempt to integrate the region into the new Russia by force led to a civil war that threatens to destabilise the whole Caucasus and has damaged Russia's international position.

Mental accommodation to the new state has proven more difficult than the resolution of political and organisational problems. As late as 2001, 79 percent of Russian citizens regretted the fall of the USSR, according to an opinion poll conducted by the Public Opinion Foundation (Fond Obshchestvennoe Mnenie 2001).The Russia of 1992 did not correspond to either the Soviet Union or to the Tsarist Empire. It possessed only three quarters of the territory of the USSR and just half of its population. It was also considerably smaller than the Tsarist Empire before 1917. A new state ideology could only draw on Soviet and Tsarist concepts to a limited extent. A national identity that was capable of integrating the new, smaller Russia had not yet been developed. The search for a "Russian idea", which President Yeltsin tried to speed up through the announcement of a competition, belongs in this context (Uhlig 1997: 1191-1206; Migranyan 1997; Sieber 1998; Vujacic 2004: 164-194), as does the discussion on the flag, coat of arms, and national anthem. Not until Putin became president was a compromise found that tied together Soviet and Tsarist-Russian elements in the symbolism of the state (de Keghel 1999, 2003).

The attempts to develop a new statehood could not but have an influence on the political process. In the interaction of centre and periphery, regional actors won a high degree of independence and influence on politics at the centre. Not until the regional reforms of 2000 and 2004/05 that were introduced by Putin were their roles again limited. The lack of a state ideology accepted throughout society offered room for a broad discussion of national identity, which referred to both the Russian and the Soviet past, and which was taken up and used by political movements and actors. The group rivalries and ideological tensions that became visible in the context of these conflicts gave the political process its particularity.

The other factor that enduringly shaped the development and orientation of Russian politics was the reconstitution of society in the context of the transition to democratic political procedures and the introduction of market principles of distribution. With the transition to the market and the end of a party and state hierarchy that had previously determined social status and levels of consumption, property gained new importance as the basis of the social system. Social position was now measured in the same way as in other market societies, according to income and wealth. In Russia, too, the phrase "money matters" began to apply. A redistribution of public wealth within society went hand in hand with this change in values. The liberalisation of the economy and privatisation led to the descent of a large part of the population into poverty, while a minority became extremely rich. Even official statistics show that during the period from 1990 to 1995, the financial situation of the fifth of the population with the highest incomes improved markedly (see Figure 1.1 and Table 1.1). It is noteworthy that this process was fundamentally over by the middle of the 1990s, and that later movements between income groups have not been large. This suggests that – if redistribution is a key process of transformation – the transition in Russia was completed around 1995/96. By this time, the restructuring of power relations in society was over. A continuation of democratic developments was only conceivable if it did not contravene the interests of the new elite.

A fundamental result of this process of redistribution of wealth was the creation of a new upper class that had adapted to the new political and economic situation and understood how to take advantage of it. The groups that formed this stratum were markedly heterogeneous in their background, education, and behaviour. After 1995, however, they were all equally interested in the preservation of the political and social *status quo* – that is, in the maintenance of the power they had acquired. This created the preconditions for the emergence of a cartel of elites (whose composition is constantly changing), which has decisively influenced Russian politics up to the present. The influence of this grouping can be seen in the in the re-election of Yeltsin in 1996 and in the selection of Putin as Yeltsin's successor at the end of 1999. Political developments during the period of transformation cannot be understood outside this context.

The counterpoint to the creation of a new elite is the social decline of the majority of the population. For a large part of Soviet society, the period of political and economic reforms was connected with material loss and a drop in social status. This experience of decline has shaped Russian society. Already by 1999, 70 percent of those asked felt that they belonged to the underclass (see the doctoral research of Mrowczynski: 2007). Russian society is now deeply divided. A numerically small group of the affluent and rich faces a large stratum of the population that can only get by with difficulty. According to surveys conducted by the Levada Center in December 2003, 15 percent of respondents said that their money was barely sufficient for foodstuffs; 36 percent had to economise in order to buy clothing; and another 34 percent found it difficult to buy large consumer goods like a television or refrigerator (Levada Center 2003). A middle class that corresponds in its behaviour and level of consumption to Western patterns – or at least is satisfied with its material situation – so far exists only in an embryonic state. The basic model is the sharp opposition within society of rich and poor: a fissure that will determine Russian politics over the next decade.

The restructuring of the social hierarchy and the related changes in the redistribution of wealth mark a sharp contrast between the transformation of the majority of "Socialist" states and the processes of transformation in Southern Europe and Latin America. Here, too, political and social change was connected, but there was not a comparably radical change in the social order. In Russia, society was reconstituted; this created new conditions that gave the political process a specific character. It was really only the elite groups that were politically active. The mass of the people were objects, not subjects of political life. The cartel of elites shaped the public sphere and organised majorities in support of their policies, while the majority of the people had no opportunity to take an active part.

This circumstance hindered the development of the institutions of civil society, which were traditionally weak anyway. In the Soviet Union, the monopoly of the Communist Party had effectively prevented public self-organisation. In contrast to Poland, there was neither an opposition elite nor were there organised groups that could bring together and realise public interests. This inheritance represents a burden that is difficult to overcome even under favourable conditions. Putnam, looking at Italy, has demonstrated the ways in which the development of a civil society is determined by historical experience (Putnam 1993: 182). Certainly, even historically disadvantaged regions can undergo a change for the better: "[C]hanging formal institutions can change political practice" (ibid.: 184). However, this maxim is no real comfort in Russia, given the existing power relations in society.

The political process in Russia is shaped by social upheaval, the rebuilding of the state, and the lack of a tradition of public self-organisation. These preconditions caused the character of politics following the fall of the Soviet regime to be determined by cartels of elites, who were not subject to public control. The process of the redistribution of wealth split society into rich and poor. Political competition only took place between the different factions of elites acting within the framework of the institutions they had themselves established under the constitution of 1993.

The regime: stable and effective?

More than a decade after the change of regime and the adoption of its new constitution, the political system in Russia seems to be comparatively stable, not least because it appears to have broad support among the population (see Balzer 2003: 189-227; Brown 2001; Kuchins 2002; Mommsen 2003; Sakwa 2004; Shevtsova 2005). This does not mean that it has managed to establish a working parliamentary or presidential democracy. Virtually all commentators agree that this is not the case. Nevertheless, post-Soviet governments, based on a changing cartel of elites, have possessed political authority, carried out the business of government, and enjoyed, especially in recent years, a high degree of public acceptance.

In view of this situation, Richard Rose, Neil Munro, and William Mishler have argued that analysis should not be orientated towards the traditional understanding of transformation, which measures the quality of politics according to how democratic it is, but rather towards a general model of political authority, regardless of whether the regime is democratic or not (Rose et al. 2004: 196f.). Rose and his co-authors are not alone in this approach. Other writers (for example, Rudra Sil and Cheng Chen) are also seeking new ways of looking at the post-Soviet system. Like Rose, Munro, and Mishler, they see research on transformation based on theories of democracy as inherently unproductive. They suggest placing the question of state legitimacy at the centre of inquiry (Sil and Chen 2004: 347-368).[4] As different as these starting points are, they both try to

---

4 See Sil and Chen (2004: 347): "[...] the debate over the prospects of democratic consolidation and civil society in Russia can be given new life only if subsumed within a more general problematique focusing on the level and sources of state legitimacy."

get away from the categorisation of transforming regimes in terms of theories of democracy and open up a discussion that had become bogged down. Indeed, this broader approach enables one to make statements about the stability of the political system and its perspectives for development.

In this paper, we can only look at a few of the many questions that arise in the context of such a new approach. Two will be dealt with, albeit briefly: the public acceptance of the regime and the effectiveness of Russian policymaking during Putin's period in office. Both aspects – acceptance and the efficacy of politics – interact: A high level of public acceptance makes political action easier, and effective action in the solution of political problems can in turn increase acceptance. If both elements exist, then the regime gains stability and at the same time acquires prospects for the future.

The work of the executive is conveyed to the public through people and institutions. In the Russian case, one must look at two constitutional organs: the president and the cabinet of ministers (the second of which the public is aware of through the person of the prime minister). Almost all polling institutes dealing with political and social topics have collected corresponding data that, on the whole, concurs. The activity of the president is without exception seen positively (see Figure 1.2). In the polls regularly conducted by the Levada Center, the overwhelming majority of respondents endorse Putin and his exercise of presidential responsibilities. In January 2000, immediately after he became acting president, three-quarters of respondents supported Putin. During the elections of 2003-4, which had an intensely propagandistic impact on the electorate, this number rose to four-fifths. Not until 2005 did his approval rate fall to two-thirds; increasing concern about social reforms may have played a role in this. Throughout, the data indicates an extremely high rate of approval for the president and his administration.

One can see a somewhat different picture if one looks at the assessment of the prime minister and the cabinet (see Figure 1.3). There were three prime ministers between January 2000 and June 2005: Putin briefly held the office in January 2000; he soon handed it over to Mikhail Kasyanov, who at first occupied the position in an acting capacity and after Putin's election as president assumed the post on a more formal basis. In the March 2004 government reshuffle, Kasyanov was replaced by Mikhail Fradkov. As prime minister, Putin had an approval rate of 80 percent. His successor Kasyanov was seen by 40-50 percent of those questioned as worthy of support. Not until the turn of the year 2002/3 did negative judgements outweigh the positive. The figures for Prime Minister Fradkov, who came into office in March 2004 through the change in government, are much lower than those for his predecessor. Following the conflict over social reforms in particular, more than half of respondents disapproved of him. If one looks at the evaluation of the government as a whole, the approval rates correspond to the assessment of the prime minister, although they are generally a few points lower. Without exception, disapproval exceeds approval. In the first half of 2005, over two thirds of those questioned gave the government poor marks.

The discrepancy between the positive assessments of the president and the poor ones of the prime minister and cabinet is striking. At first glance, it is difficult to explain. The president chose the government; he controls it; it is directly answerable to him. Policy is jointly developed and implemented by the presidential administration and the cabinet. Strictly speaking, there is no reason why the president should not be held liable for the shortcomings of his government. The perception of the public, however, obviously follows different rules.

A similar discrepancy is apparent when one looks at another area of inquiry. The Levada Center regularly asks its respondents which politicians they trust (see Figure 1.4). According to this data, since the beginning of his presidency, Putin has occupied a special position – between 40 and 50 percent of those questioned declared their trust in him. The next candidates, Emergencies Minister Sergey Shoigu and the leader of the Communists, Gennady Zyuganov, lie some distance behind. When the Levada Center offered the response "I do not trust any of them" (up to November 2003), this was the second most popular answer. Thus, Putin occupies a unique position in the public's esteem.

Two facts are worth mentioning about the trends of trust in the president. Firstly, no other politician benefits from a decline in Putin's ratings; if they do fall (for example, following the Kursk disaster in September 2000), the percentage of those questioned who claim to trust no politician rises. Secondly, the number of people supporting Putin, which was already significant, increased considerably between November 2003 and March 2004. Obviously, the extensive pro-Putin propaganda during the Duma and presidential elections had an effect. One can see from this rise that the high rate of trust is evidence of an excellent image-building campaign.

If one then asks about trust in institutions (see Table 1.4), it is clear how strongly acceptance of the regime is mediated through the person of Putin.

About half of those asked replied that they trusted the office of president. Forty percent trusted the church, and 30 percent trusted the army. The institutions that really constitute the political system – the executive at all levels, representative bodies, and the judiciary – enjoy practically no trust. Approval of political parties, the actual bearers of parliamentary democracy, is even lower than that of the notoriously corrupt and despised police. In other words, the new Russian state as represented by its constitutional organs has little support among the population; acceptance is only created through the person of the president. This difference between high personal trust and low institutional trust is characteristic of the political system as a whole, which achieves a certain degree of legitimacy solely through the plebiscitary approval of the person of the president. This instrument creates a fragile balance in a potentially unstable situation. It is as of yet unclear to what extent the political system has been able to keep its borrowed legitimacy since Putin stepped down as president in 2008. The fact that Putin has not left the political stage indicates that he is still a key player.

The effectiveness of the political system is far more difficult to gauge than its acceptance. Putnam has pointed out that assessment of the efficacy of governments is one of the fundamental questions of political science, but has also shown how difficult it is to answer.[5] On the one hand, one must determine the tasks that a government actually has to accomplish. On the other, it is necessary to develop concepts with which it is possible to measure the level of achievement in these areas. In this chapter, there is room only to outline the direction in which such an approach might be developed.

The Russian authorities do indeed have to deal with a long list of problems. These include those of a strategic nature, such as the development of democratic political processes to include a greater degree of public participation; the establishment of structures founded on the rule of law; the bridging of the gap in society between rich and poor; and the completion of the transition to a working market economy. In addition, there are short-term, tactical tasks that consume an increasing share of the gross domestic product, such as reducing poverty, the struggle against corruption, the stabilisation of the social system,

---

[5] "'Who Governs?' and 'How well?' are the two most basic questions of political science. The former raises issues of distribution and redistribution: 'Who Gets What, When, and How?' Such issues have been at the forefront of the discipline's debates in recent decades. By contrast, rigorous appraisals of institutional performance are rare, even though 'good government' was once at the top of our agenda." See Putnam 1993: 63; for Putnam's thoughts on the evaluation of politics, see ibid. 63ff.

and ending the crisis in the army. The effectiveness of state policy is also measured by the extent to which it is able to resolve these problems (Iasin 2005: 3).[6] However, this abstract list does not indicate whether the government, the elites, or the people are really aware of these as problems and are interested in their solution. One may reasonably assume that the predominant cartels of elites are not overly interested in an increase in participation by the wider society. At least a part of the state apparatus benefits too much from corruption to be inclined to bring an end to it. The stabilisation of the social system, which must be accompanied by an increasing burden on the people, is not met with deep sympathy among broad sections of the population. The question of which tasks should be prioritised depends on different interests and is therefore difficult to answer in the abstract. Therefore, in the following, two perspectives will be outlined: on the one hand, that of Putin's administration, which is expressed in its programmatic statements; on the other, that of the society as a whole, whose expectations of the government are regularly investigated in opinion surveys.

The official catalogue of tasks that the executive has set for itself is presented every year in the president's address to the Federal Assembly (Putin 2005; 2004; 2003; 2002; 2001; 2000). Its character and emphasis change from year to year, even if there are certain recurring themes. In the year 2000, the first year of his presidency, Putin emphasised the necessity of strengthening the state and dwelt in detail on the reform of the federal structure. He mentioned as concrete tasks a tax reform, a law that would strengthen political parties and civil society, and the creation of the framework for a working market economy in which everyone would have an equal opportunity to compete. A realistic social policy and administrative reform were further points. The following year, the relationship between the centre and the regions was in the foreground. Putin dealt comprehensively with legal reform and the necessary structural reorganisation of the economy. The material goals he set were administrative reform, legal reform, and the restructuring of the management of state property.

In reaction to the attacks in New York and Washington in September 2001, Putin introduced a new element in 2002: combating terrorism. Nevertheless, he also covered familiar areas such as administrative reform and legal re-

---

6   In 2005, Iasin listed the following urgent, concrete objectives: 1) pension reform, 2) reform of the housing and utilities market, 3) educational reform, 4) reform of the health system, 5) military reform, 6) the replacement of social privileges with cash benefits, and 7) administrative reform; ibid.

form. His concrete objectives were the reform of the housing and utilities markets, the modernisation of the armed forces, and the restructuring of the management of state property. The 2003 address underlined the necessity of making Russia a strong power. In this context, Putin demanded the doubling of GDP, the reduction of poverty and once again an improvement in the army. Again, in 2004, the main theme was the strengthening of Russia's position in the world, but this time, the president linked this topic with democracy, a high standard of living, and a developed civil society. He again demanded a doubling of GDP, the alleviation of poverty, a resolution of the housing problem, modernisation of the health system, reform of the education system, and, once again, military reform. The presidential address of 2005 presented Russia as a democratic state oriented towards European values. Putin touched on social policy and freedom for entrepreneurs; a new element was strong criticism of the inefficient and corrupt bureaucracy.

Altogether, the speeches suggest some change of emphasis, but at the same time, a number of themes remained constant: high economic achievement, an effective system of education, modern armed forces, a working legal system, and a good social and health system are always set as policy goals. In this, the governmental programme is not so far removed from the ideas of the experts (Iasin 2005).

Whereas the president sets out the political objectives of his government in a formal way, the aspirations of the wider society must be examined through opinion surveys. Of course, hopes "from below" and goals "from above" are not formulated independently of one another. The government reacts to the mood of the people in the formulation of its programmes. The people, in turn, take up issues that the government puts forward and propagates. Both react towards perceived shortcomings. It is therefore not surprising that the two share common ground. Despite this, differences in emphasis can be seen. On the evidence of the data issued by the Levada Center (see Table 1.2), ordinary Russians are most interested in the improvement of their material situation, social security, and the fight against crime and corruption. They are not overly interested in goals such as the modernisation of the army, preserving the right of property, or a working market economy, nor do they have a strong desire for legal reform and the reorganisation of the education system. Instead, immediate material and existential worries come to the fore, and politics is judged by the extent to which it deals with these concerns.

Between the aims of the executive and the expectations of the people, there are differences of substance, even if the former is more oriented towards "input" and the latter towards "output". However, one can identify areas that are important in both cases and assess how successful government has been in these respects. This is not an evaluation of the effectiveness of the Putin administration in general – this would require a study of far broader scope than is possible in the space available – however, there are at least indications of how seriously the government takes its goals and how politics is perceived by the wider society.

Two topics suggest themselves in this connection: the struggle against crime and material security. There is data in relation to both of them that provides some evidence of success or failure.

The official statistical agency has published figures for crime between 1990 and 2004, and provides a record of the development of the standard of living over the period 1992-2004 (see Table 1.3). The figures show that the government's performance in dealing with crime is unimpressive. After a sizeable increase in crime in the early years of transition, the number of crimes reached a high plateau. Neither has there been any marked success in reducing crime during Putin's term in office. A rather different picture emerges in respect of the standard of living. Following the social collapse of the first half of the 1990s, which saw a fall in real wages and high rates of poverty, the situation has gradually improved. The number of people who live below subsistence level is falling, real income is rising slowly, and household consumption is increasing. The general standard of living still remains low; however, the situation is improving noticeably. Thus, the government cannot claim success in the realm of fighting crime. However, it can point to progress in the securing of material needs, although the question of whether this achievement is a result of political action remains open.

Therefore, we are dealing with a political system that, in the form of its institutions, is not really accepted as such by the wider society. One can imagine that the reason for this is the experience of decline during the period of transformation and the perception that the executive is often unsuccessful in important areas of policy.[7] In this respect, two central processes of the transition pe-

---

7   Rose et al. (2004: 204) have rightly pointed out that the motives for accepting the regime are complex: "Differences in approval of the new regime and endorsement of un-

riod – the collapse of the state, which was only gradually overcome through the rebuilding of statehood, and the redistribution of public wealth, which led to the division of society – continue to exert their influence. A political regime has developed in the process of transformation that replicates the power relationships in society. The mistrust between the elite and the rest of society is great. This fragile socio-political construct is only integrated through trust in the individual. The person of the president, who as a "good Tsar" corresponds to traditional expectations and is supported by skilful control of the mass media, seems to be the only factor that really does achieve acceptance for the regime. All in all, this is not a good precondition for the creation of a stable political system. Tensions between groups of elites and latent social conflicts offer radicals a fertile breeding ground. By contrast, the forces that could promote democratic development are much weaker.

---

democratic alternatives may be influenced by: (1) socialization; (2) political values; (3) economic performance; (4) Putin's personal appeal; and/or (5) expectations."

Appendices: Graphs and Tables

Figure 1.1: Distribution of income in the USSR and Russia, 1990-2005

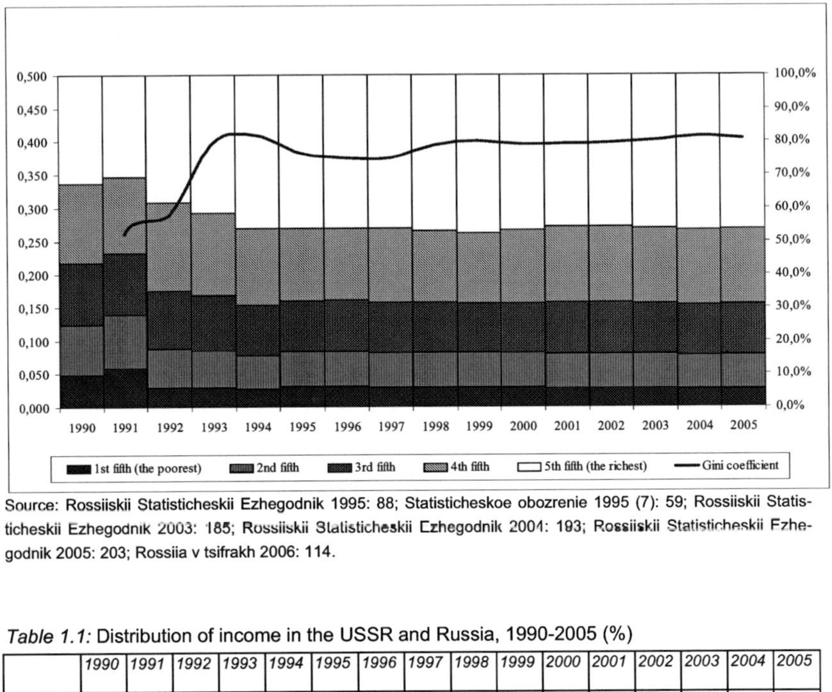

Source: Rossiiskii Statisticheskii Ezhegodnik 1995: 88; Statisticheskoe obozrenie 1995 (7): 59; Rossiiskii Statisticheskii Ezhegodnik 2003: 185; Rossiiskii Statisticheskii Ezhegodnik 2004: 193; Rossiiskii Statisticheskii Ezhegodnik 2005: 203; Rossiia v tsifrakh 2006: 114.

Table 1.1: Distribution of income in the USSR and Russia, 1990-2005 (%)

	1990	1991	1992	1993	1994	1995	1996	1997	1998	1999	2000	2001	2002	2003	2004	2005
1st fifth (poorest)	9.8	11.9	6.0	5.8	5.3	6.1	6.1	5.8	6.0	6.0	5.8	5.6	5.6	5.6	5.4	5.5
2nd fifth	14.9	15.8	11.6	11.1	10.2	10.7	10.7	10.5	10.5	10.4	10.4	10.4	10.4	10.3	10.2	10.2
3rd fifth	18.8	18.8	17.6	16.7	15.2	15.2	15.3	15.2	15.0	14.8	15.1	15.4	15.4	15.3	15.1	15.2
4th fifth	23.8	22.8	26.5	24.8	23.0	21.7	21.8	22.3	21.5	21.1	21.9	22.8	22.8	22.7	22.7	22.7
5th fifth (richest)	32.7	30.7	38.3	41.6	46.3	46.3	46.1	46.2	47.0	47.7	46.8	45.8	45.8	46.1	46.6	46.4
Gini coefficient		0.260	0.289	0.398	0.409	0.387	0.385	0.390	0.394	0.400	0.395	0.398	0.398	0.398	0.408	0.404

Sources: Rossiiskii Statisticheskii Ezhegodnik 1995: 88; Statisticheskoe obozrenie 1995 (7): 59; Rossiiskii Statisticheskii Ezhegodnik 2003: 185; Rossiiskii Statisticheskii Ezhegodnik 2004: 193; Rossiiskii Statisticheskii Ezhegodnik 2005: 203; Rossiia v tsifrakh 2006: 114.

Table 1.2: "In your opinion, which tasks should the government concentrate on?" (in percent)

	1999	2000	2001	2002	2003	2004
Reducing prices	46	46	41	44	47	45
Tackling corruption	22	37	33	34	36	40
State control of prices	37	35	28	31	36	36
Regular adjustment of pensions and income	25	35	33	38	34	34
Fighting crime	18	31	27	33	29	31
Strengthening the rouble	40	37	28	29	33	30
Subsidies to agriculture	17	31	24	20	26	27
Paying overdue wages	55	26	20	22	22	24
Support for state-owned companies	18	20	15	18	18	20
Renationalisation of core industries	14	17	16	19	17	19
Reinforcement of defence capability	9	15	9	16	15	15
Civil concord and harmony	9	14	12	14	15	12
Guaranteeing the banking system and savings	7	5	5	6	6	8
Protection of private business	6	7	8	9	9	8
Increasing taxes	10	7	9	9	7	7
Improvement of the range of goods available	12	3	3	3	4	3
Other	1	1	1	1	2	1
Don't know	1	1	3	1	1	1

Source: Levada Center, http://www.levada.ru/press/2004073007.html, accessed 2 August 2004.

84 HANS-HENNING SCHRÖDER

Table 1.3: Crime rate in Russia, 1990-2005 (thousands)

	1990	1991	1992	1993	1994	1995	1996	1997	1998	1999	2000	2001	2002	2003	2004	2005
Murder	15.6	16.2	23.0	29.2	32.3	31.7	29.4	29.3	29.6	31.1	31.8	33.6	32.3	31.6	31.6	30.8
Grievous bodily harm	41.0	41.3	53.9	66.9	67.7	61.7	53.4	46.1	45.2	47.7	49.8	55.7	58.5	57.1	57.4	57.9
Rape	15.0	14.1	13.7	14.4	14.0	12.5	10.9	9.3	9.0	8.3	7.9	8.2	8.1	8.1	8.8	9.2
Robbery (grabezh)	83.3	102.1	165.0	184.4	148.5	141.0	121.4	112.0	122.4	139.0	132.0	149.0	167.0	198.0	251.0	344.0
Aggravated robbery (razboi)	16.5	18.5	30.4	40.2	37.9	37.7	34.6	34.3	38.5	41.1	39.4	44.8	47.1	48.7	55.4	63.70
Theft	913.1	1,242.7	1,651.0	1,579.6	1,314.8	1,368.0	1,207.5	1,054.0	1,143.4	1,413.8	1,310.0	1,273.0	927.0	1,151.0	1,277.0	1,573.0
Drug related crime	16.3	19.3	29.8	53.2	74.8	79.9	96.8	186.0	190.1	216.4	244.0	242.0	190.0	182.0	150.0	175.0
Hooliganism	107.4	106.9	120.3	158.4	190.6	191.0	181.3	130.0	131.1	128.7						
Traffic offences	96.3	95.6	90.1	51.7	51.2	50.0	47.7	48.0	52.4	53.7	52.7	54.5	56.8	53.6	26.5	26.6
Of which ended in death	15.9	17.1	17.5	17.0	15.8	14.4	13.1	13.2	14.4	15.1	15.4	15.5	16.1	17.6	16.0	15.7
Others	535.0	516.4	583.2	621.6	700.9	782.5	842.1	748.0	820.3	502.2	1,084.4	1,107.2	1,039.2	1,025.9	1,036.3	1,274.8
All registered crimes	1,839.5	2,173.1	2,761.0	2,799.6	2,632.7	2,756.0	2,625.1	2,397.0	2,582.0	2,582.0	2,952.0	2,968.0	2,526.0	2,756.0	2,894.0	3,555.0
All crimes (minus traffic offences)	2,077.5	2,670.9	2,747.9	2,581.5	2,706.0	2,577.4	2,349.0	2,529.6	2,528.3	2,899.3	2,913.5	2,469.2	2,702.4	2,867.5	3,528.4	

Source: Rossiiskii Statisticheskii Ezhegodnik 1997: 269; Rossiia v tsifrakh 1999: 145; Rossiiskii Statisticheskii Ezhegodnik 2000: 243; and http://www.gks.ru/free_doc/2006/b06_11/11-01.htm, accessed 28 August 2009.

RUSSIA'S POLITICAL REGIME 85

Figure 1.2: "How do you rate Putin's activity as president?"

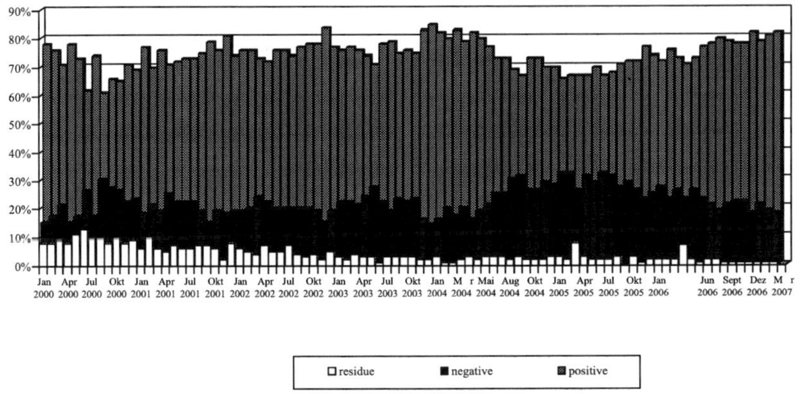

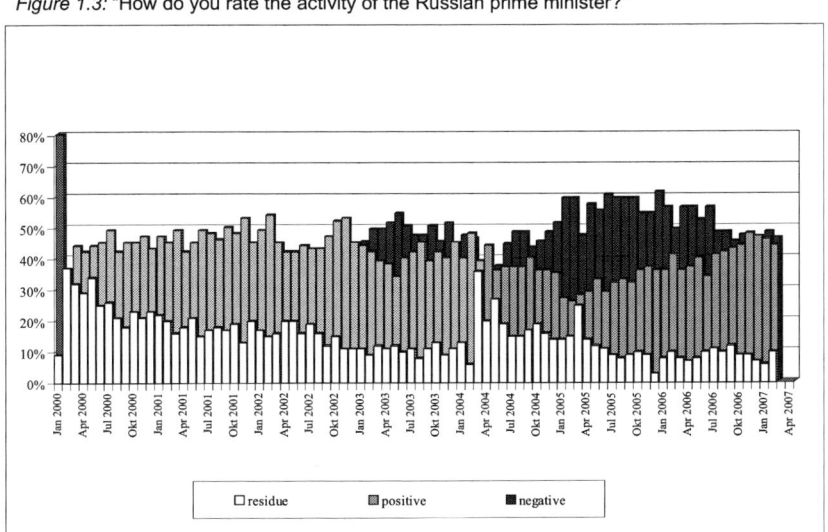

Source: Levada Center data, http://www.levada.ru/prezident.html, accessed 2 April 2007.

Figure 1.3: "How do you rate the activity of the Russian prime minister?"

Source: Levada Center date, http://www.levada.ru/pravitelstvo.html, accessed 2 April 2007 (up to Jan 2000, Putin; Feb 2000-Feb 2004, Kasyanov; since March 2004, Fradkov).

Table 1.4: "To what degree do the following institutions deserve trust?" (in percent)

	They deserve trust			They do not deserve complete trust			They deserve no trust whatsoever			Other answers		
	2002	2003	2004	2002	2003	2004	2002	2003	2004	2002	2003	2004
The president	45	58	56	33	29	28	9	5	8	13	8	8
The church	39	40	43	22	20	22	11	10	8	28	30	27
The army	35	28	30	35	32	34	16	22	20	14	18	16
The press, media	26	23	26	44	40	45	18	23	18	12	14	11
State security services	21	20	21	36	33	32	22	21	23	21	26	24
Regional government	20	17	19	36	36	37	28	31	29	16	16	15
Local government	19	16	19	37	35	37	30	36	33	14	13	11
Federal government	20	15	17	43	44	41	20	27	26	17	14	16
The courts	-	11	14	-	32	34	-	30	29		27	23
Prosecutor's office	-	11	12	-	30	34	-	30	26		29	28
Federation Council	12	8	12	40	36	36	23	24	23	25	32	29
The Duma	10	9	11	43	43	44	30	36	34	17	12	11
Trade unions	11	10	11	28	22	24	29	32	31	32	36	34
The police	14	10	10	39	34	35	36	44	43	11	12	12
Political parties	7	5	5	31	29	29	34	39	39	28	27	27

Source: derived from Levada Center data, http://www.levada.ru/press/2004092702.html, accessed 28 August 2004.

Figure 1.4: "Name five or six politicians whom you trust"

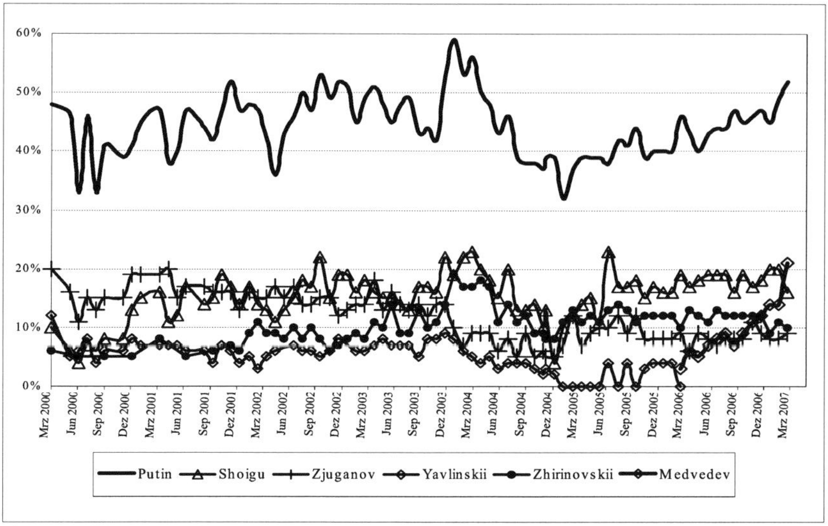

—Putin —△—Shoigu —+—Zjuganov —◇—Yavlinskii —●—Zhirinovskii —◆—Medvedev

Sources: VTsiom/Levada Center data, 2002-2005, http://www.wciom.ru; from September 2003: http://www.vcioma.ru; from 2004: http://www.levada.ru/politiki.html, accessed 23 June 2005.

(Translated by Christopher Gilley)

Bibliography

Balzer, H. 2003. "Managed Pluralism: Vladimir Putin's Emerging Regime". *Post-Soviet Affairs* 19, 3. 189-227.

Brown, A. ed. 2001. *Contemporary Russian Politics. A Reader*. Oxford: Oxford University Press.

Bunce, V. 1995a. "Should Transitologists Be Grounded?". *Slavic Review* 54, 1. 111-127.

—— 1995b. "Paper Curtains and Paper Tigers". *Slavic Review* 54, 4. 979-987.

Carothers, T. 2002a. "The End of the Transition Paradigm". *Journal of Democracy* 13, 1. 5-21.

—— 2002b. "Debating the Transition Paradigm. A Reply to my Critics". *Journal of Democracy* 13, 3. 33-38.

De Keghel, I. 1999. "Die Moskauer Erlöserkathedrale als Konstrukt nationaler Identität. Ein Beitrag zur Geschichte des 'patriotischen Konsenses'". *Osteuropa* 49, 2. 145-159.

—— 2003. "Die Staatssymbolik des neuen Russland im Wandel. Vom antisowjetischen Impetus zur russländisch-sowjetischen Mischidentität". Bremen, December (Forschungsstelle Osteuropa an der Universität Bremen. *Arbeitspapiere und Materialien*, 53).

Fond Obshchestvennoe Mnenie 2001. "Referendum o sud'be SSSR: 10 let spustia". http://bd.fom.ru/report/map/dominant/dominant2001/142_4455/dd010927 [accessed 29 August 2009].

Gans-Morse, J. 2004. "Post-Communist Transitions and the Myth of a Dominant Paradigm". *Post-Soviet Affairs* 20, 4. 320-349.

Gel'man, V. 2001a. "Postsovetskie politicheskie transformatsii: nabroski k teorii". *Obshchestvennye nauki i sovremennost'* 1. 55-69.

——— 2001b. "'Stolknovenie s aisbergom': Formirovanie kontseptov v izuchenii rossiiskoi politiki". *Politicheskie issledovaniia* 6. 6-17.

——— 2000. "Demokratizatsiia, strukturnyi pliuralizm i neustoichivyi tsentrizm: Volgogradskaia oblast'". *Politicheskie issledovaniia* 2. 111-132.

Gorshkov, M.K., N.E. Tikhonova, and A.Iu. Chepurenko, eds. 1999. *Srednii klass v sovremennom rossiiskom obshchestve*. Moscow: RNISiNP/ROSSPĖN.

Hanson, P. 1997. "How Many Russias? Russia's Regions and Their Adjustment to Economic Change", in *L'Evoluzione della Russia e i suoi rapporti con alcuni paesi Europei*, edited by Istituto Affari Internazionali. Rome: Laboratorio di Politico Internazionale, Gruppo Russia. 35-44.

Heinemann-Grüder, A. 2000. *Der heterogene Staat. Föderalismus und regionale Vielfalt in Rußland*. Berlin: Berlin Verlag Arno Spitz.

Iasin, E. 2005. "Al'ternativy i perspektivy. Glavy iz novoi knigi Evgeniia Iasina 'Prizhivëtsia li dcmokratiia v Rossii'". 28 June, http://www.polit.ru/research/2005/06/28/ [accessed 29 August 2009].

Institut kompleksnykh sotsial'nykh issledovanii Rossiiskoi Akademii Nauk (IKSI RAN). 2003. *Rossiiskii srednii klass: dinamika izmenenii (1999-2003 gg.) Analiticheskii doklad*. Moscow: IKSI RAN.

Kirkow, P. 1998. *Russia's Provinces. Authoritarian Transformation versus Local Autonomy?*. Basingstoke: Macmillan.

Kuchins, A.C., ed. 2002. *Russia after the Fall*. Washington, D.C.: Carnegie Endowment for International Peace.

Levada Center 2004. "V 2003 godu otnositel'no bogatykh stalo bol'she, absoliutno bednykh ne stalo men'she".
http://www.levada.ru/press/2004011302.html [accessed 22 August 2009].

Lewitsky, S. and L.A. Way. 2002. "The Rise of Competitive Authoritarianism". *Journal of Democracy* 13, 2. 51-65.

Merkel, W. 1999. "Defekte Demokratien". In *Demokratie in Ost und West. Für Klaus von Beyme*, edited by W. Merkel and A. Busch. Frankfurt am Main: Suhrkamp Taschenbuch Verlag. 361-381.

Merkel, W. and A. Croissant. 2000. "Formale und informale Institutionen in defekten Demokratien". *Politische Vierteljahresschrift* 41. 3-30.

Merkel, W. et al. 2003. *Defekte Demokratie*. Vol. 1: *Theorie*. Opladen: Leske + Budrich.

Migranyan, A. 1997. *Rossiia v poiskakh identichnosti (1985-1995)*. Moscow: Mezhdunarodnye otnosheniia.

Mommsen, M. 2003. *Wer herrscht in Rußland. Der Kreml und die Schatten der Macht*. Munich: C.H. Beck.

Mrowczynski, R. 2007. Im Netz der Hierarchien. Sozialstruktur, informelle Beziehungen und Mittelschicht im entwickelten Sowjetsozialismus. PhD diss., Hannover.

O'Donnell, G. 1994. "Delegative Democracy". *Journal of Democracy* 5. 55-69.

Perovic, J. 2001. *Die Regionen Russlands als neue politische Kraft: Chancen und Gefahren des Regionalismus für Russland*. Berne: Peter Lang.

Przeworski, A. 1988. "Democracy as a Contingent Outcome of Conflicts". In *Constitutionalism and Democracy*, edited by J. Elster and R. Slagstag, 59-80. Cambridge: Cambridge University Press.

Putin, V. 2000. "Poslanie Federal'nomu Sobraniiu Rossiiskoi Federatsii". http://www.kremlin.ru/appears/2000/07/08/0000_type63372type63374type82634_28782.shtml [accessed 29 August 2009].

―――― 2001. "Poslanie Federal'nomu Sobraniiu Rossiiskoi Federatsii". http://www.kremlin.ru/appears/2001/04/03/0000_type63372type63374type82634_28514.shtml [accessed 29 August 2009].

―――― 2002. "Poslanie Federal'nomu Sobraniiu Rossiiskoi Federatsii". http://www.kremlin.ru/appears/2002/04/18/0001_type63372type63374type82634_28876.shtml [accessed 29 August 2009].

―――― 2003. "Poslanie Federal'nomu Sobraniiu Rossiiskoi Federatsii". http://www.kremlin.ru/appears/2003/05/16/1259_type63372type63374type82634_44623.shtml [accessed 29 August 2009].

―――― 2004. "Poslanie Federal'nomu Sobraniiu Rossiiskoi Federatsii". http://www.kremlin.ru/appears/2004/05/26/0003_type63372type63374type82634_71501.shtml [accessed 29 August 2005].

―――― 2005. "Poslanie Federal'nomu Sobraniiu Rossiiskoi Federatsii". http://www.kremlin.ru/appears/2005/04/25/1223_type63372type63374type82634_87049.shtml [accessed 29 August 2009].

Putnam, R.D. 1993. *Making Democracy Work. Civic Traditions in Modern Italy*. Princeton: Princeton University Press.

Rose, R., N. Munro, and W. Mishler. 2004. "Resigned Acceptance of an Incomplete Democracy: Russia's Political Equilibrium". *Post-Soviet Affairs* 20, 3. 195-218.

Rossiiskii Statisticheskii Ezhegodnik 1995. 1995. Moscow: Goskomstat Rossii.

―――― 1997. 1997. Moscow: Goskomstat Rossii.

―――― 2000. 2000. Moscow: Goskomstat Rossii.

―――― 2003. 2003. Moscow Goskomstat Rossii.

―――― 2004. 2004. Moscow: Goskomstat Rossii.

―― 2005. 2005. Moscow: Goskomstat Rossii.

Rossiia v tsifrakh 1999. 1999. Moscow: Goskomstat Rossii.

―― 2006. 2006. Moscow: Goskomstat Rossii.

Rüb, F.W. 2002. "Hybride Regime – Politikwissenschaftliches Chamäleon oder neuer Regimetypus? Begriffliche und konzeptionelle Überlegungen zum neuen Pessimismus in der Transitologie". In *Zwischen Demokratie und Diktatur. Zur Konzeption und Empirie demokratischer Grauzonen*, edited by P. Bendel, A. Croissant, and F. W. Rüb, 93-118. Opladen: Leske + Budrich.

Sakwa, R. 2004. *Putin. Russia's Choice*. London and New York: Routledge.

―― 2005. "The 2003-2004 Russian Elections and Prospects for Democracy". *Europe-Asia Studies* 57, 3. 369-398.

Shevtsova, L. 2005. *Putin's Russia*. Washington, D.C.: Carnegie Endowment for International Peace.

Sieber, B. 1998. *"Russische Idee" und Identität: "Philosophisches Erbe" und Selbstthematisierung der Russen in der öffentlichen Diskussion 1985-1995. Studien zum russischen Konservatismus*, vol. 1. Bochum: projekt verlag.

Sil, R. and C. Chen. 2004. "State Legitimacy and the (In)Significance of Democracy in Post-Communist Russia". *Europe-Asia Studies* 56, 3. 347-368.

Shlapentokh, V., R. Levita, and M. Loibserg, eds. 1997. *From Submission to Rebellion. The Provinces versus the Center in Russia*. Boulder: Westview Press.

Solzhenitsyn, A. 2005. TV interview with Alexander Solzhenitsyn, TV Russia, 5 June, http://www.fednews.ru, quoted in *Johnson's Russia List* 9174, 10 June.

Stoner-Weiss, K. 1997. *Local Heroes. The Political Economy of Russian Regional Governance*. Princeton: Princeton University Press.

Tikhonova, N.E. 2000. "The Influence of Market Reforms on the Self-Identification of Russians", paper presented to the 2000 BASEES Conference, Cambridge.

Uhlig, C. 1997. "Nationale Identitätskonstruktionen für prosowjetisches Rußland". *Osteuropa* 47, 12. 1191-1206.

Vujacic, V. 2004. "Perceptions of the State in Russia and Serbia: The Role of Ideas in the Soviet and Yugoslav Collapse". *Post-Soviet Affairs* 20, 2. 164-194.

Way, L.A. 2004. "The Sources and Dynamics of Competitive Authoritarianism in Ukraine". *The Journal of Communist Studies and Transition Politics* 20, 1. 143-161.

The Specific Features and Future of Post-Soviet Transitions

Andrey Ryabov

No single theory has yet been able to explain the diverse transformations taking place in Eastern Europe and the post-Communist space. Nonetheless, the author believes that an analysis that compares Russia's transformation with that of other countries in the region is able to place it in a wider political context and characterise it as particular manifestation of a general process. He argues that, unlike many Eastern European countries, the post-Soviet space did not experience a "revolution of values". Thus, Russia and other countries remain stuck in a suspended "transition within transition". The systems are characterised by weak political institutions (with the exception of the presidency), informal centres of decisionmaking, and rising social tensions. While the "Colour Revolutions" could not live up to their promises, the author nonetheless believes that they started processes – such as more influence for parties and independent media outlets – that could lay the groundwork for more democracy in the region.

After the fall of Communism, the states within the Central and Eastern European (CEE) region and the post-Soviet space headed in different directions. Countries of the CEE region developed Western-style democratic regimes based on liberal market economies, the post-Soviet states adopted authoritarian models of governance with the state having a firm grip over the economy. No single theory has yet lived up to the challenge of explaining the great diversity in the transformation that took place over the past 20 years. Nevertheless, among all the various theoretical strands, including the promising discourse theories such as those proposed by Ernesto Laclau and Chantal Mouffe (2001), this chapter argues that the "classical" transformation theories are by no means dead, but can make a useful contribution in explaining the different trajectories.

I will not attempt to work out a new theory of transition, but rather seek to compare the general features and peculiarities of the transitional processes in the former Communist countries. Most likely, a comparison will allow us to identify the different types of post-Communist political systems. For Russia, the task is to consider its post-Communist development not as a unique case, but rather through the prism of the fundamental political and social changes common to all states formed on the territory of the former Soviet Union. Such a comparative analysis will firstly help to place Russian transformation in a wider political context and characterise it as particular manifestation of a general process. Secondly, it will bring researchers closer to refining the theoretical model of post-Soviet transition, which today looks like a dead-end without a visible "final destination", a suspended "transition within transition".

The main goal of this article is thus to identify and describe the key features of post-Soviet transition and to demonstrate how they manifest themselves in contemporary Russia.

Ready for transition?

In order to gain a better comprehension of the specific features of the post-Soviet transition period, it is fruitful to examine it in comparison with comparable changes in the states of Central and Eastern Europe. The USSR (excluding the Baltic states[1]) was the birthplace and the core of the global Communist system. Traditions of authoritarianism, vertical solidarity, and weakness of civil society (features dating back to Tsarist times) were stronger than in any other CEE country where the Communist system was established after World War II and largely imposed from abroad (with the exception of former Yugoslavia and Albania). The length of the Communist period and the even longer traditions of authoritarianism in Russia lie at the root of the large differences between the CEE and the post-Soviet states regarding their structural preconditions for post-Communist transitions.

The difference was most visible in the sphere of political culture and ideas. The national consensus on the necessity of liberal and democratic changes and the return to Europe began to emerge and take shape in CEE countries many years before the "Velvet Revolutions" in 1989 brought down the political institutions of the Communist system. The struggle against the Communist system was visible in the uprising in the German Democratic Republic of 1953, the Hun-

---

1 When speaking of the USSR or the countries of the post-Soviet space (PSS), we usually refer to the 12 former Soviet Union Republics that formed the Soviet Union. Unless otherwise stated, we do not include here the Baltic states, which broke all political ties with this space in 1991.

garian anti-Stalinist uprising of 1956, the anti-Communist disturbances in Poland of 1956, 1968, 1970, and 1980, and the "Prague Spring" in former Czechoslovakia in 1968. No comparable anti-Communist mass revolt took place in the USSR after World War II.

Revolutions in mentality and values paved the way for the political revolutions in CEE countries. As a result, the populations of the CEE countries were more likely to back the new system of values and understood the goals of political change; they were ready to face the inevitable difficulties and obstacles on the way to achieving a new social order. If in the CEE countries there was a movement from below, in the USSR, reforms were initiated exclusively from the top and only because of the decisiveness and insistence of the general secretary of the Communist party, Mikhail Gorbachev, and his team.

The Soviet Union republics did not experience "revolutions of values" before the collapse of the old political order in 1991. Gorbachev did not manage to bring about deep changes in the mentality of the Soviet people. He offered them an attractive version of democratisation as an effective instrument to improve their well-being in the near future. But this instrumental approach was not a sustainable motivation for democratic behaviour. The citizens of the post-Soviet countries, coming up against difficulties in the process of market reforms, were soon disappointed by ideas of democracy and liberal economy. This explains why the national leaders that came to power in some of the post-Soviet states in the period of 1990-1991 were replaced by the generation of "stabilisers" – members of the former Soviet nomenclature – between 1992 and 1994.[2] In Russia, Boris Yeltsin also changed his strategy after he had violently suppressed the mutiny of the supporters of the former Supreme Council in October 1993. He refused to continue the policy of market reforms and instead began to support those forces that could ensure political and social stability in the country.

The population of the post-Soviet countries at the beginning of transition was not ready to embark on a long trip fraught with significant obstacles towards the final goal – building a democratic society. Therefore, the people who had gone only part of the way from the Communist system to the new social order agreed to accept the transitional and eclectic social model that combined elements of the new realities (officially recognised private property, political and ideological pluralism, multi-party elections) as well as the heritage of the Soviet

---

2   For example, in Azerbaijan, Georgia, Moldova, Ukraine, and Tajikistan.

era (authoritarianism of the executive branch, lack of institutions of public control over the elite, nomenclature power relations). As a result, the bulk of people were neither ready to move forward towards building a democratic society based on a free market economy nor prepared to go back to the Communist order.

Thus, decisive cultural differences between CEE and the post-Soviet countries at the beginning of transition caused further deep divergences in their development in the 1990s. Moreover, CEE countries subjected their evolution to the clear goal of accession to the European Union. Therefore, their domestic policy was conducted under the strong influence of EU recommendations. Russian political scientist B.I. Makarenko has stated:

> "There is no doubt that the 'European choice' played a decisive role. It had the character of consensus for the majority of the elite and society and represented the strategic resource of development. Firstly, consensus around a strategic course caused the disagreements between the key political forces to be non-antagonistic. They fought for power and discussed concrete program issues, but did not doubt the aims of development. Secondly, orientation towards Europe prompted political elites to behave as if they were in Europe: they observed the standards of European policy in different spheres of public life. Thirdly, the 'European choice' assumed close interaction with institutions and politicians of the Western European countries that strengthened the European vector in policy." (Makarenko 2008: 108, author's translation from Russian)

The post-Soviet countries in the 1990s resembled societies that had lost their point of reference. There were huge discrepancies between the objectives of the new elites and those of the bulk of the population. At a time when elites concentrated their efforts on privatising former state ownership, the mass of the population was forced to think only about how to adapt to the new order. In fact, two parallel social spaces were formed in the post-Soviet countries – the elite's space and the people's space. Interaction between them functioned like a non-aggression pact. The elites rid themselves of any social obligations. In turn, the ordinary people were allowed to behave irresponsibly (e.g., shirking tax duties). The future of these countries, and even the prospects of building nation-states, seemed unclear. The formation of a national consensus regarding the positive goals of development was impossible under these circumstances. The only aims shared by the elites and the population were the preservation of, or the return to, stability and the necessity of nation-building.

Common features of post-Soviet transition countries

Despite variations between political regimes in the countries that once constituted the Soviet Union, some common features marked the post-Communist development of these countries' economic and social systems. One such common feature is the fact that the political predominance of the new elites became the main feature of the new order in the post-Soviet countries. Post-Soviet elites were in reality transfer classes – privileged anti-Communist groups that were not interested in building democratic societies based on open political and economic competition. Their aim was to realise a social system that would combine the market economy with old power relations and somewhat modernised political institutions of the Soviet epoch. These elites have preserved administrative skills, models of social behaviour, and devotion to the principles of a strict hierarchy from the Soviet era. These groups, above all, were represented by those strata of the state bureaucracy that realised the benefits of a transition to a market system and by the major corporations that were closely tied up with the post-Soviet bureaucracy.

In post-Soviet states such as Russia, Ukraine, and Kazakhstan, where there was widespread privatisation of formerly state-owned assets under the conditions of a weak state in the 1990s, large sections of the economy were controlled by the so-called "oligarchs" that managed to capture entire segments of the government apparatus and played an important role in shaping the political course of these countries. In the states where privatisation was insignificant (Uzbekistan) or where it was not implemented at all (Belarus, Turkmenistan), dominant groups were represented only by the state bureaucracy.

The economic predominance of the post-Soviet elites was based on their monopoly over the main resources and assets, and on the preservation of the market of administrative services that had existed since the Soviet epoch, but was privatised after collapse of the Communist system. While the ruling transfer classes conducting reforms under pressure and supervision of the European Union in the CEE countries were gradually forced to share their leading positions with other social groups, there were no restraints on the predominance of the elites in the post-Soviet states.

A low level of political participation and the lack of independence from the government on the part of various actors (political parties, NGOs, the media) characterised the political process in the post-Soviet space in the 1990s. These actors were not able to exert a strong influence on the process of decisionmaking. The extent to which independent actors were able to exert pressure on authorities and ruling elites became a factor that determined what type of political system would be established in the respective countries. The spectrum of possible systems was not a broad one. At the one end, there were systems with a "closed hegemony" (Dahl 1971) such as Turkmenistan and, to a lesser extent, Uzbekistan, where political infighting was either absent or took place outside of the public sphere. The other pole was represented by "competing oligarchies" – Russia, Ukraine, Moldova, Armenia, and Georgia – which were characterised by a high level of political competition of elites in the public sphere and weakness in the political participation of the people. Therefore, competitive elections and media pluralism played an important role in political life there.

The group of countries with intermediate regimes (Belarus, Azerbaijan, Kazakhstan, and Tajikistan) occupied positions between the "closed hegemonies" and "competing oligarchies". Some of them gravitated towards the "closed hegemonies" (Belarus), others towards "competitive oligarchies" (Kyrgyzstan). But despite the differences between the political systems of these countries, it is important to emphasise that everywhere in the post-Soviet space, the new elites acted largely independently from the peoples of their states. In connection with the political weakness of civil societies, it is important to note that political parties (except in Moldova) did not become influential centres of decisionmaking anywhere. In Russia, they turned out to be so weak that they were unable to carry out any of their traditional functions. They neither represented the interests of big social groups, nor did they elaborate strategies of societal development or shape the executive branches of their countries.

Among the "competing oligarchies", only two countries advanced noticeably in the process of democratisation: In Ukraine and Moldova, changes of power took place as a result of "elections of disappointment" in 1994 and 1996. Politicians who represented the political opposition won open and free elections and became the new presidents of these countries. Ukraine and Moldova, while they did not build mechanisms for the institution of a participatory democracy or the realisation of individual human rights, were nonetheless somewhat successful in instituting electoral democracies. Russia missed the chance to engage on a similar course. In the presidential "elections of disappointment" in 1996, the ruling Russian elites effectively prevented the leader of the Communist party (KPRF), Gennady Zyuganov, from becoming president, even though his party and its leadership did not present a threat that could have brought about a return to the Soviet system. The ruling elite, relying on the significant application of administrative resources and electoral fraud, made sure that the unpopular president Boris Yeltsin stayed in power. His name was closely tied up with the founding of the contemporary independent Russian state and the first attempts at market and democratic reforms. The Russian elite refused to safeguard one of the main elements of electoral democracy – namely, the principle of a changeover of power by way of alternative and unpredictable elections. Subsequently, the elite began to move down the path of curtailing democratic achievements. The political system of the country began to evolve in a reverse direction – from "competing oligarchies" to "closed hegemonies".

The institution of strong presidential systems

The different types of government in the post-Soviet space were also notable for their diversity. While either mixed presidential-parliamentary or parliamentary systems were established in the CEE countries (Poland, Hungary, Latvia, Estonia and others), presidential republics arose in all post-Soviet states (only in Georgia did a parliamentary system exist for a short time). Despite the constitutional differences – many authors in Russia still consider Russia to be a presidential-parliamentary system (Salmin 1996; Makarenko 2008) – de facto super-presidential regimes were established in most post-Soviet states. This phenomenon can be explained by another peculiarity of the post-Soviet transitions: namely, the weak institutionalisation of the political environment.

Everywhere, the presidency is the only institution that was successfully built on the basis of a legal and organisational plan. All other institutions may be both strong and weak. But the most important thing is that they are exposed to frequent changes. Since the Lower House of the Russian parliament (the State Duma) adapted the Russian constitution in 1993, this institution has undergone two major reforms. The Upper House (the Federation Council) experienced three reforms. The procedure for the election (or rather appointment) of the governors and presidents in the national republics that form the Russian Federation has been changed three times.

The weak institutionalisation of the political systems of the post-Soviet states is connected to the historical conditions in which they were built. All of these states arose as a result of the collapse of the USSR. Its disintegration was spontaneous in character and led to the failure of all institutions of the previous system. The most important of these was the Communist Party of the Soviet Union, including its branches in all Soviet Union Republics (except in the Russian Socialist Federative Soviet Republic – the RSFSR). Later, the post-Soviet elites, who concentrated all their efforts on becoming a new class of owners, were not concerned with the implementation of privatisation within a legal framework. Therefore, they were not interested in building a strong parliamentary system. Elites needed a strong political arbiter who had real power to decide conflicts that arose in the process of privatisation and could simultaneously restrain popular discontent over the unequal social order that emerged. That is why elites needed to build the powerful institution of the president.

But the establishment of a super-presidency under conditions of a weakness of other political institutions, and the refusal of the elites to accept elections with unpredictable results for the power constellation, led to a situation in which the authorities became the hostage of clan interests. The process of decision-making gradually shifted to informal centres: influential groups and the administrative apparatus serving the president. This had three main consequences. Firstly, in Russia and Azerbaijan, a new "transitional" system of changing power was established. According to this system, the outgoing president appoints his successor, who later legalises his status in presidential elections, the results of which are perfectly predictable.

Secondly, under the new situation, it became impossible to build institutional mechanisms and sustainable channels of elite recruitment. Old mechanisms of recruiting the elite through special nomenclature institutions and procedures were discarded, but the new democratic ones based on alternative elections with unclear results were not accepted.

Thirdly, "winner-takes-all" systems perpetuated the process of redistribution of property. The groups closest to the president usually initiate the redistribution of property in any new stage of political development. However, some authors suppose that a permanent process of gathering, distributing, and redistributing property is a peculiarity of Russia's political and economic history that has a centuries-old tradition (Bessonova 2006). This tradition led to a situation where the ruling elites gradually began to perceive the vulnerability of their state and the instability of the political system they had built. As a result, this system focused not on the task of developing the country, but primarily on self-survival. This factor strengthens the state of "suspended transition within transition" in post-Soviet societies.

The impact of external factors

International factors – the influence of the West in particular – also played a specific role in the post-Soviet countries in the 1990s. It differed from the influence that the West exerted in the CEE states. The pull exerted by the West's offer of close partnership and the prospect of accession as full members was far greater in the CEE countries than in the geographically distant post-Soviet states that received no such offer of cooperation. The reform process within the individual CEE states was driven, on the one hand, by a clear prospect of EU accession, and on the other, by a strong EU interest in supporting this process and bringing it to a successful end. Because the European states had never seriously considered the post-Soviet states potential members of the European Union , they never showed the same interest in the reform process in these countries.

Mainly due to overarching military-strategic considerations, the United States paid more attention to developments in the two biggest states of the former Soviet Union, Russia and Ukraine, as Washington feared a restoration of the old Communist system in these states. The main task for the US administration, considering Russia and Ukraine as "native lands" of Communism, was to prevent the Communists' return to power. In order to achieve this goal, the US administration was prepared to accept negative phenomena such as the massive corruption of the post-Soviet political regimes, the criminalisation of economic and political life, and the emergence of "oligarchs". The result was a new edition of the old doctrine of "deterring Communism", a relic of the Cold War that was modernised and applied to the post-Communist social system. In the post-Soviet states, the influence of the West generally did not contribute to the development of transformational processes, and thus helped to strengthen conservative political forces.

The formation of the new national states and their stabilisation concluded the first stage in the history of the countries that emerged on the territory of the former Soviet Union. These objectives were reached at the beginning of the 2000s. The results of the presidential elections in Ukraine in 1999 and in Russia in 2000, in which the candidates of the Communist parties were defeated, indicated that the threat of a restoration of the Communist system, as perceived in the political mentality of the ruling elites, had ceased to exist. After these elections, the Communist parties went into rapid decline.

However, the social systems built in the post-Soviet states were characterised by the low dynamics of development and the lack of long-term goals for evolution. Those systems were organised so that they primarily reflected the interests of privileged elite strata. Meanwhile, by the end of the first stage of transition, new social problems had accumulated in the post-Soviet states. For the ruling elites, these problems turned out to be difficult to solve. Since the beginning of the period of economic growth, huge social inequality has irritated huge sections of the population, amounting to millions of people, in all post-Soviet states. Economic growth increased the cost of living of ordinary people. The consolidation of the new ruling classes caused pathways of upward social mobility to be shut off. It caused the new middle class and the educated youth to despise these forms of injustice. In other words, demands for social justice became the key problem on the agenda of political life in the post-Soviet space.

The ruling elites of the post-Soviet countries reacted in various ways to the new challenges. In Russia, as in some other countries, elites relying on increased economic resources began to pursue a policy of guaranteeing the social welfare of the masses without changing actual political institutions and social relations. The revolutionary changes in power as a result of mass unrest took place in other states, where the ruling elites refused or were unable to react to the new challenges, and where powerful and influential counter-elites existed (Georgia, Ukraine, and Kyrgyzstan).

It is important to emphasise that during the "Colour Revolutions" in Georgia and Ukraine, the popularity of the idea of social justice under the new conditions was tied up closely with appeals for Westernisation and democratisation. "Revolutionaries" saw the rapprochement of their countries with the West and steps towards membership in NATO and the European Union as guarantees for the continuation of democratic reforms, which presented a real opportunity for these two countries to emerge from their transitory state.

However, the revolutions did not fulfil their promise. The new elites that came to power as result of the revolutions did all they could to become the sole beneficiaries of this process. For them, "revolution" meant the opportunity to profit from ruling, but not to change the nature and the "quality" of the development of these countries. As it became increasingly clear that the new elites did not intend to change the policy of the government in a radical fashion, the people's hopes for positive changes disappeared. It also became obvious that, without the prospect of EU membership, there are no factors in post-Soviet politics restricting the political influence of ruling elites and forcing them to change their policies.

Simultaneously, the failure of the "Colour Revolutions" to change the paradigm of development in the post-Soviet states reveals the obstacles to be overcome in order to emerge from the state of "transition within transition". Firstly, the transition to another model of evolution requires a radical change in the political-economic bases of the post-Soviet societies. Today, power and property are still under the control of a small group of elites. Secondly, the process of transition has replaced the system of nomenclature power relations with one that is based on individual and client dependence (Nisnevich 2007: 235-237). These relations determine the rentier character not only of the economy, but also of the state in the post-Soviet societies. But at the same time, it should be noted that, although the "Colour Revolutions" did not initiate a transition to another model of social and political development, they contributed to some progress in the advancement of these societies towards democratisation.

Firstly, the idea of a handover of power as a result of democratic elections was consolidated in the mass consciousness of the people in Ukraine and Georgia. The idea of holding authorities politically responsible, including forcing them to take responsibility for policy failures, became widespread in public opinion. It was closely linked with the concept of political responsibility. This means that mechanisms capable of institutionalising the demands for social and political changes are shaped in society.

Secondly, these countries made progress in building a sustainable infrastructure and the framework for future democratic society. In particular, the influence of the political parties, as connecting elements between authorities and the people, on government policies was noticeably strengthened. Societies began to regard media outlets that are independent of the government and the political opposition as natural and necessary components of the institutional design of the political system. In other words, the "Colour Revolutions" brought forth an accumulation of elements that could in the future become an institutional "trampoline" for a transition to the new system.

Conclusion

In conclusion, "post-Soviet" transition is a specific type of post-Communist transformation. We can classify it as a sort of transition only with great difficulty, because the final outcome of the changes is still not clear. The post-Soviet societies suffer from a deficit in self-development. In the absence of a strong international influence like the European Union , the prospects of the post-Soviet states making the transition to a new model of development are unclear. Therefore, regarding the evolution of the post-Soviet societies at the present stage of its development, it is better to use the concept of "destroying totalitarianism" (Gudkov and Dubin 2007: 10-14) and to focus on the attempts of elites that are tied up closely with this system to adjust the new market order to the interests of their predominance. The post-Soviet societies that did not experience a "revolution of values" because of their political passiveness and their willingness to be subjected to any conditions imposed by authorities in many senses contribute to this inert scenario of evolution.

Bibliography

Bessonova, O. 2006. *Razdatochnaia ekonomika Rossii.* Moscow: ROSSPEN.

Dahl, R. 1971. *Polyarchy: Participation and Opposition.* New Haven: Yale University Press.

Gudkov, L. and Dubin B. 2007. "Posttotalitarnyi sindrom: 'upravliaemaia demokratiia i apatiia mass'". In *Puti rossiiskogo postkommunisma*, edited by A. Ryabov and M. Lipman, 10-14. Moscow: Gvendalf.

Laclau, E. and C. Mouffe. 2001 [1985]. *Hegemony and Socialist Strategy.* London: Verso.

Makarenko, B.I. 2008. "Postkommunisticheskie strany: nekotorye itogi transformatsii". *Politeia* 3, 50. 105-125.

Nisnevich, Iu. 2007. *Audit politicheskoi sistemy postkommunisticheskoi Rossii.* Moscow: Materik.

Salmin, A.M. 1996. "O nekotorykh problemakh samoopredeleniia i vzaimodeistvia ispolnitelnoi i zakonodatel'noi vlasti v Rossiiskoi Federatsii". *Polis* 2. 7-32.

Russian Political Discourse in the 1990s: Crisis of Identity and Conflicting Pluralism of Ideas

Olga Malinova

This chapter analyses the competing discourses on the identity of the political and cultural community that constitutes the contemporary Russian state, paying special attention to different ways of conceptualising "the West" as a constitutive other. The discursive struggle of the beginning of 1990s is viewed through the lens of the discourse theory of hegemony of Ernesto Laclau and Chantal Mouffe. We argue that discourse about national/political identity fits Laclau and Mouffe's concept of dislocation; first, because there was a sharp conflict between radically different interpretations of the collective identity, and second, because the opposing discourses, due to their conceptual limits and lack of disposition for dialogue, could not grasp the complexity of current transformations. We also argue that neither the discursive conflicts of Boris Yeltsin's presidency nor the relative "stabilisation" of the discourse on collective identity during the presidency of Vladimir Putin can be explained without taking into consideration the transformation of the structure of political communications that resulted from the economic and political reforms of the 1990s and 2000s.

The collapse of the USSR and the subsequent sociopolitical transformations in Russia gave rise to a complex of social and mental shifts that are often described as a "crisis of identity". These shifts resulted not only from dramatic changes in the external environment and the internal social structure, but also from discursive struggles for interpretation of the new reality. In other words, the crisis of identity should be seen as a result not only of the new circumstances that called for reconsideration of the notion of *us*, but also of the sharp conflict over the interpretations of basic concepts on which the definition of this notion could rely. In this sense, the crisis can be well grasped in the terms of the discourse theory of hegemony of Ernesto Laclau and Chantal Mouffe (Laclau and Mouffe 2001 This process can be understood as a struggle of competing discourses for the establishment of a new hegemony (i.e., the order of prevailing norms that makes domination based on consent possible). This is especially evident in a case of discursive construction of the identity of a political and cultural community constituting the contemporary Russian state,[1] which will be the subject of our analysis.

According to our argument the situation at the beginning of the 1990s matched the concept of *dislocation* in at least two senses. First, because there was a sharp conflict between radically different constructions of the collective identity shared by the community constituting the Russian state, and hence different visions of current events and appropriate responses to them. This may be conceptualised as a competition between different discourses with many floating signifiers. Second, because the competing discourses (most of which developed basic ideas that were articulated since the end of 1980s or even earlier) were felt by many observers to be inadequate for the representation and explanation of current transformations. This would constitute dislocation in the strictest sense. In the following sections of this chapter, we will develop these arguments, outlining the structure of political discourse in 1990s and analysing some important aspects of the discourse about collective identification toward the West. But first, we must note some peculiarities of the institutional context of political discourse of 1990s as far as they are important for explaining both the discursive conflicts of the Yeltsin era and the relative stabilisation of the discourse on collective identity that took place during the Putin presidency.

Hegemonic struggles and the structure of political communications in post-Soviet Russia

When we speak about the discursive operations underlying political processes, we should remember that the problem cannot be reduced exclusively to the articulation of ideas. According to Laclau and Mouffe,

> "the practice of articulation, as fixation/dislocation of the system of differences, cannot consist of purely linguistic phenomena; but must instead pierce the entire material density of the multifarious institutions, rituals and practices through which a discursive formation is structured". (Laclau and Mouffe 2001: 109)

---

[1] In the modern Russian political vocabulary, this community is labelled "multi-national people" (*mnogonatsional'nyi narod*), "nation", "citizens of Russia", "the Russians" (either in an ethnic or in a civic sense), etc. The diversity of terms reflects discursive conflicts that contribute to the syndrome of the crisis of identity.

In particular, when discussing competing discourses in the 1990s, we should take into consideration the transformation of the institutional locus of the public sphere – the system of political communications – that took place with the collapse of the Soviet Union and the beginning of economic reforms in Russia.

As of the 1990s, the list of places where the public discourse took place, as well as the circle of its participants, had not changed much since the late *perestroika* period, with one important exception – the traditional channels of public communication were supplemented by the internet, which gained importance from the second half of the 1990sonwards. But the comparative significance of these places – as well as the rules and strategies that influenced the behaviour of those who produced, spread, and contested political ideas – changed greatly.

First of all, the changes touched the structure of the system of mass media. With the beginning of economic reforms in 1992, the press was confronted with rapidly increasing prices of paper, printing, and delivery. These problems were compounded by the shrinkage of markets caused by the collapse of the Soviet Union. The economic problems (which were experienced not only by the papers, but also by their readers) initiated a process of fragmentation of the audience for national periodicals, followed by a reduction of their circulation and influence. At the same time, the circulation and production of regional and local print media, which had certain economic advantages over the national periodicals, rose rapidly. This caused a dramatic change in the structure of political communications: The audience of periodicals decreased radically and became fragmented.[2] From 1992, the market for nationwide information was largely dominated by television. This was possible because Russia had inherited from the Soviet Union a system of nationwide television broadcasting that covered the entire territory of the Russian Federation.

In the 1990s, television played a crucial role in the production of political meanings and the structuring of the ideological spectrum. As the main channel of political communication on a national level, it became a bone of contention between political and financial groups. According to the assessments of some

---

2   According to the estimates of Resnyanskaya and Fomicheva, approximately 80 percent of the overall audience subscribed to the same centralised and local press during the 1980s. In the middle of the1990s this number declined to less than 50 percent (Resnyanskaya and Fomicheva 1999: 58). The total audience of the national newspapers by the end of 1990s was no more than 20 percent of the population (Vartanova 2000: 64).

scholars, the large commercial media holdings (such as Vladimir Gusinsky's Most-Media, the holdings in the state mass media that were controlled by Boris Berezovsky at the end of the 1990s, and the group of mass media outlets controlled by the mayor of Moscow, Yury Luzhkov) partially fulfilled the functions of political parties, such as articulating certain systems of political beliefs and cultural paradigms. In the words of Ivan Zasursky, "TV channels were the real parties. It was they who played a political performance and developed a hierarchy of roles [...] that later, before elections, were converted into the brands of political parties and movements for which the constituency was to vote" (Zasursky 2002: 98f.).

At the same time, the rules of formation and performance of the Russian parliament and government that were adopted after 1993, as well as the division of power between them, did not stimulate the political parties – the principal providers of competing programmes – to fulfil their programmatic functions, since the political course was determined by the president (who was not affiliated with any party). Due to these and other circumstances, most of the Russian parties preferred to fight for votes not by means of ideology, but by "imageology"; i.e., they preferred to identify themselves more with the images of their leaders than with particular sets of political ideas. Of course, there were also some parties that based their collective identity on certain types of ideology (the clearest examples being the Communist Party of the Russian Federation, or CPRF, and several liberal parties). But these parties' constituents were concentrated in limited segments of society. Furthermore, since the beginning of the 1990s, the interest of ordinary citizens in politics steadily decreased.

The development of asymmetric structures of public communications began in the 1990s with a "core" of major TV channels and a few periodicals with nation-wide circulation, and a "periphery" of local TV and press outlets, radio channels, and periodicals with modest circulation, all of which were channels of communication oriented at local audiences or fragmented constituencies of likeminded persons. This setting had two important implications. First, the perspectives of particular discourses depended heavily on the positions from which they were articulated: The competing explanations presented by the major outlets carried great weight; discourses that were presented mostly in the periphery had little chance of winning the struggle for hegemony. Second, for a temporary stabilisation of discourse, it was sufficient to dominate in the core of the public sphere; pluralism in its periphery did not seriously threaten the potential hegemonic discourse.

On the whole, the public sphere of the Yeltsin period was characterised by conflicts among different discourses. There was a sharp struggle for public opinion in which many actors took part, and the state did not strive to become the only player in this field (though it did not hesitate to use its resources to apply pressure; the struggle was by no means equal). It is difficult to say why the authorities did not try to use the asymmetric structure of public communication to limit the presence of unwanted discourses in the core: Was it due to Yeltsin's commitment to democratic freedom of expression, or because of the weakness of the state (Lipman and Petrov 2007: 198f.)? Anyhow, since Putin's rise to power, the situation has obviously changed. His administration sought to take control of the core of public communications, relegating annoying discourses to the periphery. This proved to be an important condition of the new stability under Putin.

The structure of the field of political discourse in the 1990s

Returning to the political debates of the 1990s, we should note that there were many competing discourses providing different ways of fixing social meanings. According to Laclau and Mouffe, "any discourse is constituted as an attempt to dominate in the field of discursivity, to arrest the flow of differences, to construct a centre" (Laclau and Mouffe 2001: 112). In these terms, there were many centres promoting their own systems of meaning, but none of them was authoritative enough to provide a "national consensus" that was felt to be an indispensible condition of the success of democratic reforms. After the break with the Communist regime and the collapse of the USSR, Russia entered into an uncertain transition; most of the previous notions about the identity of the community constituting the Russian state were no longer applicable. The new system of meaning was elaborated in the context of strict antagonism between adherents and opponents of "democratic and market" reforms that left its mark on the way the national and political identity was conceptualised in the new context.

The structure of ideological field, which was rather loose at the beginning of the 1990s, became clearly polarised by the mid-1990s. Two principal opponents competed in the public space – "Democrats" (*demokraty*) and the "Popular-Patriotic Opposition" (*narodno-patrioticheskaia oppozitsiia*). Both labels described clusters of discourses whose seeming unity was very much determined by this major opposition. Most of these discourses took shape in the previous years and relied on systems of meanings that were based on the experience of the late-Soviet period.

The discourse of the "Democrats" was a development and diversification of the "basic democratic ideology" (Golosov 2000: 79f.) that was articulated by "perestroika periodicals" and shared by many informal movements. In the 1990s, the main proponents of this kind of discourse were the major liberal parties – Democratic Choice of Russia (*Demokraticheskii Vybor Rossii*), later called the Union of the Right Forces (*Soiuz Pravykh Sil*), and Yabloko – as well as some of the mass media, mainly the television channel NTV, and other outlets that were part of Most-Media. More or less systematic versions of the ideology of the "Democrats" were produced and disseminated via limited party channels (brochures, newspapers with relatively low circulation, not all of which were regularly published, etc.). But some basic elements of this discourse were loosely used in the rhetoric of state officials and in the programmes of centrist parties (such as *Nash Dom – Rossiia*) that provided this discourse with an opportunity to be noticed by a wider audience. At the centre of this kind of discourse was the idea of reforms that would make Russia "a normal civilised country" ("the West" was more or less explicitly seen as the standard) with a market economy, private property, and democratic political institutions. There were various expectations as to the concrete design of these reforms; the particular point of disagreement and political demarcation was the attitude toward the actual course of reforms started by the government of Boris Yeltsin and Yegor Gaidar.

At the same time, the various versions of the discourse of the "Democrats" shared some common features. In particular, our analysis of the ideologies of Democratic Choice of Russia and Yabloko (Malinova 1998; cf. Sogrin 1997) revealed that both political organisations perceived liberalism primarily as the "ideology of capitalism". Both parties distinguished between economic liberalism, understood as a movement for free enterprise, competition, guarantees of private property, and a small, but effective state, and political liberalism, which was conceived as the struggle for human rights, civil society, and democracy. Economic liberalism was seen as an indispensable condition for political liberties. Thus, "civilised capitalism", free markets, and private property became the key liberal values.[3] To a certain extent, this was due to the fact that in post-Soviet

---

3   This set of ideas was the result of a selection of liberal ideas that people who called themselves "liberals" considered to be the most important. Their choice was probably

Russia, liberalism appeared as an ideology of anti-Communism, which unlike Marxism adhered to capitalism instead of Socialism, but used the same kinds of justification.[4] It was, in a way, an inversion of Marxism. It is easy to see that the discourse of the Russian "Democrats" was eminently suited to the transition paradigm.

The "Democrats'" reassessment of the national past drew a clear line between the Soviet experience (portrayed in negative terms derived from the Cold-War system of binary categories) and the future Russia that would return to the "path of civilisation". From this perspective, the country's pre-revolutionary history could not be seen very positively either since its specific course finally led to Communist rule. The novelty of democracy had two consequences for the Russian identity. On the one hand, it symbolised a desire for change, but on the other, it prompted an interpretation of the future breakthrough to "civilisation" as a demolition of the national traditions. The model of national identity constructed by the "Democrats" was strictly opposed by Communists and "Patriots". Because it was not acceptable for part of society, it was not suitable as a basis for consensus.

The discourse of the opposed camp was even more heterogeneous: It was based on a combination of different kinds of left-wing and nationalist or patriotic ideas. The synthesis of these types of discourses (which had previously been clearly differentiated and even opposed) took shape in the first half of the 1990s; it resulted from the complicated development of both the Communist and nationalist/patriotic ideologies and organisations since *perestroika*.

In the final era of the USSR, Russian nationalism was one of the currents opposed to the Communist regime (though it had sympathisers within the state structures and was more tolerable than the "democratic" wing of the dissident movement). In the years of *perestroika*, Russian nationalism became one of the main anti-Communist ideological alternatives. It had roots both in the dissident

---

not ideal: According to sociological surveys, economic liberalism was the type of liberal theory that had the least chances of being adopted in Russia (Kapustin and Kliamkin 1994: 80). Besides, the "revolutionary", "radical" liberalism of the 1990s definitely broke with the pre-revolutionary Russian tradition that insisted on moderate, graduate means for implementing liberal aims.

4   Some of the main lines of argument approximately stated that the basis of a "good society" was a "proper" form of property. Another version was that all social, political, national etc. problems would be solved automatically if Russia succeed in the main, economic task. A third often heard argument was that the main historical paths were universal, and Russia had to come back to the "road of civilization".

movement and in the circles of Soviet intellectuals gathered around the magazines *Nash sovremennik, Molodaia gvardiia,* and *Moskva.* But during *perestroika,* ideas of this type did not enjoy wide popularity: Since they were critical of the Western experience, they were not sufficiently opposed to the Soviet system. The situation changed significantly after collapse of the USSR and the beginning of economic reforms in Russia. Now the "popular-patriotic" opposition strove to distance itself as much as possible from the Yeltsin regime– and at the same time to reconsider its former assessment of the Soviet period as predominantly "anti-Russian".[5] However, it should be noted that the discourse of nationalists or so-called patriots was rather diverse: There were Russian nationalists who gave priority to the interests of the ethnic Russians and blamed the Communist regime for their violation of their rights and neglect of traditional values while for others, the ultimate value was embodied in the Russian state (Solovey 2000; Umland 2006; Sokolov 2006). The latter found it easier to reconcile themselves to the Soviet regime taking into consideration its geopolitical and social achievements. It was this *derzhavnicheskii,* or "imperial" version of nationalist discourse that in the 1990s tended to merge with certain currents of left-wing discourse to produce the joint 'popular-patriotic opposition'.

No less complicated was the development of the left/Communist wing (see Kholmskaya 1998; Kapustin 2000). After their defeat in 1993, the Communist and left-wing ideologies were revived in various forms. The most successful in terms of election results were the Communist Party of the Russian Federation and its allies in the national-patriotic bloc. They combined traditional communist rhetoric with criticism of liberalism and Westernism, and included some elements of Russian nationalism of the imperial type (Zyuganov 1995). This ideology was produced and disseminated mostly through party channels (though it should be mentioned that this network had many more members than any of the liberal parties could boast). It had fewer opportunities to reach out to a broader audience via television channels, but it was not totally neglected by the national mass media: The Communists were considered the principal opposing force, and their activities were covered regularly, though not neutrally.

---

5 According to Alexander Dugin, Marxism was a less harmful variety of Westernism than liberalism, because the essence of the former doctrine was successfully "improved" in a traditional Russian way, while the latter "includes no components that might be reinterpreted in a national way". Therefore, "Yeltsinism" is "radically oriented towards breaking with everything that constitutes a continuous history of our people" (Dugin 1994: 153).

Of course, the opposition between "Democrats" and the "populist-patriotic opposition" was not the only ideological watershed in Yeltsin's Russia. During this long period, there were a lot of issues that divided society along a variety of fault lines. But the problem of the reforms was at the centre, and the controversy between "Democrats" and Communists and their allies dominated the field of political debate. That led to a relative marginalisation of the other discourses.

The 1990s witnessed what might be described as a hegemonic struggle. There was a strict competition between various discourses that was structured by the opposition of two poles, neither of which had enough resources to win and provide the desired "social consent".[6] Remarkably, all participants perceived the conflict in terms of a zero-sum game: Neither side was ready to adopt the interpretations proposed by its opponents. This led to a lack of a "common political language available to participants" (Urban 1998: 969). The struggle for signification resulted in ascribing different, sometimes conflicting meanings to the same words. Thus, terms such as "democracy", "social good", "nation", "people", etc., became floating signifiers that could acquire radically different, and sometimes even self-contradictory interpretations in different discourses.[7]

But there was one more aspect that falls into the category of *dislocation*: both competing discourses, being based upon previous experience and not disposed towards dialogue with the opponents, described the ongoing social transformation in terms that could not be fully adequate to its complexity. In retro-

---

[6]   Remarkably, this term was an important part of the official discourse: a need for "consent", for the solidarity of society, and for power was a permanent topic of Yeltsin's speeches at least from 1994 onwards. An analysis of his discourse reveals a permanent tension between pluralism (which was considered a sign of a break with the Soviet past) and lack of solidarity that was seen as an impediment for the success of reforms.
[7]   This fact is particularly noticeable to the outside observer. See, for example, the remarks by Michael Urban on the use of the terms "nation", "state", and "minority" in the context of the discussion of "the national idea" in 1996-1997. Urban explains this "tendency to abuse language by encoding esoteric meanings into words, converting them into chattels of their users, thus retarding their capacity to communicate as words are detached from (common) sense" with an anti-dialogical form of expression that is typical for the Russian political discourse of 1990s (Urban 1998: 972). It should be mentioned that the "fluidity" of meanings of the term "nation" and its derivatives is used by many participants of the Russian political discourse: It helps to avoid some troublesome questions involved in the definition of "Russianness" in a post-imperial context. See, for example, the analysis of Yeltsin's rhetoric by Vera Tolz (Tolz 1998: 1007-1010) and the analysis of the texts of Vladislav Surkov by Oxana Karpenko (Karpenko 2007). Of course, this "fluidity" of meanings is not conducive to dialogue and the search for common grounds in discussions (Malinova 2007b).

spect, it is clear that neither the concept of "transition" as taken for granted by "Democrats" nor the various versions of the idea of "our own way" as developed by their opponents could fully grasp the contradictory trends that shaped the unprecedented experience of post-Soviet transformation. In the absence of reliable theories that could explain this kind of development, the participants of political discourse were forced to draw upon the "experience of the West" that became an important reference point for the construction of collective identity in post-Soviet Russia.

The images of *us* and *the other* in competing discourses
In the discourses of the 1990s, the collective identity of the community that constitutes the Russian state was constructed in connection with many *constitutive others* – the concepts of "the West", "the United States", "Europe", "China", "Japan", "the other post-Soviet/post-Communist countries" played more or less important roles in its definition and redefinition. But the most important of these terms was "the West". The discussions about Russia's relations with this *constitutive other* have a long and persistent tradition.

The opposition of "Westernisers" and "Nativists/anti-Westernisers" under different names and with varying agendas has been reproduced many times in Russia since the 19th century. From time to time – as in the 1990s – this opposition played the role of a major ideological watershed structuring the political spectrum (Malinova 2009, chapter 4). In the 1990s, the camp of contemporary "Westernisers"[8] consisted mainly of the liberal politicians and public intellectuals. The ranks of modern "anti-Westernisers" were more diverse: They included both left-wingers and right-wingers; Russian nationalists and advocates of imperial projects; critics of the Soviet regime and those who feel nostalgia for the USSR; faithful Orthodox Christians and those who used religious ideals quite pragmatically. The differences between these segments of the political spectrum were so significant that the only reason why they can be conceived as a single camp is because they all adhere to the empty signifier of "anti-Westernism" (which means both opposition to the government's pro-Western political course of the

---

8   The term "Westernisers" is used broadly here: It refers not so much to classical Westernism, i.e., the particular complex of ideas that took a shape in 1840s, as to the general current in the Russian intellectual tradition that viewed the West as the reference point of modernisation and progress. "Anti-Westernism", in turn, is represented by many currents that pointed to the principal disparity between Russia and Europe and the necessity of "our own way".

early 1990s and a critical attitude towards the West). Nevertheless, the models of collective identity that are promoted by "anti-Westernisers" still have much in common.

The aims of reforms that started in 1992 were formulated in clearly "Westernist" terms. It seemed that the triumph of "democratic" forces in August of 1991 opened up an opportunity to change the trajectory of Russia's historical path, to conduct reforms that would make it a prosperous democratic country with a market economy. In the words of the minister for foreign affairs in Gaidar's government, Andrey Kozyrev: "our 'super-task' is [...] to pull ourselves up by our bootstraps [...] to the club of the most developed democratic countries. Only in this way can Russia obtain the national self-consciousness and self-respect that it needs so much" (Kozyrev 1994: 22). It would be wrong to suppose that the "Democrats" oversimplified this "super-task": they confirmed that, in order to join "the club", Russia needed to make a choice about its collective identity vis-à-vis the West and the East.[9] Some of them doubted that Russia was able to walk such a difficult path without outside help. One of those who tried to mobilise external support for democratic reforms in Russia was the writer and historian Alexander Yanov. In his writings, he argued that it is impossible for a society that has harboured imperial ambitions for centuries to transform itself. He tried to persuade the Western countries to elaborate a special programme of support for democratic reforms in Russia – if only for reasons of their own security. According to Yanov, "there could be no national humiliation in accepting such help from outsiders [*variagov*]" (Yanov 1995: 21).

The model of collective identity promoted by "Westernisers" was significantly informed by a specific interpretation of the post-Cold War situation. With the collapse of the Communist regime, the ideological barriers between *us* and the *constitutive other* had fallen; Russia had declared the values that underpinned "Western" identity – the development of democracy, rule of law, and a market economy – its official aims. Of course, that does not mean that Russia became part of "the West, but it meant that it actually pursued the same goals as

---

9   Yegor Gaidar describes the problems that he and his government sought to solve in terms of a "final decision" between two paths of modernisation, the first of which supposes the development of the Western type of institutions, while the second one is aimed at extensive growth under the pressure of the state. According to this interpretation, Russia has long been unable to choose between these two ways, but now the time has come – it must walk the road of "civilized", "liberal capitalism" (Gaidar 1995: 47-75,143-144).

its *constitutive other*. Unfortunately, the chances of this model of collective identity were substantially weakened by the lack of sufficient support of reforms in Russia by Western countries. As the results of reforms became more and more problematic, the stated aims of the "Democrats" appeared increasingly unrealistic.

The anti-Westernism of the opposite camp was both a reaction to the radically "Westernist" model of collective identity promoted by the "Democrats" (and to the politics that it symbolised), and a common denominator of sorts for the rather heterogeneous doctrines that were gathered under the banner of a "populist-patriotic opposition". The main emphasis was the rejection of the idea that the West must be the model for Russia.

It is no wonder that in the writings of the 1990s, we find radically opposed representations of "the West". "Democrats" and "Westernisers" saw "The West" as an *other* that was worth to be taken as an example. First of all, "the West" is a highly developed society, the leader of progress. Therefore, its experience should be taken into consideration even if this is to be done for practical reasons. Nonetheless, the choice of Russian "Westernisers" is determined not only by pragmatic considerations, but also by values: "the West" is a liberal society.

"The West" is a society with high standards of living. That is why, from the point of view of a "Westerniser", it is appropriate to argue that it is in the national interest of Russia "to become a European country in a sense of the level and quality of consumption" (Sheinis 2000).

At the same time, the Russian "Westernisers" stressed that Russia was not the West. So they enthusiastically advocated taking a selective approach to the Western experience.

Almost the opposite picture is found in the writings of the "patriots". The dominant trait of their portrayal of "the West" might be summed up in the formula that "The West" was the *inimical other*. It is recognised as the technological leader and the symbol of a high standard of living, but these traits have negative connotations: "Patriots" argue that this prosperity was gained through the exploitation of the rest of mankind by "the golden billion" (Zyuganov 1995: 60f., Podberyozkin 1996: 41).

"The West" is pictured as a force that threatens *our* identity. Its aspiration to impose on Russia an alien culture is represented by "anti-Westernisers" as a part of a global plot, while preservation of the Russian identity is seen as some kind of mission that should be performed for the sake of all of mankind, since Russia is seen as the last bulwark of resistance to Western cultural expansion.

The "anti-Westernisers" depict the post-Soviet period as a difficult and unequal struggle with a guileful enemy who masked his attacks with the rhetoric of progress, democracy, human rights, etc. "The West" is represented not only as the *other* whose example is inappropriate and possibly dangerous, but also as the enemy who encroaches upon the power and capability of Russia.

Being unable to ignore the older repertoire of meanings that ascribe certain positive traits to the "progressive West", the modern "anti-Westernisers" represent the latter as a traitor to its own declared values. Under the cover of rhetoric about freedom, modernisation, and progress, it tries to pursue its selfish interests. This point of view can be found, for example, in the works of Sergey Kara-Murza, who applies the conception of "Euro-centrism". "Euro-centrism" depends on a set of myths that exaggerate the role of Europe and the West in world history. It supports a double standard and cultural racism. "The West" is thus accused of cultural imperialism. In a certain sense, Russian "anti-Westernism" is a reaction against this type of *othering*: representing the Russian identity as something radically different from the European one, the politicians and writers from this camp, following the definition of Iris M. Young, "find themselves defined from the outside, positioned, placed, by a network of dominant meanings they experience as arising from elsewhere, from those with whom they do not identify and who do not identify with them" (Young 1990: 59).

It is easy to notice that the images of "the West" portrayed by "Westernisers" and "Patriots" are painted in black and white and are almost diametrically opposed to each other. This indicates the intensity of the confrontation between the sides as well as the fact that the models of collective identity that they promoted were highly dependent on their ideological vision of reality.

What is more, neither of the competing camps was able to propose a model of collective identity that could provide a basis for social consent and solidarity. The mobilising potential of any model of collective identity depends on its capability to elevate the self-esteem of the respective community. In the sense, the chances of the "Westernist" model are not very high. In 1840, one could talk about Russia's "great future", leaving the task of determining its mission to the grandsons (as Vissarion Belinsky did). For the generation of "grandsons", it was much more difficult. The "compensatory potential" of the radical versions of the "Westernist" model was higher than that of liberal ones because they put forward an ideal that had not yet been achieved in "the West", leaving Russia an opportunity to outrun its opponent. But 70 years of Soviet rule totally reduced this advantage.

The "anti-Westernist" models are much more attractive in this respect as they try to raise the collective self-esteem by introducing an alternative frame of reference. However, their success also partly depends on the results of modernisation. The renewal of the conservative project requires new "outposts" that are to be defended on the basis of "ancient" traditions. Otherwise it goes out of fashion. The modern "anti-Westernisers" partly solve this problem by appealing to the new enemy – "globalism". So, Russian "anti-Westernism" with its century-old traditions becomes something like the godfather of anti-globalists. A much more difficult task for "anti-Westernist" models is the problem of how to formulate an appropriate utopia: the last centuries of Russian history have been so ambiguous that is rather hard to arrange them into any "organic" tradition. The ideological heterogeneity of modern "anti-Westernism" mentioned above is a result of this situation. Its adherents have a common answer to the eternal Russian question of "Who is guilty?" (*Kto vinovat?*), but they are not so unanimous about the other perennial question – "What should be done?" (*Chto delat'?*).

Of course, the persistence of this type of binary opposition cannot be explained solely by peculiar features of competing models of identity. The need for correlation with "the West" was determined by geopolitical and economic factors. Of course, the Russian debates about "the West" to a certain extent were a reaction to the way Russia was *Othered* by Western politicians and intellectuals (Neumann 1996; Neumann 1999; Malia 1999). Anyhow, the fact that in the end of the 20th century the Russian identity was constructed by the binary "either-or" opposition of "Westernism" and "anti-Westernism", was not conducive to the development of the flexible system of multiple identities that would be appropriate for a multi-ethnic country in a globalised world.

Conclusion

The crisis of identity that followed after the collapse of the USSR fits into the concept of dislocation as far as it was not merely a result of the structural changes of the 1990s, but also a failure to interpret social reality within pre-existing discursive schemes. None of these schemes became dominant. The analysis of political discourse of 1990s reveals permanent tension between conflicting pluralism of ideas and the lack of solidarity. During the first decade of post-Soviet transformation, the discursive struggle did not result in the establishment of the new hegemony.

For various reasons, in the process of political transformation of the 1990s, Russia did not succeed in creating institutions that could become effective channels of public dialogue. In the first decade of the 21st century, the political elite had staked their rule on the establishment of "consent from above" by implementation of more comprehensive models of collective identity. Putin, who – unlike Yeltsin – did not feel an obligation to take sides in the conflicts of the 1990s, could admit some ideas from the repertoire of Communists and "Patriots" that were taboo for "Democrats". In this way, he could mobilise "consent" by appealing to values and symbols from the Soviet past. The new, comprehensive official discourse tended to reduce tensions between competing models of collective identity by mixing their elements in eclectic construction. At the same time, it rejected (and thus marginalised) the extreme versions of competing models. However, it should not be forgotten that relative stabilisation of discourse was achieved not only due to the development of a more "fitting" discourse about collective identity (Godzimirski 2008: 23, 25), but also because of the establishment of control under the "core" of public sphere as a result of political reforms of Putin. On the other hand, the fact that the alternative discourses did not disappear, but were pushed to the periphery of public sphere, is reason to assert that Putin's efforts to establish "consent from above" did not stop the hegemonic struggle, but instead changed its conditions.

Bibliography

Dugin, A. 1994. *Konservativnaia revoliutsia*. Moscow: Arktogeia.

Gaidar, E.T. 1995. *Gosudarstvo i evolutsia*. Moscow: Evrasia.

Godzimirski, J.M. 2008. "Putin and Post-Soviet Identity. Building blocks and buzz words". *Problems of Post-Communism* 55, 5. 14-27.

Golosov, G. 2000. "Proiskhozhdenie sovremennykh Rossiiskikh politicheskikh partii, 1987-1993". In *Pervyi elektoral'nyi tsikl v Rossii (1993-1996)*, edited by V. Gel'man, G. Golosov, and E. Meleshkina, 77-105. Moscow: Ves' Mir.

Kapustin, B.G. 2000. "Levyi konservatizm KPRF i ego rol' v sovremennoi politike". In his *Ideologiia i politika v postkommunisticheskoi Rossii*, 115-129. Moscow: Editorial URSS.

Kapustin, B.G. and I.M. Rliamkin. 1994. "'Liberal'nye tsennosti v soznanii rossiian". *Polis*, no. 1.

Karpenko, O. 2007. "'Suverennaia demokratiia' dlia vnutrennego i naruzhnogo primeneniia". *Neprokosnovennyi zapas* 1, 51. http://magazines.russ.ru/nz/2007/1/kar15.html [accessed 4 September 2009].

Kholmskaya, M.R. 1998. *Kommunisty Rossii: fakty, idei i tendentsii*. Moscow: Partinform.

Kozyrev, A.V. 1994. *Preobrazhenie*. Moscow: Mezhdunarodnye otnosheniia.

Laclau, E. and C. Mouffe. 2001 [1985]. *Hegemony and Socialist Strategy*. London: Verso.

Lipman, M. and N. Petrov. 2007. "Vzaimodeistvie vlasti i obshchestva". In *Puti rossiiskogo postkommunisma*, edited by M. Lipman and A. Riabov, 163-233. Moscow: Carnegie Centre and R. Elinin.

Malia, M. 1999. *Russia Under Western Eyes: From the bronze horseman to the Lenin Mausoleum*. Cambridge: Harvard University Press.

Malinova, O. 1998. *Liberalizm v politicheskom spektre Rossii (na primere partii "Democraticheskii Vybor Rossii" i obshchestvennogo ob"edineniia "Iabloko")*. Moscow: Pamiatniki istoricheskoi mysli.

——— 2007a. "Ideologicheskii pluralizm i transformatsiia publichnoi sfery v postsovetskoi Rossii". *Polis* 1. 6-21.

——— 2007b. "Konstruirovanie identichnosti: vozmozhnosti i ogranicheniia". *Pro et contra* 11, 3. 60-65.

——— 2009. *Rossiia i "Zapad" v XX veke: Transformatsiia diskursa o kollektivnoi identichnosti*. Moscow: ROSSPEN.

Neumann, I.B. 1996. *Russia and the Idea of Europe. A study in identity and international relations*. London & New York: Routledge.

——— 1999. *Uses of the Other. "The East" in European identity formation*. Manchester: Manchester University Press.

Podberyozkin, A. 1996. *Russkii put'*. Moscow: Dukhovnoe nasledie.

Resnyanskaya, L.L. and I.D. Fomicheva. 1999. *Gazeta dlia vsei Rossii*. Moscow: IKAR.

Sheinis, V.L. 2000. "Rossiia i Evropa: interesy i mify". *Nezavisimaia gazeta* December. 20.

Sogrin, V.V. 1997. "Liberalizm v Rossii: peripetii i perspektivy". *Obshchestvennye nauki i sovremennost'* 1. 13-23.

Sokolov, M. 2006. "Natsional-bol'shevistskaia partiia: ideologicheskaia evolutsia i politicheskii stil'". In *Russkii natsionalizm: ideologiia i nastroenie*, edited by A. Verkhovsky, 139-164. Moscow: Center "Sova".

Solovey, V.D. 2000. "Natsional-radikalizm". In *Politicheskie partii Rossii: istoriia i sovremennost'*, edited by A.I. Zevelev, Iu.P. Sviridenko, and V.V. Shelokhaev, 594-621. Moscow: ROSPEN.

Tolz, V. 1998. "Forging the Nation: National identity and nation building in post-Communist Russia". *Europe-Asia Studies* 50, 6. 993-1022.

Umland, A. 2006. "Tri raznovidnosti postsovetskogo fashizma". In *Russkii natsionalizm: ideologiia i nastroenie*, edited by A. Verkhovsky, 223-262. Moscow: Center "Sova".

Urban, M. 1998. "Remythologizing the Russian State". *Europe-Asia Studies* 50, 6. 969-992.

Vartanova, E. 2000. "Media v post-sovetskoi Rossii: ikh struktura i vliianie". *Pro et contra* 5, 4. 61-81.

Yanov, A.L. 1995. *Posle Eltsina. Veimarskaia Rossia.* Moscow: KRUK.

Young, I.M. 1990. *Justice and the Politics of Difference.* Princeton: Princeton University Press.

Zasursky, I. 2002. "SMI i vlast'. Rossiia devianostykh". In *Sredstva massovoi informatsii postsovetskoi Rossii*, edited by A.A. Grabelnikov, 86-134. Moscow: Aspect-Press.

Zyuganov, G. 1995. *Rossiia i sovremennyi mir.* Moscow: Informpechat'.

Russian "Sovereign Democracy": A Powerful Ideological Discourse in a Quasi-Authoritarian Regime

Nicolas Hayoz

It is not an easy task to "deconstruct" the many meanings of the political slogan "sovereign democracy", and it is also difficult to identify the reasons that pushed the Russian regime to reproduce this discourse as part of its self-description, to describe its power structure; or to establish the extent to which the underlying ideology may be considered part of a strategy aiming at stabilising the regime. This chapter addresses these questions rather indirectly. It argues first that the discourse on "sovereign democracy" corresponds to the aims and realities of a semi- or quasi-authoritarian regime pretending to be a democracy, although one that is specifically Russian in nature. From this point of view, the chapter explores the interdependency of ideology and organisational power in Russia. The formula "sovereign democracy" is in fact part of an immunisation strategy coming from the core of the power structure of Russia, signalling to the world, the country, and the "near abroad" what Russian power is about. The war with Georgia highlighted this fact quite visibly. "Sovereign democracy" then, however useless the formula may be from the scientific point of view, reveals a lot about the way that power is exercised in a country like Russia, where a rent-seeking regime is trying to retain its power by all means.

The economic crisis of autumn 2008 appears to have affected the discursive and even the ideological levels in Russia. Proceeding from the assumption that a political discourse needs to be backed up by material resources in order to be sustainable, the Kremlin's notion of "sovereign democracy" may have lost much of its appeal. The financial and economic crisis has shown that the Russian state is not immune against failure. Ideas such as "sovereign democracy" thus may lose their legitimacy.

The stability of authoritarian regimes such as the Russian one is usually guaranteed by a combination of repression and the regime's ability to accommodate different groups and their interests through rent distribution. If the "contract" that stipulates "prosperity for loyalty" is out of balance due to a shrinking of the state's resource basis (meaning that the state is able to distribute less rents and accommodate fewer interests), the regime may become more repressive, or it will need to find an alternative source of legitimacy – possibly an ideological one. At the same time, the regime may also decide to change the metaphor on which the whole system rests ideologically – by placing the blame for the difficult situation on either external or internal factors. Eventually, the regime may be forced to invent a new ideological discourse.

One may ask: for whom and what for? But the more important underlying question is: Does the Russian regime really need a discursive strategy in order to justify the way it conceives its power and its global and regional aspirations? The answer is that it does. Like all illiberal and authoritarian regimes, Russia needs a discourse in order to justify its actions and policies, including its verbal attacks and quite often also its real wars against its proclaimed internal and external enemies. Furthermore, like other nations haunted by dark sides of their history, such as Turkey, it has enormous difficulties in facing up to its past. Established democracies based on the rule of law leave the question of "historical truth", and matters related to the interpretation of history, about past and present facts or conflicts, to a communication process in the public space involving the media, scientists, intellectuals, the public, special committees etc. In Russia, the political elite proclaims publicly that it needs to protect society and the state from false conceptions of history, or deviations from the official version of how things are to be perceived in the country and in its neighbourhood. One may find many reasons why Russia feels insecure about its past, its identity, and why it has a propensity to see enemies behind each corner. An authoritarian tradition, the legacy of Communism, and other cultural reasons such as Orthodox Christianity may explain the Russian obsession with unity and holism. This continuous emphasis on unity, of course, conceals a simple truth: the fear that things may fall apart – a risk that multiethnic democracies must also face. But multiethnic democracies are expected to handle conflicts with minorities through specific inclusive communicative devices or procedures in order to stabilise the country and to hold it together. They also stipulate procedures for a democratic handover of power, which is after all still considered one of the main stabilising factors in democracies. None of these elements are present in the Russian political system. So what holds Russia together? Ideological discourses, particularly the discourse on "sovereign democracy", are only a part of the explanation. Russia's contemporary power structure strongly resembles the Communist party structure of the former Soviet Union, where the hierarchical power of the party was backed and legitimised by the Communist ideology. This is to say that ideology does not make sense without control. The "genetic code" of Soviet Communism was always ideology *and* control. This is also the case in today's Russia: the "Putin system" has been, and remains, primarily concerned with control of a society and a nation affected by many centrifugal forces.

This chapter explores the interdependency of ideology and organisational power in Russia ("Russia, Inc."). The discourse on "sovereign democracy", which is a component of a larger ideological package, obviously serves a range of different interests, but it could not be understood without the establishment of a centralised quasi-authoritarian power structure by Putin and his allies in the state bureaucracy. An ideology is not enough to stabilise an authoritarian power structure. Stabilisation should not be confused with legitimisation. Legitimisation may contribute to the stability of power. Under Soviet Communism, the party ideology passed away long before the demise of the party structure, which managed to stabilise itself for a few years more through corruption and a system of favouritism. But once the "economic basis" had eroded, the party also collapsed. The contemporary power structure in Russia may not collapse, but since it is not based on a dynamic power that can transform itself, its stability is continuously being challenged by rival networks and conflicts between them. Moreover, the personal power of the leaders may be appreciated by a majority of a public that ignores the realities of a modern democracy, but personal power always means visible and exposed power, which can be challenged easily if it fails to produce visible results.

This is what should be kept in mind in the following journey through some of the meanings of the idea of "sovereign democracy", which fits quite well with the Kremlin's efforts to retain power and to control society. The meanings of "sovereign democracy" also raise the question of the extent to which this slogan contributes to the stability of the regime. This is again a difficult question, since it is not at all clear what "stabilisation" and "stability" really mean in a country like Russia. Stability in a democratic regime is quite easy to measure; for example, the stability of a government is based on a coalition of parties, which may or may not win the necessary majority in order to form a stable government. In Russia, where power is not based on change through elections, the stability of the supreme power, the "Kremlin", is probably based on a continuous balancing of interests among rival factions and groups in the state bureaucracy, which can be held together by the personalised power structure and its networks at the top of the hierarchy. From that point of view, the discourse on "sovereign democracy", with its implicit message "we have things under control", does not only satisfy the expectations and frustrations of a larger public, it could also be considered as a useful ideological device contributing to the coherence and discipline of an oversized and over-centralised state bureaucracy. Finally, "sovereign democracy" is also a framework that suggests to observers, be they the public, elites, opponents, or the international community, how to look at Russia and how its "collective identity" should be conceived on the level of political semantics. Stability in Russia thus has as much to do with the reproduction mechanism of power as with the more symbolic and ideological side of power, which has to find convincing words and concepts to "fix" the meanings of the nation and its identity. It is also likely that the more unsure a nation is about its past and its future, the more it tries to control the social production of meanings through ideology, state power, and legal means.

"Sovereign democracy" as an ideology and a slogan

Some argue that the successful models of economic development in regimes like Russia and China, combining an open economy with a closed political system, made them more politically attractive in a world characterised by the competition between democratic and authoritarian regimes (Kagan 2008: 69 ff.). This may no longer be the case, but it is probably safe to say that the attractiveness of a model like "sovereign democracy" follows a political conjuncture: The fact that the formula is no longer in circulation in the public space could mean that the regime does not need it anymore. But even if it may have lost its momentum, the policies behind this catchphrase have not changed. This was different a couple of years ago, when Russia felt the necessity to react to "Western interference" in Russian affairs (or in what Russia considered to be its "zones of influence"), or to triumphant liberalism in the West.

In this regard, Ivan Krastev (2008: 17) shows to what extent the formula "sovereign democracy" was, as a practice and a discourse, Moscow's answer to the danger represented by the "Orange Revolution" in Ukraine. The "Orange Revolution" brought a popular president to power and thus showed for the first time that regime change through mass revolt was possible in a former Soviet country – not least thanks to the help of Western "democracy promotion" strategies, which included material and financial aid.

The Russian leadership was clearly not prepared to allow similar scenarios emerge in other neighbouring countries, let alone on Russian soil. Putin's reestablishment of a "power vertical" was the beginning of political stability for Russia, but it was also the start of his offensive against Western interference, against Western-style democracy and its promoters. The anti-Western position in the formula of "sovereign democracy" also shows that this discourse was directed against the worldwide "hegemony" of the Western notion of liberalism. Also, in times of global crisis and with liberal capitalism at least for the moment no longer triumphant, the Russian regime seems to feel more relaxed and may see its approach of state-driven capitalism confirmed. But this could be an illusion, since the Russian version of state-driven capitalism has for the moment only benefited a small group of rent seekers on the elite level. Moreover, the way Russia "handled" the war with Georgia in August 2008 showed to the world that Russia is willing to assert its "national interests", if necessary, even by provoking a direct confrontation with the West. It is as if Russia was showing that it can be active not only at the level of a semantic battle, with "sovereign democracy" as one of the weapons, but that it can also mobilise "hard" military power in order do defend its interests. In that sense, the invasion of Georgia may stand for an actual "implementation" – although implicit – of Russia's vision of "sovereign democracy".

In order to understand what a certain discourse really means, we need to relate this discourse not only to the social and economic basis on which it rests, but also connect it to those actors within the relevant power structures who are actually responsible for the production and reproduction of a certain discourse. The structures within which those actors operate, i.e., the type of regime, are highly relevant for understanding a certain political discourse. Therefore, the following remarks will focus on Russia's political regime and the kind of discourse it produces.[1]

When thinking about Russia's political regime, autocracy is clearly the primary point of reference. It is telling that the representatives of the Russian state do not describe their regime in terms of a "normal" democracy. The Kremlin knows that its political construction has nothing in common with the institu-

---
1 See Galasinska and Krzyzanowski 2008, particularly the introduction by the editors.

tional set-up of a modern democracy. Its political discourse on "sovereign democracy" does not hide this fact; on the contrary, it is the semantic correlate of "autocracy". In other words, what is of interest here is a specific power configuration that produces specific discourses, but has to rely on huge organisational resources and organisational systems to control society.[2]

The discursive and organisational design of the Russian regime offers a lot of insights into its conception of society and the political. Russia has more difficulties than other regional societies in accepting the implications of modern society and of globalisation. It pretends to represent something different, but in fact this "difference" is only highlighted as a way of justifying a certain type of governance model that mainly suits the interests of a small and powerful ruling elite.

The difference is no longer strictly ideological, as was the case with the Soviet Union. After all, Russia is part of the globalised economy. But politically, the Russian leadership highlights its differences with the West, as it does not want Russia to submit to any supranational structure that would endanger its "sovereign" status as a leading regional power with global ambitions.[3] Russian companies are becoming integrated into the global markets, yet the Russian state restricts foreign access to its own markets. Russia deals with democratic countries and democratically organised international organisations, yet it fears the intrusion of "foreign" NGOs onto its territory. Through strict control of the mass media, the government tries to prevent critical voices about Russia from being heard. Finally, the Russian state has built up a discursive and organisational defence system – of which the slogan "sovereign democracy" is just one element – against the "hegemony" of liberal democracy.[4]

All of these elements are supposed to stabilise the system – yet, in fact, they are also geared towards preventing the loss of power and privileges of Russia's ruling elite. The Russian state has organised society in a similar way as Chinese society is structured; it is based on a specific combination of personal

---

2 We refer here to the systems theory of Niklas Luhmann and his distinction between the three types of system levels – society, organisation, and interactions. With regard to organisational systems, see Luhmann 1982, 1997, 2000a, 2000b. Concerning the differences and similarities between the theories of Laclau and Luhmann, see Andersen 2003 and Rasch 2008. For an application of Luhmann's theoretical framework to organised societies like Russia, see Hayoz 2007.
3 For these aspects, see Krastev 2008.
4 Authors like Mouffe (2005) identify the same "hegemony", but for different reasons.

power, organisational power, and functional differentiation. "Kremlin, Inc.", "Russia, Inc.", or "militocracy" are semantic shortcuts describing organised forms of societies expressing the obsessions of regimes with administrative resources and the construction of centrally controlled bureaucratic hierarchies in all social spheres. This phenomenon is reminiscent – not coincidentally – of the centralised control as exercised by the Communist Party during the Soviet era.

Authors like Robert Kagan (2008: 59) are certainly right when they observe that the Russian and Chinese leaders believe in autocracy and disdain democracy, since the latter is associated with interference, conflicts, divisions, and of course with the instability of power – a power that is under constant threat from society, unless this society is firmly controlled.

The idea of "sovereign democracy" can be viewed as an prescription for preventing Western democracy promotion in Russia and Western support for democratic movements in what Russia considers its "sphere of influence" in the neighbouring states. The meaning of political notions such as "sovereign democracy" can be controlled more tightly. Globalisation is certainly one of the driving forces behind such a "protectionist" discursive *dispositif*. On the other hand, such discursive claims on a regional level may be tested against the background of emerging global observers in a globalised world: They are subject to world opinion and criticism by global protest movements, but also scrutinised by scientific observers and their research programs on the progress or regression of democracy in specific countries.

The political function of "sovereign democracy"

The concept of "sovereign democracy" was elaborated with the intention of justifying Russia's "own path" in the eyes of a Western audience. It was thus mainly an elite project. However, to what extent has it also been successful in appealing to a broader domestic audience? That depends on what the public reads into the idea of "sovereign democracy". If it denotes the concept of a "powerful Russia", then the message appeals to a broader audience. On the other hand, if it refers to Russia being a democracy *sui generis*, then the message is probably missing its aim.

Opinion polls show that Russians are well familiar with the basic elements of a democracy – and are fully aware that their country does not meet the democratic standards. Elections at the national level, as well as at most regional levels, are not about transferring power, but about retaining it, and the aim of the state is not to protect rights, but to control society. The Russian public is one of the most cynical, distrusting, and dissatisfied of all post-Communist societies. Almost 90 percent of the country's citizens believe that their public officials are corrupt. The degree of political distrust towards almost all political institutions, with the exception of the presidency, is reason for alarm.[5] Such facts speak another language than the official statements about the idiosyncratic nature of Russian democracy.

Of course, one might find similar problems in established democracies. But the point is that in the Russian case, there are no checks and balances, political opposition, free media, or civil-society institutions that can mobilise against a corrupt power structure in order to request accountability or to replace the holders of power. There is a large gap between the state and society. If people do not trust politicians, they cannot be expected to take ideological propositions seriously either. Nevertheless, there are considerable differences between various strata of Russian society, e.g., along generational lines, when it comes to their responses towards the ideological discourses coming from the regime, attempting to gain a hegemonic status.

Since the discourse on "sovereign democracy" includes such elements as the achievement of national or elite unity, the strength of the nation, or the national interest[6] – but not Western-style democracy –, the public in Russia may perceive this strange semantic construction as part of the elites' efforts to strengthen Russian power at home and internationally, even though the average citizen probably has no clear idea as to what this notion is supposed to mean. In other words, if the majority understands "sovereign democracy" more in terms of sovereignty than democracy, then the hegemonic discourse has the effect intended by the state; e.g., to achieve elite unity and shield the country against ideological interference from the West. If, however, people perceive it as denoting a special form of Russian democracy, the discourse also serves an ideological purpose underscoring that Russia *wants* to be different from other countries and that the only way to guarantee stability is through a strong executive power that can maintain control over distrusted political parties, the parliament, and most other institutions of the Russian political system.

---

5   See Diamond 2008: 198ff., 64ff.; Rose 2009: 60ff., 153ff., 173ff. See also http://www.levada.ru/press/2007040901.html and the Freedom House Report *Nations in Transit 2008*.
6   See Krastev 2008.

In that sense, "sovereign democracy" serves interests, demands, and expectations on many different levels: From street-level communication to the supreme spheres of power, where the main question is how to guarantee stability and to assure the survival of the regime. Thus, depending on the attitudes of the public towards the regime, "sovereign democracy" can mean two things: a discourse that is an adequate description for the political practices and the core features of the current Russian regime; and an ideology or "ideological fantasy". In the latter case, the regime and parts of the public would pretend that Russia is a democracy, but at same time know perfectly well that this is not the case.[7] This may actually be a successful strategy, since the other part of the concept of "sovereign democracy", i.e., the word "sovereign", is the discursive reality that really matters and expresses the way power works in the country – as an authoritarian regime controlling the self-reproduction of power independently, without and against interference from the "West", the internal public, or political antagonists. It should be added that the critical part of the public in Russia, in particular, knows that such a discourse can only work in the context of a quasi-authoritarian regime *and* in a culture where official monologues are suppressing and dominating the culture of dialogue. "Russian democracy" then simply means that there is an official centre telling people how Russian democracy works. Of course, the regime is able and willing to back its power and its discourse with repression. However, it is well known that discourses and repression only work under specific conditions. The conditions may change, and a hegemonic *dispositif* may suddenly find itself confronted with another hegemonic discourse.

All political regimes reproduce and maintain specific discourses about the way they or their underlying political system function and how they want to be perceived by the public, whether be a domestic audience or an international one. The point is that illiberal or authoritarian regimes produce other forms of discourses than liberal democracies with the institutionalised discourses that underlie their respective constitutional architecture. In liberal regimes, the institutions and procedures include rights, freedoms, and – most fundamentally – the transfer of political power through elections. They reproduce the specific legitimacy of liberal democracy. The discourse is inscribed in the democratic institutions, "carved in stone", one might say. Of course, political parties can accentuate dif-

---

7 See Torfing 1999: 116f. Following Zizek, the author applies the notion of "ideological fantasy" to situations where people act as if the totalising forms of ideology were true, although they know they are not.

ferent views as to the interpretation of "democracy" at the level of their programmatic discourses, but that level should not be confused with the basic structure of the political system. The latter can only be called "liberal" insofar as it admits political opposition, freedoms, and checks and balances. On the other hand, even governments of liberal regimes may mobilise a specific rhetoric and discourses to justify restrictions of the established liberal order (for example, in the US after "9/11"). However, such practices are reversible and can be challenged by the legal system, by a political opposition, by critical media and, of course, by elections that bring to power another party.

Therefore, unacceptable discrepancies between the political and legal order on one hand and political practices and discourses on the other can always be checked and questioned in democracies based on the rule of law.

In authoritarian regimes, the legitimating mechanism is not based on democratic elections. Therefore, the ruler's discourse and practices are always "in line" with the principles of the established state doctrine. Democratic accountability is not at stake in such cases. However, in authoritarian regimes such as China, one may expect to see other forms of "accountability", such as the effectiveness of party cadres in resolving regional problems and reacting to emergencies. Thus, it is not completely accurate to talk about China or Russia exclusively in terms of autocracies, because they are still accountable to their populations in some ways. Therefore, it might be more accurate to conceive of these regimes as "hybrid regimes", or regimes that are positioned somewhere between the authoritarian and liberal poles in the spectrum of political regimes.

In hybrid regimes, it is not clear whether a specific regime is closer to the democracy pole – in which case one may speak of electoral democracies with deficiencies – or to the pole of authoritarian regimes with no elections. In the latter case, it would no longer be accurate to describe it as an imperfect democracy. Since in the contemporary global perception, only a democracy with elections can claim legitimacy, such regimes must at least formally declare themselves to be democratic, even if they are actually something quite different. This may be considered a more or less opportunistic adaptation to Western hegemony, at least at the discursive level,[8] that is linked to the dynamic constraints of the political system of global society: International opinion judges the realities of its state system by the question of how an established power regime in a spe-

---

8   See the contribution of Viatcheslav Morozov in this volume.

cific country deals with the political opposition. The question is, then, to what extent the distinction between government and opposition is accepted in a given political system. That would be the focus of Luhmann's theory on the political system, whereas in the theory of Laclau, one would rather speak of the acceptance of antagonism and counter-hegemonic discourses. But democracy is primarily a communicative structure in which all communications of the government have to face a second version in form of communications coming from an established opposition. Democracy is about the organised, public and legal interplay between government and opposition. In an authoritarian regime, the second version of the "official truth" would originate with the illegal opposition or protest movements which, particularly in that precise situation of an oppressed political opposition, would try to establish a counter-hegemonic discourse.

Russia as a "façade democracy"

In this regard, Russia is an interesting case, since it presents all the criteria of a semi- or a quasi-authoritarian regime, and comes close to the authoritarian pole.[9] Russia is a "façade democracy": The control of the media and of important social spheres helps to maintain the illusion, or rather to give the impression that democratic differentiations do exist, when they do not. The ruling elite monopolises access to positions of power (Krastev 2007). As Ottaway (2003: 20) puts it: "All semi-authoritarian regimes take steps to preserve their core, namely the power of the central government", and they differ in how they deal with challengers to that power."[10]

In such regimes, the difference between the governmental position and the opposition may be maintained; however, not in the sense of an exchange of positions – the democratic solution – but as fixed positions. The contingency of an election is not accepted, and a change of power in such regimes is out of the question. Opposition parties, despite their existence, are systematically disadvantaged. The illusion of a differentiated democratic system is maintained, but elections exist only in order to produce the "right" results.

One may ask what political change is good for if nobody is interested in change, or – as is the case for Russia – if people primarily desire *stability* and security. One should also not forget that "façade democracies" or "Potemkin

---

9 For the concept of semi-authoritarianism, see Ottaway 2003.
10 Such a regime may also end in full-fledged authoritarianism. For the evaluation of such risks, cf. Shevtsova 2008.

democracies" find the conditions of their existence not only in the past, but also in an extremely inegalitarian social structure with weak potential for change. On the other hand, there can be no democracy without democrats, without a public that is convinced that the essence of democracy consists of political opposition and political change. If the expression and institutionalisation of political antagonism in the public sphere is banned, then indeed democracy remains an ideological or even an empty construct. The regime may then still invent a specific qualifier, such as "Russian democracy", in order to underline the fact that Russia is using its own non-Western distinctions.

In order to preserve its power structure and present its political structure as an expression of a real democracy, a "façade democracy" needs – besides the indispensable material basis that holds out the prospect of prosperity! – a "political theory", a kind of ideological framework about itself and about its conception of future objectives, such as modernisation. Furthermore, it needs a lot of organisational power in order to realise at least parts of the regime's doctrine. The result can be an organised society that is controlled by the centre of the political system, for example, by a hegemonic political party or the power network of a political leader – such as in the "Putin system". These conditions were given under Soviet rule. The breakdown of Communism implied the bankruptcy of an economic model. It was what discourse theorists refer to as the crisis of a hegemonic discourse and its dislocation by new spaces of meanings and identities.[11]

However, a closer look at what happened in the new post-Soviet order shows how old identities have partly been transferred from the old regime to the new one. The discontinuity expressed in new symbols cannot conceal the continuity of the old regime, whose members were able to combine old and new power positions under a new rent-seeking capitalism. The representatives of the old Soviet order learned quickly how to cope with elements of the new order – elections and markets – and to use them for their own interests. Interestingly enough, the "new" power elites – of which Putin and his network of power are a part – have similar values as the older Soviet generations: confrontation with the West, a vision of modernisation without democracy, a rent-seeking mentality within the class of state officials, and a conception of politics as a zero-sum game.

---

11   See the introduction by the editors and the contribution of Aletta Norval and Ivo Mijnssen in this volume.

To a certain extent, the new Russian state order created under Putin, the so-called "power vertical", reproduces Soviet-like organisational structures and state capitalism in a globalised context. This undertaking is accompanied by discursive strategies aimed at explaining and reinforcing the existing power structure. The system of power established by Putin is a new attempt to control society, its media, its economy, its civil society, and its dynamics by means of political influence, the bureaucracy, and the courts. To be sure, the idea of a real Russian democracy would be a simple ideological product if it did not, to a certain extent, aim at becoming a practice that is different from "Western" realities.

The idea of a "sovereign democracy" corresponds to the aims and realities of a semi- or quasi-authoritarian regime pretending to be a democracy, but organising the political process in such a way as to keep the monopoly of power. In his analysis of the rise of "managed democracy" in Russia, Ivan Krastev (2006) shows how democracy's "doubles" function. The elites, with the help of so-called "political technologists", populist communication strategies, media manipulation, and administrative resources, create a "copy" of democracy, a kind of virtual reality.[12] Such an analysis focusing on the populist rhetoric of elites and their "public relations" specialists can be usefully combined with the organisational aspects of semi-authoritarian regimes.

Controlling the public space and the scope of the politically permissible always implies huge organisational power – for example, the legal and economic means to control the media. We have seen in the last couple of years how political parties have been built up in Russia as "clones" (for example, United Russia), whereas the political opposition has been neutralised.

Graph 1 expresses this marginalisation of political opposition inside and outside of the political system. The regime of "Kremlin, Inc." controls key aspects of the functional systems through organisations and highly personalised networks. Representatives of the regime's security forces dominate companies of strategic interest. It is precisely at the economic level that an observer gets the impression that Russia functions like a big bureaucratic corporation, combining highly personalised leadership structures with organisational power and networks of power (friends, loyalties, clients). This does not mean that independent economic or political activities are not possible.

---

12 In this regard, Pierre Hassner (2008) observed that virtual democracy and virtual empire go hand in hand.

They are possible and even admitted – cases in point being the small opposition parties in Russia. But no organisation gets a chance to become a real antagonist and to develop a real political opposition against the regime in the sense of becoming an alternative, a structure that is prepared to replace the incumbent power in the case of an election. This means that every organisation beyond a certain size seems to become a risk for the regime – as seen in the case of Mikhail Khodorkovsky.

Graph 1 - Marginalisation of opposition inside and outside of the political system: "real" vs. "not real" organisations

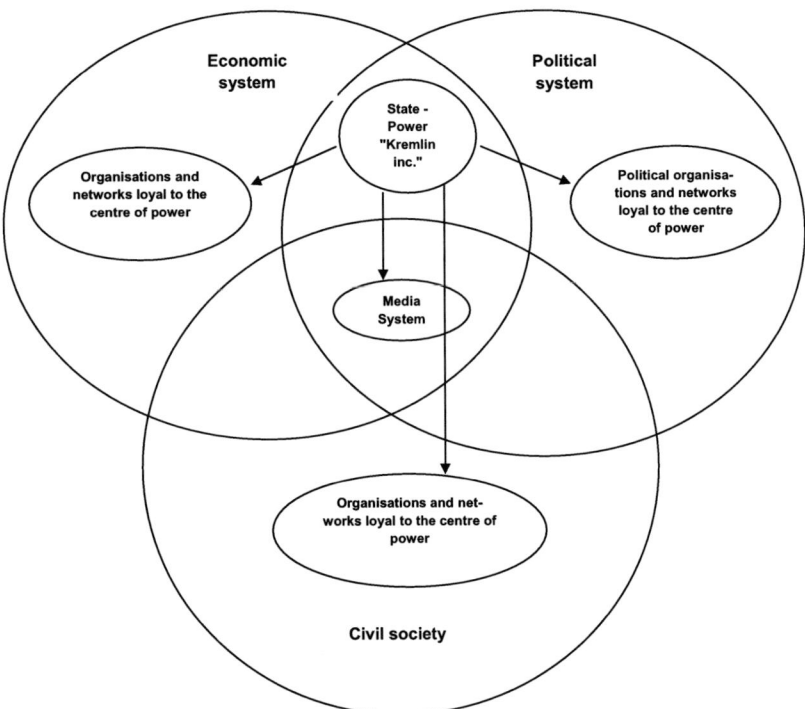

In the last couple of years, loyal economic elites have replaced those that represented a risk for the regime. Organisations of civil society lost their autonomy, and new state-driven and state-sponsored organisations (such as Nashi) have been created in order to contain and channel the dynamics of civil society. Generally, this amounts to a strategy of neutralisation and de-politicisation aimed at reducing the natural checks and balances in society as they are expressed by the pluralism of interests and organisations in politics, the economy, and society.

The regime maintains a fake double of a liberal regime and creates its own organisations and networks, through which it controls the most important social spheres. This regime is presented by some even as a "real" democracy, to be distinguished from false democratic projects in the "near abroad" or from Western liberal democracies, which are considered to be "false democracies".[13] The same logic is at work for the specific organisations of Russian society and politics. "Real" political parties created by the regime are to be distinguished from "other" parties. "Real" organisations of civil society have to be separated from "not real others" or false ones, etc. The regime uses this strategy to eliminate the pluralism of the political system and the pluralism of interests in society. Despite the fact that the regime is also "sponsoring" new political parties, United Russia is so dominant that the political system is for all practical purposes dedifferentiated.

The semantics of "sovereign democracy"

The discourse of *we* against *the others* is in fact an exclusion strategy that cannot be separated from what the elites think Russia's power in the world and in the country should look like. An unnerved nation, anxious to keep its unity and identity, will always try to shield itself behind its repressive power structure and its own ideology. Metaphorically, that is precisely what the "Kremlin" stands for: a power structure that reproduces itself behind huge walls to protect itself against *the others*, the public, opponents, "anti-Russian" movements, foreigners, terrorists, and a plethora of other foes. It is surprising to what extent old-fashioned state semantics based on the premise of the state as the centre of social order are still at work in Russia. This idea cannot be realised unless citizens are regarded as "subordinates". This is certainly also one of the biggest obstacles for building a modern democratic state based on the rule of law. The centre of power resides in the state, or more precisely, in its executive branch.

---

13 See the adherents of the notion of "sovereign democracy", such as Alexander Dugin, for whom Russian "sovereign democracy" embodies the profound will of the people and the national mindset. It is opposed to the false and demagogic democracies of dual standards. See Dugin 2006, Okara 2007.

What matters in Russia is the unity of the state and of its political top echelons against the complexity of a democracy as expressed by the presence of an opposition, checks and balances, or civil society. This ideological pretension tries to "suture" social divisions and hide dislocations or, as we prefer to call them, alternative distinctions.

Such a discourse hearkens back to the well administrated paternalist police state of imperial Russia that believed society had to be kept under control by pedagogical means and heavy-handed policing (Raeff 1994: 117f.). Transposed into Putin's Russia, the metaphor expresses the idea that there can be no political space for the expression of social autonomy. Such a conception tends to eliminate the political, if the latter signifies a continuous conflict between political parties or between different interests in society. It is precisely in this imaginary space of the political that society appears as a nation, which is being negated by a bureaucratic and hierarchic conception of society.

Unity instead of complexity: This might be considered a throwback to the pre-modern world of hierarchically conceived lacking the ability to conceive of themselves as being internally differentiated. On the other hand, the Soviet Union can be considered one of the last experiments that tried to go back to a unitary conception of power, to an indivisible sovereignty based on the idea or representation of one single people, refusing the conception of "one and the other" (Lefort). The fact that even the Soviet Union always featured several power centres does not contradict the observation that only one conception of power has been accepted. Despite the existence of several centres of power, supreme power was concentrated in the Politburo, particularly in the position of the general secretary of the Communist Party. Power was always based on the combination of strong personalised power and tremendous organisational power – the party apparatus. The so-called *nomenklatura* was based on informal rules of inclusion and exclusion, and defined the prerequisites for accessing the top positions of power in the Communist Party and the state hierarchy.

A government that cannot accept the institutionalisation of *the other* must take recourse to the archaic distinction between friends and enemies. Obviously, such a regime becomes dangerous particularly for the social environment of politics, where such a conception of the political directly contradicts the autonomous realities of other social spheres, particularly the economic system. In any case, any description of politics or society that pretends to be the only right one is totalitarian and inevitably provokes opposition: Unity necessarily produces differences and new identities based on different distinctions.

This fits quite well with what Lefort expresses in the idea of "disincarnation".[14] Social reality can neither be incarnated nor represented by a hierarchy, be it the state or a party organisation. Power is inevitably an empty place. As Luhmann puts it, state power is an exchangeable, unstable, and divided position based on the distinction between government and opposition (Luhmann 1990: 167ff. and 231ff.). Under modern conditions, sovereign power is nothing more than the contingent possibility to remain in power or to be in the opposition. This is the very essence of democratised power. Such a double codification of the political system works against the moralisation of the power position, which would reintroduce the distinction of friends and enemies based on the pretension of being in a morally superior position.

Modern politics, however, needs and involves antagonists and opponents. This crucial difference between enemies and opponents (Edelmann 1991: 131), between antagonism and agonism (Mouffe 2005), points to the core of the political in modern society and also to the problem of morals in politics: As soon as opponents are conceived of in categories of good or bad, friend or enemy, eliminating the *other* becomes the main aim of political action. On the other hand, the acceptance of the *other* as agonist implies competition focused on political victory and not on elimination. Political victory can be obtained only by respecting the rules of the game and established procedures which are shared and respected by all players in the political game. Russia and some other post-Communist regimes still have considerable difficulties in accepting the presence of agonists, i.e. of a political opposition – despite, or rather due to, the democratisation process.

If the *unity* of the political system in Russia with its "elected monarch", or now with its "double centre" at the top, is its essential feature, we can expect all official discourses to confirm this unity.

It is of course a discourse of unity of the rulers and the people. As Krastev (2006) puts it: If elections are not supposed to change anything, they still accomplish, on the level of political discourse, the function of celebrating unity. This is populism, insisting not on differentiation, but on the identity of the regime with the people.

---

14   See Lefort 1981: 172ff., 1986: 265; see also van Reijen 1992.

Such thinking is in fact reminiscent of conservative thinking along the lines of Carl Schmitt.[15] It has become fashionable again in Russia to quote Schmitt, particularly his definition of sovereign power based on decisionmaking in a state of emergency (*Ausnahmezustand*). This may be particularly useful for Russia and the conflicts at its periphery. But such thinking marks the distance to Western European political theory, which is based on how to avoid the "state of exception". The identification of sovereignty with unity is, however, problematic – particularly in the context of a quasi-authoritarian regime.

In a modern sense, as Luhmann shows, sovereignty is based on difference, not on unity: It implies the contestation of power. But such a concept of sovereignty is unacceptable for regional autocrats, since it destabilises authority.[16] A political power that is unwilling to accept such a structural destabilisation of the political system by the difference between government and opposition must necessarily re-moralise politics. It must then explain why precisely this power has the moral (Putin dixit!) right to stay in power.

On the other hand, the Russian regime – obsessed by stability – opens the door to instability precisely through its unwillingness to institutionalise political change. As Krastev (2008: 19) points out:

> "The sovereign democracy system creates relative stability (certainly compared to the Yeltsin years), but it lacks the dynamism Russia needs to genuinely transform itself into an effective polity. As things stand now, any change in the power elite takes the form of a crisis. Any loss of power means a loss of property. Any attempt to modernise the society from above clashes with the vested interests of Russia's 'sovereign bureaucracy', the real beneficiary of Putin's rule. And so the system's stability is in reality a straitjacket."

All populists must mobilise differences between the *us* and the *others*. The official nationalist discourse is "anti-Western", "anti-Orange", "anti-American", oriented against liberalism or against "enemies within". Of course, the populist distinction between "friends and enemies" has the advantage of reducing political complexity and helps to organise support for a highly personalised power structure in a system based – as several scholars have noted – on "negative in-

---

15 See also Krastev 2006.
16 For a discussion of the differences between Luhmann and Schmitt with regard to sovereignty, see Rasch 2000: 162.

tegration".[17] Moreover, in contemporary Russia, the inflationary use of the rhetoric of unity is based on the mobilisation of patriotism.[18] It is the adequate discourse for the exceptional times of crisis and war in a country where the political elite is reproducing elements of the former Soviet "garrison-state".

Conclusion

In a context where the Russian elite presents its quasi-authoritarian system as a "democratic" Russian alternative to the rejected liberal project of Western Europe and the US, criticism of Russia's façade democracy misses the point: The regime immunises itself in asserting that the country has realised its own democratic project. Usually, versions of democracy qualified by the addition of adjectives such as "illiberal" or "semi-authoritarian" serve to denote diminished democracies, but in the eyes of Russian elites, qualifiers such as "sovereign" or "directed" express the "Russian way" of thinking.

If this was certainly true for Putin's presidency, the question is whether this is still true for Medvedev. Interestingly enough, however, the new president of Russia seems to be unhappy with such a qualifier and insists on claiming that Russia is a democracy without any adjective.[19] The reasoning is right, but presenting Russia as a democracy will only further reveal the huge gap between political reality and rhetoric. Russia will be "measured" on the base of a universally accepted theory of democracy, which is rejected by the adherents of "sovereign democracy": By this standard, the emperor has no clothes, and "sovereign democracy" becomes a meaningless formula. But hierarchy, centralisation, and a powerful repression mechanism would still persist. In all quasi- or semi-authoritarian regimes, any political opposition must overcome huge obstacles to establish itself as an alternative to the incumbent power, which would also mean having an impact by promoting an alternative discourse that tries to become dominant or even hegemonic.

Nevertheless, the ideological construction created by the regime under Putin and its "political technologists" seems to work at least for the elites and parts of the Russian public. For them, the discourse on "sovereign democracy"

---

17 See March 2007.
18 See Raviot (2008), who shows that unity is an integral part of Russian political culture. It is quite impressive to what extent elites in post-Soviet countries have taken recourse to the rhetoric of unity in naming their political parties since the dissolution of the Soviet Union.
19 See Medvedev 2006.

has become reality. Concepts that circulate in society may change society and the value and thought systems of the people. Discourses are always cross-checked against reality, which is also a communicative reality if one follows Luhmann's theory of society. Political concepts such as "sovereign democracy" with strong normative implications may provide the key for a better understanding of a little-known political reality. This includes the unverifiable assertions by politicians about causality, about successful political actions, and about ways to solve big problems or overcome the current economic crisis. With globalisation penetrating every society and world region, it would be naïve to believe that regional political regimes are able to control the communicative realities of different social contexts beyond a certain extent. An economic crisis can produce new dynamics that may render the semantics of "sovereign democracy" useless.

The meanings of "sovereign democracy" are changing, depending on the expectations of the public that is addressed. For the less educated parts of the Russian public that are still oriented towards post-Soviet authoritarian attitudes and towards a highly normative worldview, "sovereign democracy" may provide the anchor of a collective identity. They regard "democracy" as being linked to conflict, weakness, and inefficiency. They hesitate to admit that conflict, competition, and cooperation can coincide in democracies. Power seems to be diluted in democracies, whereas in a "sovereign democracy" like Russia, power is concentrated in the "right" place, i.e., at the top of society.

Of course, some Russians, including some representatives of the opposition or of civil society, understand that "sovereign democracy" is a shell, a slogan, that conceals blatant autocracy. Critical political scientists in Russia know that, from a scientific perspective, the formula "sovereign democracy" is meaningless.[20] This is another example of how the meanings of concepts change from one social sphere or system to another. In trying to control the social circulation of concepts such as "sovereign democracy", the Kremlin reveals a lot about its conception of power and how it wants to confront the world of the 21st century with its rather traditional vision of control, hegemony, and domination.

---

20 For an overview of some of the positions for and against the concept of "sovereign democracy", see http://www.gazeta.ru/politics/2007/12/07_a_2398700.shtml

Bibliography

Andersen, N.A. 2003. *Discursive Analytical Strategies. Understanding Foucault, Koselleck, Laclau, Luhmann.* Bristol: Policy Press.

Diamond, L. 2008. *The Spirit of Democracy.* New York : Holt.

Dugin, A. 2006. Suverennaia demokratiia – *priznak poiavleniia u Rossii ideologii.* http://www.viperson.ru/wind.php?ID=261697&soch=1 [accessed 9 September 2009].

Edelmann, M. 1991. *Pièces et règles du jeu politique.* Paris: Seuil.

Galasinska, A. and M. Krzyzanowski, eds. 2009. *Discourse and Transformation in Central and Eastern Europe.* London: Palgrave Macmillan.

Hassner, P. 2008. "Russia's Transition to Autocracy". *Journal of Democracy* 19, 2. 5-15.

Hayoz, N. 2007. "Regionale 'organisierte Gesellschaften' und ihre Schwierigkeiten mit der Realität der funktionalen Differenzierung". *Soziale Systeme* 13, 1+2. 160-172.

Kagan, R. 2008. *The Return of History and the End of Dreams.* London: Atlantic Books.

Krastev, I. 2006. "Democracy's 'Doubles'". *Journal of Democracy* 7, 2. 52-62.

────── 2007. "Chavez, Poutine et la démocratie". *Courrier international* 891. 44-45.

────── 2008. "Russia and the European Order. Sovereign Democracy explained". *The American Interest* November-December. 16-24.

Lefort, C. 1981. *L'invention démocratique.* Paris: Seuil.

———— 1986. *Essais sur le politique. XIXe-XXe siècles*. Paris: Seuil.

Luhmann, N. 1982. *The Differentiation of Society*. New York: Columbia University Press.

———— 1990. *Political Theory in the Welfare State*. Berlin & New York: de Gruyter.

———— 1997. *Die Gesellschaft der Gesellschaft*. Frankfurt/M.: Suhrkamp.

———— 2000a. *Organisation und Entscheidung*. Wiesbaden: Westdeutscher Verlag.

———— 2000b. *Die Politik der Gesellschaft*. Frankfurt/M.: Suhrkamp.

March, L. 2007. "Russian Nationalism under Putin: A majority faith?". In *Elusive Russia*, edited by K. Malfliet and R. Laenen, 33-52. Leuven: Leuven University Press.

Medvedev, D. 2006. Dlia protsvetaniia vsekh nado uchityvat' interesy kazhdogo. Ekspert 28, 522. http://www.expert.ru/printissues/expert/2006/28/interview_medvedev [accessed 9 September 2009].

Mouffe, C. 2005. *On the Political*. London: Routledge.

Okara, A. 2007. "Sovereign Democracy: A new Russian idea or a PR project?". *Russia in Global Affairs* 2. 1-8.

Ottaway, M. 2003. *Democracy Challenged. The rise of semi-authoritarianism*. Washington: Carnegie Endowment for International Peace.

Raeff, M. 1994: *Political Ideas and Institutions in Imperial Russia*. Boulder: Westview Press.

Rasch, W. 2000. *Niklas Luhmann's Modernity*. Stanford: Stanford University Press.

―――― 2008. "Introduction: The Form of the Problem". *Soziale Systeme* 14. 3-17.

Raviot, J. 2008. *Démocratie à la russe. Pouvoir et contre-pouvoir en Russie*. Paris : Elipses.

Rose, R. 2009. *Understanding Post-Communist Transformation*. London: Routledge.

Shevtsova, L. 2004. "The Limits of Bureaucratic Authoritarianism". *Journal of Democracy* 15, 3. 67-77.

―――― 2008. *Russia Lost in Transition*. Washington, D.C.: Carnegie Endowment for International Peace.

Torfing, J. 1999. *New Theories of Discourse – Laclau, Mouffe and Žižek*. Oxford: Blackwell.

Van Reijen, W. 1992. "Das Politische – eine Leerstelle. Zur politischen Philosophie in Frankreich". *Transit* 5. 109-122.

Zakaria, F. 2003. *The Future of Freedom. Illiberal democracy at home and abroad*. New York: Norton.

Varieties of Post-Communist Nationalisms in Eastern Europe

Klaus Müller and Andreas Pickel

This analysis attempts to introduce the study of nationalism more systematically into transformation studies of Eastern Europe. Both conventional theories of nationalism and universalistic theories of democratisation and marketisation have failed to capture the particular mechanisms of nationalism in the post-Communist context. Based on a novel perspective on nationalism as a "nationalising process", we propose a number of core mechanisms to account for diversity and change in Eastern European nationalisms. Nationalism, understood as the role that a national culture plays in the relegitimation of the state as well as the justification of transitional suffering and a state's geopolitical reorientation, incorporates this important dimension into a theory of post-Communist social change. The functional as well as dysfunctional effects of nationalism on the reconstruction of post-Communist societies can thus help account for the ways in which Eastern European nationalisms are being transformed in the European integration process.

Nationalism was long an underconceptualised topic in the broad field of Communist and Soviet studies, which was characterised by "obsession with the political and lack of attention to the social and cultural; excessive focus on the Russian centre with consequent neglect of the non-Russian peoples" (Suny 1995: 105). The Soviet Union appeared as Russia writ large, and the concept of "Soviet-type societies" seemed precise enough to cover its Western "satellites" as well. Observers who were interested in nationality issues of the area at all were either focused on rather narrow ethnographic or minority topics, or engaged in grand political scenarios: National movements in the Ukraine, Georgia, or Uzbekistan were seen as a chance to subvert the unity of the Communist movement and eventually break up the "Soviet Bloc". Apart from specialists or "disintegrationist" policy advisers like Richard Pipes or Zbigniew Brzezinski, the Western academic mainstream shared the modernist outlook of the official party

VARIETIES OF NATIONALISMS 149

line: Nationalism, religion, and other traditional value orientations would be more or less dissolved by the imperatives of an industrialised society. Given these limitations, it seems only fair to say that "little attention was paid to the nationality issue by the Soviet leadership and not much more by Western students of the Soviet Union" (Laqueur 1994: 147).[1]

This changed dramatically in the late 1980s. The televised role of popular movements in the last days of Communism, the break-up of Yugoslavia and the Soviet Union, and the regained national sovereignty of the Eastern European states brought nationalism back on the agenda. Nevertheless, much of the literature was written in a narrative style, followed backward-looking approaches, or tried to capture the surprising events in historicist phrases like the "revenge of the past" (Suny 1993), the "triumph of nations" (d'Encausse 1991), or a "people's spring".[2]

Instructive though these historical accounts were, they had limited explanatory value, especially when it came to the transformative power of nationalism over the 1990s. On the other hand, nationalism was surely not central to "transitology", the new branch of the social sciences that defined the research agenda on post-Communism during the 1990s.

Understanding the different types and metamorphoses of post-Communist nationalism, therefore, remained a major challenge for the social sciences since

---

[1] Laqueur 1994, ch. 8, offers an excellent survey of failures of Western and Eastern scholars; on the politically distorted view of the "disintegrationist" school, see Xenakis (2002: 35f). Characteristically, the broad retrospective evaluation of Communist studies by Almond and Roselle (1993) hardly mentions any input from research on nationalities. On the other side, Soviet sociology did its best to confirm the illusion that the Soviet people constituted a "meta-ethnic community" represented by a "supra-ethnic state": "Under socialism, real de facto equality has been implemented for all nations and nationalities" (N.A. Aitov 1986: 263; cf. Szporluk 1989).

[2] It is not our intention to comment on this literature or the general role of nationalism in the disintegration of the Soviet Union or Eastern Europe. It may suffice to mention that references to the "explosive nature of nationalism", the "popular passion of the people", or the "restoration of national identities", etc. (Carrère d'Encausse 1991: 233) are too diffuse to explain the course of events. First, ethnic riots escalated in the second half of the 1980s as clashes between local nationalities (e.g., Azeris vs. Armenians, Georgians vs. Abkhazians, etc.), not as democratic movements against Soviet repression. Second, the strategy of national sovereignty was in many cases a political technique that allowed well-positioned regional elites to stay in power after the ethno-federal mechanisms of redistribution could not longer be fed by a stagnating economy (see Müller 1992: 128-131). Third, disintegrationist predictions expected secessionist movement primarily in Central Asia, while the first national resistance against Moscow emerged in 1987 in the Baltic republics as a protest against the Molotov-Ribbentrop treaty.

1989. Whether ignoring, underestimating, or exaggerating the power of national symbols in Eastern European politics, conventional theories for the most part misinterpreted the significance of nationalism in the transformation process. This is due in part to the great diversity of nationalisms, which are not easily captured in simple conceptions or typologies. Perhaps more importantly, the dominant transition strategies based on ideal types of Western democracy and market economy assumed the validity of universal models of political and economic order. Nationalism has played at best a subordinate role in what was generally conceived as a transition to democracy and a market economy. In this perspective, nationalism was not expected to unfold a dynamic of its own. To correct these deficiencies, this chapter will attempt to integrate the problem of nationalism into transformation theory.

The reconceptualisation of nationalism on which the following analysis is based rejects the conventional view of nationalism as a mere ideology, a view that even in the social sciences tends to be normatively anchored in an implicit understanding of good (civic, Western) nationalism and bad (ethnic, Eastern European) nationalism. While specific varieties of nationalism may indeed have positive or negative consequences, this is not the result of essential characteristics of a particular country's national culture. National cultures change over time, and even more importantly, they are at all times embedded in larger political and economic contexts. In other words, national identifications are structuring and structured at the same time. On the one hand, they structure the institutional order of modern societies by imparting legitimacy to specific forms of domination, distribution of resources, and prestige, and by interpreting collectivities in terms of common histories, destinies, futures, solidarities, and obligations. According to Max Weber's conception of communitarisation (*Vergemeinschaftung*), a sense of national belonging rests in the sphere of value orientations and feelings about which rational discussion is hardly possible. On the other hand, these are not free-floating constructions, but related to the hard realities of state power, economic efficiency, and international competition. The opportunity to stabilise national affiliations over time and against competing identifications is structured by these institutional realities – the reason why modern nationalist movements seek to achieve and maintain control over territory, the means to exert power, and the capacity to tax.[3]

---

3   See Weber 1976 [1922], ch. I, § 9 and ch. VII § 5, where he makes clear that the irreducible tension between the (specifically irrational) belief in one's nation, the behaviour

Post-Communist transformations provide a particularly clear example of this contextual dependence. Many social scientists have opted to do without the concepts of nation, national culture, and nationalism in their work, since political and economic contexts seem to be primary, and the recourse to culture, national or otherwise, fraught with conceptual and normative problems. However, nationalism – more broadly understood as the role a national culture plays in the relegitimation of the state, the justification of transitional suffering, and geopolitical reorientations – makes it possible to incorporate this important dimension into a theory of post-Communist social change that sheds light on the variety of reform outcomes. Thus re-conceptualised, nationalism's functional as well as dysfunctional effects on the reconstruction of post-Communist societies come into view, helping us account for the routes by which Eastern European nationalisms are being transformed in the European integration process.

How such "nationalising processes"[4] play out is to some extent a function of a state's regional and global environment. The Eastern European states, historically the third wave of new sovereign states, emerged from the collapse of the Austro-Hungarian, Ottoman, and Russian empires during and after World War I. In barely more than a decade, the already precarious nationalising processes in those newly independent states were derailed by Nazi conquest, World War II, Soviet occupation, and the establishment of the Communist Eastern bloc. The seriously compromised sovereignty of the new Eastern European states from the 1930s to the 1980s (i.e., spanning almost the entire "short twentieth century", cf. Hobsbawm 1994) was accompanied by a succession of powerful de-nationalising processes during which external "cultural programs" were imposed on these societies. While nationalising processes of various sorts did of course continue to varying degrees in this period, giving rise to nationally-specific Soviet-type systems, de-nationalisation was only definitively reversed with Gorbachev's reform program and new foreign policy. The subsequent collapse of Communist regimes, itself in part due to nationalising forces in each country, marked the start of an accelerated process of re-nationalisation in the

---

motivated by this conviction, and the institutional realities of one's society account for a wide variety of "national sentiments" and practices.

4   We use the phrase "nationalising mechanisms" to refer to the cultural dimensions of social processes that are composed of or related to the collective representations, discourse, and habitus of a nation as understood by the populations of existing states. This definition is neutral with respect to the particular content, historical evolution, and current contestation of a particular nation. Cf. Pickel 2006.

states of the region.[5] Unsurprisingly, "ethnic nationalisms" played a major role in the redefinition of post-Communist cultural programs everywhere. But, as we will argue, it was not their "ethnic" character that explains the political outcomes of the early re-nationalisation processes. Ethnic cleansing (Yugoslavia), the dissolution of federal states (Soviet Union, Czechoslovakia), discriminatory language and citizenship policies (Baltic States), and anti-Sovietism, anti-Socialism, and nationalist rhetoric (everywhere) were among the very different forms this re-nationalisation process could take. We will argue that the European integration process, in many respects another de-nationalisation program for the region, represents the second phase of post-Communist re-nationalisation, as East European nationalisms are increasingly taking on the "normalised" and "banal" character of West European nationalisms.

We begin by sketching the three phases through which the problem of post-Communist nationalism has evolved. Here we will further address the theoretical conceptions that have been obstacles to a proper understanding of the role of nationalism in the transformation process. The following section will then present a number of crucial nationalising mechanisms at work in post-Communist political and economic change processes. These general mechanisms have specific, and not necessarily identical, effects in different countries. Nationalism, after all, is nation-specific; there are "multiple nationalisms".

Nationalism in plural

Let us start by identifying the conventional views of nationalism in Eastern Europe. Born out of the euphoria surrounding the events of 1989, the liberal view perceived these events as democratic revolutions that would return Eastern Europe to the Western path to modernity. This teleological view implied that democratic capitalism would be the necessary outcome of post-Communist transformation. Economic liberals counted on the emergence of spontaneous, self-organising markets and a new entrepreneurial class from Prague to Vladivostok, while political scientists assumed that "liberal democracy is the only game in town" (Sartori 1991). This mood combined the *Zeitgeist* of the newly proclaimed

---

5   We think that "re-nationalisation" captures the fundamental cultural dimension of the process more explicitly than Habermas' (1990) "nachholende Modernisierung" ("catching-up modernisation"), which corresponds more closely to the universalist, acultural conception that is typical of the democratisation and marketisation literature.

era of economic globalisation, which made nationally oriented attempts at catching up futile, with the chief lesson of recent European history being the following:

> "In the postwar decades, Western Europeans enmeshed themselves in a web of transnational institutions, culminating in the European Union (EU). After the fall of the Soviet empire, that transnational framework spread eastward to encompass most of the continent. Europeans entered a postnational era, which was not only a good thing in itself but also a model for other regions. Nationalism, in this view, had been a tragic detour on the road to a peaceful liberal democratic order" (Muller 2008: 18).

Instead of the collectivist pathos of traditional social revolutions, peaceful regime change seemed to have produced a constitutional patriotism in the Western European tradition. This liberal political culture helped Eastern Europeans to transcend collectives of any kind in order to move towards an "intersubjectively dissolved, anonymous form of popular sovereignty" (Habermas 1990: 196). From this point of view, "nationalism" became a catch-all category for the various obstacles to and deviations from the path of democratisation, a defensive reaction to insecurities of regime change or the last line of defence for ideologically flexible ex-Communists. Ironically, the liberal thesis of the death of nationalism is quite similar to the view that Socialist internationalism had eliminated nationalist chauvinism – a view Gorbachev held until the end of his reign.

In the early 1990s, a second, more pessimistic view emerged as many countries returned to the old national symbols from the interwar period (Weiss and Reinprecht 1998). To some grand theorists, this seemed only normal: "Eastern Europe is not unique. On the contrary, it is typical of former imperial areas" (Chirot 1995: 60). The logic of the post-Communist situation now seemed to favour the resurgence of an aggressive nationalism for several reasons: the need for a new ideology after the collapse of old certainties, existential insecurity in the process of marketisation, and fear of a sell-out to foreign capital as a result of regional and global economic reintegration. Indeed, the reestablishment of post-Communist states was accompanied by a return to national myths, heroes, and conspiracy theories. The introduction of multi-party systems seemed to facilitate polarisation along ethnic identities. There was growing concern that the "ethnification" of politics might have much greater mobilising power than any appeal to civil society. Guaranteed civil rights were seen to be competing with discrimination, violence, forced assimilation, and even "ethnic cleansing" (Offe 1996: 61; Ignatieff 1994).

In several countries, "founding elections" were in fact instrumentalised for ethnic mobilisation. Democratic elections in the republics of Yugoslavia degenerated into the legitimation of minority deportations. The region as a whole was viewed as suffering from numerous minority problems, border conflicts, and historical animosities for which no diplomatic or political mechanisms were in place after the collapse of the Soviet Union and the Warsaw Pact. Nationalism therefore also seemed to be a threat to relations among post-Communist states that might pose serious security problems for the West (Nelson 1991). In this view, the collapse of the Communist order meant the resurrection of the traditional problem of Eastern European nationalism. "The explosive issues of 1988-92 were those created in 1918-21" (Hobsbawm 1992: 164).

We know now that neither the liberal optimism nor its pessimistic counterpart captured the complex reality of post-Communism. Transition crises were more severe and longer-lasting than anticipated, and in a number of cases, the consolidation of democracy remained precarious. On the other hand, nationalist excesses were confined to the former Yugoslavia and several post-Soviet crisis regions, especially in the Caucasus. Czechs and Slovaks separated peacefully, and no violent border changes have occurred. While nationalist parties have formed governments, such as in Slovakia, they have not shaped the political regime. Anti-state terrorism by national minorities as in France, Spain, or Northern Ireland has not occurred. Where authoritarian regimes emerged, they were not created by nationalist masses, but by former Communists. Citizenship laws and minority protection have raised complex problems, but their treatment largely follows the standards of the European Council. While problems with radical right-wing movements and the status of non-citizens cannot be denied, they are very similar to those found in Western Europe. Moreover, the willingness of post-Communist states to give up some of their newly gained national sovereignty to the supranational institutions of the EU would not seem to be a typical characteristic of nationalist regimes. Clearly, post-Communist nationalism requires a more differentiated approach that can account for its prehistory, multifunctional role, and variability.

The paradigm of the nation

It should not have come as a great surprise that nation-states and nationalism would become the dominant political paradigms in the post-Communist region. This was quite obvious in the Soviet Union, where regional Communist leaders started to transform into nationalist elites in the late 1980s. When central funds for redistribution dried up, reasserted national identities became an expression of frustrated ambitions, and autonomy became a device to keep valuable resources at home. To the surprise of those who expected anti-Soviet nationalism to be strongest in the southern republics or in the Baltic region, the final blow to the Soviet empire came from the centre itself. In 1990, Boris Yeltsin played the national card against Gorbachev's plans for a renewed union treaty and turned Russia into a sovereign nation-state for the first time in history. To be sure, this step was more than a personal stratagem. It reflected the emergence of a genuine Russian nationalism on the side of the reform-oriented intelligentsia, which perceived the non-Russian republics as a drain on the national wealth, a view shared, according to opinion surveys of the time, by a majority of the population – a surprising constellation that Zaslavsky described well before the demise of the Soviet Union:

> "In contrast to non-Russian separatisms, which habitually were in conflict with the imperial center, Russian separatism has the rather unusual form of a dominating nation which likes to free itself from an unwanted and burdening ethnical periphery." (Zaslavsky 1991: 77)[6]

Certainly, the Eastern European countries were more likely candidates for national revivals. Local Communist parties had come to power after World War II by claiming to represent the most valuable parts of their countries' national traditions. Later on, in the 1950s, Poland under Gomulka, Hungary under Kadar, and, most successfully, Yugoslavia under Tito articulated national-Communist aspirations: National traditions and interests should justify each country's own path to Socialism (Brzezinski 1960). Romania under Ceauşescu, East Germany under Ulbricht, and of course Czechoslovakia during the Prague Spring were the most significant examples of "national resistance" in the 1960s. Such ambitions inside the Communist parties had to be repeatedly suppressed by coups or military inventions. If the earliest "cracks in the monolith" (Deutsch 1963) originated from "particularism" and "national Communisms", it seems appropriate that they

---

6 According to National Russian Barometer data from 1992 (cited in Rose et al. 2006: 77), three quarters of the Russian population took pride in "one and indivisible Russia"; 39 percent preferred an independent Russia centrally governed by Moscow, while only 19 percent missed the old Soviet Union.

would fracture the system entirely after Gorbachev had lifted the Brezhnev doctrine of "limited sovereignty" of Soviet-bloc states.

Does this mean that post-Communist politics has been "unfreezing" the old Eastern nationalism that notoriously appeals to ethnic collectives instead of building a civil society? We do not think that it makes much sense to explain the recent course of events by causes from a distant past, as this would pull Eastern Europe and the former Soviet Union back into the tradition of "ethnic" as opposed to "civic states" in the West (Kuzio 2001). Nor do we think, from a neofunctionalist perspective, that "in multiethnic Soviet type societies nationalism continues to be a necessary precondition of modernization" (Zaslavsky 1992: 113). Instead, we argue that nationalism presents a precarious balance of functional and dysfunctional forces for societal transformation. The direction in which this balance will tilt depends on specific institutional capacities, regional neighbourhoods, geopolitical contexts, and domestic political processes. In order to analyse constellations of this kind, we find it helpful to treat nationalism not as a compact phenomenon or undifferentiated "legacies", but as a set of processes articulated and implemented by specific mechanisms. The "nationalizing mechanisms" (Pickel 2003) we consider to be particularly relevant to the Eastern European transformations are effective in two areas: state-building/democracy and economic policy. We will discuss each in turn.

In the first area of state-building and democracy, nationalising mechanisms are the most controversial in both theory and practice. Fears of "nationalizing states" (Brubaker 1995) trying to homogenise ethnically mixed populations by suppressing national minorities while promoting their own co-nationals in neighbouring states were not unfounded. The Baltic states used language policy to deny citizen status to considerable parts of their populations. Russia put pressure on its "near abroad" in the name of the 25 million fellow Russians outside its border and recently announced that it would introduce into its constitution provisions for sending military missions to protect its citizens living outside their home country (Russia Today, 10 August 2009). Serbian nationalism was characterised as "new" in the sense that it claimed to restore the ethnic collective without any intention of modernisation or democracy (see chapter 3 in Kaldor 1999). Evidently, strategies of state-building and democratisation are not necessarily congruent.

Robert Dahl (1990) and Juan Linz and Alfred Stepan (1996) clearly identified the problematic assumption in theories of transition to democracy according

VARIETIES OF NATIONALISMS   157

to which the territorial unit and the composition of the *demos* can be taken for granted. Normative approaches, which emphasise civil society activities, freedom of expression, or "founding elections" already presuppose a legitimate domain of political power. Surely, elections are a critical step, but no guarantee for democratic consolidation. Indeed, it is questionable whether elections are "foundational" at all. The issue that Linz and Stepan (1996) refer to as the "stateness-problem" becomes central: how to ensure the state's legitimacy in the face of competing national groups. This problem marked one critical difference between the transitions to democracy in Southern Europe and the post-Communist transformations. While in the most authoritarian systems of the South, state organisation was not contested and citizenship laws were in place, in Eastern Europe, state institutions, the degree of centralisation, and citizenship laws all had to be redefined. The resulting tensions could be diffused in several ways. The careful timing of elections, organised first on a nationwide basis and only subsequently at the regional levels, is a central mechanism analysed by Linz and Stepan. National parties tend to mobilise nationally around general issues and in this way contribute to the social and political construction of "feelings about territorial appropriateness" (Linz and Stepan 1992: 124). In contrast to Spain, the Soviet and Yugoslav cases are taken as examples that "the sequence of elections, per se, can construct or dissolve identities" (ibid.). Elections held separately in the republics of the Yugoslav Federation in 1990 deepened ethnically defined rifts. Election rules in the former Soviet Union (FSU) gave greater legitimacy to republic-level politicians than to those of the centre.

A further mechanism of creating an integral unit of political authority consists in establishing constitutional rights, including the status of minorities, and appropriate definitions of the *demos*. This seemed most problematic in multiethnic states, especially in the FSU. Socialist citizenship laws had been centred on a hyper-sovereign, unitarian state – making citizenship, as in the Soviet law from 1978, an "honorary title", leaving nearly no space for individual rights. All this changed fundamentally with the Russian citizenship laws of 1991, subsequently further amended, that enshrine human rights in the Russian constitution, extending citizenship rights to individuals in the federal state. Discrimination along racial or national lines is legally prohibited. In the member states of the Commonwealth of Independent States, national minorities are protected by bilateral agreements and a multilateral convention. Inside the Russian Federation, against the aspirations of some autonomous republics, the centre claims responsibility for a uniform citizenship that is not based on nationality (Luchterhandt 2002).

The effect of this nationalising mechanism is significant: The regional fragmentation of the Russian economy since the early 1990s did not spill over into state disintegration. A multiplication of political identities into sub-federal citizenships was successfully blocked. The political recentralisation initiated by the Putin administration was an answer to the attempt of the Yeltsin regime to create a system of local self-government, which in practice invited local and regional power elites to all kinds of corrupt and authoritarian practices, leading to a confusing tangle of special deals between the centre and the peripheries, and supplanting local democracy with "electoral clannishness", especially in the ethnic republics. However, while state-building and consolidation were necessary conditions for successful political and economic reforms, they were not sufficient, nor did they necessarily promote democratisation (Cameron 2009: 184-198).

This brings us to another area where disruptive as well as functional nationalising mechanisms are at work: the economy. While political nationalism was regarded as problematic, economic nationalism seemed simply irrelevant. The first generation of economic reform programs ignored the nation, since the rules of shock therapy – rolling back the state and opening up the economy – were considered to be basic and universal.[7] In the break-up of multi-national Communist states, economic collapse and national self-assertion were fatally intertwined. In the FSU, mistrust and the separate agendas of republican leaders undermined all efforts at coordinating credit, money, tax, or trade policies.[8] Unilateral actions to solve trade disputes and sabotage common reforms were a source of deepening conflicts. Nevertheless, blinded by a belief in the self-organising power of unfettered markets, the IMF upheld the option of a ruble zone for the FSU even after its de-facto collapse. The new republican central banks issued excessive ruble credit to support their crumbling industries with

---

7   A naiveté shared by IMF-reform programmes and the Soviet leadership: "Gorbachev did not understand the problem of collective action. He thought that economic interests, especially an understanding of the economic consequences of disintegration, would balance the impetus of nationalism" (Hough 1997: 372).
8   A coordinated reform policy to preserve a common economic space, the use of the ruble in inter-republican trade, tax harmonisation, a banking union, etc. had been agreed upon at the founding meeting of the CIS on 8 December 1991 in Minsk.

complete disregard for the inflationary consequences for all – until Yegor Gaidar pulled the emergency brake by proclaiming the nationalisation of the ruble.[9]

In Yugoslavia, too, while public opinion still held on to the ideology of "Yugoslavism", the economic malaise was fertile ground for the rise of a destructive nationalism. Since the signing of an agreement with the IMF in 1982, the republics had tried to externalise the cost of economic adjustment by the competitive issuing of credits, resulting in uncontrolled monetary emission. When hyperinflation could not be brought under federal control, central assets were secretly transferred to Serbia; Slovenia defected from the fund for underdeveloped regions; and Croatia started its own tax policy (see chapter 3 in Kaldor 2001). Only later, after economic nationalism had spilled over into open ethnic warfare, did the international financial institutions realise that nationalist strategies ("the desire to reclaim nationhood") were not simply "initial conditions" of reform, but endogenous, country-specific factors affecting the capacity of governments to adopt and sustain certain policies. Only then were ethnic or regional cleavages taken into consideration – as indicators of "extreme contestability over the boundaries of the community to be governed or who has the right to select leaders and make binding rules for that community" (World Bank 2002: 99).[10]

In addition to the newly categorised group of "war-torn regimes", there were less extreme, but no less significant forms of economic nationalism in the area of interstate economic relations. While some members of the FSU were willing to continue cooperation with Russia, others made (re-) orientation towards the West a part of their national identity.[11] Thus, differently (re-) constructed national identities had a deep impact on the region's political and eco-

---

9 This episode as well as the nationalisation of the tax system and the monetary nationalism in other East European countries are well described in Aslund (2002: 203-227). For the CIS countries, he writes: "Much of the monetary discussion was devoted to symbolic issues, such as the name of the national currency, its design, and where to have it printed. Yet, all nationalists regarded a national currency as a necessary prerequisite of an independent state" (ibid.: 204). Interestingly, at least in Central Eastern Europe, this area of national identity formation was transformed within only a decade. Now the adoption of the euro is becoming a symbol of economic strength and, more important, equal status with the Western member states.
10 The authors of this report subsequently came to regard national identity formation as a special type of "initial condition": "general development of national institutions, as determined by the length of prior experience of nationhood – are more strongly associated with variations in subsequent performance" (World Bank 2002: 15).
11 For variations of national identities as explanatory variables for post-Soviet interstate relations and economic reform, cf. Abdelal 2001, 2005; Tsygankov 2005; Eichler 2005.

nomic reconfiguration. To outline the implications of these nationalising mechanisms, we point to two observations. First, the single most important factor in the unexpectedly deep and long recessions in Eastern Europe was the national withdrawal from the CMEA (Council for Mutual Economic Assistance). Second, the single most decisive factor accounting for why the post-Communist slump did not lead the region into the worst-case scenario of instability and ethnic conflict was a transformation of "'hot nationalist passion" into Western "banal nationalism" (Billig 1995: 43-49, here 44), which thus became a variant of European political culture.

Regarding the first observation, we maintain that attributing the "external shock" of trade disruption to "geopolitics" (Roland 1997: 183ff.) is somewhat misleading. In fact it followed from internal conditions, namely from national decisions to exit from the common system. Early in 1990, Czechoslovakia and Poland decided to go their own ways and claimed sovereignty over their external affairs. The Baltic states broke radically with the Soviet past and withdrew from the Soviet Union's division of labour – precipitating dramatic output losses between 35 and 51 percent during the long post-Communist recessions. Anti-Soviet attitudes surely played a role, but only insofar as this was part of national self-assertion. Thus, the new nation states did almost nothing to rebuild regional cooperation; even the Central European Visegrad Group remained divided by tariffs and trade restrictions. It seems difficult to see an economic rationality in this kind of adjustment to a globalised economy. In fact, "from an economic point of view, it would have been probably better to find co-coordinated transitional arrangements between former CMEA countries" (Roland 1997: 182).

Instead, national economic policy styles could be observed in many areas. Foreign investment was a particularly sensitive topic in Poland and Czechoslovakia, whereas Hungary chose a more pragmatic approach in this regard. But Hungary, too, was careful to restrain foreigners, especially Germans and Austrians, from buying up forests and agricultural land. Even in technical matters such as exchange rate management, national preferences prevailed. While Estonia pegged its kroon permanently to the German mark and later the euro, Czechoslovakia marked its national tensions with Germany by choosing a US dollar peg. It is doubtful whether these hard-currency strategies made any economic sense. But the high costs of adjustment were not regarded as an obstacle since "stable exchange rates became matters of national pride" (Aslund 2002: 209).

Behind the rhetoric of "radical reform" vs. "gradualism", we find considerable experimentation with different methods of stabilisation, liberalisation, and privatisation. Generally, we maintain that the divergent histories of reform are not the simple result of unqualified "path dependencies" from the past, "initial conditions", and more or less radical commitments to market reform. What we see are essentially national responses to particular region-wide challenges with respect to trade policy, monetary arrangements, privatisation, and, above all, regional reintegration.[12] Only by taking economic nationalism into consideration can we explain why the post-Communist societies were prepared to take the risk of fundamental systemic change, and why there were no serious policy reversals, not even under re-elected post-Communist parties. Independence and national autonomy were supreme goals of post-Communist politics. Nationalism made personal sacrifice plausible and lengthened the time horizon for crossing the "valley of tears".

Europeanisation and "banal" nationalism

If anti-Soviet sentiments were formative for the post-Communist nationalisms of the Central-European and Baltic states, then their second common denominator was a normative reference to "Europe". Already under Communism, "Europe" had functioned as a cultural code to mark some distance to Moscow, and it was reinterpreted over time in several ways. "Eastern Europe" as part of the "Eastern Bloc" became "Mitteleuropa" in the 1960s, then "Central Europe", and finally just "Europe".[13] The conventional interpretation of the process is that it simply represents "Europeanisation", and for good reason, since European standards and institutional models undoubtedly played an important role in many post-Communist countries.

It is nevertheless still unclear how this Europeanisation is related to the nationalising mechanisms described so far. For many economists and for part of the region's population, the expected welfare gains of entering the common market and the convergence with Western income levels seemed most important. Many political scientists think in terms of supranational integration. Instead,

---
12 The variety of economic nationalism in the Visegrad countries in terms of different openness for foreign investments is analysed by Drahokoupil, who points out that a convergence towards a more open, "Porterian workfare postnational regime" only took place after 2000 (Drahokoupil 2009, 33).
13 This shift was expressed in the title of a 1990 issue of Daedalus (119,1): "Eastern Europe ... Central Europe ... Europe".

we conceive Europeanisation as a bundle of mechanisms that indeed transform national identities, but without leading to a post-national constellation as imagined by Habermas. Only by being transformed in this way did national identities allow for a far-reaching reinterpretation of the nation-state[14] – which is quite unthinkable in North America and South-East Asia, despite all deepening regional economic integration also taking place there. Participation in supranational arrangements and shared sovereignty in important policy areas surely cannot be taken for granted.

Thus, the phenomena we have observed during the past decade clearly were no "rebirths" or "returns". For the first time in their history, the Central and Eastern European states were prepared to accept laws, institutions, and practices designed by an external entity. Since adoption of the body of EU law is a precondition for the candidates' accession, law-making in Central Europe has to be harmonised to a considerable degree with the accession countries (European Commission 1995). As we know, the implementation of the vast *acquis communautaire* was time-intensive and complex. Of foremost interest for our purposes are those particularly sensitive areas that are essential to national identity. Subordination to international conventions and laws is probably the most unlikely restriction that states, especially nation-states, are ready to accept. But as we saw, even the core question of stateness and citizenship is being reformulated according to EU or European Council guidelines – not only in the accession countries, but even in Russia. Surely, this goes to the very core of sovereignty. At the same time, it represents a solution to the stateness problem of who should be part of the *demos*. In this sense, it was a novelty that a country with a strong national identity such as Poland was ready to open its constitution to transfer community legislation into national law. Significantly, this only happened in a second wave of constitutional reforms, after Poland had become a fully sovereign nation state by leaving the Warsaw Treaty Organisation. That this was not a matter of course could be seen in the case of Hungary, where in 1998, the constitutional court blocked a government decree translating European into Hungarian law.

On one level, it is clear by now that the EU-induced transfers of norms and institutions have helped to consolidate the post-Communist states' democratic institutions. The Copenhagen criteria made a basic set of political institutions

---

14 Csergö and Goldgeier (2004: 26-29) similarly speak of "transsovereign nationalism".

obligatory and at the same time allowed for considerable flexibility in responding to special national circumstances, legacies, and new situations: Assistance by the EU was given on a national basis in the form of National Accession Partnership Programmes. The requirement to meet the Copenhagen Criteria on a national basis mobilised energies to rebuild nation-states with strong capacities. In this way, and this should be emphasised again, Europeanisation became part of post-Communist state-building.

In addition to this nationalising mechanism related to institutional transfer, a second nationalising mechanism leading to the "normalisation" of Eastern European nationalisms was the widespread acceptance of EU membership as a part of the country's redefined national identity. In this sense, Europeanisation became part of post-Communist nation-building. Obviously, national identity formation and European integration are not always compatible. Czech and Hungarian national conservatives, right-wing Catholicism in Poland, and agrarian interest groups in all accession countries mobilised against a "dictatorship from Brussels". Politicians like Vaclav Klaus and the Czech government in general have been known for voicing strong reservations about the EU. But fears that the implementation of EU legislation as a precondition for joining the club would lead to an anti-European backlash were exaggerated. That Europe would provoke national resurgence was more a hope of right-wing populists than a reality.

This nationalising mechanism had the additional effect of "banalising" Eastern European nationalisms as Europe came to be taken for granted as part of national identities. This was powerfully underlined by the referenda on accession, in which anti-European nationalists were marginalised. Typical responses were not nationalist resistance, but apathy, cynicism, and a low voter turnout. Despite discrimination against future members and the prospect that some of the new entrants might become net contributors, accession to the EU was generally accepted.

Of some interest in our context were the motives of the voters that made this outcome likely. There is little empirical evidence for the argument that, under the guise of cosmopolitanism, Eastern Europeans tried to join the EU only for material advantages while in reality they are unreconstructed nationalists (Laitin 2002). As surveys have repeatedly confirmed, in all Eastern European countries, the majority puts the country's interests in the first place. Thus, for instance, an average 47% of the respondents to an area-wide survey expected advantages for their country, and only 34% expected to benefit for themselves personally.

The top-ranked personal advantages were not material welfare, but new opportunities for education and travel. A recent survey[15] on popular attitudes towards European institutions confirms the growing Europeanisation of Eastern European political cultures: The quality of the European institutions is regarded higher in terms of democracy than the national political systems; support for a European constitution has almost consistently been higher than in the old member countries; and even in sensitive areas such as foreign and security policy, European solutions are preferred over national solutions. We believe that this survey evidence is consistent with our argument that a majority of Eastern Europeans have incorporated a strong European component into their national identity.

Conclusion

In this paper, we have offered a reinterpretation of the character and role of nationalism in post-Communist Eastern Europe in an attempt to introduce more systematically the study of nationalism into transformation studies. Both conventional theories of nationalism and universalistic theories of democratisation and marketisation have failed to capture the particular mechanisms of nationalism in the post-Communist context. Based on a novel perspective on nationalism as a "nationalising process", we have proposed a number of core nationalising mechanisms to account for the diversity and change in Eastern European nationalisms. We have argued that the initial nationalisation process of the newly independent states of the region after World War I was interrupted early by a succession of international regimes that in effect de-nationalised these state-societies. The fundamental shift in international context as a result of the Gorbachev doctrine precipitated the collapse of Communist regimes in Eastern Europe. It marked the beginning of a period of accelerated re-nationalisation in which "multiple nationalisms" emerged. Neither the view of dangerous Eastern ethnic nationalism nor the discounting of nationalising processes in the transition literature takes account of the central fact that the same general re-nationalising process was underway everywhere, though with vastly different outcomes in the short term (from ethnic cleansing to "velvet divorce").

---

15   Data on political attitudes towards Europe can be found in the quarterly Eurobarometer surveys. The results summarised here are based on EUROBAROMETER EB60 – CCEB 2003.4: 6-10.

A highly visible dividing line separates Russia and other post-Soviet states from Central and Central Eastern Europe. Russia's state institutions and state traditions had been deeply intertwined with the imperial project of spreading a "unique" civilisation over extremely vast territories, a process in which the relations between an undoubtedly dominant Russian culture and the internationalist Soviet mission remained unarticulated. Since the institutional order of the old regime had been held together by the parallel structures of the party, the breakdown of Communism not only threw the country into institutional disarray, but also ushered in a period of disorientation. Attempts to redefine Russia's future in terms of the market, democracy, and "neo-Westernisation" foundered in the crisis of the late 1990s and buried hopes of a liberal nationalism; liberal "new thinkers" were replaced by new "state-builders" (English 2000: 235-240). "Sovereign democracy" became the latest ideological formula to legitimise the recentralised, self-centred Russian state in a more assertive way against Western expectations, to regain command over the economy, and to reclaim geopolitical weight. For a while, this seems to have created a new national consensus among the Russian leadership, the population, and even many intellectuals (cf. chapters 5 and 6 in Rose et al. 2006). Whether restorationist nationalism will serve Russia's interest in the longer term, however, is more doubtful.

The Central and Eastern European states have chosen a forward-oriented way, invoking meaningful events of their past, but making their nationalism compatible with European realities. We explained the "taming" of Central and Central-Eastern European nationalisms in terms of two fundamental mechanisms. First, the institutional transfer of norms, laws, and regulations as part of the European integration process, which facilitated the building of strong state capacity. Second, far-reaching acceptance of EU membership as part and parcel of a new post-Communist national identity, which facilitated the acceptance of this new project of – partial – de-nationalisation, thus "normalising" and "banalising" the multiple nationalisms of the region in much the same way as had happened earlier with nationalisms in post-World War II Western Europe. In Eisenstadt's terms, the unsuccessful 'second model of modernity' represented by Communism has led Eastern European countries towards adopting the first model: multiple nationalisms, one modernity.

Bibliography

Abdelal, R. 2001. *National Purpose in the World Economy. Post-Soviet States in Comparative Perspective*. Ithaca: Cornell University Press.

———— 2005. "Nationalism and International Political Economy in post-Soviet Eurasia". In *Economic Nationalism in a Globalizing World*, edited by E. Helleiner and A. Pickel, 21-43. Ithaca: Cornell University Press..

Aitov, N.A. 1986. "The Dynamics of Social Mobility in the USSR". In *The Social Structure of the USSR. Recent Soviet Studies,* edited by M. Yanowitch, 254-270. Armonk: New York.

Almond, G. and L. Roselle. 1993. "Model Fitting in Communist Studies". In *Post-communist Studies and Political Science*, edited by F. Fleron and E. Hoffmann, 170-224. Boulder: Westview.

Aslund, A. 2002. *Building Capitalism*. Cambridge: Cambridge University Press.

Billig, M. 1995. *Banal Nationalism*. London: Sage.

Bollerup, S.R. and C.D. Christensen. 1997. *Nationalism in Eastern Europe. Causes and consequences of the national revivals and conflict in late twentieth-century Eastern Europe*. London: Macmillan.

Brzezinski, Z. 1960. *The Soviet Bloc. Unity and conflict*. Cambridge: Harvard University Press.

Carrère d'Encausse, H. 1991. *The End of the Soviet Empire. The triumph of the nations*. New York: Basic Books.

Chirot, D. 1995. "National Liberations and Nationalist Nightmares. The Consequences of the End of Empires in the 20th Century". In *Markets, States and Democracy*, edited by B. Crawford, 43-69. Boulder: Westview.

Csergö, Z. and J. Goldgeier. 2004. "Nationalist Strategies and European Integration". *Perspectives on Politics* 2004, 2. 21-37.

Delanty, G. 2004. "Pluralism and the Multiple Forms of Modernity: An interview with S.N. Eisenstadt". *European Journal of Social Theory* 7, 3. 391-404.

Deutsch, K. 1963. "Cracks in the Monolith: Possibiities and Patterns of Disintegration in Totalitarian Systems". *Comparative Politics: A Reader*, edited by H. Eckstein and D.E. Apter, 457-507. New York: Free Press.

Drahokoupil, J. 2009. *Globalization and the State in Central and Eastern Europe*. London: Routledge.

Eichler, M. 2005. "Explaining Postcommunist Transformations: economic nationalism in Ukraine and Russia". In *Economic Nationalism in a Globalizing World*, edited by E. Helleiner and A. Pickel, 69-90. Ithaca: Cornell University Press.

Eisenstadt, S.M. 2000. "Multiple Modernities". *Daedalus* 129, 1. 1-29.

——— 2003. *Comparative Civilizations and Multiple Modernities*. 2 vols. Leiden: Brill.

English, R. 2000. *Russia and the Idea of the West*. Ithaca: Cornell University Press.

EUROBAROMETER EB60 – CCEB 2003.4: "Identities and values in the acceding and candidate countries", Brussels: European Commission

European Commission. 1995. "White Paper. Preparation of the Associated Countries of Central and Eastern Europe for Integration into the Internal Market of the Union". Brussels: EU.

Gellner, E. 1992. "Nationalism and Politics in Eastern Europe". *New Left Review* 189. 127-134.

Gérard, R. 1997. "Political Constraints and The Transition Experience". In *Lessons from the Economic Transition. Central and Eastern Europe in the 1990s*, edited by S. Zecchini, 169-188. Paris: OECD.

Habermas, J. 1990. *Die nachholende Revolution*. Frankfurt/Main: Suhrkamp.

Hobsbawm, E. 1992. *Nations And Nationalism Since 1780*. 2nd ed. Cambridge: Canto.

—— 1994. *Age of Extremes: The Short Twentieth Century, 1914-91*. London: Michael Joseph.

Hough, J.F. 1997. *Democratization and Revolution in the USSR 1985-1991*. Washington, D.C.: Brookings.

Ignatieff, M. 1994. *Blood and Belonging*. Toronto: Penguin.

Kaldor, M. 1999. *New And Old Wars*. Stanford: Stanford University Press.

Kuzio, T. 2001. "'Nationalizing States' or Nation-building?". *Nations and Nationalism* 7, 2. 135-154.

Laitin, D. 2002. "Culture and National Identity: 'The East' and European Integration". In: *The Enlarged European Union. Diversity and Adaptation*, edited by R. Mair and J. Zielonka, 55-80. London: Cass..

Laqueur, W. 1994. *The Dream That Failed*. Oxford: Oxford University Press.

Linz, J. and A. Stepan. 1992. "Political Identities and Electoral Sequences. Spain, the Soviet Union, and Yugoslavia". *Daedalus* 121, 2. 97-121.

—— 1996. *Problems of Democratic Transition and Consolidation: Southern Europe, South America and Postcommunist Europe*. Baltimore: Johns Hopkins University Press.

Luchterhandt, O. 2002. "Staatsangehörigkeitsrecht im Wandel von der UdSSR zur Rußländischen Föderation". Osteuropa 52, 6. 697-718.

Müller, K. 1992. "'Modernising' Eastern Europe. Theoretical Problems and Political Dilemmas". *European Journal of Sociology* 33, 2. 109-150.

Muller, J. 2008. "Us and Them. The Enduring Power of Ethnic Nationalism". *Foreign Affairs* March/April. 18-35.

Nelson, D.N. 1991. "Europe's Unstable East". *Foreign Policy* 82.137-158.

Offe, C. 1996. *Varieties of Transition*. Cambridge: Polity Press.

Pickel, A. 2003. "Explaining, and Explaining with, Economic Nationalism". *Nations and Nationalism* 9, 1. 105-128.

––––––– 2006. "The Problem of Order in the Global Age: Systems and Mechanisms". New York: Palgrave.

Roeder, P.G. 2001. The triumph of nation-states: Lessons from the collapse of the Soviet Union. Paper presented at APSA annual meeting, Chicago.

Rose, R. et al. 2006. *Russia Transformed. Developing popular support for a new regime*. Cambridge: Cambridge University Press.

Ross, C. 2009. *Local Politics and Democratisation in Russia*. London: Routledge.

Spohn, W. 2002. "Transformation Process, Modernization Patterns, and Collective Identities: Democratization, nationalism and religion in postcommunist Germany, Poland, and Russia". In *Postcommunist Transformations and the Social Sciences. Cross-Disciplinary approaches*, edited by F. Bönker, K. Mueller, and A. Pickel, 199-217. Boulder: Rowman & Littlefield.

Suny, R. 1993. *The Revenge of the Past. Nationalism, revolution and the collapse of the Soviet Union*. Stanford: Stanford University Press.

——— 1995. "Rethinking Soviet Studies: Bringing the Non-Russians Back In". In *Beyond Soviet Studies*, edited by D. Orlovsky, 105-134. Baltimore: Johns Hopkins University Press.

Szporluk, R. 1989. "Dilemmas of Russian Nationalism". *Problems of Communism* 38, July-August. 15-35.

Tsygankov, A. 2005. "The Return to Eurasia: Russia's identity and geoeconomic choices in the post-Soviet world". In *Economic Nationalism in a Globalizing World*, edited by E. Helleiner and A. Pickel, 44-68. Ithaca: Cornell University Press.

Weber, M. 1976 [1922]. *Wirtschaft und Gesellschaft*. Tübingen: Mohr.

Weiss, H. and C. Reinprecht. 1998. *Demokratischer Patriotismus oder ethnischer Nationalismus in Ostmitteleuropa? Ungarn, Tschechien, Slowakei und Polen*. Wien: Böhlau.

World Bank. 2002. "Transition. The First Ten Years". Washington, D.C.: World Bank.

Xenakis, C. 2002. *What Happened to the Soviet Union? How and why American Sovietologists were caught by surprise*. London: Greenwood.

Zaslavsky, V. 1991. *Das russische Imperium unter Gorbatschow. Seine ethnische Struktur und ihre Zukunft*. Berlin: Wagenbach.

——— 1992. "Nationalism and Democratic Transition in Postcommunist Societies". *Daedalus* 121, 2. 97-121.

Russian Nationalism and Xenophobia

Lev D. Gudkov

Xenophobia is an extreme feature of Russian nationalism. In a context of instability, tension, and social disintegration, the most meaningful collective values erode and earlier mechanisms of cultural reproduction become paralyzed. Thus, primitive forms and means of maintaining a collective us arise from the bottom of social life and begin to replace central tenets of societal self-definition. Based to a large extent on opinion polls conducted mainly by the Levada Center, this chapter looks into the various features of Russian xenophobia since the collapse of the Soviet Union.

Features of Russian xenophobia before and after the Soviet collapse

About 20 percent of the Soviet population in 1989 was openly xenophobic. Of these, six to 12 percent were aggressively ethnophobic. Zones of ethnic conflicts – especially in the Caucasus and in Central Asia – presented a different picture: There, mutual enmity, the hostility between the conflicting parties, and the corresponding inner-ethnic solidarity were so strong that they were shared by the majority of the population.

In Russia, these numbers were noticeably lower than the average values for the entire Soviet Union (between nine and 14 percent in 1989). More than half of Russia's population condemned all forms of ethnic hostility, national domination, and "moral judgment" of other peoples and also believed that an ethnic group or a nation could not be collectively held responsible for actions perpetrated by individuals or groups (for example, pogromists or extremists).

The explanation is to be found not only in the often praised "natural" tolerance and goodwill of the Russian population towards other ethnic groups, but also in the amorphous shape of ethnic identity and the extreme weakness of intra-ethnic solidarity. However, these coexist with strongly articulated great power principles and ethnocratic motives in the Russian consciousness, which do not leave the shadow of a doubt concerning the dominance of the Great Russian (later Russian) ethnos over other nationalities.

This consciousness perceives any ethnic movement's claim for autonomy as an expression of Russophobia or hostility towards Russians.[1] Russian (*russkii*) domination over other nations was perceived as the normal order of things in the sphere of relations between ethnic groups and nationalities.

The change in the structures of Russian (*russkii* and *rossiiskii*) self-awareness after the break-up of the USSR could only be a negative one –with relations with Western countries increasingly based on distrust and suspicion,[2] and the country as a whole tending towards increased xenophobia. The latter was mainly directed against the wave of successful migrants from the Caucasus and, partially, from Central Asia, or against those perceived as culturally and socially different (e.g., the Roma).

In other words, it was not the crisis of Soviet identity – caused by the breakup of the USSR – that fostered an increase in xenophobia and tendencies towards ethnic isolationism. Rather, the rise in xenophobia was the result of a process of coping with this break-up, which was accompanied by transformations in the structures of the Russian population's ethno-national identity (Dubin 2004). The Russian self reasserted itself in a positive fashion mainly through the reanimation of traditional national values and symbols or, more precisely, its latest surrogates. The accentuation of a mythologised and heroicised past redeems the rather strong emotion of ethno-national inferiority and collective masochism. The absence of significant collective achievements, which could have acted as symbols of a "new Russia", and, more tangibly, the failure to raise the level of material wealth, led to domestic discontent and displaced aggression against the rich "countries" of the West, or those neighbouring countries that were in the process of establishing closer ties to the West.

Looking out for "enemies"

Of those surveyed in 1994, 56 percent believed that the incipient reforms and privatisations would leave Russia politically and economically dependent on the West (44 percent took the opposite viewpoint). Since the educated strata of Russian society had never acknowledged the country's responsibility for the

---

1   Besides, the tough control exercised by various social institutions in the USSR forestalled any expressions of this kind.
2   Especially with the former Cold War enemy, the US.

past, the mere fact that the "younger brothers" and "allies in the Socialist camp" wanted to escape from Russia's "embrace" shocked the masses and led to childish reactions like "nobody loves us" and "everyone wishes us ill". This was especially true after the "Coloured Revolutions" in Georgia and the Ukraine, which turned these countries into Russia's biggest "enemies" (see Table 1-2).[3]

It is telling that the population did not view the conflict between the Georgian and Russian leaderships as the cause for the war between Russia and Georgia in August 2008, but rather perceived it as due to the continued opposition between Russia and the US (see Table 3-4). The latter is supposedly pushing Russia out of its traditional imperial sphere of influence. Hence, the relations between Russia and Georgia, Russia and Ukraine, and between Russia and the European Union deteriorated strongly between 2003 and 2004.

The disappointment that was caused by unfulfilled expectations of a quick bloom under new "democratic" powers was exacerbated by the negative effects of the economic slump and the restructuring of production. These brought about unemployment, delays, unpaid wages and pensions, and a change in the social status and income of a significant portion of employees. The mechanisms of social resentment converted the accumulated potential for negative emotions into an idealisation or sublimation of the Russians' ideas of themselves, on the one hand, and into serious distrust towards the power structures and hostility towards "foreigners", on the other.

The increased ethnic homogeneity in Russia after the collapse of the USSR (the percentage of Russians, of the "titular nation", increased from 52 to 83 percent), and the suppression or significant curtailment of the independence of the heads of "autonomous regions" within Russia[4] has practically denied ethnic minorities the possibility of presenting their own interpretations of the events of the past and the present in public. Since 2000, the only viewpoint that is still heard is the "Russian" (*russkii*) one.

Power and Russia's "national rebirth"

The process of Russia's "national rebirth" began already under Boris Yeltsin, with the first results of Yegor Gaidar's reforms and the unleashing of the

---

3   Data show that after Putin coming to power, public opinion on Georgia drastically worsened. Especially after 2003 and 2005 anti-Georgian and respectively anti-Ukrainian propaganda grew stronger.
4   This was one of the leading motives of presidential policies after the outbreak of the Second Chechen War.

First Chechen War, but it did not fully evolve until Putin came to power. His team turned this process into the regime's main pillar of legitimacy. The imitation of the "great power style" of Soviet and even earlier, pre-revolutionary, times,[5] with recourse to the newest technologies, was the equivalent of working out a national idea, a surrogate for big politics, that could be easily digested by a significant part of the population thanks to the monopoly of state-run television.

In the collective consciousness, Putin became the symbolic chain that linked Soviet times to the present day, healing or at least easing the trauma of the masses that had been caused by the changes under Yeltsin and the collapse of Soviet power. People did not expect the president to bring about renewal or a fresh programme, serious change, or consistent modernisation, but rather a "routinisation" of the rupture.

The increase in ethnic and national hostility among Russians living in Russia did not become noticeable until 1995 or 1996, after the political and administrative ties from Soviet times had actually dissolved. Between 1990 and 1992, according to various polls conducted by the Levada Center (which on that issue were still irregularly conducted), respondents' negative attitudes towards Uzbeks rose from 12 to 20 percent, towards Estonians from 16 to 19 percent, towards Tatars from 12 to 13 percent, towards Ukrainians from 4 to 6 percent, towards Belarusians from 3 to 4 percent, and towards Russians themselves within Russia from 2 to 3 percent. In the following 15 years, these indices hardly changed at all (see Table 5). The eruption of the financial crisis in August 1998 brought the incipient democratising and modernising processes in Russia to a halt. The beginning of the Second Chechen War in 1999 finally offered the population a "way out" of a general state of serious frustration, internal aggression, and disorientation. The war allowed for a channelling of tensions and the transfer of aggression onto the "Chechen separatists". It was presented as a fight against international terrorism, and accompanied and masked the erection of a police state.

Caucasians as main targets of Russian xenophobia

The majority of ethnic aversions today manifest themselves as hostility towards Caucasians and Roma: Overall, this accounts for about two-thirds of the

---

5 This imitation includes: manipulating imperial and Soviet symbols from the St. George Ribbon to the Red Star, ritualised parades and rallies, periodically posing of the state leadership as a resolute and concerned "father", etc.

answers of those respondents that voiced phobias against people of different nationalities (see Table 5-6).

These antipathies arise out of dissimilar outlooks on life and culture and differences in the habitual evaluation of traditional kinds of occupations. They were not articulated until the ethno-national conflicts in the Caucasus became exacerbated. Between 1987 and 1992, the Russian population began to articulate negative feelings towards immigrants from the Caucasus and from Central Asia. They followed the Armenian-Azeri conflicts, the pogroms against Armenians in Sumqayit, the expatriation of Armenians from Azerbaijan, the conflict over Nagorno-Karabakh, the Ingush-Ossetian conflicts in 1991/92, the Georgian-Abkhaz wars, and the conflict between Georgians and Ossetians in South Ossetia. All in all, however, the region is seen by Russians as harbouring the risk of ethnic tensions being diffused to other regions of the former Soviet Union, possibly excluding the Baltic states (the Chechen wars, especially the first one, were indeed not popular among the Russian public; however, they did not trigger any sympathy or compassion with the Chechens, neither with the soldiers nor with the civil population. The hidden fear that they triggered, provoked a latent hostility and aggression towards them).

A rapid increase in migration from the Caucasus followed, which raised the frequency of contacts between Caucasians and the local Russian population. The newcomers arrived with new ways of life, habits, and collective solidarity. The migrants were successful in a number of new and – to the Russians – suspicious spheres of activity, such as intermediary and retail trade and the service industry, which the core population had been weaned off during the years of Soviet power.

The onset of Gaidar's reforms coincided with massive ethnic migration.[6] This increased the prevalence of irritation and adverse views in the relations between the core population and newcomers. Sixty-eight percent of Russian city dwellers (primarily in the provinces) today harbour feelings of antipathy and discontent towards the newcomers (only 15 percent see the inflow of new inhabitants in a positive light). When they are asked to explain their hostility towards

---

6   Aggression concerned primarily those who were not ethnic Russians, although sometimes it was also directed against Russians coming from Central Asian republics. There were marked differences in terms of culture and education between the population of Central Russia, to where the immigrants went, and the population coming from Central Asia. Russians from Central Asia were better educated, more willing to work, and mostly unaffected by alcoholism, which was widespread in most of Russia.

the newcomers (non-Russians), however, people are unable to provide a common justification for their dislike. Whenever possible, they repeat arguments advanced by the press, the authorities, or their "talking heads". They claim not to like them because, firstly, they are different, and, secondly, unlike *us*, they stick together, and their solidarity is based on foundations that are both incomprehensible and inaccessible to *us* (Table 7).

Other varieties of xenophobia are more traditional (towards Jews, Tatars, and Uzbeks) and therefore subject to much larger cycles of change. Their link to current social transformations is weaker. Anti-Semitism was the first widely shared form of xenophobia in Russia, as a reaction to the role of Jews as agents of modernisation in the agrarian or traditional Russian society under the conditions of an emerging Russian national identity in a multi-national Empire, in which the Russians accounted for less than half of the total population. Jews represented the fourth-largest ethno-national or ethno-confessional group in Russia during the Russian imperial age of the late 19th and early 20th centuries.[7] Anti-Semitism gained paradigmatic character for all other pseudo-rational attempts to justify xenophobia. The attitudes of Russians towards Tatars (today the second-largest ethnic group in Russia) do not display any specific characteristic, because a majority of the latter (75 percent) live in two republics, Tatarstan and Bashkiria. This predominantly rural population is highly Russified, and their lifestyle does not differ very much from that of their Russian counterparts. The Tatars, like the Uzbeks and Kyrgyz, do not play a special role in the structure of Russian collective identity, because they do not claim autonomy, special status, or key positions in the government, and therefore the level of prejudice against them is one of the lowest. The colonisation of Tatar regions ended already in the early 19th century, after which time they never caused the Russian state any trouble.

Relations with the Baltic peoples, Belarusians, and Ukrainians, on the other hand, reflect the fluctuations in the official ideology as shaped primarily by the authorities and the mass media that are loyal to the state. One might say that the mass of Russians (*rossiianye*) still feel a general level of sympathy or goodwill towards these peoples, while they increasingly view the governments in

---

[7] After Russians, Ukrainians, and Poles; there were 5 million Jews in Russia by the beginning of mass emigration caused by the first pogroms; today, the Jewish population is 232.000 people, of which 75 percent live in Moscow, St. Petersburg, Nizhnyi Novgorod, and Ekaterinburg. A vast majority of the modern-day Russian population has never had any contact with Jews.

a negative, ideologised light. The population of the Baltic states was perceived as the most advanced already in Soviet times. They had a Western lifestyle, which was important and esteemed in Russian consciousness. Their withdrawal from the Soviet Union and rapprochement with other European states and the EU was seen as a logical step and did not garner a great deal of attention, in spite of all the anti-Estonian, anti-Latvian, and − to a lesser extent − anti-Lithuanian propaganda under Putin or the rise of national and especially ethnic hostility and dislike. Only in recent years, in connection with the intense state hysteria surrounding the memorial to the Soviet troops that died in the Second World War while liberating the Baltic states from Hitler's troops, have the attitudes of many Russians towards these states worsened. But this worsening did not provoke ethnic strife and aggression, as it primarily concerned the relationship with the state and political structures of these countries, but not the population. Belarusians are perceived as the nation closest to the Russians in terms of culture, lifestyle, and political views; hence, attitudes towards them hardly differ from those of Russians to themselves. Not long ago, that would also have been true with regard to Ukrainians, but the situation here has changed rapidly in recent years.

While about one-third of respondents in 1993 were convinced that non-Russians were to blame for the social disaster in Russia, this number rose to over two-fifths (42 percent) in 2004. Already in the early 2000s, 54 percent of respondents shared the view that people of non-Russian descent, or "other nationalities", had too much influence in Russia (41 percent disagreed with that proposition). This survey did not distinguish between people of various social-demographic categories.[8] Simultaneously, an increasing number of people became worried about the overpowering influence of foreigners, and the threat of Russia's national riches being sold out to foreigners. These ideas arose from traditional fears of conspiracies, obfuscation, secret forces and organisations, or organised crime. These laid the groundwork for ethno-national complexes and

---

8   These numbers only started to drop after Putin's fifth year in power. By that time, the Second Chechen War had ended; Russia had joined the so-called "war against terrorism" and introduced a programme to raise the level of state security. In August 2004, a similar question ("Do you agree that national minorities have too much power in our country?") returned the following responses:47 percent of respondents agreed, 44 percent disagreed (N=1600). 49 percent believed it was necessary to limit the influence of Jews in the state organs, in politics, business, education, and jurisprudence − 41 percent disagreed (Levada Center 2004: 139).

phobias (almost two-thirds of respondents harboured elements of these ideas). Table 8 summarises these results.

Social composition of the xenophobes

Nevertheless, the changes mentioned above do not simply manifest themselves in the scale of xenophobic feelings and reactions. In the years since the disintegration of the USSR, there has been a noticeable change in the social milieu of the xenophobes (Levada 1994). In the late 1980s, the level of ethnic intolerance was comparatively low, and xenophobically motivated aggression was dormant. In general, xenophobia was found among the elderly, those living on the social margins, and in small towns or in villages. Today, as in the late 1990s and early 2000s, the most intense ethnic hostility is found among two different social groups: young people with an undefined status, and "bureaucrats" and "educated people" (and, correspondingly, older people).

In the late 1980s and early 1990s, youths as a demographic cohort were far more tolerant than all other age groups, due to the rise of democracy and their hopes for change (especially because they were more educated than the preceding generations had been at the same age). Even today, 15 years later, this group remains more calm and reasonable when it comes to ethno-national relations. But the youth cohorts that supplanted them, socialised in a different socio-cultural context, are quite different.

To be more precise: Youth aggression against foreigners and anyone regarded as ethnically "inferior" or "racially foreign" exists in almost every country of Western and Eastern Europe. However, intolerance of this kind varies a great deal depending on the social surroundings. Youths are especially sensitive to changes in national self-awareness. The moments of becoming aware of large, symbolic collective entities – including ethnic entities – and of attaining political self-determination coincide with generational phases of teenage group socialisation. When earlier ideological and national stereotypes are eroded or destroyed, and new models for understanding collective reality are absent,[9] very strong and rigid mechanisms of solidarity come to bear. These are characteristic for small informal groups, and especially for teenage subcultures, which borrow from alternative Western youth cultures and counter-cultures. The latter distinguish

---

9   This applies particularly to youths from lower social strata or marginal groups, whose informational resources are very limited – not to mention their social and cultural competencies and awareness of the norms of civil society.

themselves by their inclination to stress affectively the symbolic barriers – the trademarks – that set them apart from the others.

Additionally, one finds a weak sense of empathy, responsibility, and self-control among them. Aggressive chauvinist groups – neo-Nazis, skinheads, and others – emerge primarily at the intersection of big and small towns (or, similarly, at the interface of the social environments of large cities and proletarianised suburbs and the edges of housing projects).

Moods of ethnic aggression also changed significantly in the late 1990s and early 2000s among subgroups such as students (Borusiak 2004). Today, youths, as well as the social "elite" – college-educated administrators and specialists – display the strongest aversion, which is the result of profound processes of social transformation and of changes in their social status. Although the majority of them profited from the changes, their position is insecure and unstable.

Furthermore, a significant part of the old nomenclature and management apparatus lost some of its previous status in the hierarchical system of the party-economic apparatus as a result of these changes. This diminished the societal authority and influence of these people and discredited them. As a social or functional stratum, the post-Soviet elite is in a state of slow dissolution. This leads to a discrepancy between their previous self-evaluation and self-determination[10] and that of other groups. Interestingly, this group, consisting of college-educated respondents – which is crucial for any sociological inquiry – was the only one among which complexes of injury, insult, the loss of national greatness, the fear of "selling of the national wealth" were not only preserved, but also increasing: Between 1998 and 2006, the share of this type of answer in sociological surveys almost doubled, from 39 to 69 percent. This means that these feelings have become dominant.

Even if the ethnic attitudes of society have hardly changed, there has been a rather significant shift within the politically interested part of it. Today, one can say that xenophobia and ideological nationalism[11] have merged, and that the

---

10 Which was, of course, too positive from today's point of view.
11 By "ideological nationalism", I mean Russian bureaucracy's typical apologetic stance of state policies made from the point of view of the "interests of Russians" as the "state-forming ethnic majority". Usually, these ideological constructions were used against liberals and supporters of the democratisation and modernisation of Russia (which would lead to a rapprochement of Russia to Western states). Similar points of view are not necessarily to be found in popular xenophobia or racism. But recently, the difference

perceptions of the masses, of the lower classes, and of the more educated strata of Russian society are converging. The complete inability of the educated classes (the so-called *intelligentsiia*, but also the bureaucracy) to act indicates that the representatives of humanism and the enlightenment are losing their authority: The organisations of Russian writers, film-makers, researchers from the Academy of Sciences, university teachers, professors from the influential Muscovite universities, but also from provincial higher education institutions, and many more have begun to advocate a return to national traditions, including assertions of a threat of Russian culture by the West, the necessity of uniting the secular and Christian orthodox education, and other similar demands. They try to safeguard their position by complementing it with utterly banal ideas about the shared ethnic character and quality of social groups.

The general level of xenophobic or negative national reactions among the politically active part of the population – which participated in the last Duma and presidential elections – is somewhat higher than among those who declared their indifference or disillusionment with politics. So, all in all, it is the politically active part of the Russian population that is more xenophobic than that which does not take part in politics.

Weak institutionalisation of ethno-nationalism

If one considers the significant rise of xenophobia and racism in Russia (from 12 to 16 percent in 1989 to about 40 percent in 2009), the weak support for radical organisations and extremist, neo-Nazi, or national-populist parties seems paradoxical. Parties or political organisations that have attempted to run on purely anti-Semitic, racist or anti-Western platforms have time and again lost elections and disappeared from the scene. This has happened to the National-Patriotic Front, Pamiat', Russian National Unity (RNE), Rus', the Stalinist Bloc, and others. According to opinion polls, about three to five percent of the adult population sympathised with them, but only about half of a percent was willing to support them with their vote (in 1999, 2003, and 2007).

We believe that the population's aversion is linked to its fear of the potentially destabilising effect that the aggressive actions and appearances of these organisations have. However, radical-nationalist parties do serve as triggers: They hurl those slogans at the population that other political forces dare not ut-

---

between actual xenophobia and the doctrine-driven, speculative nationalism of groups close to power has become blurred.

ter. After these "ideas" or feelings have been revised so as to appear more "respectable", parties and organisations in parliament[12] that are tied to a discontented, national-populist electorate, such as the LDPR or Rodina, adopt them. From there, these already softened – almost "refined" – arguments are taken up by the party of power or former democrats and liberals, such as Yabloko or the SPS, and begin to shape the contemporary language of Russian politics, or, more precisely the discourse of monopolised power, of the "power vertical".

If we follow the dynamics of xenophobia among the constituents of various parties and political movements in recent years, we end up with an astonishing picture. In 1993, the level of xenophobia and chauvinism among voters of democratic parties – especially, but not only, of the Democratic Choice of Russia – was very low. The inertia of the democratic rise, the illusions concerning the future, and the pro-Western orientations of those groups that put their hopes in the team of reformers under Gaidar[13] – all of these factors led to a recognition of the values of ethnic tolerance, freedom, and equal rights, as well as a rejection of ethnic domination and a relative independence from the traditional inferiority complexes and complexes of injury generally found among Russian nationalists.

On the other hand, among the Communists – which had been removed from power – a sense of national grievance, resentment, collective frustration, and suppressed aggression began to pile up. Over time, however, the link between political forces and injured nationalism began to change. The peak of mass xenophobia was reached in 2002, when Putin was at his most successful, and has dropped slowly since then (Leonova 2004).

Not only is the general increase in xenophobia and ethnic aversion striking, but so is the significant reduction in political differences between formerly "nationalist" parties[14] on the one hand, and the democratic parties as well as the "parties in power" on the other. Since the 1990s, the party in power has been the least xenophobic: This has been true for Democratic Choice of Russia, followed by Our Home is Russia, and now United Russia. The level of xenophobia or ethnic aggression, anti-Americanism, etc., increases among those who compete for power or have lost it, but not among those that already have it.

---

12 These parties tend not to be the most respected ones.
13 These were generally younger and more educated Russians, the inhabitants of the capitals and large cities, which were the most active and progressive groups with the largest amount of cultural and social capital at that moment.
14 Mainly those that formed the "national-patriotic bloc" and the "National Salvation Front" under the leadership of the Communists.

The only feature of the party of power is that it has no ideology apart from loyalty to the leader of the state. It monopolises the right to xenophobia in the sense that it has the right to designate those that are to be considered enemies at any given moment: Chechen separatists, international terrorists, the instigators and leaders of "anti-Russian" (*antirossiiskie*) revolutions of various colours, etc. The "winners" have no need for various, barely controllable phobias and ethnic aversions. The "state", i.e., those who today have appropriated the executive and judicial powers and subordinated parliament and the electoral system to their clan interests, are the most important factors in the diffusion of Russian nationalism. These people have no other means of legitimation apart from the wounded national dignity of the Russians, traditional militarism, and so on.

Conclusion

In summing up the results, we will reiterate the characteristics of Russian nationalism. In contrast to "classic" versions of nationalism or those of "catch-up modernisation", Russian nationalism does not entail a modernising vision for the development of the country or individual parts of it; hence, any such reform programmes would be seen in this context as anti-Russian and "anti-national". The components of Russian nationalism can be summed up as follows:

1. The conviction of the primacy of the Russians over other peoples making up the "empire", and accordingly, the assumption of special rights for Russians within the state – leads to advancing demands that are justified by extremely weak arguments (it would be more correct to say that they are simply proclaimed).

2. Pride in the belief that Russians are an empire-forming nation, and therefore have specific priorities and privileges concerning place of residence, as well as access to the highest posts in the state leadership, in the army, and in other power structures including the economy and educational institutions.

3. Militarism that attributes a special significance to war (based on the narrative of Victory in the Second World War) and to the army in the structure of the ethno-national identity, support for various forms of geopolitical expansion; or lately, almost burlesque attempts to keep control over the former area of the Socialist camp and the former USSR.

4. The idea of an organic unity of all Russians, as identified by blood (common origin), and the assumption of a shared historical destiny, incarnated in the symbolic character of the undivided authority of the supreme power, which

subordinates society to its goals (which accordingly implies the irrelevance of political and judicial institutions and their character, and consequently the lack of importance of evolutionary and emancipatory ideas and movements).

5. Isolationism; anti-Western sentiments; negative mechanical integration of different populations by means of repression and police control; the use of an ideology that identifies "the enemy", "hostile encirclement", negative projection of various kinds on other societies and countries; or fears of "internal enemies", strangers, a "fifth column", or the secret expansion of non-Russians endangering the existence of Russia.

Appendices

Table 1: Does Russia have an enemy?

	1989	1994	1999	2003	2008
Yes	13	41	65	78	68
No	47	22	14	9	14
Hard to answer	40	37	22	14	18
N=	*1200*	*3000*	*2000*	*2000*	*1500*

Table 2: With which countries of the world can we become friendlier, and who feels friendly towards Russia? And which countries act in a hostile manner towards Russia?[15]

Friendly	%	Hostile	%
Belarus	50	Georgia	68
Germany	51	USA	65
China	47	Ukraine	50
France	45	Lithuania	40
Japan	37	Poland	27
Italy	25	Great Britain	8
Great Britain	24	Israel	5
Turkey	23	Belarus	5
Ukraine	21	Iran	4
Spain	20	Turkey	4
Austria	18	China	4
Poland	17	Czech Republic	3

2008, N=1600

---

15 In 2007, the list of countries was widened significantly to take the republics of the former USSR into account. Hence, the column "friendly" was headed by Kazakhstan, which was not included in the 2008 survey. The column "hostile" was headed by Estonia (60%). The relations between the latter and Russia were undergoing a severe test following the removal from the centre of Tallinn of a monument commemorating the fallen Soviet soldiers from World War II.

NATIONALISM AND XENOPHOBIA 185

Table 3: In your opinion, what is the ultimate cause of the ongoing conflict in South Ossetia?

Georgian government pursues the policy of discrimination against people of Ossetia and Abkhazia	32
Authorities of recognised Republics of Ossetia and Abkhazia tries to stay in power causing tensions all the time	5
Russian officials conduct divide-and-rule policy to maintain its authority in Caucasus	5
US Administration seeks to spread its influence over countries neighbouring Russia	49
Difficult to answer	9

2008, N=1600

Table 4: In your opinion, why did Georgia use force in South Ossetia?

It was an effort to restore territorial integrity of the country	15
Georgia is through with attacks and acts of provocation on the part of South Ossetia	4
Georgia should fix its territorial issues in order to be admitted as NATO member	43
M. Saakashvili launched this campaign to boost his authority in Georgia and keep the Presidential seat	38
Difficult to answer	10

2008, N=1600

Table 5: What is your attitude towards people of the following nationalities and ethnic groups…? (Only negative replies are listed: Annoyance, dislike, distrust, fear)

	1990	'93	'95	'96	'97	2000	'02	'03	'04	'05	'06	'07
Azerbaijanis	-	43	39	27	35	29	39	33	30	33	26	30
Chechens	-	48	51	47	50	53	66	53	53	51	43	44
Gipsies	-	48	48	40	48	43	52	50	53	51	49	53
Estonians	16	16	19	12	13	14	16	14	10	14	11	15
Jews	13	17	17	10	13	12	15	11	12	13	11	10
Sum of negative replies	-	172	174	136	159	151	188	161	158	162	140	152

1990-2007, N=1600

Table 6: What do you personally feel about people who come from Southern Republics but live in your city, district?

	2002	2003	2004	2006	2007	2008
Respect	3	5	3	4	6	4
Sympathy	5	4	4	4	5	4
Irritation	25	18	23	18	16	14
Dislike	28	23	24	15	18	14
Fear	5	4	4	3	4	2
No special feelings	39	45	46	56	54	61
Difficult to answer	4	4	4	3	3	2

2002-2008, N=1600

Table 7: What should the Russian government's policy be like towards migrants (from Caucasus and Central Asia)?

	2002 June	2004 August	2005 Sept.	2006 August	2007 August	2008 October
Should try to restrict the influx of migrants	45	54	59	52	57	52
Should not have any administrative barriers against the influx, should try to use it for benefit of Russia	44	38	36	39	32	35
Difficult to answer	11	7	6	9	11	13

N=1600

Table 8: What do you think about the idea "Russia for the Russians (*russkikh*)"?

Year	1998	2000	2001	2002	2003	2004	2005	2006	2007	2008
Month of survey	VIII	XII	I	XI	XII	VII	XII	XI	XI	VIII	X
I support it, it was about time it was put into practice	15	13	15	16	16	21	16	16	15	14	15
That would be a good idea, but it should be realised within reasonable boundaries	31	30	34	42	38	32	37	37	35	41	42
I am against it, that's real fascism	32	30	27	20	26	18	25	23	26	27	25
I do not care	10	14	12	11	9	7	12	12	12	11	12
Never thought about it/hard to answer	12	13	12	11	11	22	9	10	12	7	7

N=1600

Bibliography

Borusiak, L. 2004. "Patriotism kak ksenofobiia (rezultaty oprosa molodykh moskvichei". *Vestnik obshchestvennogo mneniia* 6, 74. 58-70.

Dubin, B. 2004. "K voprosu o vybore nuti: Elity, massy i instituty v Rossii i Vostochnoi Evrope 1990-kh godov". *Vestnik obshchestvennogo mneniia* 6, 74. 22-30.

Gudkov, L. 1997. "Ethnic Phobias in the Structure of National Identification". *Sociological research* 36, 4. 60-74.

―――― 1999. "Parameters of Anti-Semitism. Attitudes toward Jews in Russia, 1990-1997". *Sociological research* 38, 4. 72-96.

―――― 1999. "Antisemitizm v postsovetskoi Rossii". In: *Neterpimost' v Rossii: starye i novye fobii*, edited by G. Vitkovskaia and A. Malashenko, 44-98. Moscow: Moscow Carnegie Centre.

Hroch, M. 1985. *Social Preconditions of National Revival in Europe: a comparative analysis of the social composition of patriotic groups among the smaller European nations*. Cambridge: Cambridge University Press.

Leonova, A. 2004. "Nastroeniia ksenofobii i elektoral'nye nastroeniia v Rossii v 1994-2003 godakh". *Vestnik obshchestvennogo mneniia* 4, 72. 83-91.

Levada, Iu. 1994. "Novyi russkii natsionalizm: Ambitsii, fobii, kompleksy". *Monitoring obshchestvennogo mneniia* 1. 15-17.

Levada Center. 2004. *Obshchestvennoe mnenie-2004. Ezhegodnik*. Moscow: Levada Center.

Mitrokhin, N. 2002. *Russkaia partiia : dvizhenie russkikh natsionalistov v SSSR, 1953-1985*. Moskva: Novoe literaturnoe obozrenie.

Mukomel, V. 2005. "Rossiiskie diskursy o migratsii". *Vestnik obshchestvennogo mneniia* 1, 75. 48-75.

III Sovereign Democracy and its Competitors

Sovereign Democracy as a Discourse of Russian Identity[1]

Victoria Hudson

This chapter focuses on the notion of sovereign democracy as developed in Russian political circles under the presidency of Vladimir Putin. These pages track the emergence of the concept as a reaction to state weakness and the absence of a coherent vision of Russia and its role in the world of the 1990s, and explore the way sovereign democracy presents Russian identity today. Sovereign democracy is conceptualised as a discourse of securitisation, which is evoked to rally patriotism and unity among elites, in particular, around a project for Russia's future as a strong and independent nation respected as an equal by the great powers of the time. This chapter also examines the efforts to present sovereign democracy as part of a wider European intellectual heritage and thereby to underpin the legitimacy of Russia's envisaged civilisational distinctiveness as an alternative path of development, rather than a distortion of the Western model.

Ivan Krastev has described sovereign democracy as the Kremlin's response to Ukraine's "Orange Revolution" (2006a). This study suggests that while this is true, sovereign democracy was also the outcome of a broader search for a vision to support the renewal of Russia as a "normal" great power. Emerging initially in 2005, the concept of sovereign democracy, with its emphasis on Russia's independence and right to determine its internal affairs free of external interference, offers an explicit rhetorical response to the perceived threat of Western-orchestrated "democratisation" (Chadaev 2006: 235). Indeed, the Kremlin

---

[1] I warmly acknowledge the support and assistance of Dr. Derek Averre, Philipp Casula, and Daniel Högger in the production of this paper. Any errors that remain are my own.

took seriously the prospect of more "colour"- and "plant-coded" revolutions in the CIS region and even a "birch revolution" in Russia itself (Tsygankov 2008: 49). However, while the need to respond to these "hostile" tendencies may have been a catalyst, sovereign democracy as a political project does not suggest a radical change of course. Rather, it develops the trends that have become visible during President Putin's presidency into a body of reoccurring, if often underdeveloped, ideas. As such, this perceived external threat constituted the impetus for a wider project to consolidate the country, which can, given the burden of domestic struggle against political weakness and instability, be depicted as a prerequisite for successful development regardless of the external political environment.

While derided by critics – both international and domestic – as an unsustainable smoke screen to legitimise authoritarian trends, sovereign democracy is understood here more subtly as a discursive attempt to reconstruct a Russian identity in the post-Soviet period. These pages seek to offer a response to the question of how sovereign democracy supports this reconstruction and will suggest that the distinct, non-Western nature of the model of state and society it envisages is itself a key factor in redefining what Russia stands for today, while providing a rhetorical basis for measures to rebuild the country's great-power status, itself a crucial element of Russian identity.

The emergence of sovereign democracy

On assuming power in 1999, President Putin inherited a country in turmoil; burdened by economic decline, stagnating living standards, and instability emanating from the conflict in the Caucasus – to name just a few domestic issues. Russia's political and economic weakness and consequent subservience to the West during the 1990s led to perceptions of a low international standing and humiliation, which undermined the national self-understanding as a "great power". President Putin's pragmatic realist approach addressed a number of critical issues during his first term in office, reflected in increased economic growth and political stability. Still, a number of structural problems in the political system remained. Indeed, Okara notes,

> "given the specificity of Russia's infrastructures [in terms of the legacy of the Communist past] a transition to strictly pragmatic utilitarian motivations cannot ensure social mobilization and hence is not efficacious." (2007)

While practical steps had been taken to restructure the state, there was a lack of corresponding attention to securing citizens' – particularly elites' – affective loyalty to the nascent polity. The Communist legacy and the chaotic experiences of the 1990s had given little cause for trust in the political system, rule of law, and the justice system, none of which had not become systematically and consistently institutionalised. Where the weak state failed, state officials pursued their own interests through rent-seeking behaviour and exploitation of the political system. A similar lack of trust existed among the citizenry because the inflow of petro-dollars had enriched only a minority of individuals – even at the expense of the state – while most of the population continued to live in relative poverty and disillusionment with the results of economic transition, public service provision, and the perceived widespread corruption.

Dmitrii Medvedev commented on the utilitarian arbitrariness in the political system, with cleavages defined more by opportunism and general populism than systemised values:

> "The programmatic goals of a significant part of the political forces are indistinct, their ideology is slippery, they do not have their own position [...]. The lack of normal rightwing ideology procreates surrogates and prejudices [...]" (2006: 28).

Indeed, the "Communist" and "extreme-nationalist" opposition have campaigned on a rather demagogic ticket appealing to the desire for social security, prejudice, and imperial nostalgia within sections of the population. Concurrently, there was much infighting among political groups surrounding the presidency, and a lack of common vision concerning Russia's role in the world, with opinions split as to whether Russia should follow the West's example, develop as a Eurasian power, or pursue a strategy in opposition to the West (Tolz 2004). Correspondingly, there was also a lack of consensus about who was signified by the term "Russian"; a topic explored later in this paper.

However, a broadly consensual understanding of identity is important for political communities, as "a polity [...] needs an identity to provide a psychological frame of reference in which to function" (Prizel 1998: 2). Indeed, without a strong identity as the rationale for collective action at state level, it is likely that dynamic sub-state actors, such as regional political and economic actors or even private individuals and criminal groups, will increasingly compete for a share of the power – and wealth – claimed by the nation-state (Tolz 1998: 1017; 2004:

166). Furthermore, without a reasonably clear and consensual notion of a state's identity – and hence its vision of the future, its fundamental socio-economic assumptions, and its possible allies and enemies, defining policy priorities is problematic. This has been reflected in international perceptions that have frequently regarded Moscow's policies as inconsistent and incoherent.

Hence, in short, this situation of a disengaged, divided elite and a base of popular discontent was seen to provide fertile ground for the transplantation of colour revolutions, should this coincide with foreign or NGO organisational support or particular triggers such as contested elections, like in Ukraine. The Kremlin appears to have reached the conclusion that pure political pragmatism and the absence of hegemonic values among the elite were untenable. This formed the background to the emergence of sovereign democracy (Medvedev 2006: 28).

Accordingly, a particular strength of this discourse has been that it not only provides for the pragmatic pursuit of interests (both state and individual) by providing a rationale and incentives for cooperation, but also transcends utilitarianism and seeks to return the "meaning" (Okara 2007), or in Surkov's terms, the "romanticism" (2007: 32) to national political life. The notion of Russia as a great power forms a focal point for unifying efforts (Medvedev 2006), as it is a value shared by different actors in the political system.

Regarding the specifics of its emergence, the concept of sovereign democracy made its first public appearance in a speech entitled "Sovereignty is a political synonym for competitiveness" by First Deputy Chief of Staff of the Presidential Administration Vladislav Surkov at a United Russia forum in February 2006. Subsequently, the notion of sovereign democracy was laid out in Surkov's manifesto-like document "Nationalisation of the Future" in November 2006. The postscript notes that the document "was compiled as the result of joint efforts by supporters and critics and is one of the interpretations of our recent past and near future" (Surkov 2006: 45).[2] The concept of sovereign democracy

---

2   Despite the unifying purpose suggested here, the term sovereign democracy has always been controversial, even among the Russian ruling elite itself. Dmitry Medvedev, a leading critic of the term (Fadeev 2006) – although no less an adherent of many of its core ideas – states that regardless of adjectival prefixes, democracy is either present or not, concluding that it is indeed in existence in Russia. Surkov relativises the terminological debate, seizing the opportunity to underline the inappropriateness of the judgements of other democracies who would criticise Russia's sovereign democracy, noting there have always been different models of democracy; majoritarian, classical etc, and,

became the *de facto* programme of United Russia in late 2006, although United Russia consistently talks about reaching out and spreading its core values beyond the ranks of its own party in its efforts to nurture the next generation of the Russian elite. Indeed, the ideas signified by the concept have coalesced into the basis of a value consensus in the Russian political system, which continues to drive domestic and foreign policy (White 2008), even if the phrase "sovereign democracy" is less explicitly cited. Given the political preoccupation surrounding it, sovereign democracy has been approached here as an elite project with which ordinary people are unlikely to be familiar, although some of its ideas do enjoy popular resonance.

Sovereign democracy as a securitising discourse

The discourse of sovereign democracy outlines a mission to secure Russia's sovereignty, which is presented as a by-word for its very political identity as a state and a "civic value" for the population (Surkov 2007: 34). While the discourse takes a proactive tone, seeking to foster a more united political leadership, its internal logic rests upon a reaction to perceived internal and external threats; particularly separatism, state ineffectiveness, the need for modernisation, and the potential of foreign indirect intervention. Therefore, securitisation theory appears to provide a useful framework through which to approach the discourse of sovereign democracy[3] (Buzan et al. 1998; Bacon et al. 2006), which will be addressed in the second part of this section.

While legislation and societal institutions play a crucial role in nation-building, it is the public discourse of political leaders that dominates everyday politics. Although "discourse" may initially refer to speeches as the main way in which leaders inform and mobilise "their" nation, it also signifies the "regime of truth" referred to in these communications. Indeed, social scientists following Michel Foucault suggest that discourses – written and spoken texts – "create not only knowledge, but also the very reality they appear to describe" (Said 1995: 94). Through repetition over time, particularly from different actors dispersed across a society, such knowledge produces a tradition, or a discourse, that signifies "what counts as true" about significant themes in society; in other words, it

---

even countries considered to be models of democracy, nevertheless practised slavery and denied the vote to women under its banner (Surkov 2006: 30).

3   I shall follow Bacon et al. in applying this approach, originally developed by Buzan et al. for analysing international politics, to an examination of domestic affairs (Bacon et al. 2006: 10).

creates a lens for the interpretation of "reality". This understanding of "truth" does not signify objective facts, but rather "the mechanisms and instances which enable one to distinguish true and false statements" (Foucault 1980: 131). In this way, discourse can be seen as core principles of knowledge that have gained the status of common sense, or, *hegemony*.

According to Gramsci (1971), while coercive methods such as military force and punishment have almost always underwritten hegemony, in the modern capitalist world, leaders also seek to gain consent for their power.[4] Disseminated repeatedly over time through the institutions of civil society – the educational system, the media, the army, the civil service, the healthcare system and so on – discourses can become hegemonic. Talking outside the discourse, on the basis of different claims to "truth", can therefore appear as a "pathology", a "deviation" (Makarychev 2008: 1), and simply unacceptable. Nevertheless, strong discourses are not monolithic, rigid or static, but can be changed over time, even quite quickly, although discursive attempts to change the regime of truth "must be similar enough to other performances to be recognizable; [...] different enough from what has gone beyond, but [...] still recognizable [since] if it is not recognizable, you're not in the discourse" (Gee 1999: 18). In this way, political actors have the possibility to reinterpret history, events, symbols, and even language to suit changing circumstances.

The emergence of sovereign democracy can be seen as an attempt to construct such a regime of truth about Russia today, which centres upon a securitisation of Russian identity and a particular portrayal of Russian history as a basis for action. As the Russian state strives to consolidate its status as a hegemonic force, in Laclau and Mouffe's terms, sovereign democracy may be seen as a *discursive formation* constructed to "provide a surface for the inscription of a wide range of demands, views, and attitudes" (Torfing 1999: 101). To the extent that one accepts the logic of sovereign democracy and its particular "regime of truth", there are conclusions for political practice to be derived from that interpretation.

---

4   It is suggested in this study that the Russian elite close to the Kremlin strives to use the discourse of sovereign democracy as the basis for establishing consensual hegemony in Russia, not least because "these new techniques are both much more efficient and much less wasteful (less costly economically, less risky in their results, less open to loopholes and resistances)" (Foucault, cited in Rabinow 1984: 61).

Securitisation provides an ideational framework whereby, in theory, any issue can be cast as an existential threat to the designated referent object.[5] The theory is less interested in "objective" security threats "out there" than in the discursive move whereby issues are taken from the domain of the normal or political and made a security threat by leading actors. Securitisation is not deemed to have successfully occurred until the audience accepts the securitising discourse – or, at any rate, not before it "just [gains] enough resonance for a platform to be made from which it is possible to legitimise emergency measures or other steps that would not have been possible had the discourse not taken the form of existential threats, point of no return and necessity" (Buzan et al. 1998, cited in Bacon et al. 2006: 12).

The main audience to whom the concept of "sovereign democracy" was initially addressed was the Russian elite itself. Without an over-arching consensus, it was felt that the political order President Putin had inherited was threatened by divisive "'reactionary fits of isolationism and oligarchy" at the hands of bureaucrats and the "off-shore aristocracy" as well as disparaged by "'intellectuals' for whom the sun rises in the West" (Surkov 2006: 38). Regardless of the heterogeneity of these groups, sovereign democracy equates and associates these groups in a "chain of equivalence" (Laclau, cited in Torfing 1999: 123ff.), which constructs them as a *constitutive other* whose apparently insufficiently patriotic behaviour endangers the viability of the state, and aligns them with external detractors hostile to Russian strength. Indeed, fostering such equivalence and thus a sense of a conspiracy against Russia can only strengthen the perception of threat.

The discourse of sovereign democracy reflects a distinctive feature of securitisation, namely "a specific rhetorical structure (survival, priority of action, because if the problem is not handled now, it will be too late), which strives to take issues 'beyond the established rules of the game'." (Buzan et al. 1998: 23) Sovereign democracy reflects the Putin regime's priority of strengthening the state (Bacon et al. 2006: 8). Accordingly, the imperative for swift, decisive action to achieve this goal is established on the basis that if the Russian elite does not address the situation now, "the risk of wasting the next ten years becomes too

---

5 The referent object of sovereign democracy is decidedly the Russian state, underpinned by the corresponding national identity. While, arguably, politicians in all states are ultimately preoccupied with preserving the structure that legitimates their power, this is more explicit in Russia, where the strong state constitutes a tradition and is seen as the bulwark against chaos.

great. And then we may never be able to elevate ourselves" (Fadeev 2006: 133). To strengthen the case for unity, the discourse of sovereign democracy appeals to both pride in Russia's history and notions of political legitimacy; "we did not assimilate these territories, we did not create this gigantic country, she was created by many generations over the course of centuries. Nobody gave us the mandate to destroy our own country" (ibid.: 137). This is clearly directed at those who have the power to effect change: not only the political elite, but also business leaders (Kokoshin 2006: 90), who, as a powerful political constituency, must be enlisted in support of the sovereignty project.[6]

As a result of this securitised interpretation, authoritarian measures such as the persecution or exclusion of certain individuals, groups, and organisations can be constructed as "justifiable" to an audience who might have shown more resistance to these tendencies. In contrast to the pluralistic, if chaotic, experiments of the 1990s, the discourse prescribes a "nationally-oriented elite" possessing "an agreed understanding of which goals the country has in sight, which means it will use to attain them and which shape of the future and how to become again one of the leaders of the world" (Fadeev 2006: 133). In brief, the Russian state should command a position of respect and strength − *sovereignty* − both domestically and on the international stage, allowing it to re-emerge as an equal among great powers.

As such, sovereign democracy's discourse of threat provides a "regime of truth" to guide elite behaviour. It strives for consensual hegemony, not only presenting a securitising logic of threat that justifies disciplinary measures to exclude as fifth columnists those who would in diverse ways resist the ruling elite's project, but also supplying the basis for "pleasurable" incentives for "nationally-oriented" (Surkov 2006: 37) persons. Indeed, as Foucault observes, regimes do not survive through top-down coercion, but rather rely on co-opting support through "inducing pleasure", or providing advantages for those who cooperate (Rabinow 1984). In the case of contemporary Russia, the disciplinary function of the preference of "nationally-oriented" persons can be seen in the growth of United Russia party membership to two million since its foundation in 2001. Such "patriotic" individuals may receive privileged access to the advantages a

---

6 Indeed, a good number of the articles in Nikita Garadzha's "Suverenitet: sbornik" concern economic matters and frame economic strength as the basis upon which to reconstruct great power status.

strong state can offer, such as lucrative state infrastructural contracts prescribed by the "need to compete".

Sovereign democracy's intellectual ambition

The concept of sovereign democracy has been a substantial topic of discussion among Russia's political elites in recent years. However, some experts suggest that even its proponents do not believe in the concept, but rather simply use the term as a "plastic bag", putting into it what they will to maintain the tenuous facade of international respectability.[7] This view is supported by the manner in which concepts such as democracy and sovereignty are discussed. Instead of a rigorous engagement with the established theory on this topic, the texts of sovereign democracy's purported authors resemble a "cacophony of voices" (Kaehne 2007: 4), tending to summarise concepts without critical engagement or even attempts at applying them to contemporary Russia. While giving an intellectual flavour, this approach leaves the task of drawing conclusions about the writer's intentions to the reader. This tendency towards the bifurcation of theory and practice also pragmatically maintains the regime's distance from fixed principles of an official state ideology, as desired by President Putin (Sakwa 2008: 216), and absolves the author from expounding what sovereign democracy might mean in concrete terms within Russia and taking responsibility for that vision or addressing contrary views.

However, despite the lack of clarity in the discourse of sovereign democracy, it is nevertheless important for Russia – an aspirant great power making distinct civilisational claims – that such a discourse should exist. Therefore, the role of sovereign democracy as an intellectual discourse that is seen as capable of "reproducing the grounds for freedom" Russian-style (Surkov 2006: 27) is significant. Garadzha, hinting at the threat of dissolution that inaction seems to imply, notes that "only if we succeed in fixing ourselves in the metahistorical space through doctrinal formulations of our state-legal system will we avoid barbarism" (2006: 229). In Foucault's terms, Russia's "nationally-oriented intellectuals" and political actors are engaged in a struggle "at the general level of the regime of truth" (Foucault cited in Rabinow 1984: 74). Their aim is for Russia's model of political organisation and the associated values to gain "fair" recognition as a

---

7   A. Moshes, V. Morozov; comments made at the workshop on "New Stability, Democracy and Nationalism in Contemporary Russia", Institute of Sociology, Basel, 26-27 September 2008.

legitimate alternative path to development, rather than a deformity of, or deviation, from the Western-led model.

Indeed, Surkov appears to see sovereign democracy as Russia's contribution to the "controversy of cultures" (2006: 38). It should possess the ability to compete with, and yet be recognised by, other centres of cultural influence. Consequently, "the Russian message must be influential and distinct; free by nature, fair in essence, interesting in form, and acceptable in tone. It is necessary to affirm our own position in the philosophical and socio-political discourses of the West" (ibid.). However, the notion of the West as a reference point for recognition must be balanced with the assumption that Russia, which stakes its claim to European civilisation, is not necessarily *of the West*, even if Moscow identifies Russia's interests and overall cultural orientation as lying in that direction. Indeed, sovereign democracy asserts its European pedigree through references to European political philosophers such as François Guizot and Carl Schmitt, and echoes of Rousseau's collectivist democracy (Okara 2007). The choice of respected European theorists, albeit illiberal and in some cases discredited, can be seen as a provocative attempt to place sovereign democracy within the normative discourse of European political theory. Starting from key words recognised in the Western discourse, such as freedom and democracy, the discursive logic of sovereign democracy strives to broaden the recognised interpretation of these concepts. Russia should thereby be presented as the author of an alternative, but equally legitimate branch of European civilisation. Whether such recognition would be explicit, based on perceived merits of the ideas, or tacit, based on the lack of leverage to force Russia – as a power in the realist sense – to consider otherwise, remains to be seen, but it would probably combine both, depending on the actor concerned.

Thus, the discourse of sovereign democracy depicts Russia as being at a fork in the road in its development, seeking to unite a divided, often pessimistic elite around a vision of restored national greatness and an attractive strategy to achieve that aim. However, the ideational foundations of the project, whatever one may think of them and their pseudo-intellectual claims, are not intended solely for internal or defensive purposes, but should enable Russia to return to the international market of ideas as an active subject of history.

Sovereign democracy's presentation of Russian identity

The first part of this chapter has pointed to the factors instrumental in the emergence of sovereign democracy as a political idea. It has shown how the discourse appeals to a tradition of national pride in Russia's history as a great power, which is funnelled to serve as an inspiration for unity to achieve pragmatic goals in response to perceived internal and external threats. According to the discourse, sovereign democracy can be seen as a *floating signifier* (Torfing 1999: 301), simultaneously articulating Russia's international standing and its internal political arrangements as well as serving as a label for the discourse overall. This second part aims to explore how Russia's post-Soviet identity is presented in the discourse of sovereign democracy.

While for Laclau, all identities are *dislocated*, that is, inherently destabilised (Torfing 1999: 301), post-Soviet identities have been in a state of extreme dislocation since the end of the Cold War and the disappearance of "Soviet citizen" as a valid identity option. While the nation-building measures of the Soviet successor states in the "near abroad" have to a greater or lesser degree resulted in a re-orientation of identities towards the respective new polity, in Russia itself, the question of identity is more problematic. Despite the civic understanding of nationality laid down in the 1993 constitution, the meaning signified by the "Russian nation" remained ambiguous. It was variously considered to refer not only to all citizens of the Russian Federation, but also by some accounts more specifically to those people of Russian ethnicity. Others understood it more broadly as a "nation of all Eastern Slavs", or alternatively in terms of a "community of Russian speakers", or even with lingering reference to a notion corresponding to the former Union identity of the *Sovetskii narod* (Tolz 1998: 995f.). As suggested above, such confusion and lack of common perspective on this key topic reflects state weakness. In response to the need for a common idea of *us*, sovereign democracy may be interpreted as a hegemonic project whose role as a discourse is to "provide the empty signifier of the nation, which symbolises an absent fullness, with a precise substantive content that people can identify with" (Torfing 1999: 195). Sovereign democracy is primarily concerned with the *rossiisskii* identity as a basis upon which to strengthen state cohesiveness. Yet, it is proposed, the standing of the "multinational people" is of direct relevance to that of the parallel ethnic Russian nation, whose worth is shored up by the reflected glory of the *rossiiskaia natsiia*. This notion is explored further towards the end of this section.

Sovereign democracy reaffirms the recognition of the separateness of the Soviet successor states, yet they are still of significance to questions of Russian identity. It is felt by many in Russia that Russian great-power status is to a considerable degree dependent on occupying the role of regional hegemon in Central Asia and the Caucasus. Not only does influence in, and cooperation with, this region serve and protect Russia's economic, political, and geo-strategic interests, it also constitutes a historically connected neighbourhood upon which to project civilisational radiance; the vitality of Russian and Russia-oriented cultural and "humanitarian" values. The export of cultural attributes is one of the very characteristics of being a great power, as it serves to demonstrate the presumed universality of its civilisational values and forms the basis of the "soft power" ties with one's allies, which should garner consent for assertive involvement in the economic and strategic affairs of the region (Popescu 2006: 1; Nye 2004).

Patriotism, therefore, is not only the inspiration and outcome, but also the means for realising sovereign democracy's vision of national greatness. This suggestion hinges upon the argument that "neighbours will only accede to the mission of Russia to be an intellectual and innovative leader if Russia believes in itself, as a feasible reality, and not as imitation and simulated politico-technological project" (Karavaev 2006). Furthermore, the necessity of overcoming national pessimism and self-doubt commonly expressed by proponents of sovereign democracy (e.g., Surkov, Kazin, Karaveav, Shevchenko 2006) goes beyond the domestic population. Increasing the levels of both international prestige and identification with Russia is seen as a prerequisite for mobilising "compatriots abroad"[8] in the neighbouring states, whose disadvantaged situation was frequently ignored in the weak years of the 1990s. Indeed, the cultivation of a supportive diaspora among the diverse community is envisaged by some as the basis for pro-Russian lobbying in those countries (Zevelev 2008: 55ff.; Solozobov 2008; Popescu 2008). Concurrently, while Russia seeks to cultivate strong relations with its neighbours, the presence of Russian or other non-titular groups with a pro-Russian identification could represent a means of exercising leverage (through supporting civil society mobilisation or even as a pretext to

---

8 The terms "compatriots" and "compatriots from abroad" were introduced into Russian legislation in 1999 by Law No. 99 "O gosudarstvennoi politike Rossiiskoi Federatsii v otnoshenii sootechestvennikov za rubezhom" (Sobranie zakonodatel'stva 1999).

threaten more direct intervention) should such states seek to pursue a strategy contravening Russia's geopolitical interests.[9]

Moving on to the specifics, it may be observed that while appealing to romantic myths of a great history, sovereign democracy is guided by hard-nosed pragmatism; it provides a vision of modernisation in a globalised world, which seeks to avoid both the Charybdis of the "national state dissolving into globalisation" (Konstantinov 2007) and the Scylla of isolationism. Both the discourse of sovereign democracy and the political measures advocated therein aim to preserve sovereignty in the face of globalisation by providing a legitimating discourse for potentially controversial state-centred economic and political measures to help Russia to compete advantageously as a great power (for a further elaboration of this topic, cf. Martin Müller in this volume). Concurrently, the discourse provides a rhetorical focus to help ward off another perceived threat of globalisation, "becoming Ivan the Downcast with an Erased Past"[10] (Orlov 2007: 8); forgetting Russia's cultural tradition as the price to pay for modernisation. The assumption appears to be that in joining the West whole-heartedly, Russia would lose something of itself, not least its *gosudarstvennost*; the strong state with a central role in society.

Sovereign democracy echoes Putin's consistent position, namely that "Russia is part of European civilisation, I cannot conceive of Russia falling out of Europe" (Putin 2000, cited in Tolz 2004: 175). The Kremlin has, however, repeatedly stated that this relationship should be one of "equal partners, not consumers of EU blessings" (Russian ambassador to the EU, Vladimir Chizhov, cited in Averre 2007), and firmly and consistently reminds other Western leaders that Russia "as a sovereign country" "is capable, and will independently define for itself the term and the conditions of its movement on the path [to freedom and democracy]" (Putin 2005). In doing this, Russia will take into account which

---

9   As an example, one could cite the cultivation of ties with ethnic Russians in the Ukrainian Crimea (Harding 2008) through a range of "soft power" initiatives, which may prove to be a useful basis for resistance and Russian leverage, should Ukraine strive to push forward its NATO membership bid.

10 Orlov uses a historically rooted expression to suggest the necessity of maintaining a sense of one's own national history. Kuzmin (2001: 227f.) provides background to this idiom: "the fugitives from Siberia's prisons who happened to get caught by police in old times did not want to divulge their real names. A fugitive would call himself 'Ivan', the most popular Russian name, and say he 'does not remember' his place of birth. Such fugitives were registered by police as 'Ivans who do not remember their descent', that is they have forgotten their root [sic] [...]. Loss of traditions is one of the feelings that gives rise to the feeling of senseless existence."

form of democracy will suit Russia's "historical, geopolitical, and other specificities" (ibid). Surkov concurs, noting that "Russia should take the lead, rather than be led, as a co-author and co-actor of European civilisation, not as a common Philistine" (Surkov 2007: 38). Rejecting the disparaging attitude of Western leaders towards Russia's post-Soviet development, he underlines the claim to the contribution made by Russia to the development of European civilisation. In this way, the "part of European civilisation" referred to by Putin may – rather than representing one component in a homogenous whole – point to a distinct centre of cultural origination within a diverse civilisational community; this is what Krastev has termed Russia's claim to be the "other Europe" (2007). Thus, in policy terms, sovereign democracy reflects "Russia's European choice" in terms of its overall orientation, which creates space for pragmatic cooperation, without boxing Moscow into a "traditional" – liberal democratic – European framework of development.

Nevertheless, not all Russian commentators acknowledge the alleged "need" for a "great power" identity distinct from the West. In some quarters, albeit ones that are relatively marginalised in Russia nowadays, the system developing in Russia today continues to be envisaged in terms of a diversion from the teleological path of development towards a Western-style liberal democracy. Lilia Shevtsova, for instance, stresses the unsustainable nature of "bureaucratic authoritarianism", citing its inability to facilitate social modernisation, while foreseeing a bleak future that holds only "continued stagnation, systemic crisis or a breakthrough to liberal democracy" (Shevtsova 2007: 911). The realisation of human potential is a recurrent theme in texts concerning sovereign democracy (e.g., Kokoshin 2006: 95; Konstantinov 2006). However, the sustainability of Russia's sovereign democratic identity surely depends on whether the politico-economic model outlined in the discourse proves to be capable of transcending mere rhetoric to defy Shevtsova's gloomy predictions by "[translating] the raw material economy into a knowledge economy" and thereby perpetuating "Russia's path to the top and into the future in the community of creative nations that make history" (Surkov 2006: 44).

Sovereign democracy's definitions of Russianness

In Russia's internal discourse, despite Western scepticism, "European values" play a significant role as a marker of identity and civilisation, being repeatedly used by political leaders in counter-position to "barbarism" in discussions of terrorism, public disorder, and fears of unspecified "demodernisation". This can be interpreted as an example of *othering*, whereby the *we* identity is demarcated against an *other*, with relative differences "totalised" (Smith 1998: 16) into absolute ones and securitised as a threat. Although by no means unique to Russia, Duncan (2008) has noted that this is a common feature of Russian, and previously Soviet politics, with successive leaders rallying the nation against an enemy other, be it the capitalist West (Soviet era), the Communist past (Yeltsin era), or Islamist terrorists and Western hegemony (Putin era). In Laclau's terms, the problematisation of the West enacted in the discourse of sovereign democracy in response to the destabilisation (or *dislocation*) of Russia's identity in the wake of the collapse of the Soviet Union (Torfing 1999: 195) can be seen as creating a *constitutive outside* that simultaneously denies and provides the conditions of possibility for that identity (Laclau 1990: 39). Thus, the identification of such others or enemies may not only serve to shift the focus away from internal problems, it unites the population against an *other* with a sense of *fullness* not achieved by simply enumerating positive national attributes.

However, while sovereign democracy follows this tradition to the extent that it attributes to the West a preference for keeping Russia weak, the difference is not inevitably totalised. Rather, it is depicted for the most part as a "normal" jostling of competitive powers, not a "clash of civilisations". The Kremlin's pragmatic approach notwithstanding, the notion of the West as a potential threat to Russia's self-realisation, which is drip-fed into the discourse of sovereign democracy, represents a reoccurring idea to be drawn upon periodically to foster a sense of unity against the outside and mobilise support, for example around election time.

The discourse of sovereign democracy also "historicises" (Smith 1998: 16) Russia's identity as a great power. It holds up selected periods of Russia's history, for example the Brezhnev period, as a "golden age", a standard "against which to measure the alleged inadequacies of the present generation and community" (Anthony Smith, cited in Smith 1998: 15) and, as such, as an inspiration for contemporary action. Indeed, the history of contemporary Russia is presented as a continuous development of Russian statehood and the legacy of great-power status. In stressing continuity, rather than rupture, with the Soviet Union, Putin casts the end of the USSR and the rejection of Communism as a historic choice, not defeat (Putin 2005). This interpretation of the past bolsters the Kremlin's dismissal of any notion of the subjection of the vanquished, and post-Soviet Russia's right to choose its own political system. Furthermore, in laying claim to the achievements of the Soviet Union, political leaders may also avail themselves of the mobilising power of nostalgia for this "golden age" among the population.

Contemporary Russian identity is cast in a rather "essentialising" (Smith 1998: 15) light by the discourse of sovereign democracy, which presents Russia's status as a great power as an "intrinsic and essential context" of its identity. As such, policy should be oriented towards restoring this status, given the risk, suggested above, that Russia will not be "itself" – figuratively or literally – if its weakness prevails. Yet sovereign democracy's "essentialisation" of Russian identity is indeed selective; it does not develop in a profound way the long history of thought on Russian exceptionalism (Krastev 2006a). This suggests that the "scholars" behind sovereign democracy are indeed political pragmatists (Tsygankov 2005) (PR specialists and the like (not true primordialists like Dugin and his ilk, and are not seeking to be hemmed in by dogma in the pursuit of modernisation.

In addition to what the concept of the Russian nation refers to, Surkov also explores who is implied by this label. Considering the nation as "the community with which the majority identifies" (Surkov 2006: 27), he describes the nation (natsiia) as a

> "supra-ethnic aggregate of all citizens of the country. Applied to Russia: that which is characterised as the 'nation' [in Surkov's text] is referred to as the 'multinational people' in the text of the Constitution. In other words, the Russian (*rossiiskii*) nation (people) unites all the peoples (nationalities?) [sic] of Russia in common borders, a common state and a common culture, past and future." (2006: 27)

This definition appears to underscore the civic nationhood outlined in the 1993 constitution, albeit in a way that stresses the belonging of many nationalities to a common nation in a manner reminiscent of the notion of the "Soviet people". However, while the constitution does not privilege any nationality, Surkov's text makes specific reference to ethnic Russians, who are described variously as the "leaders of the fate of the nation" (Surkov 2007) and the "creators of the greatest projects" (ibid.). Ethnic Russians are the only nationality to possess a distinct profile, while others are merely listed on occasion as titular appendages, with sovereign rights attached only to "their territory" (Karpenko 2007) and to the extent they do not challenge the wider order of things. This notion of ethnic Russians as the leading, "state-forming" nation (Sakwa 2008: 225) appears to be confirmed by Surkov's comment that "the Russian (*russkii*) democratic project is open and should be attractive to all Russian (*rossiiskii*) peoples" (Surkov 2006: 42). It appears to stand in contrast to the equal footing suggested by the constitution.

However, having established this pluricultural order, sovereign democracy consistently stresses the unity of the *rossiiskaia natsiia*, a reflection of the inherent fear that sovereignty will not be maintained over the entire territory of the Russian Federation, whether due to separatist tendencies or territorial challenges in the sparsely populated, underdeveloped Far East. Given the key significance of national unity, it is therefore possible to consider the incursion of ethno-national conceptualisations, at least partially, as a result of the pragmatic cohabitation of the patriotic discourse of sovereign democracy with more radical nationalist views represented by the closest opposition groups.[11]

Conclusion

This chapter has argued that the discourse of sovereign democracy draws upon the Russian past as a great power as inspiration to unite the disparate post-Soviet elites around a vision of achieving successful modernisation in the present. In doing so, it constructs a discourse about Russia with which citizens should identify and of which they should feel proud. According to the logic of this discourse, various domestic and international issues are constructed as threats to the nation. This not only enables a variety of "obstacles" to be "dealt with" as potential security concerns, but also creates a threatening *other* that serves to constitute the cohesiveness of the Russian *we* identity, particularly among the hitherto divided elites. While the discourse of sovereign democracy refers in most cases to the *rossiiskaia natsiia*, the few exceptions to this reveal the privileged position of the Russian ethnic nation envisaged, albeit mostly unspoken,

---

11 While sovereign democracy has been largely promoted by United Russia, the party has striven to reach out beyond its own ranks to some of the opposition parties in order to bring some common values to the Russian political scene, striving to create a new, patriotically-minded "political class" (Kokoshin 2006: 90; Chadaev 2006: 234).

within the discourse of sovereign democracy in the Russian Federation. While this should be borne in mind, it should equally perhaps not be overemphasised, as the sovereign democracy project is explicitly concerned with the fate of the Russian (*rossiiskii*) nation as a whole.

This discussion has highlighted the tension between the view of sceptics who regard sovereign democracy as an instrumental tool lending a veil of respectability both to authoritarian tendencies and to elite self-enrichment based on Russia cultural specificities, on the one hand, and the claim that sovereign democracy is a reflection of a discourse on national values as inspiration for societal renewal on the other. An interim assessment of where the balance lies might usefully recall the comment of Vladimir Putin in 2000 that "he who does not regret the destruction of the Soviet Union has no heart, and he who wants to see it recreated in its former shape has no brain." Similarly, in order to achieve sustainable statehood within its current borders – in other words, hegemony – the Russian state today faces the challenge of appealing to both the "hearts" and the "brains" of the elite and wider population alike. It must demonstrate its ability to be both a vehicle for facilitating the sustainable pursuit of individual and group interests and a consistent focal point for the affective loyalty of all citizens. Whether the practical and psychological aspects of the touted great-power identity can be maintained – particularly under the difficult conditions of the current economic crisis – will depend very much on whether there is sufficient genuine political will behind the sovereign democracy blueprint to facilitate development that goes beyond the much-cited stability and order to provide genuinely innovative modernisation and social development (Okara 2007). This issue will ultimately determine whether identity reconstruction retreats towards the murky path to chauvinistic stagnation, or emerges as a positive attribute of a forward-looking societal culture.

Bibliography

Averre, D. 2007. "'Sovereign Democracy' and Russia's Relations with the European Union". *Demokratizatsiia* spring. 173-190.

Bacon, E., B. Renz, and J. Cooper. 2006. *Securitising Russia. The Domestic Politics of Putin*. Manchester: Manchester University Press.

Buzan, B., O. Wæver, and J. de Wilde. 1998. *A New Framework for Analysis*. Boulder: Lynne Riener Press.

Chadaev, A.V. 2006. "François Guizot: Suverenitet protiv Revoliutsii". In *Suverenitet: sbornik*, edited by N. Garadzha, 233ff. Moscow: Evropa.

Duncan, P. 2008. "The Position of Russian Parties on Foreign Policy". Paper presented at the CREES Conference, 6-8 June, at Great Windsor Park.

Fadeev, V.A. 2006a. "Rossiia − eto energeticheskaia sverkhderzhava". In *Suverenitet: sbornik*, edited by N. Garadzha, 133-146. Moscow: Evropa.

────── 2006b. "Dlia protsvetaniia vsekh nado uchityvat' interesy kazhdogo [interview with D.A. Medvedev]". *Ekspert* 28, 24 July. 58-65.

Foucault, M. 1980. *Knowledge / Power*. London: Harvester Wheatsheaf.

Gee, J.P. 1999. *An Introduction to Discourse Analysis. Theory and Method.* London: Routledge.

Gramsci, A. 1971. *Selections from the Prison Notebooks.* Edited and translated from the Italian by Quintin Hoare and Geoffrey Nowell Smith. London: Lawrence and Wishart.

Harding, L. 2008. "Crimea: Divided Peninsula Plays Host to Russian Warships and Ukrainian Pride". *The Guardian* 16 September. http://www.guardian.co.uk/world/2008/sep/16/ukraine.russia [accessed 16 September 2008].

Kaehne, A. 2007. *Political and Social Thought in Post-Communist Russia* (BASEES/Routledge Series on Russian and East European Studies). London: Routledge.

Karavaev, A. 2008. "Ne dopustit' degradatsii russkogo smysla". *Nezavisimaia gazeta* 7, 21 January. 18.

Karpenko, O. 2007. "'Suverennaia demokratiia' dlia vnutrennego i naruzhnogo primeneniia". *Neprikosnovennii zapas* 1, 51. http://www.intelros.ru/2007/05/29/oksana_karpenko_suverennaja_demokratija_d lja_vnutrennego_i_naruzhnogo_primenenija.html [accessed 22 August 2009].

Kazin, F. 2008. "Ot 'piara' k 'kulturnoi gegemonii'". *Sankt-Peterburgskie vedomosti* 8, 18 January. 400.

Kimmage, D. 2006. "'Sovereign Democracy' in Almaty and Moscow". *Radio Liberty – Radio Free Europe*: http://www.rferl.org/featuresarticle/ 2006/07/6129BE69-8044-4EAD-A401-3AC4D549A134.html [accessed 21 May 2008].

Kokoshin, A.A. 2006. "Real'nii suverenitet i suverennaia demokratiia". In *Suverenitet: sbornik*, edited by N. Garadzha, 89-129. Moscow: Evropa.

Konstantinov, I. 2007. "Vozvrashchenie ideologii". *Zavtra* 20, 16 May 2007. 2.

Krastev, I. 2006a. "'Sovereign Democracy', Russian Style". http:// www.opendemocracy.net, 16 November [accessed 18 June 2008].

―――― 2006b. "New Threats to Democracy – Democracy's 'Doubles'". *Journal of Democracy* 17, 2. 52-62.

―――― 2007. "Russia as the 'Other Europe'". *Russia in Global Affairs* 4, October-December. http://eng.globalaffairs.ru/numbers/21/1151.html [accessed 22 August 2009].

Kuzmin, S.S. 2001. *Translators' Russian-English Phraseological Dictionary*. Moscow & Flinta: Nauka.

Laclau, E. 1990. *New Reflections on the Revolution of Our Time*. London: Verso.

Makarychev, A.S. 2008. "Rebranding Russia: Norms, Politics and Power". CEPS Working Document 283, February.

Medvedev, D.A. 2006. "Sokhranit' effektivnoe gosudarstvo v sushchestuiushchikh granitsakh". In *Suverenitet: sbornik*, edited by N. Garadzha, 25-41. Moscow: Evropa.

Nye Jr., J.S. 2004. *The Means to Success in World Politics*. New York: PublicAffairs.

Okara, A. 2007. "Sovereign Democracy: a New Russian Idea of a PR Project?". *Russia in Global Affairs* 2, July-September. http://eng.globalaffairs.ru/numbers/20/1124.html [accessed 5 April 2009].

Orlov, D. 2007. "Politicheskaia doktrina suverennoi demokratii". In his *Suverennaia demokratiia. Ot idei – k doktrine*. 3-14. Moscow: Evropa.

Prizel, I. 1998. *National Identity and Foreign Policy. Nationalism and Leadership in Poland, Russia and Ukraine*. Cambridge: Cambridge University Press.

Popescu, N. 2006. "Russia's Soft Power Ambitions". CEPS Policy Brief 115, 27 October.

Putin, V. 2005. Speech to the Federal Assembly of the Russian Federation on 25 April. http://www.kremlin.ru/eng/speeches/2005/04/25/2031_type70029type82912_87086.shtml [accessed on 22 August 2009].

Rabinow, P., ed. 1984. *The Foucault Reader. An Introduction to Foucault's Thought*. London: Penguin.

Said, E.W. 1995 (1978). *Orientalism. Western Conceptions of the Orient*. London: Penguin.

Sakwa, R. 2008 (2004). *Putin. Russia's Choice*. London: Routledge.

Shevchenko, M.L. 2006. "Opyt proshlogo i novii suverenitet Rossii". In *Suverenitet: sbornik*, edited by N. Garadzha, 201-215. Moscow: Evropa.

Smith, G. 1998. "Post-Colonialism and Borderland Identities". In his *Nation building in the post-Soviet borderlands*. Cambridge: Cambridge University Press.

Solozobov, Iu. 2008. "Agenty sliianiia". *Rossiia* 17, 22 May. http://dlib.eastview.com/sources/article.jsp?id=15052424 [accessed 22 August 2009]

Surkov, V. 2006. "Suverenitet − eto politicheskii sinonim konkurentosposobnosti". In *Suverenitet: sbornik*, edited by N. Garadzha, 43-64. Moscow: Evropa.

―――― 2007. "Natsionalizatsiia budushchego (paragrafi pro suverennuiu demokratiiu)". In *Suverennaia demokratiia. Ot idei − k doktrine*, edited by D. Orlov, 27-44. Moscow: Evropa.

Tolz, V. 1998. "Forging the Nation: National Identity and Nation Building in Post-Communist Russia". *Europe-Asia Studies* 50, 6, Sept. 993-1022.

―――― 2004. "The Search for a National Identity in the Russia of Yeltsin and Putin". In *Restructuring Post-Communist Russia*, edited by Y. Brudny, J. Frankil, and S. Hoffman, 160-178. Cambridge: Cambridge University Press.

Torfing, J. 1999. *New Theories of Discourse: Laclau, Mouffe, and Žižek*. Oxford: Blackwell.

Tsygankov, A.P. 2005. "Vladimir Putin's Vision of Russia as a Normal Great Power". *Post-Soviet Affairs* 21, 2, April-June. 132-158.

―――― 2008. "Russia's International Assertiveness. What does it mean for the West?". *Problems of Post-Communism* 50, 2, March/April. 38-55.

White, D. 2008. "Russia: 'Sovereign Democracy' Still Guides Policy". *Oxford Analytica*, 5 August.

Zevelev, I. 2008. "Russia's Policy Towards Compatriots in the Former Soviet Union". *Russia in Global Affairs* 6, 1. 49-62.

Sovereignty and Democracy in Contemporary Russia: A Modern Subject Faces the Post-Modern World[1]

Viatcheslav Morozov

The slogan of '"sovereign democracy" forms the ideological horizon of contemporary Russia. While many scholars would warn against taking the official propaganda seriously, I choose to treat it as a symptom of the discursive tensions that exist both in Russian identity politics and, more broadly, in the global debate about the future of democracy. Using a poststructuralist perspective, I explore the origins of the restorationist neo-Soviet turn in Russian identity politics. At the global level, the Kremlin attempts to redefine democracy as a truly universal value to be emancipated from Western hegemonic control. I contend that this criticism indicates a significant degree of dislocation existing in Russian domestic and global hegemonic structures. Dislocation can provoke securitising practices that lead back to a structural closure, but it can also provide foundations for emancipatory politics, if and when there is a subject willing to liberate itself.

Relations between Russia and the West are in decline.[2] Authors from across the political spectrum are warning of an imminent new Cold War. Emerging as a new global player, Russia insists on its sovereign right to conduct independent policy both domestically and on the international arena, while the United States and the European Union are unhappy about what they see as a reversal of democratic reforms and are wary of the increasing assertiveness of Russia's foreign policy. Sovereignty and democracy stand out as the two most prominent

---

1   This article was first published in: *Journal of International Relations and Development* (2008) 11: 152-180. Reproduced with permission of Palgrave Macmillan.
2   Some key arguments of this article were developed in dialogue and debate with my colleagues at the St. Petersburg State University, in particular Dina Khapaeva, Nikolai Koposov, Artemy Magun, and Alexander Semënov. The work on the initial manuscript was done at the University of Denver, CO; I am grateful to its Graduate School of International Studies for being a generous host, and to the Fulbright Program for supporting my stay. Last but not least, I thank Patrick Jackson, Pertti Joenniemi, the editors of the JIRD, and the anonymous reviewers for their extremely useful comments.

keywords in this controversy, with both sides insisting on their understanding of these notions as being self-evident and universal, and dismissing the other's vision as ideological and distorted. This relationship is becoming increasingly antagonistic and, at least in Russia's case, leading to the creation of an undifferentiated image of the West as the key opponent, very much in the spirit of the Cold War.

This article analyses some important aspects of this discursive relationship, with the primary focus on Russia. In particular, it looks into how the notions of sovereignty and democracy fit into and help reproduce the discursive reality of Putin's Russia, and examines the challenges Russia faces in its attempts to (re-) establish itself as a sovereign subject. The first section addresses the question of whether the ideological models produced by the Kremlin can be a relevant subject for academic research, given that many analysts might be inclined to view them as mere figures of speech designed for purely rhetorical purposes and not to be taken seriously – neither by the audience nor by those who produce them. Building on the existing body of constructivist and poststructuralist literature, I argue that the concern with democracy and sovereignty is symptomatic of the overall political developments in today's Russia and, moreover, essential for the discussion about the prospects for global democracy. The second and third sections address the issue of sovereign democracy as a project aimed at constructing a certain kind of political community, whose identity is firmly rooted in the Soviet version of modernity. In the fourth section, I explore some of the contradictions that become evident once we take into account the uncertain boundaries and identity of the Russian nation. Section five addresses the complications arising from the collision between sovereign democracy and the liberal universalist discourse, which views sovereignty in today's "post- modern" world as an obsolete and perhaps even reactionary notion. The challenges that Putin's modernisation has to cope with, both domestically and internationally, produce *dislocation* of the structures of meaning. Security practices emerge as a means to eliminate this disturbance, resulting in a reinforced antagonism towards the West and a crackdown on various identities that are perceived as pro-Western and therefore subversive, from the liberal opposition to ethnic Georgians. Whereas within Russia, securitisation tends to produce a closed identity and to eliminate political alternatives in favour of unity and consolidation, I nevertheless argue in the conclusion that the emancipatory potential of structural dislocation should not be underestimated. In particular, the Russian leadership's attempts to redefine democracy as a universal value to be emancipated from Western hegemonic control constitute an extremely interesting departure with a great liberating potential. This potential exists regardless of the fact that this discursive practice is currently used to justify the most undemocratic policies of the Russian government.

"Sovereign democracy" as a symptom

Analysing contemporary Russian foreign policy, one is left to wonder whether it is grounded in any ideology at all. Indeed, Stephen Hanson (2006) has argued that "the absence of *any* compelling new political ideology" is the key explanation for Russia's "weak state authoritarianism", which distinguishes it from the two similar cases of "postimperial democracies" – the early years of the Third Republic in France and Weimar Germany. President Vladimir Putin and his foreign policy officials constantly emphasise "pragmatism" as a key factor defining Russia's foreign policy goals. Foreign Minister Sergei Lavrov (2007c), for instance, taking stock of the international developments in 2006, contrasts the Western "black and white image of the world, tendency towards a re-ideologisation and re-militarisation of international relations" with Russia's ability to "reject ideology in favour of common sense" (see also Lavrov 2007a, b). Indeed, the self-description of Russia's foreign policy as "great power pragmatism" is accepted by many academic writers (notably, Tsygankov 2006: 127-166).

The recent political developments, especially the evolution of Moscow's energy policies in the post-Soviet space, seem to confirm the trend towards a more pragmatic approach. The former "strategic allies" and "sister nations" face the choice of either losing their sovereignty by "integrating" with (or, rather, into) Russia, or being treated as part of the outside political and economic space – something that, in the words of the Russian ambassador to Washington, consists in creating "a standard business relationship with every [neighbouring] country" (Ushakov 2007). This typically results in higher oil and gas prices, also meaning higher revenues for both the big corporations and the federal budget. It would seem, therefore, that the logic of pragmatism and profit is indeed replacing imperialism as the major factor determining the development of Russia's foreign policy.

At the same time, however, a new ideological horizon might be in the making. In key speeches made by President Putin (2007a, c) and other top Russian politicians in early 2007, two keywords figured prominently: "sovereignty" and "democracy". This indicates that the slogan of sovereign democracy, invented by the main pro-Kremlin ideologist, Deputy Head of the Presidential Administration Vladislav Surkov, and elaborated in the propaganda of "United Russia", the main pro-Putin party (see, in particular, Dobrynina 2006; Surkov 2006a, b), might indeed be acquiring the status of the official ideology. However, neither the president nor his likely successors ever used the slogan itself. Despite assertions to the contrary by "United Russia" (e.g., United Russia 2006), Putin is most probably not ready to accept this formula as his main policy framework. One of Putin's closest associates at the time, today's president of Russia, Dmitry Medvedev, declared in his speech in Davos in January 2007 that he wanted to see the future Russia as a "full-fledged democracy [...] without unnecessary extra attributes" (Arsyukhin 2007).

Even more importantly, domestic developments in Russia such as the increasingly limited freedom of the media, as well as a crackdown on the liberal opposition or on the non-governmental organisations (NGOs), make it hard to believe that at least one element of this new catchphrase – democracy – is taken seriously by the Kremlin. Indeed, it is difficult to argue against Artëm Magun's (2006) assertion that sovereign democracy "obviously is a hypocritical screen, a euphemism which its author himself does not believe in, to say nothing about his audience". This expression is of the same kind as the "dispute between commercial agents" – an infamous phrase coined in September 2000 by the then Prime Minister Mikhail Kasyanov in a bid to de-politicise the takeover of the independent Media-Most holding by Gazprom. Andrei Okara, an author much more sympathetic to the substance of Surkov's project, also concedes that, at least for the time being, sovereign democracy is nothing more than an eclectic combination of controversial symbols whose aim is to galvanise the electorate in the run-up to the parliamentary and presidential elections (Okara 2007: 16). Thus, it is easy to dismiss these discursive developments as insignificant, as mere manipulation aimed at concealing the true state of affairs from the Russian people.

This answer, emphasising the power of "political technologies", is very popular in the Russian context,[3] but a serious analysis must not stop at this point. First of all, in the age when talk about the death of the grand ideologies and the advent of politics as technology aimed primarily at manipulating public

---

3   For a good review that is rather sympathetic to the idea of manipulative politics, see Zvereva (2007).

opinion has become commonplace, we have to decide for ourselves whether we see manipulation as being liable to any limitations whatsoever, or whether we are facing a political subject that is absolutely free and, as a corollary, absolutely beyond our comprehension. In the latter case, Russia would figure as a society where strong and autonomous agency, personified in the figure of Vladimir Putin, has completely suppressed all social structures in terms of social institutions (political parties, civil society, etc.) as well as discourses as relatively stable, intersubjective systems of meaning that normally impose limits on political action or even, as poststructuralists argue, constitute agency as such. This transcendental subject, seeking to achieve something we can never fully understand, every time creates a new simulacrum in the place where reality used to be (Baudrillard 1988). Such an image of a quasi-divine (or devilish) Big Brother, however, is hardly at home with any social theory because it leaves us with an image of the world as a chaotic place where no rules or patterns can be taken for granted. Characteristically, even the literature on the work of spin doctors talks about linguistic structures, psychological archetypes, and myths as both preconditions and resources for political technologies, thus recognising the importance of social structures the manipulating subject has to be aware of.[4]

The next question that has to be answered is how much one should care about the "real" motives of political actors. The paradigm of technological politics seems to emphasise the central role of covert motives as opposed to public statements. If manipulation is the essence of politics, the only way to analyse the latter is to uncover the goals of political actors and to see how successful they are in achieving those. On the contrary, constructivist and poststructuralist approaches make a strong case against the obsession with the "real" motives of political actors. "The issue is not that motives do not exist [...], but that we have no systematic way of talking about – and, hence, analyzing – them without returning to publicly meaningful notions", Patrick Thaddeus Jackson (2006: 24) writes, referring to Max Weber's (1978: 5) definition of motive and to Ludwig Wittgenstein's (1958: 100) rejection of the notion of "private language" as two major arguments against prioritising "private" motives over public statements. No one, Jackson maintains, "has direct access to the motivations of another person but must instead rely on behavioral cues and accepted community standards in order to *attribute* motive" (2006: 24).

---

4   One of the best Russian books on the subject (Kara-Murza 2000) even mentions Gramsci as one of its sources of inspiration.

This important methodological consideration is echoed by Lene Hansen, who insists on the need to analyse even omissions and deception as part of the discursive articulation, and not as indications of some "evil" nature of power. In her study of the Western discourses on the Bosnian war, Hansen points out that the official documents of that period make almost no use of "Islamic threat" as a justification for the Western powers' inaction at the early stage of the conflict. This fact, according to Hansen, does not exclude the possibility that the anti-Islamic arguments were used in secret discussions and documents, but in this case "a new research question appears: why would it be that governments refrain from legitimizing their policy through recourse to an 'Islamic Other', particularly since even before September 11 this is a trope with a long history in Western thought?" (Hansen 2006: 219f.). Many recent political developments in Russia have been interpreted as indications of an inherently anti-democratic disposition of the current Russian political elite. Moreover, the identity of Putin's Russia crucially depends on the negation of Yeltsin's "democracy" as a period of chaos and destruction. Why, then, does Putin still speak about democracy with respect, and why does his team try to save Russia's democratic reputation by playing with the slogan of "sovereign democracy"? This paradox must tell us something about the structures of power in today's world, which turn "democracy" into a norm and make any deviations subject to punishment.

In sum, instead of taking "sovereign democracy" at its face value or dismissing it completely as pure manipulation, it can be useful to look in between these two extremes, assuming neither full sincerity on the part of the high-ranking ideologues nor pure contingency of the discursive articulations they are trying to establish. In this way, one would have a chance to locate the focal point of the hegemonic discourse that ensures the public consensus behind Putin's regime. As Magun (2006) rightly notes, sovereign democracy in this sense is "symptomatic". If one treats it not as a coherent ideology, but rather as one of the most characteristic manifestations of deeper, more solidly sedimented discursive structures (Wæver 2002), it can serve as a good starting point for reflection on the nature of current Russian politics and on the possible limits of something that would like to present itself as boundless sovereignty. This also points in the direction of studying the origins of Putin's Russia in the spirit of Michel Foucault's genealogy – as Foucault himself described it, "a form of history which can account for the constitution of knowledges, discourses, domains of objects etc., without having to make reference to a subject which is either transcendental in relation to the field of events or runs in its empty sameness throughout the course of history" (Foucault 1980: 117). Contrary to the paradigm of technological politics, genealogy sees power as dispersed in and constitutive of social institutions, and subjectivity as emergent out of, rather than external to, social structures.

More specifically, this study builds on the growing body of constructivist and poststructuralist literature in the field of international studies. It disagrees with mainstream constructivism, most authoritatively represented by Alexander Wendt's *Social Theory of International Politics* (1999), by refusing to treat foreign policy as an outcome of identity that has already taken shape "inside" of a political community. My take on the relationship between identity and foreign policy is much closer to David Campbell's, who in his analysis of US security practices proposes "that United States foreign policy be understood as a political practice central to the constitution, production, and maintenance of American political identity" (1998: 8).

In terms of selecting the sources, my approach is different from the inductive methodology used by Ted Hopf (2002) in his ground-breaking book on Russian identity politics and foreign policy. While Hopf bases his mapping of the Soviet and Russian identity discourses on reading a vast array of non-foreign-policy-related texts, I do not aim at justifying my findings by including as many sources as possible. Lene Hansen's approach, aimed at identifying "basic discourses" (2006: 51ff.), would also go beyond the scope of this chapter. However, the texts I use as my starting point (in particular, Vladimir Putin's Munich speech (2007c) and Vladislav Surkov's *Nationalisation of the Future* (2006a)) satisfy all three criteria for text selection put forward by Hansen: "they set out clear constructions of identity and policy; they are widely attended to by other politicians, the public and by governments throughout the world; and they are articulated by a formal political authority" (2006: 85). My goal is to explore the origins of a particular interpretation of the relationship between sovereignty and democracy offered in these texts in the genealogy of contemporary Russia, that is, in the fundamentally political process of community building on the ruins of the Soviet Union, and to assess the significance of the Russian criticism of "unipolarity" for the current debate on global democracy.

In its treatment of historical memory and its significance for the present, this article is inspired by the work of Maya Zehfuss (2001, 2002). However, I suggest a further step in the same direction by emphasising the constitutive dimension of relations with the outside world. This is invited by the very case in point: After the collapse of the Soviet Union, Russian society found itself in a situation of utter indeterminacy, with the old structures of meaning swept away by the revolutionary change, and the urgent need to define the very foundations of political community. The establishment of the new Russian nation was a foreign-policy exercise through and through. It started with Mikhail Gorbachëv taking up the theme of "universal human values" and ended, perhaps, with Putin's "sovereign democracy". During the last two decades, the predominant attitude to the notion of universal liberal democracy has shifted from enthusiastic to critical and even dismissive, but the need to relate Russian identity to the universal liberal project remained constant, and the dialectics of the universal and the particular has always been one of the key driving forces behind Russian foreign policy change. In the final part of this article, I examine this in view of the poststructuralist theory of hegemony developed by Ernesto Laclau and Chantal Mouffe (1985).[5] These two authors have recently been gaining prominence in reflectivist international studies, but while such scholars as Jenny Edkins (1999: 125-136) and Lene Hansen (2006: 18-23) are mostly interested in Laclau and Mouffe's theory of discourse and signification, I look at the Russian criticism of "unipolarity" using their work on ideology, hegemony, and universality. This new theoretical focus allows one to discuss the ideological aspects of sovereign democracy at a much more advanced theoretical level; but, more importantly, it leads to the question of whether "sovereign democracy" is a symptom of discursive tension on a much wider, global scale. The very need to emphasise sovereignty as an attribute of democracy may signal that we are moving away from the classical model of democracy rooted in the sovereign autonomy of the people. The question remains whether by abandoning sovereignty we are not running the risk of abandoning democracy as well.

Restoration: the Soviet past and the genealogy of Putin's Russia

The first important consideration one has to take into account when analysing the structures of meaning in today's Russia is that Putin's project as a whole and sovereign democracy as one of its constitutive elements are deeply rooted in the image of the Soviet past as the golden age in the history of Russian statehood. Commenting on the 2005 presidential address to the Federal

---

5   Laclau and Mouffe base their approach on a critically revised theory of hegemony developed by Gramsci (1971).

Assembly, in which Putin introduced the image of the Soviet collapse as a "geopolitical catastrophe", and which is usually referred to as spelling out the main principles of sovereign democracy without using the term, Vitalii Tretiakov rightly notes that from the point of view of Putin's political philosophy, "the Soviet period was not a 'black hole' in the Russian history, and the Soviet Union was not an 'evil empire' – rather on the contrary", if only because it was the USSR that liberated Europe and the world from Nazism (Tretiakov 2005).

Anchoring Russian national identity in the Soviet past is a genealogical feature of Putin's regime. When they arranged the first presidential succession in 1999, the pro-Kremlin elites were very limited in their strategic and tactical choices. A shared understanding of the basic constitutive principles of the political order was missing in Russia throughout the 1990s. While the elites were trying to justify the painful reforms as necessary in order to introduce pro-Western democracy and market economy, the population was doubtful about the applicability of Western standards to Russia. The painful and futile crusade for a "national idea", which was officially declared by Yeltsin after his re-election in 1996 (Breslauer and Dale 1997), testifies that the elites were deeply concerned with the means of achieving a national consolidation. Manipulation worked at the tactical level – it is enough to recall how Yeltsin went from a single-digit approval rate in late 1995 to a victory over Zyuganov in 1996. However, at the strategic level, it was useless: The pro-Kremlin spin doctors were unable to sell market democracy to the Russian public as a value worth striving for.

Although we can know very little about the actual decisionmaking in Yeltsin's innermost circle, it is probably safe to suggest that the ruling group had to choose a new strategy. This was, indeed, a strategy of manipulation that included such elements as exploiting the image of Putin as a strong leader unrepentant about his KGB past, the merciless fight against terrorism in Chechnya, and standing firm against Western pressure discarding it as a manifestation of double standards. However, what came first was the recognition of the discursive limits within which this manipulation could be deployed, and the fine-tuning of propaganda techniques to resonate with the more solidly sedimented elements of the referential system in which the majority of the Russians lived and acted.

The Great Patriotic War (i.e., the Soviet Union's war against Nazi Germany in 1941-1945) is the fundamental narrative on which the identity of the new Russia is increasingly being grounded (Gudkov 2005). The heroic narrative of the Great Patriotic War links Russia with Europe and/or civilisation, because it can be told in such a manner that the Soviet Union will appear at the centre of the struggle for genuine European values against a barbarian force (stemming, by the way, from the very heart of Europe). Sacralisation of the war narratives leads to a situation where the memory of the war becomes "implacable" (Ferretti 2005). The public discursive space is consistently purged of any stories that allow for drawing parallels between Stalin and Hitler, or between the USSR and Nazi Germany (Khapaeva 2006). Once again, there is a significant degree of conscious manipulation here: "Structural" factors cannot explain away such obvious steps as the removal from public schools of textbooks telling the story of mass repressions. In addition, Vladimir Putin bears personal responsibility for publicly refusing to denounce the occupation of the Baltics and the Molotov-Ribbentrop pact (Mendelson and Gerber 2006). At the same time, however, all these myths, denials, and suppressions should be understood as elements of discourse as a unified system, where one element cannot be changed without a corresponding adjustment of many others. Given the foundational significance of the Great Patriotic War narrative, any recognition of the negative role played by the Soviet Union in the history of the Second World War would involve reconfiguring the whole groundwork of the Russian national identity construction. There are quite a number of structural similarities between the treatment of historical memory in Russia and Germany – in the latter case, as Zehfuss (2002) finds, the Nazi past is both admitted and denied as part of the history of the Bundesrepublik, whereas Eastern Germany is almost completely excluded from the foundational narratives.

Another cause of the very low level of tolerance to critical interpretations of Soviet history in contemporary Russia is due to their firm association with the period of the Perestroika and the liberal market reforms. The revolution of the late 1980s to early 1990s has taken the place of the historical *other*, which was occupied by Tsarist Russia during the Soviet era, and then, briefly, by the Soviet Union in the early 1990s (Hopf 2002: 159-169). The criticism of "those who, at the end of the last century, led Russia to mass poverty, to epidemic bribery" (Putin 2007b) was so central for United Russia's 2007 election campaign that it became a point of reflection in the expert community (Khamraev 2007). On the one hand, this nodal point seems to be structurally given at any moment in time, since one of the means used by the current regime for its consolidation is the negation of the previous epoch as the Dark Age. This is contrasted with the present to demonstrate the progressive nature of the existing hegemonic constellation. On the other hand, this particular reading of the country's recent history stood in a mutually reinforcing relationship with the longing for "stability" – a conspicuous element of Russian political discourse ever since the violent resolution of the 1993 constitutional crisis. The simple (or even primitive) chronological scheme that described Brezhnev's "stagnation" as the golden age of stability and prosperity, Gorbachëv's *perestroika* and Yeltsin's reforms as collapse, destruction, and treason, and then Putin's restoration as a return to a new golden age (Munro 2006) proved to be such a powerful force structuring the universe of meaning that all contradictory historical narratives were swept aside as intrigues of the pro-Western opposition.

One may argue at length whether this restorationist turn was the only option available to the Russian politicians at the dawn of the century. However, the analysis of the origins of Putin's Russia seems to demonstrate that the range of choices was not unlimited, and therefore the course of events cannot be described as totally contingent or dependent exclusively on the free will of certain individuals. Moreover, the option preferred by the Western critics of Russia – a pro-Western democracy instead of a weak authoritarian system – would have had to be based on the negation of the Soviet past and require the identity of the new Russia to be created from scratch. The experience of the post-World War II Germany seems to prove that such an endeavour is not entirely impossible, but it also demonstrates the scale of the social upheaval necessary if it is to be successful. It also brings us back to the question of agency. As Marcia Weigle pointed out, a strong and autonomous state was necessary to conduct democratic market reforms; but the very process of democratisation limited the state's autonomy, which made the continuation of the reforms increasingly difficult (Weigle 2000: 199-273). It would seem logical that when the new president consolidated his power and received a mandate from the voters, he moved to restore the autonomy of the state.

Modernisation: Putin's Russia as a sovereign subject

In the state of the nation address of 2005, Russia of the 1990s is portrayed in gloomy colours: catchphrases include "the epidemic of disintegration", the destruction of the "old ideals", the omnipotence of the "oligarchic groups", "Khasavyurt capitulation" in the first Chechen war, mass poverty, the "economic downturn", and "the paralysis of the social security system" (Putin 2005). At the same time, in the president's opinion, the choice for democracy was neither reckless nor vain. During his annual live Q&A session with the Russian public in October 2006, Putin declared that "Russia played an extremely important role in bringing down the Berlin Wall and overcoming the division of Europe. Credit for that should be given first of all to the Soviet Union and to our Russia, our motherland" (Putin 2006b). In his controversial speech in Munich in February 2007, Putin similarly stressed that the fall of the Berlin Wall "was made possible by a historic choice, made also by our people – the people of Russia, the choice in favour of democracy and freedom, openness, and genuine partnership with all members of the big European family" (Putin 2007c). Foreign Minister Sergei Lavrov is of the same opinion, arguing that "Russia, having resolutely stepped out of the Cold War, ceased to be an ideological, imperial state" (2006: 12). To put it differently, the USSR, according to the president and his team, in a certain sense sacrificed itself for the sake of peace and security in the Greater Europe. Besides, the crisis of the 1990s was a necessary period for choosing a "new vector" in the "millennium-long history of Russian statehood". It was in the 1990s that Russian society "was generating not only the energy of self-preservation, but also the will for a new and free life" (Putin 2005). Thus, at the end of the 20th century, Russia once again accomplished a great historical mission, recovered its strength and became ready for new global tasks.

The need to restore or, rather, to create a modern political subject lies at the core of sovereign democracy as a project. One may therefore describe the latter not only as restoration, but as modernisation as well. It stands in opposition to the total collapse of the previous decade, characterised by the disintegration of the state, its appropriation by the oligarchs, and the resultant loss of the capacity for autonomous action. The idea of state subjectivity is pivotal for Vladimir Putin's policies ever since he came to power. Starting with the declaration of the "equal distance" between the state and the private enterprise, which effectively meant freeing the state from the oligarchs' control, his administration continued to concentrate "strategic" economic resources in state-owned holdings. As the liberal reforms of the social security system failed, the government tended to opt for paternalistic solutions, such as the measures aimed at raising birth rates,[6] demonstrating that a stronger state was better able to provide security to the people. Foreign policy came to be dominated by the idea of establish-

---

[6] This was declared top priority in Putin's 2006 address to the Federal Assembly (2006a).

ing Russia as a strong and independent player on the global stage. As long as Russia could position itself as a key member of George W. Bush's anti-terrorist coalition fighting against the new evil as an ally of the US, its foreign policy could be described as moderately pro-Western. After this setting lost its plausibility (mainly because of the US "intrusion" into what Russia considered its natural sphere of influence), Moscow surprised the world with its new assertiveness in the old geopolitical arena (the post-Soviet space) as well as in the relatively new sphere of energy politics, which had never before been so deliberately politicised. The instrumental nature of the "energy superpower" discourse is nicely summed up by a pro-Kremlin analyst: "If Russia itself does not become an actor in the global game, the other actors will tear it apart [...] Russia comes back to the global 'top league' using the tools which it has at hand" (Leontev 2006). In the 2007 address to the Federal Assembly, Putin (2007a) emphasised the spiritual dimension of state autonomy and quoted the prominent nationalist scholar Dmitry Likhachëv: "State sovereignty is defined inter alia by cultural criteria."

Even the notorious amendments to the law on NGOs, introduced in late 2005 and significantly increasing the burden of financial and other controls on NGOs, can be interpreted in this context not as a measure directly aimed at suppressing civil society,[7] but rather as an attempt to secure the autonomy of the domestic political space, to protect it from outside influences, and to guarantee the sovereignty of Russian democracy. The measure is thus motivated not by the abstract hatred of all elements of democracy, but rather by the perception, spread widely in Russia, of the NGO activists as a fifth column (first, because their activity is often financed from abroad, and second, because they are trying to "impose" values which are perceived by Russian public opinion as inherently Western) (Morozov 2002). President Putin summed up this attitude very well in his February 2007 talk in Munich: "when the non-governmental organisations are in essence financed by foreign governments, we consider this as an instrument used by the other states in their policy towards our country [...]. This is hidden financial support [...]. What is democratic about that?" (Putin 2007c). The anti-liberal measures are designed to secure freedom, but instead of liberating the individual, the concern is the freedom of the common will, the national self-fulfilment by means of a great state. Politics as such – as a way of constructing the common good of the national interest out of an irreducible plurality

---

7   This is how the law was interpreted by its critics both in Russia and abroad: see Zaiavlenie (2005) and United States Department of State (2005: 110f., 134f.).

of private wills (cf. Kapustin 1996; Edkins 1999) – disappears in contemporary Russia. What is left is the higher domain of sovereign freedom and everyday depoliticised activity of the executive structures, which, under Putin, included the legislature and the judiciary (cf. Makarychev and Reut 2006). The position of the representative institutions, at least, was precisely defined by the State Duma Chairman Boris Gryzlov, who declared soon after the 2003 elections that the parliament "is no place for political discussions" (Ostrovsky 2004).

The political subject that is coming into being before our eyes does not look like some ahistorical monster whose decisions are extraordinary to the extent of being beyond our comprehension. On the contrary, its features are easily recognisable, because today's elites borrow the criteria for political subjectivity from the Soviet era. That is hardly surprising in view of the fact, pointed out in the previous section, that the origin of Putin's Russia is rooted in the historical narrative of the Soviet golden age. This narrative stems from the classical tradition of modern political thinking, which assumes that the default form of political organisation is the sovereign nation-state based on the notion of the national interest as an objective reality that does not require any critical reflection. However, the specific meaning of the national interest is defined through the comparison between the present-day situation and the idealised image of the Soviet modernity. Sometimes, this takes grotesque forms – for instance, when Khabarovsk Governor Viktor Ishaev reports to the president, "[i]n the best years of stagnation, they were not building as much as we have recently" (Kolesnikov 2006).[8] However, even given all the attendant irony, the customary reference to the standards of Brezhnev's time suggests an image of an ideal Russia – a global power with a strong technologically advanced economy. From this vantage point, state property looks much more reliable than private ownership. Political pluralism is perceived as a threat to national security (inter alia, this is reflected in the name of the ruling party – United Russia), while the West appears as the main geopolitical adversary and opposing "unipolarity" gives meaning to foreign policy. Putin's approach to modernising Russia thus assumes the form of the restoration of Soviet symbols and practices.

---

[8] Interestingly, the Russian word "zastoi" in contemporary usage has lost all its direct negative meaning when used to describe Brezhnev's epoch, and therefore in Russian, "luchshie zastoinye vremena" sounds much less paradoxical than its English equivalent, "the best times of stagnation".

Fuzzy boundaries and the ethnonationalist challenge

Restorationist modernisation as a political project inevitably faces two groups of contradictions that produce dislocation of the current hegemonic articulation. The first group of contradictions has to do with the nature and boundaries of the political community that is being constructed through the constitutive references to the Soviet past. Today's Russia differs from the Soviet Union in both quantitative and qualitative terms, and it is the qualitative difference that has led to a tragic indeterminacy as regards the boundaries of the Russian nation. In order to fill the abstract idea of common good with political substance, to proceed from the general "national interest" to concrete policy measures, it is not enough to define a system of coordinates through references to the Soviet past. What is also necessary is to answer the question "who belongs?" (Thomas 2002), to specify, in Alexander Wendt's terms, the corporate identity of the political community. Contrary to what Wendt (1999: 224-230, 2006: 206) seems to suggest, corporate identity, at least in Russia's case, should not be assumed as given or described as "constituted by self-organizing homeostatic structures" that are "constitutionally exogenous to Otherness" (1999: 224f.). As Bahar Rumelili (2004: 32) rightly notes, "[t]he assumption of a self-organizing collectivity presupposes unequivocal bounded-ness", an unproblematic internality that somehow produces the initial, non-social *self*, which then engages in social interaction. What is missing in Wendt's description of states as self-organising units is the key poststructuralist point that the boundaries of political community are part of an integral relational system of meaning. Therefore, a change of social identity always redraws the boundary between *self* and *other* by making certain "external" identities part of *us* while expelling others as incarnations of the dangerous outside world (the image of the "fifth column"). Patrick Jackson nicely summarises this point in his study of the post-World War II debate on German reconstruction:

> "I am not 'inside' my head, any more than 'Germany' is completely 'inside' of its boundaries; both 'I' and 'Germany' are rather the results of boundary-drawing processes which never completely 'contain' us. Both 'I' and 'Germany' are empowered to make certain decisions in certain contexts about where our proper boundaries lie, and therefore we somehow transcend our boundaries." (2006: 25)

On the contrary, Wendt's "quantum social science", developed partly in response to the criticism against his *Social Theory*, easily accommodates the poststructuralist perspective, since "[i]n their subjective or wave aspect states are not prior to the relationships in which they are embedded, and as such state identity is indeed social all the way down." However, Wendt still insists that "in their objective or particle aspect the ontological priority of the state remains" (2006: 209), and claims that failure to recognise a relative stability of state identity would amount to a statement that state identities are "chaotic" (2006: 206). What is missing in this latter argument is, in my view, the possibility that, in some cases, alternative articulations of community boundaries can produce radically different identities that are not completely haphazard and unpredictable, but still hardly compatible with each other. To use Wendt's terms, the particles that are produced as a result of the collapse of a particular wave function are not necessarily similar to each other, so when we measure a state identity we get several sets of contradictory outcomes. Russian identity, understood as a wave function, contains the possibility of at least three different sets of boundaries between the inside and the outside, which are embedded in three different relational systems of meaning and, as a result, lead to different types of policies when they become actualised (or articulated). Not only are these identities "social all the way down", but they also necessarily influence each other, as meanings inherent in one of them often cause dislocation in the other two. If this is the case, even "endogenizing" corporate identities (Cederman and Daase 2003) does not really do the job. As we analyse the empirics, the link between the two aspects of Russia's identity becomes so strong that one has to question the very possibility of analytically separating them instead of treating boundaries and corporality as an essential relational component of social identity.

Depending on a particular articulation, the political community of today's Russia defines itself in three ways – as a civic nation (Russia as a state of all Russian citizens, *rossiiane*), as an ethnic nation (as a state of the ethnic Russians, *russkie*), or, finally, as a supranational imperial unity, which potentially includes the so-called "compatriots" in the former Soviet republics. Whereas the imperial model is compatible (although not without tension) with both civic and ethnic ones, the latter two types of nationalism are contradictory in many crucial aspects (cf. Miller 2007). The danger of ethnic nationalism for the unity of the state was clearly understood by Vladimir Putin's administration from his very first years in office. This understanding resulted in some conscious and more or less consistent steps towards the creation of a civic nation (Tolz 2004). Civic nationalism is explicitly proclaimed by Vladislav Surkov. His article on the key principles of sovereign democracy, entitled "Nationalisation of the Future", is provided with a note explaining what type of nationalism he subscribes to. It deserves to be quoted in full because the terminological uncertainties the author is struggling against are very indicative of the ambiguous character of contemporary Russian nationalist discourse:

> "The nation is understood here as a supra-ethnic totality of all citizens of the country. As applied to Russia: "the nation" in this text [is equivalent to] "the multinational people" in the text of the Constitution. I.e. the Russian nation (the people) incorporates all the peoples (nationalities?) of Russia in the shared boundaries, state, culture, past and future" (Surkov 2006a).

Despite all these efforts, Russia, at present, faces an enormous challenge on the part of ethnic nationalism. When the Kremlin shifted the public holiday from 7 November, the day of the October Revolution of 1917, to the 4th of the same month to commemorate the surrender of the Polish garrison in Moscow in 1612, the goals were probably to further marginalise the Communist opposition and to provide a reference point for a moderately anti-Western consolidation (specifically directed against the former satellites who are now the main troublemakers for Russia within the EU) (Zorin 2005). However, the very first celebration in 2005 resulted in the ultranationalist "Russian March" with thousands taking part under xenophobic anti-Semitic and anti-immigrant slogans. The fact that the authorities were frightened by the magnitude and radicalism of the manifestation is indirectly confirmed by their desperate efforts to prevent similar large-scale events in the subsequent years. In 2007, this even included "preventive" detention of nationalist leaders and "educational" interviews with activists held by security services (Savina 2007). However, by November 2006, the atmosphere in the country had changed. The ethnic clashes in Kondopoga, Karelia caused a nationalist outcry throughout the country, and the state itself was violating the principles of civic nationalism by targeting ethnic Georgians, regardless of their citizenship, in the course of the intense conflict with Tbilisi.[9]

The growth of ethnonationalism can be partly explained by a changing balance on the domestic political scene. The liberal opposition, perceived as a pro-Western fifth column and associated with what many describe as "anti-national" reforms of the 1990s, was an easy target for the Kremlin as it consoli-

---

9 For a detailed account of these and other developments in 2006, see Kozhevnikova (2007).

dated the "vertical of power". However, having eliminated its democratic critics, the regime found itself facing a much more vocal and increasingly powerful nationalist opposition. The radical nationalists have been able to consolidate into a viable alternative to the Kremlin while what was meant to become a strong and autonomous state now looks increasingly helpless and indecisive. The scale of the ethnonationalist challenge is certainly appreciated by "United Russia", which is also starting to play with the word *russkii* and even trying to redefine the traditional right-wing slogan "Rossiia dlia russkikh" ("Russia for the [ethnic] Russians") to fit the inclusive civic version of patriotism (United Russia 2007).

At a different level, the strength of the ultranationalist opposition exposes the structural limitations of the consolidation of the political subject which have to do with the very nature of Putin's project, with its foundation in the Soviet past. The Soviet Union, the "affirmative action empire" (Martin 2001), was a society in which ethnicity was institutionally and discursively embedded through the system of "national" autonomies and the organic idea of ethnicity as the only "real" foundation for nationhood. This legacy is reflected, inter alia, in the fact that Surkov (2006a) combines his definition of the Russian nation as a civic community with talk about the ethnic Russians as "tireless masters of the lofty fate" of Russia as a whole, while other ethnic groups figure, to use the words of Oksana Karpenko (2007: 137), as "a background mosaic highlighting the greatness of the main protagonist". Besides, when the sovereignty of the Russian state is measured in comparison with the USSR, the question inevitably arises about the status of various "grey zones" left behind by the Soviet collapse and, in particular, the status of the "compatriots abroad". In his 2005 address to the Federal Assembly, Putin spoke about the "tens of millions of our co-citizens and compatriots" who "found themselves outside of the Russian territory" (Putin 2005), describing that as one of the catastrophic consequences of the collapse of the Soviet Union. This ambiguous description of the citizens of other states as "our co-citizens and compatriots" underscores the precarious condition of the civic nationalist project in Russia. It is evident that belonging to the "compatriots" is a matter of ethnic identity and language. Most often, the concept refers to the ethnic Slavs (preferably Russian-speaking) (Malakhov 2006: 150f.). The neo-imperial identity thus serves as a link to the ethnic nationalist discourse, which creeps back into official policy statements.

Reactionary modernisation? Russia faces the "post-modern" world

The previous section has shown that, domestically, the construction of Russia as a modern sovereign subject is hampered by the ambiguity about the nature and boundaries of political community. The international scene presents an even more significant challenge to the Kremlin. Sovereignty is out of fashion in the contemporary world – at least in as much as the hegemonic articulation succeeds in promoting liberal universalism in its various incarnations, from neo-conservative to cosmopolitan. Against this background, the very emphasis on autonomy, control and sovereignty that the Russian diplomacy is trying to present as a pragmatic shift and a move away from foreign policy driven by ideology becomes desperately ideological in the Marxian sense of the word. Sovereignty, far from being a neutral constitutive principle, has turned into one of the most important battlegrounds of today's global politics (Scheipers 2007: 223f.). Despite the conflicting philosophical and ideological traditions underlying the liberal universalist agenda, nearly all of them insist that sovereignty be limited for the sake of spreading democracy and/or protecting human rights. This constitutes a new time scale on which modernisation aimed at the (re-) establishment of an autonomous sovereign subject becomes reactionary in the sense that it means moving back in historical time from post-modernity into the modern world. Thus, from the point of view of the discursive articulation, which arguably occupies a hegemonic position in the contemporary world, Russia's insistence on sovereignty becomes a manifestation of "false consciousness", an ideologically skewed position out of touch with reality.[10]

David Chandler (2006: 489) refers to what is perhaps the most explicit elaboration of the topic in a book by Robert Cooper, the policy advisor to UK Prime Minister Tony Blair and EU High Representative Javier Solana. Cooper divides the world into the pre-modern, modern, and post-modern states. He then argues that the latter states (the EU members and to some extent the US) are primarily concerned with democracy and justice, having no traditional foreign policy interests. However, when the post-modern world has to face the modern and pre-modern states, it cannot treat them as equals:

---

10   I here subscribe to the conventional view of the Marxian interpretation of ideology as false consciousness, which is disputed by some authors (McCarney 1980), but defended by others (Pines 1993).

"[...] When dealing with more old-fashioned kinds of state outside the post-modern limits, Europeans need to revert to the rougher methods of an earlier era – force, pre-emptive attack, deception, whatever is necessary [...]. In the jungle, one must use the laws of the jungle." (Cooper 2003: 62)

Echoing John Rawls (1999), Cooper goes on to advocate a neo-Wilsonian interventionist agenda, which does not tolerate modernity and pre-modernity as co-existing worlds, but insists on the need to reshape them by introducing "universal" norms and institutions.

A crucial point to be made here is that Western discursive hegemony cannot be understood in purely geographical terms. Poststructuralist theory describes hegemony as a situation of antagonism and domination; but hegemonic domination is always contingent, and the boundaries that separate the antagonistic forces are unstable (Laclau and Mouffe 1985: 136). Hegemony is power that is accepted through (partial and hesitant) identification with the source of power and challenged by means of drawing a boundary between the "oppressors" and the "oppressed". It is a system of social institutions and practices (and the underlying discursive articulation) based on a decision whose political nature is still very much alive and can be reactivated. The fact that democracy today comes close to being universally accepted as a point of reference is a result of the hegemonic position of one particular subject of history – the West. There is no doubt that the West as a place is very diverse – this is where the war of position around the notion of democracy is most intense and where the very identity of the West itself is often questioned. However, the presence of the West as an *other* within political communities that construct themselves as non-Western is a very different story. First of all, drawing a boundary between the West and *us* is often a constitutive exercise for the non-Western communities. Fully in accordance with the logic of hegemony, the boundary between the West and any of the non-Wests is seldom absolute. While challenging the Western dominance, leaders all over the world, with a few exceptions, subscribe to the idea of democracy as the only legitimate form of government and refer to the West as setting the standards for this form. At the same time, as Western hegemony consolidates, the communities that are (self-) excluded from the West feel an ever more pressing need to define their identity in opposition to the dominant Western *other*, which makes the West ever more real as a subject of global politics.

Besides, the Western debates about the nature of democracy do not fully, or at all, translate into other discursive spaces or into political action on the global arena. While Americans and Europeans might be in disagreement about the meaning of democracy and sovereignty (as demonstrated, inter alia, by the heated debate on the future of the EU) and argue about the democratic credentials of their own political systems, the policy impact felt by the people in the periphery and semi-periphery of the world makes them think of the West as a single undifferentiated force. This is true both in the case of the US "democratic crusade" and its "with us or against us" logic and in the case of the EU policy of conditionality, which strives to remodel its neighbours from Montenegro to Russia to Libya in its own image. In Richard Cheney's talk in Vilnius (2006), "a return to democratic reform in Russia" is synonymous to Russia's "aligning with the West", and this statement by the US vice president is no less indicative than many others from the same speech. As Chandler argues, Western interventionism "delegitimates the political process of the state intervened in" (2006: 485) and thus replaces the fundamentally political process of constituting political community through everyday decisionmaking by the autonomous people with technocratic management: "[D]emocracy is often presented as a solution to the problems of the political sphere rather than as a process of determining and giving content to the 'good life'" (2006: 483). Similarly, Alexander Astrov (2007) notes that popular legitimacy in the EU accession countries has been replaced to a significant extent with vicarious power – a rule in the name of external authority. This leads to politics being substituted with management and to a disproportionate expansion of the executive prerogatives.

One of the most characteristic examples of the deep mistrust of local politics, manifest in the very idea of exporting democracy, was the 2006 elections in the Palestinian autonomy. On the one hand, "democracy promotion" has been a special focus of the US foreign policy in the Middle East after 11 September 2001, but on the other hand, both Washington and Brussels refused to accept the outcome of the democratic process – the victory of Hamas – and went on with their usual interventionist approach (Sayigh 2007). Sergei Prozorov (2006) maintains that the failure, resulting from the inherent paradoxes of the cosmopolitan integrationist discourse, to recognise the difference between the EU and Russia as legitimate is a major source of conflict between the two parties. Helle Malmvig argues that, in the EU's approach to its Mediterranean neighbours, "liberal reform discourse" draws "a sharp boundary" between the democratic

Europe and "the troubled and unstable space" of the Mediterranean region. This, in turn, undermines the EU's own efforts to create a security community through a "cooperative security discourse", deepens and reinforces the already prevalent "feeling of distrust and suspicion about the EU's real intentions", and thus "enhances representations of an occidental Other" (2006: 358, 365). Olivier Roy points out that the efforts to promote "civil society" in the Middle East and Central Asia often consist in the "importation of ready-made frameworks", which "often offends the receivers", and concludes that "there is no way to root democracy without addressing the issue of political legitimacy and nationalism" (2005: 1008, 1010). In sum, the liberal democratic idea does indeed have an infinite number of incarnations, yet the resultant hegemonic force of the war of position inside the West is the insistence that sovereignty be limited for the sake of spreading democracy and/or protecting human rights. While arguing among themselves, the Europeans and the Americans may envisage the ideal world as a community of sovereign republics, but when they operate globally, they tend to spread uniform norms and practices. The West thinks Kantian, but acts Bushian.

One could, of course, argue that the Bushian image of the West is constructed by its Russian and other interlocutors in line with *their* respective traditions of imagining the West as the *other*. This is certainly correct in the sense that the identity of the West as a unified global actor, like all other identities, is not contained within itself. It is shaped *both* inside and outside of the Western political community, by the debates about the nature of "Westernness" in Western Europe and North America (O'Hagan 2002; Bonnett 2004; Jackson 2006) *and* by the construction of the West as the *other* in Russia (Neumann 1996, 1999: 161-182) and elsewhere. Indeed, as Heller (2006: 149-237) has demonstrated, Russian identity construction from the mid-19th century onwards played a key role in establishing the West as a point of reference in the global discourse. However, the recognition of the external dimension as crucial for identity construction must not obscure the fact that current Western hegemony relies on *one* global relational network of meaning, which defines the West as a unified democratising actor. It might be defined differently in alternative articulations that challenge the hegemonic one, but the very fact that they are not accepted outside of the Western community and do not resonate with non-Western identity discourses indicates their relatively marginal position worldwide.

The risk of potential confrontation resulting from the global sovereign's insistence on the old-fashioned, futile, and even threatening nature of all other sovereignties was fully recognised in Russia at the beginning of NATO's military operation in Kosovo (Arbatova 2001) and has remained on the lists of threats to Russia's national security ever since (Kontseptsiia 2000; Solov'ëv 2007). This anxiety has been repeatedly spelled out by Putin. In his Munich speech, he described the "unipolar world" promoted by the West as "a world of one master, one sovereign", where "nearly the entire legal system of one state, first of all, of course, of the United States, has transgressed its national boundaries and [...] is being imposed on other states". "Unilateral, illegitimate actions" of the US and its allies are detrimental to global security because they produce new conflicts and wars, intensify the nuclear arms race, and lead to a situation where "no one feels secure. Because no one can find refuge behind the stronghold of the international law" (Putin 2007c).

It is important to emphasise that the overall argument of the speech is framed in global, rather than personal or national, terms. Unlike the hawks in the military establishment and the Duma, the top people in the Kremlin are not comfortable with the prospect of an open confrontation with the West. Hegemony works in Russia as well. Opposing the West, the Russian leaders have not given up on the idea of establishing Russia as a full member of the "community of civilized nations", as demonstrated, inter alia, by their attempts to prove that the Soviet Union is to be credited with the end of the Cold War (also O'Loughlin et al. 2004). Thus, Putin and his team, including his successor Dmitry Medvedev, are busy arguing that "real democracy exists in Russia", even if "there is still room for progress" (RIA Novosti 2007). Speaking in Munich, Putin emphasised that the system with one global sovereign is "pernicious" for everyone, including the sovereign itself, and "has nothing in common with democracy" (Putin 2007c). In his Davos speech, Medvedev maintained that democracy, "as a social phenomenon, as a legal construction [...] is a totally universal term [...]. Humankind knows what it is and is able to see when one speaks about real political democracy, and when this word is used in vain" (RIA Novosti 2007).

This last quote demonstrates particularly well that the case Putin, Medvedev, Surkov, and others are trying to make can be described as an attempt to overcome the logic of proper names or of thinking based on prototypes (Koposov 2001: 93-121). The argument is that democracy exists above all as an abstract principle (something that people, as Medvedev argues, know almost intuitively, because "freedom is better than the lack of freedom" (Arsyukhin 2007)), and this principle can be put into political practice in many different ways. The problem is that, in the practice of liberal universalist hegemony, the standards of democracy are set by comparison with the US and the EU as prototypes of democracy, democracies par excellence. Both Surkov's sovereign democracy and Medvedev's real democracy are trying to create one more proper name for democracy, "Russia". Speaking more broadly, this constitutes an exercise in representational politics: Facing what it perceives as a single and unified West trying to impose its values and practices on all other civilisations, Russia claims to represent the "true" universality. It attempts to fill in the universal that is always empty because "society consists only of particularities, and [...] all universality will have to be incarnated in something utterly incommensurable with it" (Laclau 2000: 80f.). In the Russian discourse, sovereignty becomes the universal value that Russia strives to protect, acting in the name of humanity. Its criticism against the West as being ideological in its policies is pointed against the failure to recognise the fundamental nature of sovereignty for the global political order. Thus, both liberal universalism and sovereign democracy represent "false consciousness" in each other's terms.

At a more general level, however, both discourses are ideological in as much as they constitute "a critique of the lack of structuration accompanying the dominant order" and refuse to accept "the precarious character of any positivity, of the impossibility of any ultimate suture" (Laclau 1990: 62, 92). Russia is unhappy with the fact that the world today is "no longer" neatly divided into sovereign territorial states and the ideological moment in this position consists in the failure to recognise that the world has never been like that, nor could it have been. For the US and the EU, Russia's and others' insistence on their sovereignty challenges their view of global democracy understood as a universal value, but modelled on their own historically contingent social institutions and practices.

This predicament, like any structural dislocation, has a strong emancipatory potential since Russia could, theoretically, embark on what Ernesto Laclau (1996: 34) calls "a systematic decentring of the West" by exposing the Eurocentric nature of Western discourse "which did not differentiate between the universal values the West was advocating and the concrete social agents that were incarnating them". This could expand the horizon of universal democracy by undermining the link between universal values and their particular cultural context, and could be useful for both the West and the non-West. Unfortunately, Russia compromises its own position as the protector of global diversity by its attempts to install uniformity within the limits of the nation. As a member of Putin's audience in Munich aptly noted, while criticising the Western-dominated unipolarity, the Kremlin continues to create a unipolar political space within Russia (Putin 2007c).

Even though the Kremlin's desire to protect and enhance Russia's sovereignty is framed in opposition to the West, Moscow's policies actually mirror those of the West in one important respect. Russia claims for itself the role of the ultimate political centre that simultaneously figures as the only locus of politics and as a depoliticised, disinterested subject catering exclusively for common good. David Chandler argues that the emphasis on "good governance" in various projects aimed at exporting democracy is based on "[t]he rejection of the domestic political sphere as a vital constitutive sphere, in which social and political bonds are constituted and strengthened, and the re-representation of this sphere as essentially one of division and conflict" (2006: 486). The external intervening powers are portrayed as being "above politics" (2006: 485) and aimed essentially at administering and policing, rather than at taking decisions in a situation of indeterminacy. This has a striking parallel in the Russian domestic discourse, where the ruling party presents itself as a party of "the real deeds" taking care of the de-problematised national interest, while the opposition is scorned as trying to split society and capitalise on social problems instead of solving them. Both strategies originate in the inherent mistrust of all "local" politics and grassroots democracy, and both consist in monopolising the power to take decisions while presenting these decisions as non-political in nature.

Moreover, it can be argued that by mistreating the NGO activists, the Georgians, the Chechens, the liberal politicians, etc., the Russian authorities engage in a practice that, rephrasing Ernesto Laclau, may be called a representational inversion of the relations of oppression. Facing what it perceives as unjust Western dominance in global affairs, on the one hand, and the disturbing uncertainty at home, on the other, Russia is tempted to define its identity in radical opposition to the West. Even if it could win this battle and inverse the oppressive relationship (i.e., if it started a new Cold War and won it), oppression as a form would still be there, the only result being that the oppressor and the oppressed would have exchanged places (Laclau 1996: 31). This is why Russia's criticism of the West from the vantage point of universal and abstract democracy is a very encouraging sign. It is a move in the direction of opposing the form of oppression as such and towards the expansion of the horizon of global democracy. The opposite trend, however, is also present and might be gaining the upper hand. Being unable to win the confrontation with the West, Russia turns against what it sees as Western agents, clients, and proxies – everything that *represents* the West in its domestic political space. The result of this representational inversion is that the oppression is not only preserved, but doubled. Western hegemony is still there and is still perceived as oppressive, but internal hegemony within Russian society is also built on the oppressive treatment of various "pro-Western" identities.

Conclusion

This article has explored the way in which the Russian leadership deploys two key concepts of modern political discourse – sovereignty and democracy – at the intersection of the universal and the particular in the current global discursive setting. It presented a case in favour of studying discursive articulations as reflective of power structures limiting, but also empowering political agency. To that end, it supplemented the approach to foreign policy as identity construction common to poststructuralist international studies with Ernesto Laclau and Chantal Mouffe's theory of ideology, hegemony, and universality.

As empirical analysis confirms, discursive hegemony is never unproblematic. In the Russian case, the dominant theme of the official discourse is sovereign autonomy, which presupposes the ability of the state to control all significant domestic and transnational processes in and involving Russia. This focus on control corresponds to the arcane interests of the top managers of the corporatist state, but it would be naïve to describe and explain the discursive developments only in those terms. As the broader analysis suggests, the prioritisation of sovereignty in contemporary Russia is an ideology of modernisation, since it aims to establish the nation as a sovereign subject in Westphalian terms. At the same time, this is a restorationist project inspired by the image of the Soviet modernity as the golden age in the history of the millennium-old Russian state. From the point of view of the liberal universalist discourse, this project may even look reactionary, since the global hegemonic articulations tend to view sovereignty with suspicion and as a rudiment of the past that impedes the spread of democracy.

Anchoring Russian national identity in the Soviet past does not help in solving one of the crucial problems of contemporary Russia – that of the boundaries of the political community. No vision of the Russian nation – either civic or ethnic – can be fully realised under the current conditions. Additionally, the identity of the new Russia as a "sovereign democracy" does not receive a positive external confirmation. The resulting frustration reinforces the feeling that the "enemy is at the gate" (Surkov 2004; Lynch 2005). The fuzzy inside/outside boundaries in a situation where the official discourse emphasises the feasibility and necessity of certainty and stability create a painful dislocation, which leads to an increased feeling of vulnerability and, as a result, to the constant witch hunt in search for aliens to be blamed for all failures. The irritation with partners in the West as well as with neighbours in the Commonwealth of Independent States who are unwilling to buy into Russia's image of itself as a great power also outgrows the limits of everyday politics and becomes a question of national security. As the 2006-2007 crisis in the Russian-Georgian relations demonstrated, securitisation of domestic and international concerns is mutually reinforcing and contributes to the growth of ethnic nationalism, which comes too close to becoming an official ideology. Paradoxically or not, the unfeasibility of all existing versions of Russia as a project helps one of them, the most dangerous and potentially destructive one, to gain the upper hand.

Dislocation is celebrated in the poststructuralist tradition as preventing structural closure and therefore creating the possibility of liberation. The analysis presented here draws attention to another consequence of the in-built structural contradictions – the structural drive to eliminate dislocation, which takes the form of securitising practices. This, however, should not be taken to mean that structural limitations on human agency will necessarily prevail. On the contrary, as this article has shown, the structural limits that strongly determine certain political outcomes are likely to produce new dislocations further down the road. Thus, even if the restorationist turn of identity politics under Putin was at a particular historical conjuncture almost predetermined, it has at the same time produced a glaring uncertainty in the definition of boundaries of the political community of Russia. This uncertainty, in turn, can facilitate an ethnic nationalist backlash, but the very possibility of the latter creates ground for possible political mobilisation in favour of defining Russia as a civic nation.

The criticism of unipolarity, presented by the Kremlin, should also be considered along these lines. On the one hand, sovereign democracy certainly contributes to the new antagonism between Russia and the West, which reinforces existing political boundaries and marginalises oppositional discourses as being "pro-Western" and thus belonging to the threatening world located beyond the limits of the domestic political space. On the other hand, Putin's insistence on the universal nature of democracy, as opposed to its particularist representations by the West, opens up the possibility to argue that democracy *within* Russia can be defined in numerous ways, and thus to revitalise the irreducible diversity of local politics. This leaves open the question as to the possible subject of such discursive transformation, but at least one can see that there is a *possibility* for this subject to emerge.

Bibliography

Arbatova, N. 2001. "European Security after the Kosovo Crisis: The Role of Russia". *Southeast European and Black Sea Studies* 1, 2. 64-78.

Arsyukhin, E. 2007. "Davos vziat'"". *Rossiiskaia gazeta* 30 January. http://www.rg.ru/2007/01/30/davos-medved.html [accessed 22 August 2009].

Astrov, A. 2007. *Samochinnoe soobshchestvo: politika men'shinstv ili malaia politika?* Tallinn: Tallinn University Press.

Baudrillard, J. 1988. "Simulacra and Simulations". In *Selected Writings*, edited by Mark Poster, 166-184. Stanford: Stanford University Press.

Bonnett, A. 2004. *The Idea of the West: Culture, Politics and History*. Basingstoke: Palgrave Macmillan.

Breslauer, G. and C. Dale. 1997. "Boris Yeltsin and the Invention of the Russian Nation State". *Post-Soviet Affairs* 13, 4. 303-332.

Campbell, D. 1998. *Writing Security: United States Foreign Policy and the Politics of Identity*. Revised edition. Minneapolis: University of Minnesota Press.

Cederman, L. and C. Daase. 2003. "Endogenizing Corporate Identities: The Next Step in Constructivist IR Theory". *European Journal of International Relations* 9, 1. 5-35.

Chandler, D. 2006. "Back to the Future? The Limits of Neo-Wilsonian Ideals of Exporting Democracy". *Review of International Studies* 32, 3. 475-494.

Cheney, R. 2006. Vice President's Remarks at the 2006 Vilnius Conference, 4 May, Vilnius, Lithuania. http://www.whitehouse.gov/news/releases/2006/05/20060504-1.html [accessed 27 January 2007].

Cooper, R. 2003. *The Breaking of Nations: Order and Chaos in the Twenty-First Century*. New York: Atlantic Monthly Press.

Dobrynina, E. 2006. "Prishli k soglasiiu". *Rossiiskaia gazeta* 6 September. http://www.rg.ru/2006/09/06/diskussia.html [accessed 24 August 2009].

Edkins, J. 1999. *Poststructuralism and International Relations: Bringing the Political Back In*. Boulder and London: Lynne Rienner.

Ferretti, M. 2005. "Neprimirimaia pamiat': Rossiia i voina". *Neprikosnovennyi zapas* 2-3. 76-82.

Foucault, M. 1980. *Power/Knowledge: Selected Interviews and Other Writings 1972-1977*. Hemel Hempstead: Harvester Wheatsheaf.

Gramsci, A. 1971. *Selections from Prison Notebooks*. London: Lawrence & Wishart.

Gudkov, L. 2005. "Pamiat' o voine i massovaia identichnost' rossiian". *Neprikosnovennyi zapas* 2-3. 46-57.

Hansen, L. 2006. *Security as Practice: Discourse Analysis and the Bosnian War*. London and New York: Routledge.

Hanson, S.E. 2006. "Postimperial Democracies: Ideology and Party Formation in Third Republic France, Weimar Germany, and Post-Soviet Russia". *East European Politics and Societies* 20, 2. 343-372.

Heller, K.M. 2006. *The Dawning of the West: On the Genesis of a Concept*. PDE diss., Cincinnati Union Institute & University.

Hopf, T. 2002. *Social Origins of International Politics. Identities and the Construction of Foreign Policies at Home*. Ithaca: Cornell University Press.

Jackson, P.T. 2006. *Civilizing the Enemy: German Reconstruction and the Invention of the West*. Ann Arbor: University of Michigan Press.

Kapustin, B. 1996. "'Natsional'nyi interes' kak konservativnaia utopiia". *Svobodnaia mysl'* 3. 13-29.

Kara-Murza, S. 2000. *Manipuliatsiia soznaniem*. Moskva: Algoritm.

Karpenko, O. 2007. "'Suverennaia demokratiia' dlia vnutrennego i naruzhnogo primeneniia". *Neprikosnovennyi zapas* 1. 134-152.

Khamraev, V. 2007. "Proiski proshlogo". *Kommersant* 23 November. http://www.kommersant.ru/doc.aspx?DocsID=828434 [accessed 24 August 2009].

Khapaeva, D. 2006. "Goticheskoe obshchestvo. Stalinskoe proshloe v rossiiskom nastoiashchem". *Kriticheskaia massa* 1. http://www.artpragmatica.ru/km_content/?auid=25 [accessed 1 November 2007].

Kolesnikov, A. 2006. "Vladimir Putin prishël v Khabarovskii krai truboi". *Kommersant* 26 September.

Kontseptsiia. 2000. "Kontseptsiia natsionalnoi bezopasnosti Rossiiskoi Federatsii". http://www.scrf.gov.ru/documents/1.html [accessed 1 November 2007].

Koposov, N. 2001. *Kak dumaiut istoriki*. Moskva: Novoe literaturnoe obozrenie.

Kozhevnikova, G. 2007. *Autumn-2006: Under the Kondopoga Banner*. Moscow: SOVA Center. http://xeno.sova-center.ru/6BA2468/6BB4208/884A3C7 [accessed 4 February 2007].

Laclau, E. 1990. *New Reflections on the Revolution of Our Time*. London: Verso.

——— 1996. *Emancipation(s)*. London: Verso.

——— 2000. "Identity and Hegemony: The Role of Universality in the Constitution of Political Logics". In Laclau, E., J. Butler, and S. Zizek, *Contingency, Hegemony, Universality: Contemporary Dialogues on the Left*, 44-89. London, New York: Verso.

Laclau, E. and C. Mouffe. 1985. *Hegemony and Socialist Strategy*. London: Verso.

Lavrov, S. 2006. "60 Years of Fulton: Lessons of the Cold War and Our Time". *International Affairs: A Russian Journal of World Politics, Diplomacy & International Relations* 52, 2. 8-12.

——— 2007a. "The Present and the Future of Global Politics". *Russia in Global Affairs* 5, 2. 8-21.

——— 2007b. "Sderzhivanie Rossii: nazad v budushchee?". *Rossiia v global'noi politike* 5, 4. 8-21.

——— 2007c. "Vneshnepoliticheskaia samostoiatel'nost' Rossii – bezuslovnyi imperativ". *Rossiia v Global'noi Politike* 19 January. http://www.globalaffairs.ru/articles/0/6770.html [accessed 24 August 2009].

Leontev, M. 2006. "Kontsept 'Rossiia kak energeticheskaia sverkhderzhava'". *Russkii zhurnal* 27 October. http:// 2005.russ.ru/docs/ 132446829 [accessed 3 February 2007].

Lynch, D. 2005. "The Enemy is at the Gate". *International Affairs* 81, 1. 141-161.

Magun, A. 2006. "'Suverennaia demokratiia', ili 'Otchaiannyi konservatizm'". *Russkii zhurnal* 24 October. http://2005.russ.ru/docs/ 132197879 [accessed 3 February 2007].

Makarychev, A. and O. Reut. 2006. "O de-politizatsii i de-suverenizatsii". *Tsentr internet-politiki MGIMO(U) MID Rossii. Statyi chlenov ekspertnogo soveta.* http://www.netpolitics.ru/public.php?doc_id=166 [accessed 15 February, 2008].

Malakhov, V. 2006. "Nastoiashchee i budushchee 'natsional'noi politiki' v Rossii". *Prognozis* 3. 144-159.

Malmvig, H. 2006. "Caught between Cooperation and Democratization: The Barcelona Process and the EU's Double-Discursive Approach". *Journal of International Relations and Development* 9, 4. 343-370.

Martin, T. 2001. "Affirmative Action Empire: The Soviet Union as the Highest Form of Imperialism". In *A State of Nations: Empire and Nation-Making in the Age of Lenin and Stalin,* edited by R. Suny and T. Martin, 67-90. Oxford: Oxford University Press.

McCarney, J. 1980. *The Real World of Ideology.* Sussex: Harvester Press.

Mendelson, S. and T. Gerber. 2006. "Failing the Stalin Test". *Foreign Affairs* 85, 1. 2-8.

Miller, A. 2007. "Natsiia kak ramka politicheskoi zhizni". *Pro et contra* 11, 3. 6-20.

Morozov, V. 2002. "Resisting Entropy, Discarding Human Rights: Romantic Realism and Securitization of Identity in Russia". *Cooperation and Conflict* 37, 4. 409-430.

Munro, N. 2006. "Russia's Persistent Communist Legacy: Nostalgia, Reaction, and Reactionary Expectations". *Post-Soviet Affairs* 22, 4. 289-313.

Neumann, I. 1996. *Russia and the Idea of Europe: A Study of Identity and International Relations.* London: Routledge.

———— 1999. *Uses of the Other: 'The East' in European Identity Formation,* Minneapolis: University of Minnesota Press.

O'Hagan, J. 2002. *Conceptions of the West in International Relations Thought: From Oswald Spengler to Edward Said*. Basingstoke: Macmillan.

Okara, A. 2007. "Sovereign Democracy: A New Russian Idea or a PR Project?". *Russia in Global Affairs* 5, 3. 8-20.

O'Loughlin, J., G. Ó Tuathail, and V. Kolossov. 2004. "A 'Risky Westward Turn'? Putin's 9-11 Script and Ordinary Russians". *Europe-Asia Studies* 56, 1. 3-34.

Ostrovsky, V. 2004. "On eshche i istorik...". *Nevskoe vremia* 24 December. http://www.nevskoevremya.spb.ru/test8/3323/on_eshe_i_istorik/ [accessed 24 August 2009].

Pines, C. 1993. *Ideology and False Consciousness: Marx and His Historical Progenitors*. Albany: State University of New York Press.

Prozorov, S. 2006. *Understanding Conflict Between Russia and the EU: The Limits of Integration*. Basingstoke and New York: Palgrave Macmillan.

Putin, V. 2005. "Poslanie Federal'nomu Sobraniiu Rossiiskoi Federatsii'. 25 April. http://kremlin.ru/appears/2005/04/25/1223_type63372type 63374type82634_87049.shtml [accessed 4 November 2007].

—— 2006a. "Poslanie Federal'nomu Sobraniiu Rossiiskoi Federatsii'. 10 May. http://kremlin.ru/appears/2006/05/10/1357_type63372 type63374type82634_105546.shtml [accessed 4 November 2007].

—— 2006b. "Stenogramma priamogo tele- i radioefira ('Priamaia linia s Prezidentom Rossii')". 25 October. http://president.kremlin.ru/ appears/2006/10/25/1303_type63381type82634type146434_112959.shtml [accessed 1 November 2007].

—— 2007a. "Poslanie Federal'nomu Sobraniiu Rossiiskoi Federatsii". 26 April. http://kremlin.ru/appears/2007/04/26/1156_type63372type 63374type82634_125339.shtml [accessed 1 November 2007].

―――― 2007b. "Vladimir Putin: Nasha obshchaia tsel' – pobeda 'Edinoi Rossii' na vyborakh v Gosdumu". Speech at the Forum of Putin's supporters, Moscow, 21 November. http://www.edinros.ru/news.html?id=125609 [accessed 17 December 2007].

―――― 2007c. "Vystuplenie na Miunkhenskoi konferentsii po voprosam politiki bezopasnosti". 10 February. http://president.kremlin.ru/appears/2007/02/10/1737_type63374type63376type63377type63381type82634_118097.shtml [accessed 1 November 2007].

Rawls, J. 1999. *The Law of Peoples*. London & Cambridge: Harvard University Press.

RIA Novosti. 2007. "Medvedev: v Rossii sushchestvuet demokratiia, no ei est' kuda dvigat'sia", 27 January, http://www.rian.ru/world/foreign_russia/20070127/59781269.html [accessed 5 February 2007].

Roy, O. 2005. "The Predicament of 'Civil Society' in Central Asia and the 'Greater Middle East'". *International Affairs* 81, 5. 1001-1012.

Rumelili, B. 2004. "Constructing Identity and Relating to Difference: Understanding the EU's Mode of Differentiation". *Review of International Studies* 30, 1. 27-47.

Savina, E. 2007. "'Krovnye druz'ia". *Kommersant* 1 November. http://www.kommersant.ru/doc.aspx?DocsID=820946 [accessed 24 August 2009].

Sayigh, Y. 2007. "Inducing a Failed State in Palestine". *Survival* 49, 3. 7-39.

Scheipers, S. 2007. "Civilization vs Toleration: The New UN Human Rights Council and the Normative Foundations of the International Order". *Journal of International Relations and Development* 10, 3. 219-242.

Solov'ëv, V. 2007. "Vragov stalo bol'she, vragi stali agressivnee". *Nezavisimoe voennoe obozrenie* 22 January. http://www.ng.ru/nvo/2007-01-22/1_enemies.html [accessed 24 August 2009].

Surkov, V. 2004. "Putin ukrepliaet gosudarstvo, a ne sebia". *Komsomol'skaia pravda* 29 September.http://www.kp.ru/daily/23370/32473/ [accessed 24 August 2009].

―――― 2006a. "Natsionalizatsiia budushchego". http://www.edinros.ru/news.html?id =116746 [accessed 2 February 2007].

―――― 2006b. "Suverenitet – eto politicheskii sinonim konkurentosposobnosti". Transcript of talk to the students of the Centre for political education and personnel training of the United Russia party, 7 February. http://www.edinros.ru/news.html?id=111148 [accessed 2 February 2007].

Thomas, E. 2002. "Who Belongs? Competing Conceptions of Political Membership". *European Journal of Social Theory* 5, 3. 323-349.

Tolz, V. 2004. "A Search for a National Identity in Yeltsin's and Putin's Russia". In *Restructuring Post-Communist Russia*, edited by Y. Brudny, S. Hoffman, and J. Frankel, 160-178. Cambridge: Cambridge University Press.

Tretiakov, V. 2005. "Suverennaia demokratiia. O politicheskoi filosofii Vladimira Putina". *Rossiiskaia gazeta* 28 April. http://www.rg.ru/2005/04/28/tretyakov.html [accessed 24 August 2009].

Tsygankov, A. 2006. *Russia's Foreign Policy: Change and Continuity in National Identity*. Lanham: Rowman & Littlefield.

United Russia. 2006. "Prezident podderzhal ideiu suverennoi demokratii", http://gov.cap.ru/hierarhy.asp?page=./75063/187503/255513 [accessed 4 September 2009].

United Russia. 2007. "'Edinaia Rossiia' otkryvaet 'russkii proekt'". http://www.edinros.ru/news.html?id=118052 [accessed 8 February 2007].

United States Department of State. 2005. "Supporting Human Rights and Democracy: The U.S. Record 2006". http://www.state.gov/documents/organization/80699.pdf [accessed 12 June 2007].

Ushakov, Iu. 2007. "From Russia with Like". *Los Angeles Times* 1 February. http://articles.latimes.com/2007/feb/01/opinion/oe-ushakov1 [accessed 24 August 2009].

Wæver, O. 2002. "Identity, Communities and Foreign Policy: Discourse Analysis as Foreign Policy Theory". In *European Integration and National Identity: The Challenge of the Nordic States*, edited by L. Hansen and O. Wæver, 20-49. London, New York: Routledge.

Weber, M. 1978. *Economy and Society*, vol. 1. Berkeley: University of California Press.

Weigle, M. 2000. *Russia's Liberal Project: State-Society Relations in the Transition from Communism*. University Park: Pennsylvania State University Press.

Wendt, A. 1999. *Social Theory of International Politics*. Cambridge: Cambridge University Press.

—————— 2006. "*Social Theory* as Cartesian Science: An Auto-Critique from a Quantum Perspective". In *Constructivism and International Relations: Alexander Wendt and His Critics*, edited by S. Guzzini and A. Leander, 181-219. London & New York: Routledge.

Wittgenstein, L. 1958. *Philosophical Investigations*. New York: Macmillan.

Zaiavlenie. 2005. "Zaiavlenie rossiiskikh nekommercheskikh nepravitel'stvennykh organizatsii". 6 December. http://www.hro.org/ngo/about/2005/11/text.php [accessed 12 June 2007].

Zehfuss, M. 2001. "Constructivism and Identity: A Dangerous Liaison". *European Journal of International Relations* 7, 3. 315-348.

―――― 2002. *Constructivism in International Relations: The Politics of Reality.* Cambridge: Cambridge University Press.

Zorin, A. 2005. "A New Holiday for Old Reasons: Taking A Day Off to Remodel the Past". *Russia Profile* 20 January. http://www.russiaprofile.org/page.php?pageid=Politics&articleid=479 [accessed 24 August 2009].

Zvereva, G. 2007. "Postroit' Matritsu: diskurs rossiiskoi vlasti v usloviiakh setevoi kul'tury", *Vestnik obshchestvennogo mneniia* 1. 21-33.

Ordering Chaos: Russian Neo-Fascist Articulation[1]

Zachary A. Bowden

This chapter argues that Russia's various neo-Fascist and ultra-nationalist groups are articulating a populism-in-formation around the signifiers "order" and "people", and through the narrative of mischief. The processes of signification and context are added to Ernesto Laclau's understanding of the process and politics of the articulation of hegemony. The chapter suggests that Russia's National Bolshevik Party, insofar as it articulates a discourse that mobilises resonant versions of "order" and "people", and as its narrative mode highlights the mischievous version of masculinity that is dominant in Russian culture and politics, represents the potentiality of Russian neo-Fascism to articulate a hegemonic populism.

This chapter brings a sociolinguistic approach to the study of post-Soviet Russian politics. A focus on discourse and identity provides a fruitful starting point for understanding contemporary Russian politics and culture, opening doors not only to the analysis of the actions and policies of the Russian state or political parties, but also to the everyday negotiations of identity and politics on the ground, in effect covering a realm of politics that is sometimes excluded. Sociolinguistics can teach us much about the relative stability of a political order, but, more importantly for my own work, it can also provide significant insights into the challenges to established order. Indeed, the link between discursive theories and social movement theory is not new. Alberto Melucci, among others, pioneered the analysis of social movements through a discursive lens, highlighting the links between cultural codes, identity construction, and the challenging of such codes (discourses) (1996).

This chapter explores the articulatory practice of a social movement that sought to challenge the established order in post-Soviet Russia. This challenge

---

[1] This chapter is based largely on my "*Poriadok* and *Bardak* (Order and Chaos): The neo-fascist project of articulating a Russian 'People'" (2008).

reached a crescendo during the years of Vladimir Putin's presidency, but it continues to thrive today.

My argument is that the discursive challenges posed by extremist youth movements in Russia provide an important insight into the power of language in Russian politics culture. Furthermore, I argue that a sociolinguistic and discursive analytic approach to the study of these movements teaches us much about both the groups and their politics, and about the theories involved in the approach. I show this by briefly introducing the field/movement(s), analysing the primary signifiers of these movements, and analysing these movements and their signifiers through a lens comprised of a combination of Laclau's theories and Greimas' method of the semiotic rectangle. This combination helps us understand that not only are the semiotic challenges posed by Russian youth extremist movements quite powerful, but also that, viewed through a discursive lens, groups and movements that might appear fragmented, disparate, and even opposed might be considered as being in the process of constructing a larger collective identity.

Post-Soviet ultra-nationalism: a brief historical and positional introduction

Following the *bardak* (chaos)[2] of the 1990s in Russia, many groups, both formal and informal, sought seek to restore order – in one form or another – to Russia. This impulse found institutional expression in the presidency of Putin, and his program of the "dictatorship of law". Beyond the institutionalisation of a discourse of stability, however, the very signifier of order itself, *poriadok*, seemed to attain privileged status in Russian culture and politics.[3]

With the rise of Putin, the Kremlin swiftly colonised much of the formal political sphere. To many observers, it seems that as the Kremlin continued to dominate all aspects of "formal" politics (including "opposition parties"), the only remaining oppositional politics, as well as the only youth politics in contemporary Russian society, is that of extremist Fascists, neo-Fascists, skinheads, and

---

2   Joma Nazpary has shown the moral implications of *bardak* (2002). *Bardak*, he suggests, has become what post-Soviet citizens consider the structuring principle of post-Soviet life. *Bardak* means chaos, but it also means "whorehouse". It carries with it a moral judgment that signifies the decay of society, the amorality of post-Socialist leaders and elites, and the general depression of non-elite citizens. *Bardak*, itself, is a powerful signifier.

3   *Poriadok* may, in fact, be one of Russia's most important master signifiers.

thugs (Likhachev, 2002). Indeed, post-Soviet Russia has been the stage of an astonishing and disheartening explosion of racially motivated violence and youth extremism. While the issues of "civic" nationalism, far-right political parties, historical xenophobia, and organised ultra-nationalism are well researched, Russian youth extremism, neo-Fascism, and ultra-nationalism have received less scholarly attention, particularly from a discursive point of view. This article, therefore, focuses on the contemporary and local issue of a surging youth extremist movement in Russia.

The field of youth extremism in Russia is extremely fluid, for there are many different groups, "parties", organisations, and informal groupings that appear, disappear, reappear, remain hidden, and change their names and labels frequently. Nonetheless, there seem to be three primary discursive positions that most groups fit in: The ultra-nationalist, the neo-Nazi, and the national-Bolshevik. While below I provide historic examples for each of these camps, many of the groups I introduce have since declined in significance, or disappeared from the field into the internet, where they maintain an exclusively electronic presence. My understanding of the situation, however, is that while some specific organisations come and go, the underlying discursive positions (camps) remain.

Pamyat and the Russian National Unity party (RNE) represent two historical examples of the most extreme, organised, and visible organisations with a specific Russian face and are thus treated in the following as exemplars of the ultra-nationalist camp. Theirs was a politics of ethnic nationalism, based on the idea that Russia should be for (ethnic) Russians, and the desire for monarcho-Fascism or a "national/authoritarian" state. Blood and Honor and the Freedom Party are semi-organised gangs of skinheads with closer ties to "Western" forms of neo-Fascism, which I will call the neo-Nazi camp. The groups of the neo-Nazi camp resemble closely the Nazi Skins of the United States and Western Europe, with some variation.

The National Bolshevik Party (NBP) is the manifestation of the combination of left and right extremism that I refer to as the national-Bolshevik camp. This national-Bolshevik camp combines elements of radical left and ultra-rightist ideology, philosophy, and symbolism. The NBP differed from all of the above groups in its size, visibility, and popularity, all of which were surprisingly high.[4]

---

4   This grouping of the differing camps is my own. It is employed merely as an organisational tool. I use this tool to suggest that while the various groups on the field of the

During the later years of Putin's presidency, all of these groups were structurally opposed both to the Kremlin-sponsored youth "democratic anti-Fascist movement" Nashi (Ours), which engaged in both "mainstream" political actions and outwardly violent clashes with any group opposing the Kremlin, as well as to their traditional enemies, the more informal forces of the Russian anti-Fascist movement.

I hypothesise that as "normal" (i.e., constitutional and/or legal) opposition becomes increasingly difficult, if not impossible in today's Russia, those groups that are well organised and active, and that present resonant, yet challenging, cultural (semiotic) frames will be best equipped to oppose the Russian state.[5] In 2007, it seemed that the two main "players" in youth politics (the NBP and Nashi) as well as their anti-Fascist others in the punk movement provided the most important insights into the struggles taking place in contemporary Russian politics. That is to say, as Russia's most visible (and seemingly popular) opposition movement, the NBP seemed to provide some of the most important insights into opposition and youth politics in Russian culture.

An underlying argument in my work is that rather than being analysed as separate movements and organisations, the seemingly separate, and sometimes opposed, groups that make up the field of Russian extremism, including at certain moments the Russian state, can be understood as constituting a discursive whole, a new social movement.[6] In this work, rather than analysing this larger grouping through social movement theory, I will focus on the discursive work of the groups and suggest that it is a populism-in-formation. Laclau's work on the use of the people helps us explain the formation of social movements. Laclau insists that articulation must take place to form equivalence, but says little about the actual process of articulation. One way to analyse articulation is at the level of signification.

Russian far right are segmented and outwardly separate, if not opposed, through the process of articulation, it is possible that these camps come to form a discursive bloc.

5   The fact that the Kremlin launched its own youth movement to engage in non-"normal" politics (i.e., the politics of youth street violence) seems to strengthen this claim, demonstrating that even the state is not engaging in "normal" politics.

6   Alberto Melucci (1996) stressed that social movements are always in the process of constructing and negotiating a collective identity. One of the most important ways in which collective identity is constructed is through discourse. This is the underlying link between the sociolinguistic analysis of this chapter and the larger project of an analysis of Russian youth extremism as social movement.

Articulation and discourse analysis: theoretical background

The analysis of the formation of equivalence is founded upon, in addition to a theory of equivalence, a theory of signification and an examination of signifiers themselves. Discourse analysis helps us understand this process of articulation, or how equivalence is formed. We can look to A.J. Greimas and his work on signification to explore further the process of articulation. From a discursive analytic point of view, then, Greimas can be added to Laclau to gain a more vivid understanding of the process of articulation, introduce a framework for textual analysis, and expand an understanding of the process of movement/equivalence formation.

If my use of Greimas' methods represents a structural moment in my analysis, the work of Ernesto Laclau represents the poststructuralist moment. Inherent in this work is the assumption that both of these moments are needed. The structuralist moment promotes analytic clarity and narrative coherence, while the poststructuralist moment serves to remind us that the un-centredness and impossibility of a stable unity is always present when considering discourse, identity, and political projects. In fact, as I will argue below, understanding and utilising Laclau's work on the empty signifier, an impossible totality, is aided by a return to Greimas via Fredric Jameson and the semantic rectangle. In addition to the philosophical overlap between Jameson's Greimas and Laclau, it is my argument that because Laclau provides little explanation of how particularities are articulated into a totality, Jameson's work on signification provides us, via the semantic rectangle, with a much-needed explanation and understanding of the discursive aspect of the work of articulation.

In his book *On Populist Reason*, Laclau suggested that at the heart of any political project resides a populist logic (2005). That is to say, a political project must, at some level, strive to create a people, constituted by a chain of equivalence symbolically integrating diverse groups, and their semiotic demands. This creation of the signifier people involves both the process of positing equivalents, and that of enforcing distinctions among differing versions of the people. Political discourse, then, is a process of simultaneous positing of difference and equivalence. This suggests that the analyst's first goal in beginning a discursive examination of particular discourses is to identify the equivalences and differences posited in a given set of texts and discourses. The articulation of equivalence and difference is indeed at the core of much of the process of constructing and negotiating identity, both personal and collective.

That process seems to be largely reliant upon a binary of *nash/ne nash* (ours/not ours, or us/not us). Many social theorists of post-Soviet life, politics, and culture point to the centrality of the *us/not us* binary in post-Soviet life (Ries 1997; Tishkov 2004; Urban 1996; Shevchenko 2002; Caldwell 2002). The *nash/ne nash* binary, it seems, may be the most significant way in which Russians (and other post-Soviet peoples) construct their versions of personal, ethnic, group, and political identity. This binary is crucial factor in the analysis of the textual and discursive oppositions posited by the various camps of Russian extremism.

Previously, I have provided a more in-depth analysis of the texts and images of the three camps of youth extremism (Bowden 2008). There, I argued that each discursive movement on this field is working with the binary of Russian/Non Russian. This appears in many different forms, such as Orthodox/Non-Orthodox (Jewish), white/not white, active/not active, committed/not committed, Fascist/statist, etc. (ibid.). The similarities in the oppositions projected by these various groups and organisations are the first points from which we can begin to understand them as all distinct, but (becoming) equivalents in a discursive formation. From these oppositions, and the signifiers that express them, we can begin to engage with the process of articulation, or the process of discursively negotiating a new popullsm.

Signifiers, equivalences, squares and chains

The following section will examine the semiotic implications of the surface signifiers that the various neo-Fascist and extremist groups share. I will then suggest that we see the various groups as representing discursive moments that are undergoing an articulation of equivalence. I will then introduce the role of the empty signifier the people and link this to the *nash/ne nash* binary to suggest that the Russian neo-Fascist formulation demonstrates a populist logic struggling around the definition of the people based on the *nash/ne nash* opposition.

Laclau argues repeatedly that the semiotic project of any political struggle is to create hegemony (Laclau 1996; 2005). Hegemony, according to Laclau, is the creation of a chain of equivalence; that is to say, it is the creation of a unity out of disparate discursive elements. Equivalence, as well as its negotiation and articulation, here become the primary loci of attention for the analyst interested in how disparate discourses congeal into a political project. This focus has particular relevance for us insofar as we are attempting to suggest that neo-

Fascism in Russia, rather than being a set of disparate political groups, parties, and movements, represents a coherent bloc. To identify equivalence, we should therefore begin with an analysis of the shared demands (signifiers) of these various groups. Laclau provides many important insights into the study of empty signifiers and their deployment in politics, particularly in his "Why do Empty Signifiers Matter for Politics?" (1996) and *On Populist Reason* (2005).

Laclau states: "an empty signifier is, strictly speaking, a signifier without a signified" (1996: 36). This, in the strictest sense, is nonsense – an impossibility. Rather than this purely empty signifier, the analyst has to deal with signifiers that are empty in themselves, but nonetheless signify. "We do not have to deal with an excess or deficiency of signification, but with the precise theoretical possibility of something which points, from within the process of signification, to the discursive presence of its own limits" (ibid). That is to say that "language is a system of differences, that linguistic identities – values – are purely relational and that, as a result, the totality of language is involved in each single act of signification" (ibid.: 37). In this system, however, the possibility of the totality of the language, and thus signification, is predicated on the limits of the system and "to think of the limits of something is the same as thinking of what is beyond those limits" (ibid). The process of signification is, therefore, always founded on exclusion: to a creation of both the limit of signification (meaning), and thus the outside of meaning. The implications lead Laclau, and us with him, directly to the empty signifier.

The first of these implications is that signifiers only signify insofar as they project exclusion. "Each element of the system has an identity [meaning] only so far as it is different from others: difference=identity" (ibid.: 38). But all of the identities (which for us, at this point, are equivalent to "meanings") mean only insofar as they all share a limit, a larger exclusion. They all mean, and share an assumption about what does not mean. The empty signifier, then, is that signifier that cancels all of the differences of the system. Because of the fact that in a system of meaning, both difference and equivalence are in constant tension, it is possible that any signifier will come to represent the impossibility of the lack of difference. "We see here the possibility of an empty signifier announcing itself through this logic in which differences collapse into equivalential chains" (ibid.: 39). It is the goal of hegemonic or populist projects to create and utilise these empty signifiers to create a chain of equivalence out of the different elements in

ORDERING CHAOS 255

a discursive system. Before we move to this process, the articulatory practice, a few more words regarding the process of signification are needed.

The process of signification is a process of articulating the limits of a given signifier. What is excluded is what is beyond these limits. Jameson argues that Greimas' semantic rectangle is highly suitable for representing this process of the articulation of limits (1972: 163). He suggests that each signifier not only implies its own opposite (differentiation), but also its inverse, and the inverse of its opposite (ibid.). Figure 1 shows Greimas' semantic rectangle, which can be seen as representing the semiotic drawing of a particular signifier's limit.

Figure 1:

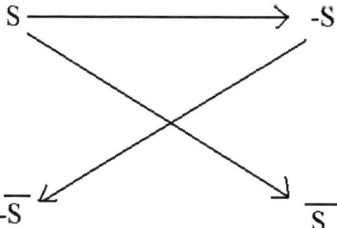

S in this diagram represents the signifier. -S represents the anti-S. The third position (clockwise from S) represents the not-S, and the fourth represents the negation of the negation of S (the not-anti S) (Jameson 1972: 163). I call these positions S1, S2 (anti-S), S3 (not-S), and S4 (not-anti-S). S1 and S2 represent simple opposition. The idea is that every signifier gains meaning, and thus implies its opposite. S3 and S4 point to the fact that language is not simple opposition, but rather the range (limits) of meaning, the possibilities of the system. It should also be stated that S2 and S3 represent affinity, as do S1 and S4 insofar as both S2 and S3 are opposed to S1, and both S1 and S4 are opposed to S2.

My argument here is that we see the semantic rectangle as a method for representing the process by which every signifier posits its own contradiction, opposite, and inverse. In other words, the rectangle can be seen as a visual representation of Laclau's theory of signification. The formulation of the semantic rectangle provides an explanatory aspect to the process of articulation, about which Laclau is silent. Accepting this combination, we can move toward an analysis of the master signifiers of neo-Fascism in Russia.

The most common signifiers found across the spectrum of Russian neo-Fascism appear to be *poriadok* (order) and *narod/natsiia* (people/nation). These are found in the posters, slogans, and literature of most extremist organisations and groups (Bowden 2008).[7] A central factor to remember here is, that while many organisations employ these signifiers, they imply different things to each camp. That is to say, the signifiers may be the same, but what they signify varies. The process of these signifiers moving toward a more cohesive meaning is the very process of articulation with which this chapter is concerned. If we are to understand the signification of these signifiers, then, we must consider their projected limits and exclusions. The semantic rectangle helps us here.

If we place *poriadok* in the place of S1, the opposite of order, chaos (*bardak*), becomes S2. Its inverse is, in this formulation *bezpredel* (S3). *Bezpredel* is an interesting word. Literally, *bezpredel* means "without limits", it seems to be a version of *bardak* that is free of the moral implications chaos carries with it. In another instance, *bezpredel* is the gangster's equivalent of lawlessness. It implies that some illegitimate group is not following the codes of the criminal world.[8] I have left the fourth position, the limit of the signifier, blank, for as Jameson notes, "in actual practice [...] it frequently turns out that we are able to articulate a given concept into only three of the four available positions; the final one [...] remains a cipher or an enigma for the mind" (ibid.: 166). The fourth position, as I have argued, represents the limit of signification. It is also the negation of negation. Because of the richness of Russian words for "outsiders", "foreigners", and others, and to lay the advance ground for our arguments regarding populist articulation, I suggest replacing *narod* with *nash*. *Narod/natsiia* are also fairly unambiguous versions of *nash*.

In Figure 2, we see that in the signification of ours (*nash*), the second term is the primary structuring position. The third term is a relatively simple notion of other.[9] The fourth term in this formulation is pure negation of negation: Not-not-ours. S4 here can be seen as purely empty, and below I will argue that the two S4s represent the primary empty signifiers being filled in the struggle for hegemony that Russian neo-Fascists are engaged in with the Russian state.

---

7   See also: http://www.rne.org; http://www.pamyat.ru and http://www.nbp-info.ru.
8   See the film "Bumer" (2001) for entertaining uses of *bezpredel*. Pamyat also describes the chaos of democracy as *bezpredel*.
9   It is possible that, depending on the particular version of *nash*, *ne-nash* could float between S2 and S3, represent both simultaneously, or at least, inform each.

Figure 2:

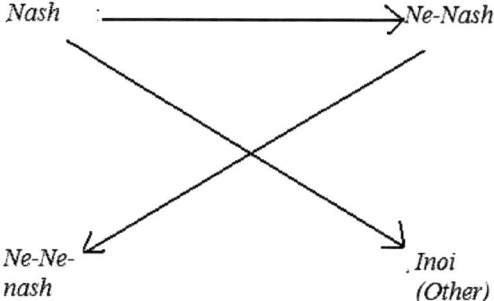

Laclau calls the process of creating equivalence out of difference "articulation" (2005). Articulatory projects, for Laclau, are the projects of both hegemony and populism. They are the attempts to create chains of equivalence and entail the projection of a version of the people based on those excluded from the people. It should be clear by this point that these two discursive aspects, which Laclau declares to be common to all political projects, are easily identified in the discourse of Russian neo-Fascism. Explicit definitions (and therefore, exclusions) abound in the discourse of neo-Fascism.

The project of hegemony, according to Laclau, "is the possibility that one difference, without ceasing to be a particular difference, assumes the representation of an incommensurable totality" (2005: 70). This is the point at which we can fully understand the significance of the empty signifier. "The hegemonic identity becomes something of the order of an empty signifier, its own particularity embodying an unachievable fullness" (ibid.: 71). This "difference" begins as a "social demand" (ibid.: 73), which moves into a chain with other demands, and in the process of articulation comes to signify the equivalence of these heterogeneous demands. That is to say, a hegemonic struggle is constructed around a particular signifier, or demand, which is employed to speak equivalence across a heterogeneous social field. This is done through the tensions that exist in the field of language introduced above: the fact that both difference and equivalence are central to the identity of a given demand (to the meaning of a given signifier). Articulating a hegemonic project, then, is the process of moving from each particularity toward an equivalence-in-tension. This cannot be done from the myriad particular signifiers, but rather involves a changing of the meaning (identity) of each. The semantic rectangle again becomes central to our understanding of this project.

If the project of articulating a hegemonic formation of Russian neo-Fascism involves the creation of equivalence among heterogeneous demands, it implies changing the identities of these demands. From the point of view of the semantic rectangles, this involves moving beyond the various S1s of the particular signifiers toward a common signifier. This should be seen as moving from heterogeneous S1s to a common S4. S2 and S3 are unavailable to the project of articulation because they mark the more (S2) or less (S3) radical opposites and negations of each S1. S4, on the other hand, is the relatively available negation of the negations of S1. Articulating a neo-Fascist hegemony, then, involves one S1, the master signifier, taking the place of each particular S1 in the field of demands (these can be the various claims of each particular group on the field) and simultaneously shifting its meaning, and thus the meanings of the system of S1s.

I hypothesised above that the master signifier on the field of Russian neo-Fascism is *poriadok*. If this is true, then the project of hegemony implies *poriadok*, in some form, taking over as the point of equivalence. That is to say, something within the signification process of the meanings contained in the demand for social order will, through articulation, come to represent the equivalence of the heterogeneous demands of neo-Fascism. The nature of articulation, which requires each point in the chain of equivalence, as well as the master signifier itself, to be fundamentally altered, precludes the possibility of the link between *poriadok* and its clear signification of order. In other words, *poriadok* as S1 cannot create equivalence. As I noted in the preceding paragraph, *poriadok's* S2 and S3 are also precluded by the logic of signification. That leaves us with the space I left blank in the semantic rectangle of *poriadok* above. This S4, it seems, remains as the point of equivalence, the particularity that through articulation will come to signify equivalence in the chain of neo-Fascist hegemony. S4 in the *poriadok* rectangle also remains to be determined.

As S4 is essentially an open signifier insofar as it is the negation-of-negation, and can thus be filled, often, in several positive terms, any naming of S4 is essentially preliminary and partial. That being said, within the very structure of the discourse, the tales being told, we can identify a prominent version of the fourth term in the *poriadok* rectangle. Let us review: *poriadok* (order) is opposed to *bardak* (chaos) both semiotically and morally. In the discourse of neo-

Fascism, *bardak* signifies the evils of the chaotic established order. *Poriadok* is also not *bardak* (rule-lessness). Order in this rectangle signifies a rejection of the chaos of the powers that be (the established order). Where, in the discourse of neo-Fascism, do we find the narration of the rejection of order? In the tales of mischief.[10] Mischief is the rejection of order that the forces of *poriadok* enact in the tales they tell.[11] *Khuliganstvo* (mischief), then, appears as the S4 of *poriadok*. It is semantically linked to order as the negation of the opposite of S1.

Khuliganstvo,[12] then, is the not-anti order, when order is opposed to the established order. Mischief is the narrative rejection of the established order, which in our square is chaos. From this point of view, any particular demand that can be articulated into an aspect of a narrative of mischief-making can be seen as a potential point of equivalence in the chain of neo-Fascism. At this point, it may appear that the equivalential chain of neo-Fascism is open enough to be able to create equivalence wherever tales of mischief-making are a prominent component of a political discourse. This conclusion, however, would be misleading.

Khuliganstvo, or mischief, can also be mapped onto the semantic rectangle of *nash*, insofar as the making of mischief can be seen as acting against the *ne-nash* of the version of *nash* posited by neo-Fascist discourse. The *ne-nash*, of course, represents all parties outside of the shared *us* of neo-Fascism. Active struggle against them represents the position of S4, and can also be conceptualised as articulated in the tales of mischief identified in neo-Fascist discourse.[13] Inherent in the assumptions made above regarding the particular natures of these two S1s (*poriadok* and *narod/nash*) are particular assumptions regarding

---

10 Nancy Ries noted that litanies and tales of mischief provide conversational methods of identity construction and negotiation in Russia (1997). She suggested that litany and mischief represent feminine and masculine modes of speech. Tales of mischief come to represent a potent linguistic method for marking both difference and opposition for Russian men. Furthermore, fighting is a common aspect of tales of mischief. "Tales of drinking, brawling, and sexual wildness" are the core of the narratives of mischief (ibid.: 65).

11 The irony of a valorisation of mischief for the demanders of order should not be lost on the reader.

12 My thanks to Nancy Ries for her suggestion of this term, which is the way her respondents refer to their own activities, and the way she translates "mischief" back into Russian for the recent translation of her *Russian Talk* (2005). Ries also noted that *khuliganstvo* carries with it an *ordered* mischief. Personal communication.

13 The NBP seems, at this point in my analysis, to be the group, and the discourse, that most fully articulates these meanings, and most clearly embodies the narrative and discursive structure of these modes of signification.

the projected version of *us*, and thus of the people. It is to the role of the people in political projects that we now turn.

Narod, floating signifiers, and Populist Reason

In his recent work, Laclau extends his theories of hegemony and equivalence a step beyond hegemony and into the realm of populist reason (2005). In *On Populist Reason*, he argues that a particular definition of the people that both includes heterogeneous elements and excludes other versions is central to any hegemonic project, and thus any political articulation.

> "On the one hand, all social (that is, discursive) identity is constituted at the meeting point of difference and equivalence [...] a certain identity is picked up from the whole field of differences, and made to embody this totalizing function [...] in the case of populism: a frontier of exclusion divides society into two camps. The 'people' in that case, is something less than the totality of the members of the community: it is a partial component which nevertheless aspires to be conceived as the only legitimate totality." (Ibid.: 80f.)

That is to say, when combined with the notion of hegemony, the equivalential chain articulated by the particular demand standing in for the whole will contain within it a particular definition of the people that through its implications simultaneously defines the forces of the enemy as illegitimate versions of the people. Laclau argues that this takes place in a broken social space (ibid: 85). Insofar as demands attempt to fill a lack (most often, the lack of order),

> "the construction of the 'people' will be the attempt to give a name to that absent fullness. Without this initial breakdown of the social order – however minimal that something could initially be – there is no possibility of antagonism, frontier, or, ultimately, 'people'." (Ibid.)

Russia, from this perspective, seems to be the ideal space for positing the people, for the space of Russia is not only discursively divided, but following the collapse of the Soviet Union, and the ensuing tumult of the 1990s, seemed socially broken.[14]

Furthermore, the positing of opposing camps of the people and the people's enemies, "presupposes [...] the presence of some privileged signifiers

---

14 See for instance, Shevchenko 2002.

which condense in themselves the signification of a whole antagonistic camp" (ibid.: 87). It should not involve a cognitive leap, at this juncture, to see how *poriadok* (more importantly, mischief), has come to involve within it a particular version of the people (recall my discussion of *narod/natsiia* and *nash/ne nash*). It is felicitous that Laclau himself links order and the people in his discussion of populist reason.

> "In a situation of radical disorder, the demand is for some kind of order, and the concrete social arrangement that will meet that request is a secondary consideration [...]. The semantic role of these terms is not to express any positive content, but as we have seen, to function as the names of a fullness which is constitutively absent." (Ibid.: 96)

Order, then, should not be seen as a demand for any thing, but rather as the supplemental name of the people. Order carries with it a particular definition of the people, and stands in for a particular notion of *nash*, and thus, of *ne-nash*. This can be represented as a combination of the semantic rectangles of *poriadok* and *narod* (*nash*), as seen in Figure 3.

Figure 3:

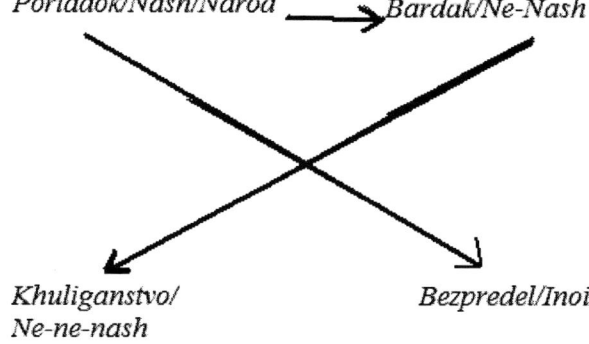

We can now suggest that it is not just any mischief-makers that can become points in the chain of equivalents of neo-Fascism, but only those that relate to, or can speak with the particular notion of the people that the *poriadok/nash/narod* triad carries with it. Also, in the same way that *khuliganstvo* becomes the face of equivalence in this chain, we reach the strange conclusion that, rather than a pure *nash* being the version of the people in the populist equivalence of neo-Fascism, the *ne-ne-nash* gains prominence. *Ne-anti-nash* can be seen as the oppositional identity par excellence in Russian politics, for it is truly open to speak for all those who are not representative of the *ne-nash*, the perpetuators of *bardak*; the powers that be. It is the pure negation of the negation of the people. In this way, we can suggest that neo-Fascism has completely consumed and occupies the only available position for real opposition in Russian politics, because of the various ways in which the Russian state has arrested the possibility of "normal" politics.[15]

Evidence backs this conclusion up. The oppositions found in neo-Fascist texts posit pure rejections of all those associated with the current state of affairs: the Jews, the democrats, the state, the inactive population, all non-Orthodox Christians, all non-Slavs, etc. These oppositions, paired with the internal nature of the tales being told, and the symbols being utilised, signal a pure rejection of all aspects of the current order. They carry with them a radical version of the people as pure, active, and committed (which is also a full rejection of most Russians). They represent the *ne-anti-nash* so completely it is astounding. Nevertheless, these discourses carry with them the only current political option for opposition to the state: the pure rejection of all that the state stands for, which simultaneously posits a version of the people that most could access, or identify with.

Poriadok and *nash* (and by extension, *narod*), however, represent not only empty signifiers in the populist project of neo-Fascism, but floating signifiers being struggled over on the discursive field (the social, albeit broken, order). They are not only the master signifiers for Russian neo-Fascism, but also the key signifiers in the discursive struggles of Russian politics in which the neo-Fascists take place. The major opponent in this struggle is, of course, the Russian state. Before describing the actual struggle over these signifiers, let us outline Laclau's theory of the floating signifier.

A signifier can be said to be floating insofar as it is the master signifier for more than one hegemonic bloc, whose meaning is subject to contention among these positions. Master signifiers (versions of the demands that come to stand

---

15 By "normal", I refer here to the politics of political science and civil society. "Normal" opposition takes place, so the story goes, in civil society through non-state actors, political parties, lobbies, and "normal" processes of interest politics and legislation. None of these take place independently of the state in Russia.

for totalities, with their particular definitions of the people) are not owned exclusively by one equivalential bloc, but rather are struggled over; they can come to be "articulated to entirely differential links" and "in that case the same [...] demands receive the structural pressure of rival hegemonic projects" (ibid.: 131). That is to say, these signifiers become representative of (at least) two differing equivalential chains. Furthermore, because every positing of a political project requires, on the one hand, the attempt to create a hegemonic formulation (where one demand takes the place of a totality of demands), and, on the other, the positing of a particular version of the people, floating signifiers represent the site of all political struggles. These struggles will always be over a particular signifier (standing in for the whole) and involve radically opposed versions of the people.

> "Does this mean that the political become synonymous with populism? Yes [...] since the construction of the 'people' is the political act par excellence [...] which involves, as we know, the production of empty signifiers in order to unify a multiplicity of heterogeneous demands in equivalential chains [...] there is no political intervention that is not populistic to some extent." (Ibid.:154)

The discursive struggles of neo-Fascists can therefore be seen as populist and based on the struggle over the meaning of order and the particular conception of the people that this meaning carries with it. *Poriadok* and *nashi* are, therefore, the points of political struggle in the discourse of neo-Fascism, and the state is the major opponent in these struggles.

Vladimir Putin's regime promised to bring order to Russia. This involves a particular definition of order as a reduction of the chaos involved in semi-democratic politics and bandit capitalism. Putin's Kremlin projects a version of order that is much different than that of the neo-Fascists, and carries with it a radically different definition of the people. Naming the Kremlin's youth movement (which is supposedly anti-Fascist at that[16]) *Nashi* signifies the Kremlin's attempt to re-define *ours* (the people). This is the state's attempt to fix the floating signifier order and its attendant version of the people in ways that serve its particular articulated equivalence. The struggle over *order* and *ours* is that between two hegemonic blocs: The state and neo-Fascists.

---

16 See: "Democratic, anti-fascist youth movement: Nashi", http://www.nashi.su, accessed 21 May 2006.

It is not within the scope of this work to make predictions regarding the outcome of this populist struggle. However, let me suggest that insofar as neo-Fascists and youth extremist discourses are able to project a version of the people through its supplement order, and its narrative mode, mischief-making, that makes sense to Russians in an atmosphere of social disintegration (*bardak*!), they do, indeed, present a credible and potentially powerful alternative to the discourse of the Kremlin.

Furthermore, as Yuri Lotman demonstrates in his *The Semiotics of Russian Culture*, the specific structure of discourse in Russia is that change occurs through the radical replacement of the present with inverted forms of the past (1984). This is an aspect that Urban has taken from Lotman's work, calling it the "binary structure of representations" in Russian culture (2006: 5). This binary structure requires, for things to mean, that they represent radical replacements of the other term. We can identify neo-Fascist discourses, and the semantic rectangles introduced above, as clear examples of this binary structure. The binary structure of representation, then, should be read into, and be read as an integral part of, the struggles for hegemony that the competing populist formations are engaged in. Finally, these nationalist versions of political identity, we-articulation, and empire are by no means limited to the rightist fringe. Rather, they are particular expressions of a growing trend in even the most mainstream political discourses to highlight a desired return to Great Russian empire status (Rumer 2005: 47). This is intimately tied to a mythical heroic past, and the lived memory of the "great power" of Soviet Russia.

Conclusion

By examining the semiotic work of the NBP and other Russian neo-Fascist and youth extremist movements, we can now conceptualise how groups that might sometimes be considered merely disruptive (at best) can actually be seen as posing one of the most important non-institutional challenges to the current arrangements of hegemonic codes and institutional configurations in today's Russia. Furthermore, we can now understand how deepening an analysis of the process of signification can add to Laclau's theories of articulation and how this combination can further the study of the work of social movements engaging in discursive struggles.

In concluding this article, several ironies must be highlighted. I have suggested above that the equivalential face of a neo-Fascist populist formation will be one that appears as a mischief-based version of order, which articulates *poriadok* as *khuliganstvo*. This appears counter-intuitive. I am arguing that mischief is the narrative and semiotic mode of a version of order that is creating equivalence in neo-Fascist discourses. Furthermore, the chaos that these versions of order oppose represent the forces of social order: the Russian state and its organs. I have, as of yet, neglected to note that in the process of creating a populist formation, each particular discourse (and therefore the group that espouses it) undergoes change. Furthermore, it follows that a particular political identity (group) must come to represent the whole of differential groups. Several years ago, it seemed that the NBP, insofar as its narrative mode of communication and the openness of its symbols can embody the myriad particular identities of groups (from ultra-nationalist and neo-Nazi to radical-Communist) under the rubric of mischief/order (*khuliganstvo/poriadok*), had great potential to become the party of equivalence in Russian youth extremism, and opposition politics in general.[17]

This can also be represented in a semantic rectangle where the differential S1s (in this instance, S1=organisation) are articulated as a single S4. Until June 2007, it seemed that the NBP had great potential to become this S4, a populist articulation that may be able to achieve some sort of alternative, or anti-hegemony. Who, if anyone, will next take up the mantle of making mischief into a potentially hegemonic challenge to order remains to be seen.

Bibliography

Bowden, Z.A. 2008. "Poriadok and Bardak (Order and Chaos): The neo-fascist project of articulating a Russian 'People'". *Journal of Language and Politics* 7, 2. 321–347.

Caldwell, M.L. 2002. "The Taste of Nationalism: Food Politics in Post Socialist Moscow". *Ethnos* 67, 3. 295-319.

---

17 It could be argued that their combination of such contradictory, indeed oppositional, political discourses, symbols, and programs is an explicit attempt to draw such equivalences. Much of my interview data backs this up, as I have been told of NBP efforts to attract and recruit both Nazi-Skins and anarchist punks.

Cheles, L., R. Ferguson, and M. Vaughan, eds. 1991. *Neo-Fascism in Europe.* London: Longman.

Greimas, A. 1984. *Structural Semantics.* Lincoln: University of Nebraska.

Holmes, D.R. 2000. *Integral Europe: Fast-Capitalism, Multiculturalism, Neofascism.* Princeton: Princeton University Press.

Jameson, F. 1972. *The Prison-House of Language.* Princeton: Princeton University Press.

Kaplan, J. and L. Weinberg, eds. 1998. *The Emergence of a Euro-American Radical Right.* London: Rutgers.

Laclau, E. 2005. *On Populist Reason.* London: Verso.

——— 1996. "Why Do Empty Signifiers Matter for Politics?" In: Emancipation(s). 36-46. London: Verso.

Likhachev, V. 2002. *Nacizm v Rossii.* Moscow: Panorama.

Lotman, Yu. and B. Uspenskii. 1985. "Binary Models in the Dynamics of Russian Culture". In *Semiotics of Russian Culture: Essays*, edited by Y. Lotman, L.I. Ginsburg, and B. Uspenskii. 30-66. Ithaca: Cornell.

Lotman, Yu. 1990. *Universe of the Mind: A Semiotic Theory of Culture.* London: I.B. Tauris.

Melucci, A. 1996. *Challenging Codes: Collective Action in the Information Age.* Cambridge: Cambridge University Press.

Merkl, P.H. and L. Weinberg. 1997. *The Revival of Right-Wing Extremism in the Nineties.* London: Frank Cass.

Nazpary, J. 2002. *Post-Soviet Chaos: Violence and Dispossession in Kazakhstan.* London: Pluto Press.

Ries, N. 1997. *Russian Talk: Culture and Conversation During Perestroika.* Ithaca: Cornell.

Rumer, B., ed. 2005. *Central Asia at the End of Transition.* Armonk: M.E. Sharpe.

Schreck, C. 2006. "Websites Under Scrutiny After Wake of Extremist Acts". *Saint Petersburg Times* 2 May. http://www.sptimes.ru/index.php?action_id=2&story_id=17489 [accessed 2 September 2009].

Shevchenko, O. 2002. "'Between the Holes': Emerging Identities and Hybrid Patterns of Consumption in Post-Socialist Russia." *Europe-Asia Studies* 54, 6. 846-866.

Tishkov, V. 2004. *Chechnya: Life in a War-Torn Society.* Berkeley: UC Press.

Urban, M. 2006. "Post-Soviet Political Discourse and the Creation of Political Communities". In *Lotman and Cultural Studies*, edited by A. Schonle and A. Malkinger, 115-135. Madison: University of Wisconsin.

―――― 1996. "Stages of Political Identity Formation in Late Soviet and Post-Soviet Russia". In *Identities in Transition*, edited by V. Bonnel. Berkeley: International and Area Studies.

Websites

"Fight Club 88 Moscow, Outlaw Hammerskins".
http://www.outlawhammerskins.info.
Pamyat. http://www.pamyat.ru.
Nashi. http://www.nashi.su.
National Bolshevik Party. http://www.nbp-info.ru.
Ruskoe Natsionalnoe Edinstvo (RNE). http://www.rne.org.
The Freedom Party. http://svobodarus.ru/artikl/patrul.htm.

IV Symbols and the Past

The Symbolic Politics of the Putin Administration

Ivan Kurilla

This article deals with the use of symbols by the Putin administration and its deliberate strategy of creating a new national identity as part of the re-articulation of a hegemonic discourse in the Russia of the 2000s. After a decade of dislocation and state neglect of the symbolic universe, Putin started his presidency by shaping Russian identity according to his own preferences – and many Russians agreed with his approach, while others simply preferred any fixation of identity over the symbolic chaos and uncertainty. On his way towards achieving that goal, Putin's moves included establishing state control over TV and history textbooks, and frequent appeals to the memory of the Second World War and especially the victory in Stalingrad, while avoiding the use of symbols with great potential for controversy (such as the rehabilitation of Cossack ataman and Nazi collaborator Pyotr Krasnov, renaming Volgograd "Stalingrad", or returning the statue of Dzerzhinsky to Lubyanka Square).

In their seminal work *Hegemony and Socialist Strategy*, Ernesto Laclau and Chantal Mouffe (Laclau and Mouffe 1985) offered an analytical framework that is increasingly used in contemporary social science. However, it has only recently started to be applied to the dynamics of Russian politics (See, for instance, Morozov 2009, esp. 431-445). This approach is particularly suited for analysing the period of change from the perestroika era of the late 1980s until the recent "stabilisation" under President Vladimir Putin. This approach allows us to theorise Russian political discourse, in which some Soviet elements were maintained, outlasted the Yeltsin period, and emerged anew quite recently under Vladimir Putin: Discourse theory would frame this process as the *dislocation* of a hegemonic discourse, followed by hegemonic struggles and the renegotiation of values and symbols, eventually resulting in a new hegemonic discourse. The major tool for reconstructing national identity was a renewal of the symbolic universe. In this article, we will analyse the use of symbols by the Putin administration and its deliberate strategy of creating a new national identity as part of the re-articulation of a hegemonic discourse in Russia. The demand for the articulation of a new symbolic landscape was present by the late 1990s in many competing discourses; however, it was Vladimir Putin who became the voice of the new approach and reaped the benefits of its introduction.

How it happened

During the first years after the collapse of the Soviet Union, the administration of then-Russian president Boris Yeltsin attributed little or no value to the old symbols of Russian national pride. The only symbolism Yeltsin introduced was an attempt to restore the legitimacy of the pre-revolutionary Russian political heritage by using the tri-coloured Russian flag instead of the Soviet red banner. However, liberal ideology as Yeltsin's advisers understood it had nothing to do with the symbols of the Soviet past. The revolutionary wave that Yeltsin rode destroyed those symbols, crushed monuments, and changed city and street names. Such policies permitted oppositional political and economic forces to rally around a programme of saving Russia's historical identity. In the terminology used by Laclau and Mouffe, the political situation in Russia created by the reforms would be referred to as a situation of *antagonism*, when "the world divides, through a system of paratactical equivalences, into two camps" (Laclau and Mouffe 1985: 129). Moreover, the forces opposed to Yeltsin's reforms appropriated some of the major symbols of national pride and thereby took the political initiative away from the authorities.

Vladimir Putin brought a significantly different attitude to the Kremlin. His advisor Gleb Pavlovsky was famous for his ability to use political symbols for the president's benefit. Today, as the period of revolutionary activity has turned into a period of stabilisation, the Putin administration's most impressive achievements lie in the sphere of symbolic politics.

Putin started his presidency by shaping Russian identity according to his own preferences – and many Russians agreed with his worldview, while others simply preferred any fixation of identity to symbolic chaos and uncertainty. We do not mean to give the second Russian president too much credit for the fixation of this identity; however, he managed to turn the presidency into the symbolic centre of power on the Russian political stage.

During the first two years of his presidency, Putin succeeded in creating the base for a new Russian identity in a new symbolic landscape. Some of the most important steps were: the exiling of former media magnates Boris Berezovsky and Vladimir Gusinsky (who controlled, respectively, the First Channel and NTV) and a drastic change of the political positions of these TV stations; the legislation to re-introduce the old Soviet anthem with slightly updated lyrics; and a return to tsarist state symbols such as the double-headed eagle. Those were the first visible signs of the Putin administration's efforts to appropriate previously *floating signifiers* and thereby to reshuffle the symbolic space.[1]

Since that time, Putin's team has been steadily increasing its hold on all significant symbols of the Russian past. This applies particularly to the victory in the Great Patriotic War – the universally recognised reference point for all Russians. Thus, Putin devoted special attention to appropriating this part of the symbolic space, including the Battle of Stalingrad.

"Stalingrad": a short history

The following analysis will begin with Putin's attitude to Stalingrad/Volgograd. It is an important city in Russian politics. Not only is it valued for its economic role and the activities of local elites, but it is also very important symbolically. The city was founded in 1589 as Tsaritsyn, a fortress and trading post on the Volga River. The name Tsaritsyn was derived from the Tartar language, but in Russian, it sounded like its root had evolved from the title of a tsar's wife, "tsaritsa". Not surprisingly, the Bolsheviks renamed the city "Stalingrad" in 1925, in remembrance of Joseph Stalin's role in the Red Army during the Russian Civil War battles that took place nearby.

But the city is most famous for the role it played in World War II. In 1942–43, the Battle of Stalingrad was fiercely waged in the streets of the city and its immediate vicinity. Indeed, it was in part the symbolic importance of Stalingrad that compelled Hitler to press for its conquest, and that led Stalin to issue his famous command to the Red Army "not one step back" to prevent the Soviet city from falling to the Germans. The battle, in terms of its scope, importance, and

---

[1] "It is not the poverty of signifieds but, on the contrary, polysemy that disarticulates a discursive structure. That is what establishes the overdetermined, symbolic dimension of every social identity" (Laclau and Mouffe 1985: 113).

casualties on both sides, was the greatest battle in history. The hard-fought Soviet victory was the turning point in the fight against Nazi Germany. For the Soviet Union, the battle of Stalingrad was the first major victory after months of defence and retreat.

During the de-Stalinisation campaign, launched by Nikita Khrushchev, Stalingrad's name was changed again. Khrushchev did not restore the city's tsarist name. The city was rechristened Volgograd, meaning simply "city on the Volga". The numerous portraits and statues of Stalin were removed from their pedestals. The huge bronze statue of the former leader above the first lock of the Volga-Don ship canal made way for a concrete Lenin statue that was only half as large.

In the 1960s and 1970s, Volgograd continued to be a place of pilgrimage for foreign leaders – from Fidel Castro to Charles de Gaulle. Under Leonid Brezhnev, a war veteran himself, victory in the Great Patriotic War became a central source of legitimacy for the Soviet regime. It became a *nodal point* in Soviet discourse. As part of this program, Volgograd was proclaimed a "hero city", along with five other Soviet cities. Such a title had been in use since 1945, but the Supreme Soviet only made it an official honorary title on 8 May 1965. By 1967, the memorial designed by the sculptor Evgeny Vuchetich had been built on Mamayev Kurgan in Volgograd, crowned with the huge Statue of Mother Russia. Brezhnev visited the opening of the memorial on 8 November 1967 and delivered a speech he had prepared with the help of the famous Soviet poet Konstantin Simonov. There is an often-told story about the preparation of the speech that is, however, not confirmed by the participants themselves: Allegedly, Brezhnev told Simonov that people only needed to hear one truth about the war: "The main truth was that we won the Victory" (see, for instance, Kolesnikov, 2008). Many veterans, however, considered the speech one of Brezhnev's best.

In the late Brezhnev era, regional party leaders considered restoring Stalin's name to the city. They hoped that "Stalingrad" would be a more important city on the Soviet map than "Volgograd", but the last such attempt (timed to coincide with the 40th anniversary of the victory in May 1985) was refused by the new CPSU Secretary General Mikhail Gorbachev.

In the 1990s, the Yeltsin administration paid little attention to the city. As a result, "Stalingrad" became a rallying cry for the "patriotic" and Communist opposition. From their point of view, the westernisation of Russia had to be stopped in the same way the Nazi invaders had been turned back at Stalingrad.

Opposition leaders from across the country annually converged in Volgograd on 2 February (the last day of the Battle of Stalingrad). In February 1993 – the 50th anniversary of the Stalingrad victory – the residents of Volgograd witnessed a huge rally led by politicians from across the opposition spectrum, ranging from orthodox Communists to nationalist extremists. The government did not participate in the celebration. At the time, Yeltsin officials seemed afraid of visiting a city occupied by the "National-Patriotic" forces. It was there that the opposition called for a "second Battle of Stalingrad" to be fought against President Yeltsin and his reformist team, associating the administration with the Nazi invaders of 50 years earlier. Six months later, those who had met in Volgograd led the anti-Yeltsin coup that resulted in the October 1993 violence in Moscow.

Perhaps beginning to realise the power of symbols, the presidential administration stepped up its efforts to gain the support of a larger segment of the "patriotic" field. The problems that the reformist government faced in view of the protests against a rapidly decreasing standard of living in the early 1990s were connected with the identity crisis of the Russian people. On the other hand, the opposition succeeded in constructing a symbolic universe.

It was not until Yeltsin's campaign for re-election in 1996 that his advisors, seeking to win public support, paid more attention to popular attitudes and included Volgograd in the presidential program. His campaign stop on Victory Day, 9 May 1996, was in Volgograd. The Russian president was met with great warmth by the population of Volgograd, who crowded around the Central Embankment, the traditional place for celebrations and meetings. He had ample company, as candidates from across the political spectrum – including Mikhail Gorbachev, Gennady Zyuganov, and Alexander Lebed – also chose Victory Day to converge on the city. Even the president of Belarus, Alexander Lukashenko, who considered himself a major player in the Russian political field, frequently visited Volgograd. After the election campaign of 1996, the Yeltsin team called on scholars and PR agents to invent a new "national idea" to fill the ideological vacuum of the new political system. It was not successful. The attempt to wrest the patriotic symbols from the opposition was too little, too late.

"Stalingrad" and the Putin administration

Yeltsin's government had missed its chance. Putin's did not. He started his presidential campaign by catering to the electorate of the "patriotic" opposition. As acting president, Putin visited Volgograd on 22 February 2000, on the eve of a Russian military holiday, to make a patriotic appearance. The official reason for his visit was a conference on social security services for military personnel. However, Putin started by attending the Mamayev Kurgan war memorial, laid a wreath on the grave of the Unknown Soldier and the bed of honour, met war veterans, and visited regional veterans' hospitals. Putin left a few lines in the guest book on Mamayev Kurgan:

> "During a visit to places like Mamayev Kurgan, one's breath is taken away by sorrow and, at the same time, by the greatness of our Fatherland. Special words of gratitude go to the veterans of the Great Patriotic war, and the participants of the Battle of Stalingrad. A deep bow to Volgograd residents who keep sacred the memory of the fallen defenders of our Motherland." (Prezident Rossii 2002a)

Since that time, Putin has visited Volgograd almost every year, either on 2 February (the date of the German surrender in Stalingrad) or on other patriotic holidays. In February 2003, on the 60th anniversary of the Battle of Stalingrad, he took part in the celebrations. Putin emphasised the importance of the event, concluding with words of praise to veterans:

> "By their lives they reaffirmed that our country was always good at defending itself, and good at uniting against common trouble and for big common work; that our people's union, our century-long victorious tradition is the most valuable and precious heritage that you leave to your descendants. It will be passed on from one generation to another." (Putin 2003a).

When Putin visited Volgograd on 19 February 2007 to lead a State Council conference on the military-industrial complex, he did not mention the war victory, but the place, month, and topic were chosen to link everything in one (Prezident Rossii 2007). In 2008, however, 2 February was celebrated without Putin. He sent Dmitry Medvedev to Volgograd.

Vladimir Putin was so successful in linking his personality to the politically powerful symbol of the victory in Stalingrad that even the semi-official hymn of the youth organisations supporting "United Russia" (*Nashi, Molodaia Gvardiia Edinoi Rossii, Rossiia molodaia*), the song "A v chistom pole" ("In the Open Field") by the pop group "Belii Orël" (White Eagle), includes a line that combines everything "great": "There is a Grad system in the open field, Putin and Stalingrad are behind us!"[2]

Other patriotic symbols of war memory are also appropriated by the state, even if they emerged from a grassroots movement. Such has been the case with the ribbons of the St. George Cross. The latter stems from tsarist times, but it was also used as part of the Soviet Order of Glory and as a symbol of the elite Guards regiments. On Victory Day in 2005, people began to decorate their cars and clothes with St. George ribbons in order to display their patriotism and respect for the veterans. Two years later, it was already state-controlled TV that urged people to use the ribbon of St. George for the same purpose. Vladimir Putin himself appeared on that day wearing the ribbon.

Clash of symbols

Although the personality of Vladimir Putin is very influential in fixing the significance of major symbols, some continue to have multiple meanings, and are used by competing discourses. The Volgograd region was situated at the epicentre of such a clash.

This region was historically divided into diverse territories inhabited by Don Cossacks, Volga Germans, Russians, Ukrainians, and other peoples. That is why regional identity construction was a very complicated task. Nationwide "umbrella" identities are much easier to accept for such a diverse population. Cossack influence in the region is especially strong; even most of the employees at the Regional Committee on Nationalities and Cossacks Affairs wear Cossack paramilitary uniform. That is why a recent initiative of Don Cossack leaders caused much commotion in Volgograd.

In the winter of 2007/08, Don Cossack officials residing in Rostov demanded the rehabilitation of Ataman Pyotr Krasnov, a Cossack leader in the Civil War. Such a claim would have been considered legitimate in the course of national reconciliation after the Civil War. However, Krasnov was not just a White general; he later allied himself with the Germans during the Nazi invasion of the USSR and was hanged in 1946 as a war criminal.

In this case, the name of Ataman Krasnov served not just as a pre-Revolutionary symbol, but as a part of a regional discourse juxtaposed to the

---

2 "A v chistom pole sistema Grad, / Za nami Putin i Stalingrad!" "Sistema Grad" refers to the Grad multiple rocket launcher. For details about the song: "A v chistom pole", see: http://dic.academic.ru/dic.nsf/ruwiki/469251.

"national" one. Some Cossack leaders claimed (based on the rehabilitation of the Ukrainian national leaders Stepan Bandera and Roman Shukhevych) that Krasnov had fought for a Cossack "nation" against Russian "occupants". Such a clash of symbols strongly resonated in Volgograd: The regional identity contains strong Cossack elements (although fewer than neighbouring Rostov-on-Don), but also deeply patriotic and anti-Nazi ones. In the clash between symbols, the more Russian "patriotic" theme prevailed. It was, however, not the nationwide indignation, but the personal intervention of the president (who flew to Rostov to meet with the initiators of the idea) that forced Cossacks to repudiate the move (Kislitsyn 2008: 80).

After having established control over TV channels, the Putin administration aimed "to fix" history school textbooks. Learning about history is an important step in the socialisation of school children; it helps to establish the symbolic universe in which the child will live. Which figure is a symbol of heroism? Who is a "traitor"? If our analysis ignored this kind of symbolism, it would be hard to understand the arguments between Russian and Ukrainians about many personages of their common history, or to gauge the meaning of the debates over Stalin or Krasnov. "Who owns history?" – in the words of the prominent historian Eric Foner – is an urgent question in contemporary Russia (Foner 2002). Putin first began to pay attention to the problem of "right" and "wrong" textbooks after his visit to Volgograd in 2003. The day after the celebration of the 60th anniversary of the Stalingrad victory, he connected his meetings with veterans to the demand to check history textbooks: "Yesterday, as you know", Putin started his meeting with members of government, "I was in Volgograd, due to the 60th anniversary of victory in Stalingrad, and practically during every meeting with veterans the question was raised about teaching history in our schools, about the content of our teaching texts" (Putin 2003b).

From that moment on, the Russian state tried to regain control over historical narratives. War descriptions were not the only new subject of inquiry. The first victim of the struggle was a textbook by Igor Dolutsky that challenged high school pupils with a provocative assessment of Putin's regime by two oppositional figures (Dolutsky 2002). The textbook was excluded by the Ministry of Education from a list of recommended reading and disappeared from the classrooms.

In 2007, President Putin endorsed a school textbook that provided pupils with the emerging "official" view of recent Russian history. The main idea of the book (Danilov, Filippov, Utkin 2007) was to eliminate the harsh critique of the regimes that existed in Russia and the Soviet Union in the 20th century. Any critical assessment is "counterbalanced" with a list of the country's achievements during the same period. Putin and his associates have since repeated the idea that, in order to form the patriotic consciousness of the country, a heroic version of history needs to be taught in schools, and all dark pages of the national past need to be omitted from school texts. The move was criticised by parts of Russian society (including former Soviet President Mikhail Gorbachev). They saw government attempts to "explain" Stalin's policies as steps toward his vindication. However, the overarching demand, above and beyond the issue of Stalinism, was the elaboration of a common national identity by way of avoiding a discussion of the painful pages of the national past.

One of the problems the Russian authorities faced in this respect was the quick development of alternative versions of history in the neighbouring countries of the former Soviet Union, especially in Ukraine. Their system of symbolic references clearly contradicts the one that emerged in Russia. It is difficult to project the symbolic landscape of Putin's Russia abroad when Russia's neighbours are actively creating their own symbolical universes. Putin (and Medvedev after him) even put the shared history at the top of the agenda of Russian-Ukrainian relations, along with natural gas transit. However, the international clash of symbolic universes is a topic that deserves special attention (see Morozov in this volume).

Finally, Russian television showed several TV projects in 2008 that were aimed at constructing a pantheon of Russian heroes and Russian wonders. The project "Seven Wonders of Russia" ended on 12 June 2008; among the winners, along with natural wonders, were three historical monuments that represented three periods of Russian history: St. Basil's Cathedral (from the so-called Moscow, or Tsar epoch), the Petergof architectural ensemble (Petersburg, or Imperial period), and the Statue of Mother Russia in Volgograd (Soviet period). Another project aimed at selecting the most "important" people in Russian history: "Name of Russia" produced a scandal when the leading figure for several weeks of internet voting was Joseph Stalin. In the end, it produced a similar result as the project "Seven Wonders of Russia": the three top names represented the same three epochs – medieval prince and saint Alexander Nevsky; Pyotr Stolypin, an influential statesman of the early 20th century; and Joseph Stalin.[3]

Why did Putin not push through?
Many Russian politicians noticed the president's special attention to symbols. Aiming to win Putin's appreciation, Moscow mayor Yury Luzhkov in September 2002 suggested to return a statue of Cheka founder Felix Dzerzhinsky to Lubyanka Square. The removal of this statue, which was broadcast around the world, was a profound symbol of the dismantling of the Soviet regime. Returning the statue to its former pedestal would have been of equally high symbolic value. The arguments made in favour of Dzerzhinsky's return to Lubyanka Square included his role in helping street children, and his activity in the Russian High Economic Council. Furthermore, the monument's role as the architectural centre of the square was emphasised. However, all these factors have so far failed to outweigh the legacy of cruel fanaticism that placed him at the head of the Bolshevik secret police.

One of the other controversial issues concerning Soviet symbols was Volgograd governor Nikolay Maksyuta's suggestion in 2001 to restore the name of Stalin to his city. As mentioned above, the roots of this idea go back to the 1960s. In the early 1990s, though, the idea was proposed yet again, this time by "National-Patriots". They made common cause with leftist and veteran organisations, who supported the return of the name "Stalingrad" as a commemoration of the battle, not the Soviet leader.

In 1998, when then-deputy of the State Duma Alexander Vengerovsky (LDPR) proposed the idea of returning Stalin's name to Volgograd, no serious debates arose. Local polls demonstrated that the majority of Volgograd residents did not want to change the city's name. This proposal resembled Luzhkov's proposal to restore the monument to Dzerzhinsky in that it posed many of the same problems.

Symbols such as the Dzerzhinsky statue and "Stalingrad" are used within two competing discourses and may thus re-open antagonisms in society. For many Russians, renaming Volgograd as Stalingrad would be a celebration of the

---

3   All three individuals represented a statist tradition in Russian history, which was also celebrated on the eve of the Second World War when Alexander Nevsky was introduced into the contemporary pantheon with the motion picture "Alexander Nevsky" by Sergey Eisenstein (1938).

name of Joseph Stalin rather than that of the place of the decisive battle. Stalin was the head of the Soviet Union during the Great Patriotic War and during a time of "repression" of the Soviet people on a massive scale. There are two competing interpretations of the figure of Stalin in Russian society: the first tends to see him as a paranoid dictator who rivalled Adolf Hitler in his cruelty, while the other emphasises the achievements of the USSR during his leadership, plays down the scope of executions, and sees the Stalin period as a model for an efficient and incorrupt Russian state. Within the latter group, there are two different (although partially intersecting) sub-groups who support the idea of renaming Volgograd Stalingrad – "patriotic" forces including veterans, to whom Putin often panders, and pro-Stalin Communists. Liberal and democratic forces, not surprisingly, oppose the proposed renaming. Putin's approach, however, seemed to be based on providing a version of history that is acceptable to both camps. Thus, he avoids the use of symbols with a large controversial potential whenever possible.

Putin decided to change the plaque with the name "Volgograd" to "Stalingrad" near the Tomb of the Unknown Soldier in Alexanderovsky Park near the Kremlin in 2004. He responded in the negative, however, to a direct request to rename the city during the "Direct line with the President" show in December 2002. Putin answered as follows:

> "Certainly, the Stalingrad Battle has its place in the history of our Fatherland, and in world history as one of the brightest episodes of the Second World War. All of us are rightly proud of it. And, naturally, the question appears: why is there, say, in France, a Stalingrad Square, and here they were all of a sudden renamed? That question, of course, should be addressed not to us, not to me; it happened. I think that […] the return of the name Stalingrad today in our country (and we are not France) would give rise to some suspicions that we are returning to the times of Stalinism. I am not sure it would be beneficial to us. […] That problem should be settled by the local legislature, and the final decision must be taken by the State Duma. What I have no doubts about, what I am absolutely sure of is that we all should be proud of those people who won that victory at Stalingrad, as well as of those who won the victory near Leningrad at the Leningrad siege, as well as of all those who won us Victory in the Great Patriotic War. We are all in a great debt that we are unable to repay." (Prezident Rossii 2002b).

Putin refused to side with anybody, and at the same time used the opportunity to re-emphasise his devotion to the memory of the great Victory.

Conclusion

As the Russian journalist Yury Bogomolov put it, paraphrasing Vladimir Lenin, "present-day Russia is secular power plus semiotization of all the country" (Bogomolov 2008). The symbolic discourse on Russian identity is therefore of crucial importance.

Putin's presidency proved to everybody in the Russian political elite that the politics of symbols were the "real" politics. Putin's success as a politician was the result of a combination of favourable economic conditions and his skilful management of the symbolic universe.

However, as Laclau and Mouffe put it, "the more unstable the social relations, the less successful will be any definite system of differences and the more points of antagonism will proliferate. This proliferation will make more difficult the construction of any centrality and, consequently, the establishment of unified chains of equivalence" (Laclau and Mouffe 1985: 131).

The global economic crisis has already hit Russia and started to have negative political consequences for the ruling elites. Among other problems, it may damage all symbolic frames of reference created during the last decade. The change in political agenda under the new conditions could force the ruling elite to either emphasise different symbols that are currently existing in the shadow of the hegemonic discourse, or to side with one or another more radical variant of political symbolism. The first alternative was hinted at by a recent suggestion to make 19 February (the anniversary of the abolition of serfdom in 1861) the national holiday instead of 4 November (the day of the expulsion of Poles from the Kremlin in 1612). The second was promoted by some Communists, who advocated going further towards "rehabilitating" Stalin and renaming Volgograd Stalingrad. The new president, Dmitry Medvedev, is very cautiously trying to amend the legacy of his predecessor: One step in this direction was his meeting with the editor of the opposition newspaper *Novaia Gazeta*, Dmitry Muratov, in February 2009. His famous tautology "freedom is better than unfreedom" has been understood as a challenge to the purely statist attitude of Putin and was praised by liberals. However, Medvedev acts within the symbolic universe established in the previous period. He is thus obliged to refresh many of the appeals of that epoch. He develops the Patriotic war discourse further and instructs historians on how to teach it (Medvedev 2009; Prezident Rossii 2009).

Economic prosperity went hand in hand with the consolidation of national identity under Putin. The time has come to see whether the new Russian identity will be strong enough to withstand economic dislocations. We believe it will be difficult to battle the crisis efficiently without correcting some identity myths. This process is unlikely to topple the heroes in the textbooks and the symbols in the public sphere. Rather, it will reemphasise other elements of their significance. The Battle of Stalingrad itself may be potentially re-constructed in a less "statist" way by paying more attention to the sufferings of privates and local populations, and portraying the Victory as a people's victory achieved despite commanders' mistakes. Moreover, other "victories" could be elevated to the same level as those attained in wars: not just peaceful achievements in science and culture, but also victories of the people over its own past, as those achieved during the de-Stalinisation campaign. Thus, the polysemy of the set of signifieds in Russia could once again help to change the hegemonic discourse.

However, the current symbolic universe seems very firm, which leaves us with the more cautious expectation that it will be modestly embellished, rather than totally changed.

Bibliography

Bogomolov, Iu. 2008. "Samyi pervyi chelovek". *Gazeta.ru* 23 May 2008. http://www.gazeta.ru/comments/2008/05/22_a_2731729.shtml [accessed 28 February 2009].

Danilov, A., A. Filippov, and A. Utkin. 2007. *Istoriia Rossii, 1945-2007, 11 klass*. Moskva: Prosveshchenie.

Dolutsky, I.I. 2002. *Otechestvennaia istoria. XX vek. Uchebnik dlia 10-11 klassov obshcheobrazovatel'nykh uchrezhdenii. V 2 chastiakh*. 7th edition. Moscow: Mnemozina.

Foner, E. 2002. *Who Owns History? Rethinking the Past in a Changing World*. New York: Hill and Wang.

Kislitsyn, S.A. 2008. "O sootnoshenii rossiiskoi i regional'noi identichnosti v issledovaniiakh po istorii kraev i oblastei Rossiiskoi Federatsii". In *Istoriia kraia kak pole konstruirovaniia regional'noi identichnosti*, edited by I. Kurilla, 75-88. Volgograd: Volgograd University Press.

Kolesnikov, A. 2008. "Apelliaciia k VOVe". *Gazeta.ru* 5 February 2008. http://www.gazeta.ru/column/kolesnikov/2625484.shtml [accessed 28 February 2009].

Laclau, E. and C. Mouffe. 1985. *Hegemony and Socialist Strategy*. London: Verso.

Medvedev D. 2009. "Zakliuchitel'noe slovo na zasedanii rossiiskogo organizatsionnogo komiteta 'Pobeda'".http://www.kremlin.ru/appears/2009/01/27/2210_type63376type63378_212143.shtml [accessed 05 April 2009].

Morozov, V. 2009. *Rossiia i Drugie: identichnost' i granitsy politicheskogo soobshchestva*. Moscow: Novoe literaturnoe obozrenie.

Prezident Rossii. 2002a. "I.o. Prezidenta, prem'er-ministr Vladimir Putin posetil raspolozhennyi na Mamaevom kurgane pamiatnik-ansambl' 'Geroiam Stalingradskoi bitvy'". http://www.kremlin.ru/text/news/2000/02/121894.shtml [accessed 28 February 2009].

―――― 2002b. "Stenogramma priamogo tele- i radioefira ('Priamaia liniia s Prezidentom Rossii')".http://www.kremlin.ru/text/appears/2002/12/29647.shtml [accessed 28 February 2009].

―――― 2007. "Dossie sobytii". http://www.kremlin.ru/events/sched/2007/02/118615.shtml [accessed 28 February 2009].

―――― 2009. "Nachalo rabochei vstrechi s Ministrom obrazovaniia i nauki Andreem Fursenko". http://www.kremlin.ru/appears/2009/03/18/2006_type63378_214115.shtml [accessed 5 April 2009].

Putin, V. 2003a. "Vystuplenie na torzhestvennom zasedanii, posviashchennom 60-letiiu Stalingradskoi bitvy". http://www.kremlin.ru/appears/2003/02/02/0001_type122346_29750.shtml [accessed 28 February 2009].

―――― 2003b. "Vstupitel'noe slovo na soveshchanii s chlenami pravitel'stva". http://www.kremlin.ru/text/appears/2003/02/29751.shtml [accessed 28 February 2009].

An Old Myth for a New Society

Ivo Mijnssen

Myths are important moments in the construction of national identity. The devaluation of the Soviet myths has been a significant factor in the prolonged identity crisis of post-Soviet Russia. It was not until the presidency of Vladimir Putin that the Russian identity was stabilised to a certain extent: An important moment in this stabilisation was the renewed articulation and adaptation of a mythologised narrative of the Soviet victory in the Great Patriotic War. This chapter thus tracks the rise, fall, and re-emergence of this myth. The myth is seen as a discursive response to dislocations of the 1980s and 1990s in Russia. The myth articulates a unified and powerful Russian state that will prevail against all enemies – as it did in the past. Since the myth articulates these demands on the basis of the Soviet territory and its peoples, it also gives rise to controversies and is challenged from various sides – both inside and outside of Russia.

"Victory Day is the most important holiday": this is an often-heard statement in Russia – in the media, in the street, but also in academic circles. Doubtlessly, the anniversary of the victory in the Great Patriotic War[1] is and was a cornerstone of Soviet and post-Soviet national identity in Russia. Along with many others in Russia, president Vladimir Putin called Victory Day "a sacred day" in his speech on the 60th anniversary in 2005 (2008: 292). Pundits referred to it as "an eternal commemoration (*pamyat*) of those who [...] liberated Europe" (Iakovenko 2005: 4) and a "truly observed holiday" (Rossiiskaia Gazeta 2005a: 3). Scholars, while using a language that is less dramatic, agree in essence: Lev Gudkov points to the "sacred status" of the holiday as a symbol of collective identity (2005: 59). Boris Dubin cites a survey indicating that 86 percent of Russians consider 9 May the most important date of the year (2005: 1). Last but not least, Thomas Sherlock refers to the victory in the Great Patriotic War as a "foundation

---

1   The Great Patriotic War began with the German invasion of the Soviet Union on 22 June 1941 and ended with the Soviet victory of 9 May 1945.

myth" that provides the citizens of the Russian Federation with "a sense of unity and purpose" (2007: 166).

The dimensions of suffering – but also the relief that followed the unconditional German surrender on 8 May 1945 – are hard to gauge. This is reflected in the Russian political discourse about the war. Even today, it is still set in a "lyrical tone" (Gudkov 2005: 63). Victory has become a historical myth that official discourse has made use of in response to various dislocations in the last 60 years. It originated in the 1960s and collapsed in the 1980s and 1990s as a result of revelations about historical events – the Molotov-Ribbentrop Pact and mass repression, among others – that could not be articulated in the myth. In recent years, however, there have been attempts to rearticulate the myth of Victory and use it to strengthen Russian national identity. The official narrative maintains that the Soviet Union was the largely innocent victim of Nazi aggression. Under the leadership of the state, however, the Soviet people united without regard to nationality or political preferences to face and repel the German aggressor and thereby save the nation.

For analysts of contemporary political discourse in Russia, the paramount position of the Great Patriotic War provides a number of interesting starting points. Following Ernesto Laclau and Chantal Mouffe (2001), one could see the myth of Victory as one important discursive response to the dislocation that accompanied the collapse of the Soviet Union. It contains moments – elements that are articulated in a discourse – that make it possible to construct a specific kind of national identity and a vision of a strong Russian state with a distinct place in the world.

Theory and analytical strategy

Historical myths are powerful foundations of official discourses in particular and of collective identities in general. Lene Hansen sees national identities as being made up of spatial, temporal, and ethical moments (2006: 37). A historical myth can contain all three: Sherlock defines it as "a narrative of past events that gives them special significance for the present and the future" (2007: 3). The myth links various temporal levels in "a single symbolic universe" (ibid.). The retelling of historical happenings of great national importance creates a legitimising genealogy in which the identities of "the people" or "the state" are grounded. Often, these mythological narratives show how a certain type of social order – often the presently dominant one – arose out of the struggles of the past. Rather than incorporating various viewpoints, these narratives idealise the "deeds" of one national community and leave out elements that can subvert this image. A historical myth thus provides a kind of certainty and imaginary unity, particularly in times that are perceived as unstable or difficult. A myth can become a discursive moment that is "above politics" or even "sacred" and thus unassailable or at least difficult to challenge (Torfing 1999: 123).

Laclau's conception of the myth is somewhat broader. He sees a myth as a discursive, hegemonic response to structural dislocation (Laclau 1990: 61). Both he and Mouffe reject the idea of essential social identities. The latter are always constructed within a discourse:[2] Discourses are symbolic attempts to "suture" the social space through the establishment of a symbolic order, articulated around a number of nodal points.[3] If these attempts are successful, a stable, or *hegemonic*, discourse is established.[4]

However, no articulatory practice is complete, and no hegemonic discourse manages to articulate all the elements into moments because it only partially fixes meanings. The discourse tries to arrest the play of differences and fix the various moments of a discourse in a chain of equivalence, which simplifies the social and political space (ibid.: 97) and distinguishes between those that are part of a community and those that are not. Every identity has to define itself in opposition to something – a *constitutive other* – that cannot be articulated within the hegemonic discourse. This *constitutive other* is the basis of every identity, but at the same time threatens to destroy it by undermining its claim to universality.

According to Laclau and Mouffe, there exists "a vast area of floating elements and the possibility of their articulation to opposite camps" (2001: 136). The struggle to articulate these *floating signifiers*[5] is never finished. If they become too numerous, the discourse collapses (Laclau/Mouffe 2001: 113). The "disruption of the symbolic order by events that cannot be represented or do-

---

2   The two authors define discourse as a "system of differences" in which identities are articulated. For details, cf. Laclau/Mouffe 2001: 105.
3   "Any discourse is constituted as an attempt to dominate the field of discursivity, to arrest the flow of differences, to construct a centre. We will call the privileged discursive points of this partial fixation, *nodal points* […], privileged signifiers that fix the meaning of a signifying chain" (ibid.: 112).
4   Such a discourse establishes certain "norms, values, views and perceptions through persuasive redescription of the world" (Torfing 1999: 302).
5   "The status of the 'elements' is that of floating signifiers, incapable of being wholly articulated to a discursive chain" (Laclau/Mouffe 2001: 113).

mesticated" (Torfing 1999: 53) leads to a "dislocation" of the order. The latter will be followed by renewed attempts at "suturing" the social space.

This "suturing" involves signifiers that are "overdetermined" – they represent something beyond themselves. At this point, the myth plays an important role: It becomes a metaphor for a specific demand, or, alternatively, even for a fullness that is absent from any discourse:

> "[a]ny frustration or unsatisfied demand will be compensated for or offset by the myth of an achieved fullness. This indetermination of myth – as the means of expression by which specific dislocations might be overcome – is a direct consequence of its metaphorical nature, of the possibility it opens for the expression of the form of fullness itself, beyond any concrete dislocation. This means that myth functions as a surface on which dislocations and social demands can be inscribed." (Laclau 1990: 63)

While a myth often arises in reaction to a specific – economic, social, or cultural – dislocation, its metaphorical nature leaves open the possibility of it becoming something larger.[6] If a myth is dislodged from any concrete demand, it turns into a "social imaginary", an "unlimited horizon of inscription of any social demand and any possible dislocation" (ibid.: 64). A social imaginary is pure positivity, the inverted image of any possible dislocation. The myth is then a space of representation that is located on a different discursive "plane": it is presented "as an alternative to the logical form of the dominant structural discourse" (Laclau 1990: 62).

As a social imaginary, the myth promises a kind of "new order". It "is often accepted by several sectors, not because they particularly like its content but because it is the discourse of an order, of something that is presented as a credible alternative to a crisis and a generalized dislocation" (ibid.: 66). This new order will, however, only be accepted if it rearticulates elements that are already present in the social space.

In practice, myths maintain an unstable balance between the literality of the demands they promise to suture and their embodiment of an absent fullness. In both cases, their strength is simultaneously their weakness: Either the myth keeps absorbing countless new demands and becomes deformed; or, alternatively, the literal demands might predominate, which weakens a myth's ability to

---

6   Since "the relation between the surface of inscription and what is inscribed on it is [...] essentially unstable" (ibid.: 63), the demands that are inscribed in a myth can keep changing.

absorb new demands and present itself as fullness: "for longer or shorter periods they [myths] have a certain relative elasticity beyond which we witness their inexorable decline" (ibid.: 67). Myths are thus important discursive tools for the establishment of a new hegemonic discourse, but they cannot provide a lasting discursive stability unless they are supplemented by other moments in a discourse. To what extent the myth has been a social imaginary or an embodiment of a concrete social demand is an empirical question.

This chapter will explore the emergence and decline of the myth of Victory in Russia. In its analytical strategy, it borrows heavily from Lene Hansen (2006). Hansen suggests that, in order to analyse discourses, individual texts need to be seen simultaneously as unique and embedded in a contextual web. Each one draws upon the past and rearticulates it into a new text (Hansen 2006: 56). This chapter will thus, in a first part, draw a sketch that outlines the development of the historical myth of Victory in the Great Patriotic War – mainly through secondary literature. In doing so, this chapter will trace "the genealogy of the dominant representations" (ibid.: 82).

The kinds of texts one includes in the examination determine how broad the conclusions are that can be drawn. This chapter focuses on official discourse as articulated by political leaders (ibid.: 60ff.): Vladimir Putin's speech on the 60th anniversary of Victory is the most important source. In it, one can find the nodal points of a rearticulated myth of Victory. Besides, it was held at a moment in time that crystallised discourse. According to Hansen, such a moment "will often have a striking character and be the subject of intense political concern" (ibid.: 78). In particular, secondary sources, written by political scientists and sociologists, will help to access the symbols and signs that the text makes use of. Additionally, primary texts will be included in the analysis as "intertextual links" that "stabilize the discourse" (ibid.: 60). They are taken from the government newspaper *Rossiiskaia Gazeta*. The assumption is that the latter will articulate a version of official discourse that follows its basic premises, but adds its own elements, as well as references to the events taking place around Victory Day 2005.

The emergence of a myth

For the first 20 years after the war, Victory Day was rarely celebrated. Even though it initially had the status of an official holiday, it was demoted to a workday in 1947: The scars left by the war were still too visible to be glorified (Tumarkin 1994: 98).

This changed when Leonid Brezhnev took power. He reinstated 9 May as an official holiday and started the Soviet tradition of grandiose celebrations and military parades on this day. Under his rule, the myth of Victory started to take shape:

> "The master narrative's basic plot: collectivization and rapid industrialization under the First and Second Five-Year Plans prepared our country for war, and despite an overpowering surprise attack by the Fascist *beast* and its *inhuman* wartime practices, despite the loss of twenty million *valiant martyrs* to the cause, our country, under the leadership of the Communist Party headed by Comrade Stalin, arose as one *united front* and expelled the enemy from our own territory and that of Eastern Europe, thus *saving Europe* – and the world – from Fascist enslavement." (Tumarkin 1994: 134, emphasis added)

In the ensuing two decades, the government tolerated little deviation from this "master narrative".[7] Numerous moments of discourse were articulated through the myth: heroism, Communist leadership, national unity, and the awareness of being part of a great power that had saved the world. The constitutive outside took on demonic features: Fascists who wanted to enslave the world. The myth became a social imaginary, pure positivity, opposed to a nonplace, "a transcendent point" (Laclau 1990: 62) of pure negativity.

The potentially subversive element – that an unimaginable number of people had died – was rearticulated in such a way as to become an important moment of the myth: They were "valiant martyrs". The government began to set up memorials all over the Soviet Union – most prominently the Tomb of the Unknown Soldier with its eternal flame, lit in 1967. Simultaneously, a kind of hero worship emerged that assumed traits similar to the adoration of Orthodox saints. There were other quasi-religious aspects of the myth of Victory: "the Victory Banner gained the epithet 'holy of holies', [...] an embodiment of the collective virtue implied in the official remembrance of the victory" (Tumarkin 1994: 137). The myth cleansed the historical events of their "affective radicality" (Gudkov 2005: 6) and transposed them to a transcendent level.

---

7   According to Tumarkin, the Ministry of Defence determined what the "right" version of history was (1994: 134f.).

Nonetheless, the concrete social actions accompanying the establishment of the myth of the Great Patriotic War were very real. The government started a campaign of "military-patriotic" upbringing that was to serve as an antidote against the individualistic international youth culture of the 1960s. Adolescents spent time with veterans and visited war memorials on school excursions. The campaign connected the element of respect for the heroism of the war generation with an attempt to stabilise a Communist discourse that was under pressure due to competition from other discourses.[8]

Along with this renewed emphasis on Communist discursive moments, imperial and nationalist elements were articulated into moments of the myth. They were to "boost" the "decaying official ideology of Marxism-Leninism" (Dunlop 1994: 609, cf. Sakwa 2008: 210). Thus, in 1975, during the celebrations for the 30th anniversary of the Victory, the latter was presented as having resulted from the combined efforts and the unity of all the peoples of the Soviet Union, regardless of class or race (Vyzhutovich 2005a: 6). It was Victory that had made an empire out of the Soviet Union, a great power, even a superpower.

The myth was a hegemonic response to the dislocations resulting from social changes.

> "A fractionated culture of insularity, self-protectiveness, and an unsettling sense of estrangement that sociologists used to call 'anomie' was replacing the revolutionary and post-revolutionary culture that had valued self-sacrifice, devotion to a cause, communality, faith in, or at least respect for, or at the very least, fear of, political authority. [...] In its idealized form, the war had everything: violence, drama, martyrdom, success, and a chic global status." (Tumarkin 1994: 131f.)

The quote above illustrates that the Soviet discourse was increasingly hard pressed to articulate various newly emerging elements. De-Stalinisation had dislocated the Stalinist order, centred on the image of the leader. Among younger people, demands for more individual, political, and cultural freedoms were on the rise. The number of floating signifiers was increasing. The myth of the war was a hegemonic response to these demands: The space of representa-

---

8 Under Brezhnev, Soviet citizens had come to enjoy a higher standard of living than any of the generations before them. Technology was increasingly available and affordable, and educational levels were relatively high. It appears plausible that these factors contributed to the decline of the mobilising power of the Communist discourse. Still, even today, many people remember Brezhnev's rule as a kind of "golden era" of Russian history (Dubin 2005: 5). Others refer to it as the "era of stagnation".

tion that the myth articulated created a renewed, symbolic universe that upheld the Communist values that had led to the defeat of Nazi Germany and had made the USSR what it was today.[9] However, this original embodiment of a literal demand absorbed an increasing number of demands and turned more and more into a social imaginary. Its expanding chain of equivalence came to include nationalist and quasi-religious moments, which slowly began to loosen the clear link of the myth to a Communist social order. The new demands that it allowed to emerge contributed to the collapse of a Communist discourse.

A myth in decline

In 1985, the Brezhnevite narrative was still mostly in place. However, the overall Soviet discourse had already started to change. During the late 1980s, the Soviet discourse was marked by a series of *dislocations* that increasingly threatened it. The economic and military strength that the social imaginary of Victory had promised was being challenged from all sides: The United States appeared to be winning the arms race, the Soviet Army was bogged down in Afghanistan, the European satellites and the Baltic States were on their way to national independence, and ethnic conflicts were breaking out in various parts of the Soviet Union.[10] Last but not least, the political ideals of Communism were challenged by conceptions of democracy that assumed increasingly central places in competing discourses.

The official narrative of the war began to be challenged from various sides. Veterans published memoirs that related the horrors and abuse of life on the front. Gorbachev abandoned the magic number of 20 million "martyrs" and set the number of soldiers and civilians who had died at 27 million. In 1988, Stalin's orders 227 and 270 were published.[11] When Poland and, later on, the Baltic

---

9   Catherine Merridale writes: "From the 1960s, the Great Patriotic War provided the most important images. The memory of it was genuinely sacred for whole generations. As time went by, however, it also became a convenient distraction from economic and political stagnation" (2003: 17).
10   The fact that the official discourse had admitted the moment of nationalism contributed to this.
11   Stalin signed both orders in 1942 to stabilise the collapsing fronts. The first one is also called "Not One Step Back!" (*ne shagu nazad!*) and threatened those who did with the harshest punishments – summary execution or service in penal battalions that were sent on suicide missions (Overy 1998: 159f.). Order 270 labelled all those who were captured by German units "traitors". Their families were subject to imprisonment, and many of them were sent to prison camps after the war (ibid.: 80f.).

states became independent, demands for the acknowledgement of the secret protocol to the Molotov-Ribbentrop Pact began to emerge.[12]

The revelations about the Great Patriotic War eroded the official discourse's ability to fix the meaning of the war: Victory, which had been a nodal point of this discourse, became a floating signifier.

Throughout the 1990s, the meaning of Victory was contested. The government under Yeltsin struggled with the question of how to approach the Soviet past. On the one hand, it tried to reject it: "[c]ondemning the Soviet past was also an essential act of identity creation, enabling Russian liberals to define themselves by rejecting the Soviet 'Other'" (Sherlock 2007: 157). The government ended the military parades on 9 May and attempted – with little success – to institute "peace parades" that were sponsored by various international corporations, in an effort to endow the independent Russian state with "a new non-militaristic tradition" (Smith 2002: 86). This unwillingness or failure to cultivate this hitherto central myth, on the other hand, made the government vulnerable to attacks from the Communist and nationalist opposition, who decried it as "unpatriotic".

In an attempt to win back symbolic control over the past, the government marked the 50th anniversary of the Victory with large celebrations attended by heads of state from all over the world, military parades, and speeches in downtown Moscow. Yeltsin paid tribute to the Soviet military and appealed to the patriotism of the population. This tribute was linked to the war in Chechnya that had begun six months earlier: "[T]he heroic Russian soldiers killed on the other side of the Terek River were seen as carrying on the heroic tradition of the Soviet fighting men who died on the fronts of the Great Patriotic War" (Vyzhutovich 2005a: 6). The enemy was no longer Nazi Germany – its government representatives were guests of honour – but the "terrorists in Chechnya".

The celebration of the Victory and the war against the "separatists" in Chechnya were parts of an attempt by the government to respond to the perceived disintegration of the Russian state and its political community. Russia was to regain its status of a great power, for which a strong state and a powerful military were seen as preconditions. The defeat in Chechnya and the default cri-

---

12   "The classic Brezhnevite narrative of the war had involved a massive cover-up" of the Pact (Tumarkin 1994: 175). Given the importance of the "Fascist beast" as the *constitutive other* of a victimised, but heroic Soviet Union, it is not surprising that this fact was omitted from the discourse surrounding the Great Patriotic War.

sis in 1998, however, only produced new dislocations. This prepared the ground for a new leader who could bring order to Russia.

A refreshed myth under Putin

Putin came to power in 2000 and instantly adopted a different style of leadership than Yeltsin. Compared to the latter, he appeared youthful and resolute. He promised to fight terrorism relentlessly, began a second war in Chechnya, and spoke of the need for a patriotic education for Russia's youth. He passed a law that established the tricolour as the official flag of Russia. At the same time, the Duma decided to make the two-headed eagle the new state emblem, and the Soviet national anthem was resurrected with new lyrics. "It thus appeared that all three periods of Russian twentieth-century history had been reconciled: The Tsarist, Russia's brief experiment with democracy in 1917, and the Soviet." (Sakwa 2008: 224) Soon, Victory in the Great Patriotic War also began to re-emerge as a symbol of national unity. Calls were heard for a more "balanced" assessment (Afanasiev 2007: 2) of history in general and of the Great Patriotic War in particular. After the chaos of the 1990s, it was time for Russia to "get up from its knees" and stop the masochistic and "unpatriotic" depiction of past events (Sherlock 2007: 159). The cultivation of a more positive image of the Great Patriotic War produced a noticeable effect: Lev Gudkov cites a survey that asked Russians which past event filled them with the largest amount of pride. In 1996, 44 percent answered "the Great Patriotic War", compared to 87 percent in 2003.

In 2005, Russia celebrated the 60th anniversary of the Victory. It was a three-day-long affair, lasting from 8 to 10 May. There were concerts for veterans, a parade with thousands of former *frontovniki* (front soldiers) in historic costumes, and air shows, all broadcast live on television. The administration made sure that everybody was aware of the significance of the holiday: Russia's two official television channels "tele-bombarded" (Dubin 2005: 4) the people with broadcasts about the war.[13]

The Russian government took control of the format of the celebrations and connected traditional elements with others that highlighted Russia's important position in the world. Before Victory Day was re-articulated in this way, most people had seen it as a private holiday. Between April and May 2005, the num-

---

13   Normally, six to eight percent of broadcasting time is reserved for shows about the war. Around important holidays, this number rises significantly (Gudkov 2005: 7).

ber of those who saw *Den' Pobedy* (Victory Day) as an official state holiday rose from 26 percent to 55 percent (ibid.).

Putin began his speech on Victory Day, held at the parade in Moscow, by addressing the citizens, visitors, soldiers, officers, generals, and admirals:

> "I would like to congratulate you on the anniversary of the great victory, on the day of peace and triumph of justice, on the day when good triumphed over evil and freedom triumphed over tyranny." (2008: 291)

Victory Day is articulated as a highly overdetermined moment when the war once again becomes a social imaginary that encompasses all kinds of demands. Here, Victory Day stands for peace and for the triumph of justice, freedom, and goodness in general. The discourse even accentuates this condensation by calling Victory Day "the day on which the world was saved" (ibid.: 292) from the absolute evil of Fascism. Victory thus assumes a mythical, transcendental quality of pure positivity. The imaginary quality becomes even more noticeable when Putin states: "9 May is a sacred day" (ibid.). This "sacralization" of the past that the myth of Victory provides allows a distancing from the dislocated space of disorder and political weakness that surrounded the collapse of the Soviet Union and the emergence of an independent Russian state. The "new order" that the discourse of the Putin regime promises thus constructs itself in opposition to the "temporal Other of its own past" (Hansen 2006: 49). Rather than being the successor of a weak government and state, the Putin regime discursively becomes the successor of the Soviet great power that won the war.

Putin describes the events of the war as follows:

> "Fascists expected to enslave our people in an instant. In fact, they counted on destroying the country. Their plans failed. The Soviet army first stopped the Fascists outside of Moscow. And over the three subsequent years, it managed not only to resist the assault but also to force the enemy back into his lair. The results of the battles near Moscow and in Stalingrad, the courage of Leningrad under siege, the success in the Kursk and Dnieper battles, determined the outcome of World War II. The Red Army marked the victorious end to the war by liberating Europe, waging the battle for Berlin." (ibid.: 291f.)

According to this narrative, the Soviet Union was the victim of inhuman "Fascist" aggression, yet the strength of the Red Army repelled the enemy and pushed it back into its "lair" – also a metaphor that indicates that the enemy is not human – in Berlin. By articulating the enemy in such a way as to make him appear solely bent on destruction, the narrative forecloses any possibility of commonalities existing between the Soviet Union and Nazi Germany.

With this official discourse, Putin reactivates at least parts of the Brezhnevite myth of the Great Patriotic War. He mentions the same canonical "cities of heroes" and constructs the Soviet history of the war as a series of successes (Afanasiev 2007: 3) that culminated in the liberation of Europe.

To interpret this as a re-Sovietisation of history, as some observers do (Smith 2008: 5), would be imprecise and simplistic, however. Since "the myth of the Great Patriotic War outlived the polity" in which it emerged (Weiner 1996: 639), it has changed. For one, Communism does not appear in the official discourse. In Putin's speech, the real significance of Victory lies in the defence of the "nation": "Our grandfathers and fathers gave their lives for the honour and freedom of the nation. They were united and defended their Fatherland" (2008: 294). National unity and the willingness to sacrifice one's life for the Fatherland turned the Soviet Union into a great power. Following the traumatic experience of weakness in the 1980s and 1990s (Gudkov 2005: 62), the reference to past greatness is equivalent to the articulation of a demand: to become a great power nation once more.

One aspect of this demand is contained in the articulation of Russia's position in the world. The post-war Soviet Union was the antagonist of its former Western allies: The enemy of that period was no longer Nazi Germany, but the "Fascists" and "imperialists" in the West.[14] Under Putin, official foreign policy was ambiguous: It emphasised Russia's status as a great power and opposed the US invasion of Iraq. At the same time, Russia wanted to be a constructive partner in the international system, "but on Russia's terms, not as a supplicant but as an equal, retaining Russia's own identity and defending its interests" (Sakwa 2008: 378).

This conception of Russia's international role also bears on Putin's articulation of the Great Patriotic War. He underlines that the Soviet Union and its Western Allies won this war together and mentions that "80 percent of the planet's population" was affected by it. At the same time, he emphasises that its

---

14   Tumarkin points out that the term "Fascist" lost its concrete, Nazi German, identity in the course of the decades after the war and came to signify simply "enemy" in the Russian political discourse (1994: 222).

"most brutal and crucial events" took place on the territory of the Soviet Union (Putin 2008: 291). Implicitly, this signifies that Russia bore the brunt of the suffering and deserves most of the credit for Victory.[15] It has thereby gained its rightful and powerful place in the world order. The alliance of different actors against a common *constitutive other* is, however, held up as a model for a contemporary world order.

> "History teaches nations to do their best, not to ignore the emergence of new deadly doctrines, the origins and environment in which new threats evolve. [...] In the face of today's real *terrorist threats*, we must remain faithful to the memory of our fathers. We must defend the world order based on security and justice, a new culture of relations which does not allow for a repetition of cold or hot wars." (2008: 292f., emphasis added)

Stability is the key moment of the contemporary world order. Victory has created a peaceful world. However, a new constitutive outside threatens the world order, just as "Fascism" did: terrorism. It is the enemy not only of Russia, but also of the whole world. The enemy is as inhuman as the Fascists, and no separate treaties – other writers at times liken the appeasement of Hitler to negotiations with terrorists (cf. Iakovenko 2005) – can solve the problem. The international community has to actively defend its values – peace, justice, dialogue, tolerance (Putin 2008: 293) – against an enemy that shows "disdain for human life" (Iakovenko 2005: 4). Also, just like in the Great Patriotic War, the official discourse maintains, Russia is once more "at the centre of the struggle for genuine European values against a barbarian force" (Morozov 2008: 160).

How does Putin define these European values? "Since the epoch of global confrontation came to an end, we[16] have made significant strides toward the

---

15 Incidentally, Gudkov cites a survey that shows that two thirds of the Russian population believe today that the Soviet Union could have won the war without the help of its Western allies. In ethnic-nationalist discourses, this fact leads to an antagonisation of the West: "Mehr noch, mit dem zu beobachtenden Anstieg des ethnisch-russischen Nationalismus und mit wachsendem zeitlichem Abstand fügt sich der Krieg allmählich in den traditionellen Rahmen der russischen messianischen Idee und der Rivalität mit dem Westen ein" (Gudkov 2005: 66).
16 Whether this "we" refers to the Russian government, the nations of Europe, or to the "civilised nations", all of which are actors in Putin's speech, remains somewhat ambiguous. This is consistent with earlier discursive attempts at constructing a universalised, shared identity in opposition to the terrorist threat. Seen through the lens of the discourse theory of Laclau and Mouffe, the international community in this discourse has a negative identity that is only held together through its constitutive other.

lofty goal of ensuring peace and calm in Europe." Only "the right of every state to choose its path of development independently", as well as "international dialogue and co-operation", can lead to "a civilized future for all nations" (Putin 2008: 293). On the one hand, these demands call for unity against a common enemy. On the other, they carry an implicit warning: Attempts to subvert the system of collective security and co-operation by mingling in other countries' internal affairs are detrimental to a civilised future. One suspects strongly that this is directed against unilateral tendencies in the United States. Equally, it can be interpreted as a warning against the West not to act against the national interests of Russia and to endanger the post-Cold War system of security – key issues here are the expansion of NATO into Russia's "backyard" and plans to welcome the Ukraine or Georgia into the alliance. In hindsight, one can already perceive the first signs of the more antagonistic Russian attitude towards the West that have since become more pronounced.

Laclau claims that if a myth wants to present itself as an actual space, it must be opposed to a "non-place where a set of dislocations are added together" (1990: 62). Thus, the dislocations of the current global discursive order – among them antagonistically articulated "national interests" – are glossed over. It seems doubtful, however, whether the chain of equivalence that is opposed to it is strong enough to outweigh them. As soon as the *constitutive other* "terrorism" disappears from the discourse, antagonisms reappear.

Challenges to "the nation"

This is all the more problematic because the "nation" that repelled the Germans in the Great Patriotic War is not the same as the one inhabiting the Russian Federation today. The Soviet Union was more than the Russian Federation. The example of the myth of Victory shows quickly, just how "fuzzy [Russia's] inside/outside boundaries" are (Morozov 2008: 175). In an interview with CBS on Victory Day 2005, Putin deplores the "tragedy" of the collapse of the Soviet Union and mentions as the main reason that "after the break up of the Soviet Union 25 million Russians (*russkie*) found themselves outside of the newly created Russian Federation" (Rossiiskaia Gazeta 2005c: 3). The issue of the Russian successor state's unclear boundaries presents a large problem for Russian political discourse in general and for the discourse surrounding the Great Patriotic War in particular. Putin articulates this issue in the following way: "9 May is a sacred day for all nations in the Commonwealth of Independent

States. We are united by our anguish, our memory and our duty to future generations. [...] I am convinced that there is no alternative to our friendship and our fraternity" (2008: 292). By evoking the unity of the past, Putin articulates the demand for unity in the future. The discourse draws an imaginary political community that involves not only the Russian Federation, but also its neighbouring "little brothers". The present was, however, more marked by antagonistic relationships between Russia and the CIS. In the two years before the 60th anniversary, the "Rose Revolution" and the "Orange Revolution" took place in Georgia and the Ukraine. Mikhail Saakashvili did not attend the celebrations in Moscow (Vyzhutovich 2005b: 3); neither did the presidents of Estonia and Lithuania. Furthermore, the talks during Victory Day that were to bring a new vision for the future of the CIS yielded more disagreements than concrete results (Sakwa 2008: 225). The moment of "unity" mainly represents a demand. The mythical political community that won Victory in the Great Patriotic War no longer exists.

This demand highlights the fact that the meaning of "the nation" is the object of some uncertainty. The myth functions as a hegemonic response to a dislocation. However: "Anchoring Russian national identity in the Soviet past does not help in solving one of the crucial problems of contemporary Russia – that of the boundaries of the political community" (Morozov 2008: 174).[17] In order to articulate a strong, undivided Russia, official discourse incorporates elements of "statism" (Bacon et al. 2006: 8) – the demand for a strong state circumvents the problem of having to pick one specific type of national identity. Hence the emphasis on the sovereign development of the state: Russia repeatedly went through traumatic periods of state failure and imposition of identities and concepts from outside. Sovereignty "presupposes the ability of the state to control all significant domestic and transnational processes in and involving Russia" (Morozov 2008: 174). The demand for "unity" is all the more important as a nodal point. Within the myth of Victory, Russia is articulated as a unified people, a powerful state, and a great power on the international stage. Insofar as the discourse is aimed at an audience within Russia, it fulfils a hegemonic function and presents itself as a credible alternative (Laclau 1990: 66) to the crisis of the 1980s and 1990s.

---

17   The endless academic debates about which term is the appropriate one for "Russians" – *russkii, rossiiskii, rossiian*, etc. – illustrate this problem.

Besides, by referring the concept of unity back to a social imaginary, it can be portrayed as being above politics and thus be "securitised".[18] Consequently, any challenge to this unity is framed as "an existential danger" (Bacon et al. 2006: 10) that has to be fought with any means at the state's disposal. Putin in his speech linked unity against the Fascists to unity in the face of terrorism. While the vagueness of the *constitutive other* creates the semblance of universality in Putin's speech, a political commentary that was printed in the *Rossiiskaia Gazeta* on 4 May reveals how quickly this loss of the *constitutive other* can change its content depending on the context. Iakovenko writes: "Fascism was the plague (*chuma*) of the 20th century. It was replaced by the plague of the 21st century – terrorism" (2005: 4). However, when Putin rephrases the *constitutive other* in a later section of the article, it has turned into "the forces of separatism and extremism" (ibid.). It is therefore not surprising that attempts towards secession by the Chechens were portrayed as an existential threat to the Russian state (Bacon et al. 2006: 178).

Challenges from the "inside"

The official discourse adopts different strategies of de-politicisation (cf. Makarychev in this volume) against antagonistic social forces inside of the Russian Federation. "These days, any holiday, even 9 May, serves as pretence for a brawl. Yesterday, the Moscow police carried out preventive arrests all day: members of the council 'for the Fatherland', the 'Avant-garde of the red youth', and the 'National-Bolsheviks'" (Rossii-skaia Gazeta 2005b: 5). The youth organisations mentioned above are relatively marginal in political terms. But they are also portrayed as a security risk against which "measures outside the formal norms and procedures of politics" (Bacon et al. 2006: 10) are necessary. The sacred nature of Victory Day justifies these measures.

However, the concept of securitisation does not apply to all the discursive strategies that the official discourse uses against its antagonists. According to the same news report, both the Communist Party and the liberal Yabloko-Party were able to hold legal gatherings. The latter is apparently too marginal to deserve any further mention: The *Rossiiskaia Gazeta* only writes that party leaders met veterans in a park. The Communists, however, are an antagonistic force that carries a certain weight – especially when it comes to historical myths.

---

18 Bacon et al. (2006: 12) work with Wæver's (1998) concept of securitisation and apply it to various sectors of Russian politics.

Referring back to Communist traditions linked to Victory Day, Gennady Zyuganov demanded the right to follow the traditional route on his march, which led through downtown Moscow.[19] The government granted the request. It would appear that the Communist Party is the only political force in Russia today that can articulate a similarly coherent version of the myth of Victory. The Communists claim to be in possession of the "true" meaning of Victory – as the political force under whose leadership the war was won. Official discourse disputes this, albeit not directly. Afanasiev writes: "[...] the Soviet Union was victorious under the leadership of Soviet power, and we – we are its legal successors" (2007: 2). The Communists reply: "[T]he course of the government betrayed *our* Victory, *our* country" (Vyzhutovich 2005b: 3, *emphasis added*). By referring to an ill defined *we*, the Communist discourse attempts to articulate a different kind of "people", and a different *nation*. It claims that the victory was a Soviet and Communist achievement, and thereby exposes the extent to which official discourse has adapted the classical Brezhnevite narrative to contemporary conditions. The Communists portray the government not as the successor of the Soviet state, but rather of the "Democrats" who destroyed the Soviet Union. In this way, they articulate elements with a potential for dislocation, such as the collapse of the Soviet Union and the economic hardships of the 1990s.

On Victory Day, the Communists protested against the government's pension reform and thereby articulated the issue of economic degradation in relation to the veterans (ibid.). The discursive moment of veterans living in poverty appears to carry some weight. Numerous articles describe the poor living conditions of many veterans (cf. Pavlovskaia 2005: 26). By presenting themselves as the champions of these veterans, the Communist discourse challenges a nodal point of the myth of Victory: respect for veterans. Rossiiskaia Gazeta's Valerii Vyzhutovich (2005b) responds directly to this challenge and uses the moment "respect for veterans" against the Communists. He deplores how "out of place" demonstrations are on Victory Day. By politicising the holiday, Vyzhutovich holds, the Communists try to "privatise" it. He deplores the fact that even Victory Day has now become the subject of political "bickering".

He reduces the significance of the Communist challenge by portraying them as eternally unhappy with any government: "[T]his is normal. [...] What is

---

19 The security measures in Moscow for Victory Day gave rise to a number of heated polemics in newspapers, which accused the government of having taken the holiday away from "the people" (cf. Radzikhovsky 2005: 3).

not normal is something else – when Communists campaigns take place on 9 May. This is not normal because, unlike 22 April, May Day, and 7 November, which are occupied by the Communists, this is the only date that is capable of uniting the nation" (ibid.)

9 May is the only Soviet-era holiday that the new state has managed to appropriate. It provides an important link. In order to show to what extent Victory Day is above politics, Vyzhutovich takes the image of the veteran and uses it against the Communists. He talks about an encounter he had with a veteran of the Great Patriotic War at Poklonnaia Gora – the official war memorial in Moscow. The veteran tells him about how the oligarchs have too much power, the politicians are liars, and how the pension pays for nothing but his medication – "the usual song". But when the journalist asks the veteran what he thinks about the Communists' protest march against the government on 9 May, the old man's opinion is clear. "Unfortunately, his words are not fit to be put down on paper" (ibid.). The implication is, of course, that a politicisation of Victory Day is offensive to the veterans.

As a political strategy, the depiction of one's opponents as "politicians" serves the function of "naturalising" the myth as it is articulated in official discourse. The latter is presented as being "above politics" and therefore universally valid: "What is politically constructed is presented as normal, or natural, and resistance is constructed as deviant, or unnatural" (Torfing 1999: 123). This applies to the *constitutive other* of terrorism and its opposition to universal values, as discussed above, but also to the challenges to the myth stemming from internal opposition forces in the Russian Federation. It is a consistent strategy of denying the fact that any discourse rests on the basis of "contingent articulation" (Laclau/Mouffe 2001: xii). Nevertheless, any discourse is political because identities are not fixed, and the articulation of a discourse requires the political act of deciding something that is fundamentally "undecidable" because no essentialist identities exist (Torfing 1999: 63).

Even though official discourse in Russia takes recourse to a historical myth, its version of history is presented as non-ideological. In another commentary for the *Rossiiskaia Gazeta*, pundit Valerii Vyzhutovich writes that in the past, Victory Day celebrations were always used in such a way as to serve the ideological interests of Russia's rulers – from Brezhnev to Yeltsin.

"This time the Victory was deideologized. [...] In the year of the 60th anniversary of the Victory, the authorities have decided not to try to manipulate memory. They have given society an opportunity to do its own probing into the tumultuous events of the war years [...]" (Vyzhutovich 2005a: 6)

The discussions in this chapter show that this claim is dubious. The government may not imprison anyone for articulating elements of the war that do not fit into the narrative of the myth. Rather, the official discourse deals with them according to the formula: "silence, praise, and criticism – in that order" (Sherlock 2007: 283). The main Russian media outlets broadcast the official discourse and a mythologised version of the war. Presenting this as a "deideologised" approach only makes the discourse more powerful.

Conclusion

The adapted myth of the Great Patriotic War is doubtlessly a nodal point within the official Russian "statist" discourse.[20] Within this nodal point, it is possible to articulate a chain of equivalence that contains moments of national unity, pride in Russian history, and a Russian state that is a globally respected great power and guarantor of stability.

Empirically, this has several implications. First, the myth can contribute to the re-articulation of a national identity that is dislocated because of the collapse of the Soviet Union. In the space of representation of the war, there was only one unified Soviet people that fought a transcendental constitutive other. If, secondly, this myth is used to describe the world, it can articulate a powerful Russian state with a strong global position. At the same time, however, the myth articulates a political community that has been dispersed by the collapse of the Soviet Union. It thus dislocates rather than stabilises the social order, as it calls attention to the unclear boundaries of the Russian Federation's political community. Third, the myth articulates a strong, hierarchically organised state that is capable of controlling internal and external processes and of defending its interests against its constitutive other.

Still, the fact that the boundaries of the Russian political community are so blurry has problematic implications regarding the definition of the constitutive other. If, furthermore, the myth is dislodged from the concrete dislocation it re-

---

20 "Er ist ein Referenzpunkt, ein Massstab zur Bewertung der Vergangenheit und teilweise auch zum Verständnis von Gegenwart und Zukunft" (Gudkov 2005: 64).

sponded to in the first place, it turns into a social imaginary that stands for a nonexistent fullness. The "unity of the nation" can easily be interpreted as an embodiment of this absent fullness. But if the boundaries of this community are as unclear as they are in contemporary Russia, challenges to this mythological unity are more likely to be perceived as existential threats that need to be combated at all costs. The war against Georgia in fall of 2008 is a case in point.

Interestingly, however, one can also observe a securitisation of the literal content of the myth. In May 2009, the new president, Dmitry Medvedev, founded the "Commission to Counteract Attempts at Falsifying History to Damage the Interests of Russia". The Duma plans to pass a law that allows the courts to pass long jail sentences for researchers, politicians, or journalists who do not present the "right" version of history – particularly that of the Great Patriotic War. It is too early to say what will come of these initiatives. What can be said, however, is that the myth of Victory seems to be so central to the official discourse on Russian national identity that the state is willing to defend it with all the means at its disposal.

The question is whether a myth that tends towards "the construction of a somewhat totalizing and reductive discourse" (Torfing 1999: 115) provides a foundation for a national identity that is broad enough in the long run. In order to attain lasting stability, Russian official discourse may not be able to avoid offering a "persuasive redescription of the world" (ibid.: 302) in which its population currently lives.

Bibliography

Afanasiev, Iu. 2007. "Tragediia Pobedivshego Bolshinstva: Pasmyshleniia ob Otechestvennoi Istorii i ee Interpretatsiiakh". http://www.yuri-afanasiev.ru/tragedy.html [accessed 22 November 2008].

Dubin, B. 2005. "Bremia Pobedy. Boris Dubin o Politicheskom Upotreblenii Simvolov". *Kriticheskaia Massa* 2. http://magazines.russ.ru/km/2005/2/du6.html [accessed 22 November 2008].

Dunlop, J.B. 1994. "Russia: Confronting a Loss of Empire, 1987-1991". *Political Science Quarterly* 108, 4. 603-634.

Gudkov, L. 2005. "Die Fesseln des Sieges: Russlands Identität aus der Erinnerung an den Krieg". Translated from Russian by Mischa Gabowitsch. *Osteuropa* 4-6. 56-73.

Hansen, L. 2006. *Security as Practice: Discourse Analysis and the Bosnian War.* London: Routledge.

Iakovenko, A. 2005. "Nasha Obshchaia Pobeda – Pamiat', Uroki, Dolgi". *Rossiiskaia Gazeta* 4 May. 4.

Laclau, E. 1990. *New Reflections on the Revolution of Our Time.* London & New York: Verso.

Laclau, E. and Mouffe, C. 2001 [1985]. *Hegemony and Socialist Strategy: Towards a Radical Democratic Politics.* London & New York: Verso.

Merridale, C. 2003. "Redesigning History in Contemporary Russia". *Journal of Contemporary History* 38, 1. 13-28.

Morozov, V. 2008. "Sovereignty and Democracy in Contemporary Russia: A Modern Subject Faces the Post-Modern World". *Journal of International Relations and Development* 11. 152-180.

Overy, R. 1998 (1997). *Russia's War: A History of the Soviet War Effort: 1941-1945.* New York: Penguin Books.

Pavlovskaia, T. 2005. "Byvshii Frontovnik Shivët v Zemlianke". *Rossiiskaia Gazeta.* 6 May. 26.

Putin, V. 2008. "Vystuplenie na Voennom parade v chest 60-y godovshchiny Pobedy v Velikoi Otechestvennoi voine". *Izbrannye rechi i vystupleniia.* Moskva: Knizhnii Mir. 291-294. English translation available at http://news.bbc.co.uk/2/hi/europe/4528999.stm [accessed 22 November 2008].

Radzikhovsky, L. 2005. "Strana Bednykh Evgeniev". *Rossiiskaia Gazeta.* 19 April. 3.

Rossiiskaia Gazeta. 2005a. "Politika v Den Pobedy". 6 May. 3.

―――― 2005b. "Den Pobedy s partbiletom". 10 May. 5.

―――― 2005c. "Interviu non-stop". 10 May. 3.

Sakwa, R. 2008 (1993). *Russian Politics and Society*. London & New York: Routledge. 205-448.

Sherlock, T. 2007. *Historical Narratives in the Soviet Union and Post-Soviet Russia*. New York: Palgrave MacMillan. 1-27, 149-185.

Smith, K.E. 2002. *Mythmaking in the New Russia: Politics and Memory During the Yeltsin Era*. Ithaca & London: Cornell University Press.

Smith, M.A. 2008. "The Politicisation of History in the Russian Federation". Shrivenham: Defence Academy of the United Kingdom. Available at: http://www.defac.ac.uk/colleges/arag/document-listing/russian [accessed 12 December 2008].

Torfing, J. 1999. *New Theories of Discourse: Laclau, Mouffe and Žižek*. Oxford & Malden: Blackwell Publishers.

Tumarkin, N. 1994. *The Living and the Dead: The Rise and Fall of the Cult of World War II in Russia*. New York: BasicBooks.

Vyzhutovich, V. 2005a. "Two Days Till Victory: The Best Way to Set the Tone of Citizens' Feelings on the Eve of the Celebration Might Be a Moment of Silence". *Current Digest of the Post-Soviet Press* 18, 57. 6.

―――― 2005b. "Okkupirovannaia Territoriia". *Rossiiskaia Gazeta* 11 May. 3.

Weiner, A. 1996. "The Making of a Dominant Myth: The Second World War and the Construction of Political Identities within the Soviet Polity". *Russian Review* 55, 4. 638-660.

Russia in Plural: (Re)Constructing Otherness, (De)Constructing Power

Andrey Makarychev

Despite Russia's reputation as a country with an authoritarian regime, there are various spaces for alternative discourses beyond the control of the state. Even though they operate within a non-political, cultural space, they can convey powerful political messages. This tells us a lot about the way power is organised in Russia. Instead of banning seemingly alien – though not necessarily inimical – discourses, today's ruling elite takes advantage of a growing variety of cultural narratives and representations in Russia. The state welcomes the proliferation of a culture of entertainment, which fits into the de-politicised model of governance pursued by the Putin-Medvedev regime, which relies upon administrative procedures and is sceptical towards public activity on the part of citizens. The state is keen to instrumentalise literary and cinematic narratives as effective tools for delivering political meanings. However, the increasingly diversified discursive landscape of Russia will ultimately challenge – and probably undermine – the dominant discourse.

Despite Russia's reputation as a country run by an authoritarian regime, there are various spaces for alternative (non-state-controlled) discourses that – even though they operate within a non-political, cultural space – can convey political messages that are even more powerful than any message the state, through its administrative machinery, can convey. This argument, which is pivotal for this chapter, can be placed conceptually at the intersection of social constructivism and a variety of poststructuralist theories, where one may discover a growing body of literature arguing that "the sovereign order is no longer simply that of decision, but also of imagination." (Aradau et al.: 2008) Therefore, the key political question of "who decides" has to be complemented by "who gets to imagine the future?" (ibid.: 152). The linkage between imagination and political acts was nicely encapsulated by Derrida (2005: 67): "Without the opening of an absolutely undetermined possible, without the radical abeyance and suspense marking a perhaps, there would never be either event or decision."

This approach might be conceptualised even more straightforwardly: "objects of popular culture are not simply treated as mirrors of existing norms, ideas and identities, but as mutually constitutive of those norms" (Muller 2008). What might be dubbed "cultural governance" is a set of representational practices never fully controlled by the state; by the same token, it is in these practices that the struggle for national identity is located and the (counter-) performances of statehood take place.

The main goal of this chapter is to uncover the ways in which cultural discourses contribute to a variety of political articulations that are constitutive for identity construction in today's Russia. More specifically, I argue that the concept of Russian identity is developed at the intersection of discourses emanating from both the '"holders of power" (i.e., the governing elite) and a wider cultural milieu where alternative political articulations may appear. This tells us a lot about the way power is organised in Russia. The more or less liberal attitude of the Kremlin towards the variety of discourses generated outside of the locus of power is a strong argument against those who deem that practices of the bygone Soviet era are constitutive for today's Russian politics. They are not, since instead of banning the seemingly alien – though not necessarily inimical – discourses, as was the case in the Communist era, today's ruling elite is keen to take advantage of a growing variety of narratives and representations across the entire range of Russia's cultural life. The state certainly does not object, and even welcomes, the proliferation of the culture of entertainment, which logically fits into the de-politicised, technocratic model of governance pursued by the Putin-Medvedev regime that relies upon administrative procedures and is sceptical towards public activity on the part of the citizens. By the same token, the state is keen to instrumentalise literary and cinematic narratives as effective tools for delivering political meanings.[1] Yet – and this is also part of my argumentation – in spite of the ability of certain discourses to stabilise the dominating regime, the increasingly diversified discursive landscape of Russia will challenge – and probably undermine – the dominant discourse.

---

1   Thus, the 2009 movie "Taras Bulba" sends two interrelated messages of evidently political background to a wider audience: One is the iteration of the argument of Russian and Ukrainians as a single people, while another one presents Poland as their historical enemy.

This chapter will be divided into four parts. Part 1 is a description of theoretical assumptions. Parts 2 and 3 will discuss how the concept of otherness is inscribed into the discursive construction of Russian identity through the stories of war and historical narratives. Part 4 will demonstrate how the idea of power is attacked by deconstructing discourses. These points will be illustrated with reference to the most prominent examples of contemporary Russian cinema and literature, which, as I will argue, contain strong – though still understudied – political messages.

Theoretical premises

In recent years, the interest in a variety of artistic narratives as means of conveying political messages has grown considerably (Bulloch 2007). This can be explained in part by the fact that some of these narratives possess the power to uncover and publicise what remains concealed by political correctness and other discursive constraints. Nevertheless, there is a deeper explanation for this phenomenon:

> "The shift from the political to the aesthetic is inherent in the political itself. The aesthetic metaphor, in which a particular element stands for the Universal, is enacted in the properly political short-circuit [...]. These poetic displacements and condensations are not just secondary illustrations of an underlying ideological struggle, but the very terrain of this struggle" (Zizek 2004: 76f.).

Against this background, one may argue, on the one hand, that "calling something unthinkable or unimaginable is a strategy of depoliticization" that pushes free political debates out of the spheres controlled by the power establishment. On the other hand, the "cultural constitutive work" based upon "genealogies of the creative imagination" performs a deeply political function: "the visualization of some futures and not others entails profoundly political work that enables and constrains political decision making" (de Goede 2008: 171).

In order to uncover the plurality of cultural representations of Russian identity, I will attempt to combine the Russian semiotic tradition as exemplified by figures like Yury Lotman and Mikhail Bakhtin with a number of poststructuralist departures (grounded, in particular, in the writings of Ernesto Laclau and Jacques Derrida). Lotman is known for approaching semantic interpretation as a search for correlations between two (or more) "structural rows" (Lotman 1970: 90), which in our case have to be understood as discourses that are closely interwoven with (even presupposing) each other. Paradoxically, discourses produced by the governing elites might be technological and seem apolitical, while cultural representations and narratives can generate political meaning.

Mikhail Bakhtin (1990: 8-109) focused on what he calls "a carnival-type popular culture of laughter" which drastically differs from the "serious" discourses of officialdom and, therefore, constructs an imaginable "non-state world" free of dogmatism and indoctrination. "Seriousness" was historically the hegemonic way of ascertaining the "official truth". By contrast, the "culture of laughter" is grounded in emancipatory narratives, including parodies and caricatures that help to deflate the "official truth", debunk its hierarchy, decompose established norms, efface bans, and deconstruct privileged speaking positions. Unlike the centralised discourses predicated upon fixity and uniformity, the culture of laughter is inimical to everything finite, stable, and allegedly "universal". Presuming that the "seriousness" of "official discourse" conceals violence, threats, fear, and domination, Bakhtin looked for what turns this discourse inside out, demolishes the symbols of power, and destroys the rituals of submission. In this playful culture of grotesque and relativity, all claims and appeals to eternity are doomed. Laughter cannot be an instrument for domination; on the contrary, it helps people liberate themselves from presumably undisputable impositions from the top of the political hierarchy. Bakhtin's theory thus supports the idea that the hegemony of state discourse is inherently unstable.

In Bakhtin's reading, the spread of these "alternative counter-languages" is a reaction to state-sponsored rationality, authoritarian ways of thinking, and "bureaucratic optimism". It is the language of merriment and gaiety that destroys the fear of a foreclosed and presumably static world with clear-cut borders and thus demonstrates the emptiness and incompleteness of power. This language demolishes the false image of power as something unshakable and unquestionable, and calls for the freedom to fantasise and get rid of the undue constraints.

In this chapter, the hegemonic discourse will be understood as being grounded in such signifiers as "sovereign democracy", "the vertical of power", "unity", "patriotism", "Putin's plan", "national projects", "energy superpower", etc. It is based upon what might be called "official discourse", yet it stretches far beyond the speech acts of the Kremlin and includes a variety of narratives that have the effect of strengthening the dominating articulations. A hegemonic discourse is "that which is seen to be common sense, the bounds of the reasonable" (Croft 2006: 389). However, this type of discourse, despite its intention to bring more clarity and uniformity to the construction of Russia's identity, is inherently dislocated in two aspects. Externally, it depends heavily upon a constitutive outside (Russian identity can be formulated only through the constant references to Europe, the West, and the international community, while internally, it is fragmented into a multiplicity of subject positions. Thus, the Kremlin agenda may be interpreted as one reviving the imperial legacy, on the one hand, and as one that is turning Russia into a de-politicised type of corporate actor motivated chiefly by material gains, on the other; the hegemonic discourse presents Russia as the heir to the Soviet traditions and simultaneously as a country that voluntarily liberated itself from the vestiges of Communism. The examples of inconsistencies embedded in Russia's hegemonic discourse confirm that Russia is not an empirically fixed entity, but is rather symbolised and imagined as a nation.[2] "Russia" as an open concept includes multiple meanings and invites a clash of interpretations; hence, I have borrowed the term "Russia in plural" from a colleague (Joenniemi 2008). This incompleteness is in no way an annoying imperfection, but rather the condition of existence of Russia as a complex semiotic structure embedded in multiple conceptualisations, performances, and representations that fuel the endless process of Russia's (re-) signification.

Otherness and identity: The *self-other* divide and representations of war

In this part, I intend to demonstrate that there are various inter-related dimensions of otherness that play constitutive roles in the process of Russian identity building.

In hegemonic discourse, the concept of war maintains its validity (Zvereva 2005), and many pieces of contemporary Russian cinematography underline the importance of the military argument for Russian identity. The motion picture "We Are From the Future" is perhaps one of the best examples that shows that the Great Patriotic War as well as the *self-enemy* division in general are indispensable elements of the Russian *self* that can be rediscovered only through the bygone war (Izvestiia 2008). The plot is grounded in the genre of war fantasy: A group of cynical young diggers busy with illegal excavation of wartime military accessories suddenly traverses time and finds itself right in 1942. The movie fixes the transition from the virtual (war as "archaeology", rendered visible only

---

2   This is, of course, not unique to Russia.

through the remnants of the fallen soldiers) to the real (war as a painful experience with the possibility of death). The message delivered by "We Are From the Future" seems to be a political one: It is only through the redefinition of the war experience that the younger generation might be capable of uncovering its true identity. However, there is another forceful message inscribed into this story: The past war appears to be more real than the contemporary reality itself, and thus turns into a background for all social identifications and relations of power.

"The Rifleman of the Voroshilov Regiment" (1999) – directed by Stanislav Govorukhin – conveys a similar message: The heroic war legacy is manifested as a resource to be re-actualised, while the present is portrayed as a regretful denigration of the good old times. The movie hero, a veteran of the Great Patriotic War, takes revenge on a group of young yobs for the rape of his granddaughter and shoots each of them dead. The sympathies of the authors are clearly with the old soldier, who embodies the spirit of the past distorted and betrayed by the new generation.

Nevertheless, in other cultural narratives, the situation looks strikingly different: there, one increasingly finds portrayals of a strange war that fulfils neither mobilising nor identity-building functions. The *self-other* distinction is culturally blurred and even disavowed, and the very idea of enmity is sometimes effaced through either mockery or parody. For example, in the interpretation of Dmitry Bykov, war is degenerative, irrational, and even comic, and it splits, divides, and ultimately deconstructs Russian identity. In his anti-utopia "Zh.D." (an acronym that, according to the author, can mean a lot of different things, including a derogatory Russian word for Jews), he describes Russia in a not-so-distant future entangled in a sort of civil war between the "Varangians" ("Northerners") and the "Khazars" ("Southerners"). Bykov evidently derides this weird opposition: Both parties appear to be ethnically and historically "non-Russian", but fight for their "own Russia" and accuse each other of being occupants. The war between them resembles, in Bykov's reading, a "skirmish of two viruses", "two models of extermination": The Varangians' aim is empire, while the Khazars intend to build a capitalist corporation. No final victory is possible in such a war in principle; it is infinite in its purest sense: All of Russian history is depicted as an everlasting battle between the invaders and the invaded, inevitably followed by endless repressions among the winners, whoever they may be. Against this background, the essence of Bykov's Russia is exemplified by the metaphor of "colony", a highly hierarchical expanse only held together through violence and force. Russia is portrayed as a captive nation, always suffering from excessive oppression, the expulsion of its own population, and revolutionary terror. The vicious circle of cruel brutality and self-extermination seems to be unbreakable to Bykov, which explains why wars in Russia are immanent and, in a way, "normal" events.

The internal war depicted by Bykov starts from spontaneous, yet quite recognisable clashes between "the fighters against immigration" and non-Russian ethnic groups, including Jews, Caucasians, and others. Bykov insists that it was not the authorities that initiated the hostilities – the conflict is a grass-roots phenomenon. "Usually wars renovated and purified nations", Bykov speculates, "but this new war was radically different from the previous ones. Officers not only were almost unable to mobilize soldiers for battles, but themselves were hesitant to attack" (Bykov 2007: 344). Later, he explains:

> "[I]n a country where everything is spoilt and tainted, not much is left from the war. Indeed, it was not a war but contempt for its very idea [...]. The Varangians were shooting their own soldiers for desertion, while the Khazars had no idea what to do with the conquered land. Consequently, both sides tried to evade mass-scale collisions: the Varangians forgot how to die for this soil, while the Khazars were not sure that it was worth dying for at all. There was no point in waging war anymore; it appeared to be shameful to disperse and go home, yet there were no forces left to destroy each other [...]. Even properly killing each other was an unsolvable problem." (Author's translation, p.212)

The double game that the author skilfully plays with his readers must be understood against this background: On the one hand, he seemingly erases the political from his picture of Russia: "the structuring enemy [...] ceases to be identifiable and thus reliable"; and instead, he observes "a mobile multiplicity of potential, interchangeable, metonymic enemies, in secret alliance with one another" (Derrida 2005: 84). At this point, Bykov might agree with Derrida that "losing the enemy would simply be the loss of the political itself" (ibid.: 84). In his description of an anti-Schmittian world, Bykov goes much further than simply describing a senseless, languid, and illogical war; he claims that militaristic nationalism is both archaic and ridiculous. In his anti-utopian Russia, the so-called "patriots" sympathise with insane ideas, such as introducing the practice of imprisoning conscripts' relatives to ensure soldiers' bravery, or shooting citizens for childlessness.

On the other hand, Bykov portrays "the invention of the enemy", which repoliticises the whole situation. "No enemy? We'll fabricate him, bring him up, make him confess under torture to his enmity" (Bykov 2007: 406), one of the characters exclaims. Therefore, the war he describes only virtualises the figure of the enemy, which turns into a dubious, yet inevitable figure. In his interpretation, Russia remains a country that is unable to identify its friends and enemies and thus fails to identify itself properly. His portrayal of Russia seems to be in line with Derrida: "The enemy is then my best friend. He hates me in the name of friendship [...]. The two concepts (friend/enemy) consequently intersect and ceaselessly change places" (Derrida 2005: 72).

The issue of dislocated identity is quite salient for Russian cinema as well. Alexey Uchitel' in "The Captive" tells the story of two Russian officers who are guarding a captured Chechen soldier. The relations of the presumed enmity are gradually transformed into a more subtle and nuanced mix of feelings that include tacit sympathy and hidden solidarity. In the resultant inter-subjective space of forced interaction, the supposedly rigid self-enemy distinction softens, yet the initial rigidity is ultimately restored in its most tragic form – the Chechen soldier is shot dead by Russian troops.

"The Muslim" shows the intrusion of religious *otherness* into Russia's rural heartland in the aftermath of the Afghanistan war. A Russian soldier who converted to Islam in captivity and then returns to his native village becomes a bearer of a Muslim identity, which does not fit into the rigid structure of established beliefs and traditions. A former soldier's new religious identity becomes dangerous and challenging to the traditional Russian way of life. The message of the movie is rather clear: Individual – exceptional – choice is always problematic in the intolerant atmosphere of communitarian traditionalism.

Identity conflicts could be transposed to the most recent cinematographic excursions to the times of the Great Patriotic War. In "Franz + Polina", a young German soldier in love with a Belarusian girl has to join the locals that are escaping from Nazi troops. The story shows how a person with a split identity divides others as well: Partisans and their families must make ethical decisions on whether to accept Franz's mimicry or not. The plot could be approached from the viewpoint of what Derrida dubbed "the suitability of the enemy at one's own convenience": "the enemy had indeed to be there already, so near. He had to be waiting, lurking close by, in the familiarity of my own family, in my own home, at the heart of resemblance and affinity" (Derrida 2005: 172). The end of the movie is quite traditional, however: In an act of brutal revenge, a Russian boy kills the German soldier, who has almost become a part of the community of displaced people looking for refuge from the Nazi army. The lesson of this gesture may be interpreted as a triumph of the inevitable pressure of the traditional divides and the tragic impossibility of communicative bridges between enemies. In a wartime milieu, alterity is not tolerated even as an exception, and dividing lines persist.

In "Ours", the story of "Franz + Polina" is told in reverse: Soviet officers have to escape from the Germans and pretend to change their identity. The movie portrays a series of confusions between *us* and *them* in a war atmosphere where no one can be trusted or even properly identified. Paradoxically, what ultimately unfolds within this seemingly post-modernist situation of distorted roles and masked identities is a very Hobbesian world that reifies the reality of an everlasting battlefield.

A similar message is inscribed in "The Enemies", a movie depicting an interactive situation in a village occupied by German troops that turns into a site of communication between the invaders and the oppressed. The very possibility of such an interaction appears to be a revision of canonical interpretations of the Great Patriotic War in which the Soviet *self* was clearly divorced from the German *other*. However, the end of the story reasserts the dividing lines: The emerging communication instantaneously collapses as soon as the Germans shoot dead a local woman and thus restore the *self-enemy* dichotomy in its sharpest form.

All the examples here tell the story of a demarcation line between the *self* and the *enemy* that becomes blurred in wartime and is then reasserted, which testifies that Russia's troubles with its past are crucial for today's identity construction. All attempts to forge a consensus on "national identity" (as exemplified, for example, by the establishment in 2008 of the Presidential Commission on Countering the Attempts to Falsify History to the Detriment of National Interests) are constantly undermined, which testifies to the dislocated nature of that identity. I will turn to this issue in the following section.

Identity and history: the temporal dimension of otherness

Russian hegemonic discourse is based on historical narratives that are closely tied to a glorified and cherished past, re-actualised by events such as the conflict with Estonia over the removal of the "Bronze Soldier" monument in Tallinn in 2007, political frictions with Poland grounded in their conflicting interpretations of World War II/The Great Patriotic War, and the steady politicisation of the 9 May celebrations in Russia.

However, these hegemonic articulations are constantly undermined by multiple stories that construct Russian identity to a significant extent in contrast to the practices of the past. Movies like "East – West", "Burnt by the Sun", "The Children of Arbat", "The Moscow Saga" and others are classical attempts to lambaste the Soviet times from the viewpoint of the past as Russia's *other*. Alexei Balabanov's movie "Cargo 200" is a tough portrayal of the late Soviet regime, where tyranny, cruelty, and corruption created an atmosphere of steady social degeneration. The drawing of a line of distinction between the repulsive and unfree past and a presumably new post-Communist Russia is constitutive for this type of cultural discourses.

The past not only tends to be dangerous and threatening; what is more important is that all attempts to remodel, reconsider, rethink, or rewrite the scripts of the past have potentially deadly consequences. In contemporary Western cinema ("The Butterfly Effect", "The Outpost", "A Sound of Thunder", "The I Inside", etc.) one finds an entire performative tradition that follows this reasoning. In Russian cinema, the idea that "inroads" into the past are perilous adventures is best staged in "The Soviet-era Park". The plot is a combination of playful imagination and reality, portraying the revival of the Communist past in the form of a business entertainment project which, nevertheless, tends to transgress its functional boundaries and forcefully intrude into reality. You cannot control the incursions into your past, which is always annoying, menacing, troublesome, excessive, and intrusive – this is perhaps the most evident lesson of the story.

Karen Shakhnazarov's movie "The Disappeared Empire" portrays the routine – and seemingly de-politicised – everyday life of the Soviet Union in the beginning of the 1970s, which is narrated along with archaeological allusions to the perished empires of the past. Archaeology here may bear a double meaning – as a science that restores the traces of antiquity and as a Foucauldian concept of discourse analysis. "The reality that surrounds the main protagonist strongly resembles the last stage of an ancient empire: everything is false, unreal, disintegrating" (Volodikhin 2008).

In his novel "Pravda", Bykov creates an absurd version of the Communist revolution that turns into a combination of post-modernist imagery and a deeply sarcastic disdain of power as such. In this funny interpretation of the idea of contingency, Lenin joined the Bolshevik party by mere incident, and his major incentive – a clear allusion to "Lord of the Rings" – was to find a magical ring that can turn someone into a new Russian tsar (Chertanov and Bykov 2005). This strikingly "untrue" story merits conceptual interpretation: For Bykov, power is, firstly, radically contingent (in the sense that it lacks a "grand design" and represents a series of chaotic moves made by either ethically corrupted or perverted human beings). Secondly, it uncovers non-political motives in the behaviour of the so-called power holders, including greed and vengeance.

But the past is not the only temporal dimension in which Russian identity is constructed. According to a sociologist, Russian identity is swept out either to the incorrigible past, or to the impossible future. Consequently, the future is discursively modelled after a distant past, thus paving the way for a "simulative identity" (Dubin 2004). This argument is nicely illustrated by the intellectual exchange between the two authors Vladimir Sorokin and Maxim Kononenko.

The novel "Day of the Oprichnik" by Sorokin (2006) is a caustic satire, a parody that mocks the widespread fascination and admiration of authoritarian rule by anti-Westerners (in one of the book's most absurd scenes, he depicts the masses of ordinary Russians voluntarily burning their international travel passports in a collective gesture of disdain of the West). This old-new Russian state-to-be erects a wall separating the country from the West, closes all international supermarkets, introduces Cyrillic for computer programs, and legalises the practice of publicly flogging dissidents. Sorokin describes a future Russia that restored major attributes of totalitarianism (strong religious rhetoric, undisputable authority of the Father of the Nation, etc.). The core of Sorokin's argument, however, lies in the deconstruction of the image of the past-in-the-future in a number of ways. Firstly, he explicitly questions the archaism of the "good old days" lifestyle by multiple references to the most sophisticated gadgets widely used by the new "oprichniks" (a military squad created by Ivan the Terrible for political repression). Secondly, he uncovers the hidden motivations of the "oprichniks" – neither political loyalty nor ideology, but simply money and obscene sex. Thirdly, the anti-Western paranoia conceals, in Sorokin's interpretation, the factual colonisation of Russia by the Chinese, who not only dominate the Russian economy, but – most ironically –even make the emperor's children speak Chinese among themselves.

Maxim Kononenko's "Day of the Otlichnik" (2008) is a direct – and no less sarcastic – reaction to Sorokin. The novel describes an opposite type of anti-utopia – a Russia dominated by pro-Western liberals who acceded to power after the so-called "Birch Revolution" (a clear allusion to Boris Berezovsky's family name). The narration is regularly interrupted by obviously irrelevant slogans like "Long live Procter & Gamble!" and other virulently satirical references to Western consumerist culture. The name of the country is "Another Russia", referring to an anti-Putin oppositional group. Among the most cherished heroes of a post-"Birch Revolution" Russia are Mikhail Khodorkovsky "the Saviour" (canonised in Kononenko's imagery as a national symbol for his refusal to leave prison even after his acquittal) and Alexander Litvinenko (whose murder in London some see as having been instigated by the Russian secret services). Moscow's toponymical landscape nicely reflects the spirit of this caricature of a liberal Russia: the Red Square is renamed after Viktor Yushchenko, while a military base bears the name of Mikhail Saakashvili. The Kremlin is repainted in black as a sign of the nation's repentance for its historical wrongdoings, while the symbol of Soviet-era progress Yury Gagarin is dubbed the "so-called cosmonaut". Russia acknowledges its status as a "junior brother of the Ukrainian-Georgian liberty"; Estonian language is introduced at schools, and the denial of the Federal Security Service's complicity in the explosions of several residential buildings in Moscow in 2000 is equated with a crime against humanity. The Ministry of Defence is dismantled, while conscription is reduced to ten days. Chechnya has been granted full independence, and Russian gold reserves are used for paying reparations to former Soviet republics for occupation.

Kononenko's satire boils down to uncovering the existential un-freedom of Russia's liberals who have to wear talismans clumsily dubbed "Human Rights Watch" and read "The Gulag Archipelago" before going to bed. Governmental officials salute each other with the standard exclamation "Be free!", which must be answered with "Always free!" (a clear reference to the Soviet-era slogan of pioneers). The alleged freedom leads, in the author's eyes, to the complete legitimacy of terrorists who are granted the status of a "free people". In a radical, mocking disavowal of liberalism, Kononenko describes the surrealistic procedures of submitting applications to authorities for staging terrorist acts, which are perceived as a peculiar type of public spectacle to meet the identity needs of terrorists. All political practices, therefore, turn into a series of bizarre shows (like, for instance, ritualistic arrests of former dissidents during national festivities).

In Kononenko's Russia, freedom presupposes the right to die in an act of public self-destruction and, therefore, is reduced to the toleration of violence, to be enjoyed by everybody. Human rights turn into a type of religion to be adored and worshiped ("rights precede human beings"). Like monks, human rights defenders are deprived of marital rights; like freemasons, they meet secretly in hidden places, isolated from the general public. Everything seems to be secure and sterile in this supposed liberal paradise – including "safe terrorist acts" ("It is unbelievable that some time ago terrorist acts brought pain to people", one of the protagonists confesses) and "harmless coffee", which has only to be smelled. There is a clear parallel with Zizek's critique of the West as a civilisation of objects without essence (from coffee without caffeine to war without casualties).

"We people can be wrong, but the procedure can't" (Kononenko 2008: 173) – this is a concise description of the triumph of administrative prudence and continuity as understood by the liberals. In Kononenko's imagery, human rights and democracy undermine themselves due to their striking and overwhelming triumph. In this utopian universe, everything can (has to?) be democratic, including the room set-up, a cemetery, a dance, a shower, a pill, a psychoanalyst, etc. Everything can be of "human rights nature" – even a sweater. References to freedom unnaturally permeate people's entire lives, including sexual intercourse (the lovers confess to each other to enjoy the sense of "freedom", not feelings of carnal intimacy with each other).

It is telling that both anti-utopias conceal a certain type of dictatorial regime (Kovalyov 2008) that was introduced with the overwhelming consent of a population that turns into an anonymous and anomic mass unable to generate political impulses. The totalitarian temptation is always there, warn both Sorokin and Kononenko, but in two different ways. For both writers, some kind of *constitutive other*, against which contemporary Russian identity can be defined, is indispensable. For Sorokin, this *constitutive other* is grounded in the times of Ivan the Terrible and the experiences of medieval repressions. For Kononenko, *otherness* is associated with an imagined society in which "everything becomes visible and transparent, everything is 'liberated'" (Baudrillard 2005: 17), yet total liberation paradoxically turns "into a duty, a moral obligation", which reveals "a secret awareness of the illusoriness of freedom", or, more bluntly, a "voluntary servitude" (Baudrillard 2005: 54).

In this sense, the Sorokin-Kononenko dispute is a manifestation of a political debate in the form of literary narratives that spell out alternative interpretations of what Russia is. Identity, therefore, "is a matter of political struggle rather than of some kind of deduction. And this assertion of openness, in turn, serves as another condition for the possibility of the formation of particular social imaginaries" (Brockerman 2003).

These two sections can be concluded by noting the idea of identity in Russian cultural discourses can be conceptualised in at least two ways. Firstly, there is ample room for a *self-other* divide and its strong bordering effects. Secondly, there are more subtle poststructuralist departures that admit the unstable/displaced nature of identities and decompose the stringency of ideological borderlines. These two approaches are quite visible within the various representations of history, politics, and war that seem to be constitutive for the conceptions of alterity.

Deconstructing power

Anti-hegemonic narratives respond to the multiplicity of state-sponsored speech acts that place Vladimir Putin at the very centre of the sacral place of power. A number of documentary motion pictures (such as "55" by Nikita Mikhalkov or "President's Group Portrait" by Leonid Mlechin), as well as a series of public initiatives (for example, those purporting the erection of monuments to Putin and his dog Cony) are testimonies of this trend. There are indeed visible proofs of Putin's "cult of personality", yet in the meantime, for most Russian officials "the personality of Putin is under taboo" (Vernidub and Pismennaya 2006).

It is against this background that one has to assess the appearance of multiple cultural discourses with a clear deconstructive potential. One of the strongest moves here is Bykov's radical disavowal of the strength of power per se:

"the main paradox is that the accession to the highest stage of power presupposed the transit to complete impotence. Anyone who conquered power was destined to experience such a shock because they comprehended its illusoriness [...]." (Bykov 2007: 185)

A number of Putin-focused discourses that have emerged in contemporary Russian literature belong to the same anti-hegemonic tradition. Most interesting among them are those that reduce Putin to "just an ordinary man" who lacks what might be dubbed a sense of "finalité politique". Thus, in Andrey Kolesnikov's series of essays, Putin is a simple and sometimes funny personality who could, for example, offer his already used pocket handkerchief to his French counterpart in a gesture of spontaneous and sincere friendship (Kolesnikov 2005).

In Kononenko's literary project "Vladimir Vladimirovich",[3] Putin is portrayed in a much more ironic way, as a character in a series of short anecdotes. The Putin imagined by Kononenko eviscerates politics; he is presented as someone who became president almost by accident, without any sort of "grand project". He is ignorant of the names of the leading Russian pop stars, top business figures, and the geographic location of some Russian regions. He is frivolous in his comments, and may fall asleep in his office. When his limousine breaks down, he takes a taxi to the Kremlin. In complicated situations, he is completely dependent on his advisers (and even the Dalai Lama). He also fears being arrested and jailed. Kononenko's Putin makes several attempts to resign, complaining that he is "the least needful person in the whole country". To entertain himself, he dreams about fishing or taking a space trip. He frankly confesses that he desperately misses his family and thinks about leading a secluded life. The deep dissatisfaction of the state of affairs is expressed in his phrase: "Even war is awkward; it's not war at all – a kind of anti-terrorist operation." His communications with other people in power are deficient: "Presidents come and go, but mayors stay", – this is how Kononenko imagines the way Yury Luzhkov, the mayor of Moscow, talks to Putin.

Kononenko makes Putin face himself as a virtual creature. Thus, in one of the anecdotes, he surprisingly finds out that a certain commercial firm offers to its customers a "President's visit to your business company, corporate party of family celebration". However, what resurfaces against this radically apolitical background is Putin's immanent and instinctive zeal for power. Having learned that salaries (a word he could not grasp at the outset) are strikingly low, he orders: "Let my people rob Yukos of money." In one of his dreams, huge Russian military aircraft are on duty in the Persian Gulf, and Coca-Cola is replaced by Russian kvas in all McDonald's restaurants.

The harshest deconstructive critique of Putin is found in Sergey Dorenko's "2008" (2005), a novel ironically dedicated to "the memory of Vladimir Putin, someone whom I recall with regret, understanding, bitterness, pride, and irony. How else can I recall my credulousness?" (Dorenko 2005: 7) In Dorenko's vi-

---

3   This project consists of an ongoing series of short stories about "Vladimir Vladimirovich" that can be found at http://vladimir.vladimirovich.ru.

sion, Putin is a man of "inaction", someone who "lets matters realize themselves, following events without forming them". Putin's is the "art of infiltration and mimicry"; he does not create situations, but decodes the course of events and tries to be in the right place at the right time. In times of crises, he finds himself in a kind of trance. He does not generate ideas, but follows his spin doctors. He looks at the world through them, smells through them, eats through them, etc. This is exactly what Zizek ventured to dub "interpassivity", or the relegation to others of one's "passive authentic experience" (Butler and Stephens 2006). Putin as imagined by Dorenko suffers from defencelessness, vulnerability, and the fear of losing control and being "out of context". He can only pretend to perform the role of political subject; his natural environment is one composed of simulacra. "People love you. – No, they simply watched me on TV" (Dorenko 2005: 213) – this is an anecdotal remark pointing to the virtual nature of Putin's leadership. The president, therefore, is rather a "ritualized public function which can be neither good nor bad. It is the subject of mythologized conscience [...] rather close to traditional folklore [...]. [His] texts might be interpreted in thousands of ways" (Plutzer-Sarno 2000).

In his narration, Dorenko quite frequently refers to the metaphor of emptiness, which arguably had been introduced a few years earlier by Viktor Erofeev, a Russian writer who described Putin as "the tsar of Russian dream", "an artist capable of playing any role staying in the meantime indifferent to its content". In this interpretation, Putin plays this "emptiness in which each of us is free to locate his/her feelings [...] and fill it out with one's fantasies" (Erofeev 2004). Very much like Dorenko and Kononenko, Erofeev denies Putin's subjectivity, depicting him as an "empty figure" (perhaps, an empty signifier) who in each critical case waits for "a master" who will tell him how to behave ("Does Putin exist at all?", asks Erofeev with unexpected radicality). Putin therefore symbolises a void that corresponds logically to Russia's "facelessness" predetermined by its location between West and East; therefore, Putin appears to be in paradoxical harmony with the enigmatic "Russian soul" (Erofeev 2004).

The state imagined and symbolised by Dorenko is built upon the emptiness uncovered by Erofeev; the government is devoid of any content and limits its activity to defending and protecting itself against something external to it. What is inside power, he wonders, and then argues: Perhaps there is nothing inside at all. This utterance should probably not be understood as one supporting the poststructuralist idea of democracy as being analogous to an "empty place of power"; Dorenko rather sustains a vision of politics as a sphere devoid of its "own" content. There are two interpretations of this argument. On the one hand, following traditional realism, it might mean that power is a goal in and of itself (Legro and Moravcsik 1999: 22). On the other hand, in a more postmodernist interpretation, one may find clear parallels with the concept of the "non-place, or ou-topia": "there is no place of power – it is both everywhere and nowhere" (Hardt and Negri 2000: 190).

This "emptiness" conceals striking instability within society. Putin's reign, in Dorenko's utopia, ends in a revolution: National Bolsheviks led by Eduard Limonov, and allied with Chechen military units, take Moscow. "We'll shoot all moguls" – Dorenko predicts a continuation of the vicious cycle of the Russian tradition of violent revolt against power. Mikhail Khodorkovsky, released from jail, is recruited by the new Revolutionary Council as Russia's new prime minister, empowered to reassemble the rapidly disintegrating country. It is this critical situation that unveils Putin's inappropriateness: He tries to call the US president and the German chancellor in order to find out what is going on. Consequently, Putin is accused of soliciting US military intervention in Russia and overthrown.

Unlike hegemonic discourses, a variety of literary narratives deconstruct power and identities. It is the "empty place of power" – nicely described by Bykov, Dorenko, Kononenko, and partly Kolesnikov – that allows for (and fosters) the multiplicity of identity discourses. Power is not "pre-empted", fixed or given from above, but has to be constructed and placed in the referential context of competing identities.

Conclusion

There are no doubts that the Russian state – as, perhaps, many other states – for the sake of its own endurance wishes to control intellectual and ideational practices emanating from the outside of the political elite and, whenever feasible, to use them for its own purposes. However, for a technocratic state predominantly concerned with stability – understood basically in materialistic terms as accumulation of the critical mass of resources – the sphere of ideas is only of secondary importance. It is at this juncture that the crucial challenge to the official regime lies: In traditions of political realism, it treats power as a possession, rather than as a delicate and sophisticated type of inclusive relationship, which is nicely articulated in critical theory starting from Foucault. This is why the Russian government appears to underestimate the constitutive force of free-floating discourses that are themselves potentially capable of shaping the contours and the content of power relations.

What I have ventured to show in this chapter is that the hegemonic discourse is not in a position to keep its monopoly in the interpretative field of politics and power. There are always "deviant languages" (Joenniemi 1995) of identity-building that stretch far beyond the limits imposed by official conceptualisations with their pre-fixed and sometimes exclusionist articulations. These alternative languages are more flexible in their articulations and may convey deeply political arguments, thus challenging the primacy of state politics.

In Soviet times, the ruling elite was enormously sensitive to any alternative discourses (those of dissidents, for example), which were automatically eliminated from the legitimised and authorised public space. That is why Soviet power could be challenged by a variety of seemingly non-political discourses (from famous "kitchen anecdotes" to pop music). The current Russian regime leaves ample space for alternative discourses and makes every effort to take advantage of them. Cultural narratives may represent a form of cultural resistance, yet they can also stabilise the hegemonic discourse. That is why the distinction between "official" and "non-official" (i.e., ironic, popular culture, etc.) discourses cannot be maintained in a strict fashion.

Against the background of the immanent fluidity and instability of the hegemonic discourse, it is questionable whether alternative discourses can be regarded as ostensibly distinct from – and necessarily challenging – it. Arguably, a more nuanced approach can consist in viewing cultural discourses as strengthening and exacerbating the dislocations embedded in each discourse, either supporting or opposing the ruling elite and its political preferences. Since the hegemonic discourse is so intrinsically variegated and multi-faced, it is not always possible to say whether a certain cultural narrative sustains or disavows it. The borderlines between discourses are shifting, and are sometimes far from evident.

What the analysis undertaken above has also made clear is that the deconstruction of hegemonic discourses and identities cannot be effectuated in the very political language that constructs and sustains them. Dominating power can be most deeply challenged by switching to a different language of communication. To speak – even critically – about power in the language register authentic to this very power means accepting – and abiding by – its discursive rules. That is why all attempts to dislocate sovereign power structurally from the political terrain it firmly occupies (as exemplified, for example, by political parties) appear to be either ineffective or tend to even strengthen this sovereign power, which has proven to be capable of imposing its discursive framework and rules on other political agents.

Thus, the picture of identity moulding consists of a "grand narrative" of the Kremlin and a multiplicity of "small narratives" that infuse more ambiguity, indeterminacy, and uncertainty into the efforts of explaining what Russian identity is. As one commentator put it, "Russia is a matter of taste," a "poly-semantic cloud" devoid of permanent and unquestionable core, a subject of disputation and controversies (Gornykh 2003). Its identity is a moving target; it always demonstrates the capability to rid itself of one set of meanings and acquire another one (Timofeev 2005). Identity and otherness thus have to be understood as consisting of symbols and metaphors that are usually undetermined and open to interpretation in the everlasting discursive process.

Bibliography

Aradau, C., L. Lobo-Guerrero, and R. van Munster. 2008. "Security, Technologies of Risk, and the Political: Guest Editors' Introduction". *Security Dialogue* 39, 2-3. 152.

Bakhtin, M. 1990. *Tvorchestvo Francois Rabelais i narodnaia kul'tura srednevekovia i Renessansa*. Moscow: Khudozhestvennaia Literatura.

Baudrillard, J. 2005. *The Intelligence of Evil, or the Lucidity Pact*. Oxford & New York: Berg. 17.

Brockerman, T. 2003. "The Failure of the Radical Democratic Imaginary. Žižek versus Laclau and Mouffe on vestigial utopia". *Philosophy and Social Criticism* 29, 2. 189.

Bulloch, D. 2007. "V is for Vendetta: P is for Power. A film reading of V for Vendetta". *Millenium: Journal of International Studies* 35, 2. 431-434.

Bykov, D. 2007. *Zh.D.* Moscow: Vagrius.

Croft, S. 2006. "Images and Imaginings of Security". *International Relations* 20, 4. 389.

Chertanov, M., and D. Bykov. 2005. *Pravda*. St.Petersburg: Amfora.

Derrida, J. 2005. *The Politics of Friendship*. London and New York: Verso.

Dorenko, S. 2005. *2008*. Moscow: Ad Marginem.

Dubin, B. 2004. "'Protivoves': simvolika Zapada v Rossii poslednikh let". *Pro et contra* 8, 3. 31.

Erofeev, V. 2004. "Rossiia i Pustota Putina". *InoSMI*, 15 March. Translated from *Die Welt*. http://www.inosmi.ru/print/208430.html [accessed 2 January 2009].

De Goede, M. 2008. "Beyond Risk: Premediation and the Post-9/11 Security Imagination". *Security Dialogue* 39, 2-3. 171.

Gornykh, A. 2003. "Rossiia kak delo vkusa". *Neprikosnovennyi zapas* 4, 30. http://magazines.russ.ru/nz/2003/4/gorn.html [accessed 31 August 2009].

Hardt, M. and A. Negri. 2000. *Empire*. Cambridge & London: Harvard University Press. 190.

Joenniemi, P. 1995. "Regionality: A Sovereign Principle of International Relations?". In *Peaceful Change in World Politics*, edited by Heikki Patomaki, 361. Tampere Peace Research Institute, Research Report N 71.

────── 2008. "Russia's Narrative Resources". *Journal of International Relations and Development* 11, 2. 122.

Kolesnikov, A. 2005. *Vladimir Putin. Mezhdu Evropoi i Aziei*. Moscow: Exmo and Kommersant Daily Publisher.19.

Kononenko, M. 2008. *Den' otlichnika*. Moscow: Folio Press.

Kovalyov, V. 2008. "Rossiiskaia fantastika kak politologiia". *Politicheskii klass* 29 February. http://politklass.ru/cgi-bin/issue.pl?id=954 [accessed 31 August 2009].

Legro, J. and A. Moravcsik. 1999. "Is Anybody Still a Realist?". *International Security* 24, 2. 22.

Lotman, Iu. 1970. *Struktura khudozhestvennogo teksta*. Moscow: Iskusstvo.

Muller, B. 2008. "Securing the Political Imagination: Popular Culture, the Security Dispositif and the Biometric State". *Security Dialogue* 39, 2-3. 200f.

Izvestiia. 2008. "My iz proshlogo". *Izvestiia* 55, March 28. 14.

Plutzer-Sarno, A. 2000. "Ritual i mif v sovremennoi politike". *Logos* 2, 23. 15.

Sorokin, V. 2006. *Den' oprichnika*. Moscow: Zakharov.

Timofeev, M. 2005. *Natsiosfera. Opyt analiza semiosfery natsii*. Ivanovo: Ivanovo State University Publishers. 54f.

Vernidub, A. and E. Pismennaya. 2006. "Mif-universal". *Russian Newsweek* 6, 84. 17-18.

Volodikhin, D. 2008. "Imperiia riadom". *Russkii zhurnal* 18 March. http://www.russ.ru/layout/set/print/lyudi/imperiya_ryadom [accessed 2 January 2009].

Zizek, S. 2004. The Lesson of Ranciere, in Jacques Ranciere. The Politics of Aesthetics. London & New York: Continuum. 69-79.

Butler, R. and S. Stephens, eds. 2006. *Slavoj Žižek. The Universal Exception. Selected Writings*, vol. 2. London & New York: Continuum.

Zvereva, G. 2005. "Natsionalisticheskii diskurs i setevaia kultura". *Pro et Contra* 2, 29. 35.

Rethinking Identification With the Hegemonic Discourse of a "Strong Russia" Through Laclau and Mouffe

Martin Müller

From the conceptual perspective of poststructuralist discourse theory as developed by Laclau and Mouffe, this contribution rethinks the project of a strong Russia. Drawing on material gathered during nine months of ethnographic research at the Moscow State Institute of International Relations (MGIMO), the premier school for educating future Russian elites, it argues that identification with a strong Russia is inherently ambiguous: Articulations of a strong Russia are always accompanied by the imminent possibility of a weak Russia. This constant possibility of a weak Russia prevents the full realisation of the identity of a strong Russia. The project of a strong Russia is therefore structured around a constitutive lack: It is always incomplete, but this incompleteness, at the same time, is the condition of its very possibility.

Russia as a great power?

The war in South Ossetia in August 2008 once again fuelled discussions on Russia's re-emergence as a great power in world politics – a great power that flexes its military muscle and asserts its influence in the post-Soviet space and beyond. Arguments to this effect have dominated the news coverage at least since President Vladimir Putin's second term in office and flared up in the aftermath of the South Ossetian incident: Headlines announced that "The bear is back" (The Australian, Dibb 2008), that the West faces "The Russian threat" (Die Zeit 2008) or, reminiscent of the epic Star Wars saga, that "The empire strikes back" (Time; Baer 2008). Even broadsheets such as the leading German Süddeutsche Zeitung ran headlines like the following: "Russian foreign policy strategy still knows only one idea: the tank" (Zekri 2008).

In an editorial, Thomas Kleine-Brockhoff, senior director for policy programs at the German Marshall Fund of the United States, claims that the world is witnessing "the attempt of a country to return to the centre of world politics with force. The Russian occupation tanks in Georgia are a symbol for the attempt to re-establish old patterns of geopolitics. To create a belt of satellite states with limited sovereignty is Moscow's aim. [...] Backed by an exploding oil price, Moscow has started a kind of rollback" (Kleine-Brockhoff 2008: 2).

Diagnoses of a resurgent Russia are not confined to the public media, though. Many foreign policy scholars, while adopting a more toned-down voice, arrive at broadly similar conclusions. Gone seem the days of the 1990s when a staggering, unstable Russia appeared to be on the brink of collapse and could easily be dismissed in international politics. Since the start of the new millennium, Russia has exhibited new self-confidence and stability as it emphatically asserts its place in the international arena. Scholars observe that the country is pursuing an increasingly confrontational course vis-à-vis Western states and is attempting to restore its status as an influential world power and return to past greatness (most recently Allison 2008; Kanet 2007; King 2008; Trenin 2006, 2007). This literature forcefully makes the point of Russia's re-emergence as a great power and chronicles Russia's re-assertion in international politics.

Rethinking the identification with a strong Russia, this chapter locates itself within a body of critical discourse scholarship at the intersection of political geography and international relations. In political geography, what has become known as "critical geopolitics" examines the social construction of global space. How do certain narratives of world politics become seemingly objective points of identification? Adopting "discourse" as a conceptual linchpin, critical geopolitics views geography as being imbued with struggles for the power to organise, occupy and administer space (Dodds 2001; Ó Tuathail 1996). In a similar vein, discourse takes centre stage in critical international relations theory (e.g. Edkins 1999; George 1994; Milliken 1999): It constructs meaning within systems of signification and produces the subjects it speaks of. The clarion call of such work has been "to demystify the process by which political subjects are made" (Kuus 2007: 91; see especially Campbell 1992). The analysis of global politics through a discursive lens then is not so much an effort to measure the objective interests of states as rational actors entrenched in struggles for power and security, but rather an interpretation of how meaning and subjects in international politics are constituted in specific contexts.

Such a perspective has recently begun to take hold in the analysis of Russian foreign policy, enlisting the ideas of various post-positivist theorists such as Alain Badiou (Prozorov 2008), Michel Foucault (Neumann 2008), or Ernesto Laclau (Makarychev 2005; Morozov in this volume). Drawing on the work of Laclau and Mouffe (Laclau 1990, 1996; Laclau and Mouffe 1985), this chapter follows in the footsteps of poststructuralist discourse theory to show that the hegemonic project of a strong Russia is a highly ambiguous one. It is shot through with intense doubts and misgivings about the very possibility of a strong Russia. Many accounts of Russian great-power fantasies fail to problematise this ambiguity. Instead, they diagnose the emergence of a Russia triumphant in which great-power ideology rules almost completely unbridled. The discursive construction of a strong Russia, however, is bound up with fears of a weak Russia – a Russia that fails to realise its ambitious plans to live up to its great-power potential, that is perceived to be marginalised, or is even excluded from world politics.

By way of empirical illustration, this chapter employs material collected during ethnographic research at the Moscow State Institute of International Relations (MGIMO), the premier institute for teaching international relations in Russia (see Müller 2009). What makes MGIMO interesting for studying identification with a strong Russia is its affiliation with the Russian Ministry of Foreign Affairs and the Russian state apparatus more generally. Not only does the institute train future Russian diplomats, but it also serves as a preparatory school for students who are to later occupy influential positions in Russian politics and society. Thus, the following is more than an isolated case study. Given the pivotal role of MGIMO in the reproduction of Russian elites, looking at the way discourses are recited in elite education may even provide a glimpse of the geopolitical thinking of the future Russian elites.

Ethnography and discourse analysis

Prima facie, the liaison of ethnography and discourse analysis may seem odd. A large number of discourse analytical approaches originate in linguistics, which makes for their fixation on discourse as text and talk, or as "language in use" (Taylor 2001: 6). The linguistic turn in the social sciences with its interest in the semiosis of representation further reinforced this linguistic focus. Given their conceptual lineage from language philosophy, structuralism and poststructuralism served to cement a take on discourse research that owed much to Derrida's famous and often misinterpreted dictum that "there is nothing outside of the text" (Derrida 1976: 158). It is not surprising, then, if discourse analysis is considered the paragon of the linguistic turn in the social sciences (cf. Neumann 2002: 629).

Ethnographic research, on the other hand, is mostly concerned with the everyday practices and interactions of social groups in a particular setting (Denzin 1997). In this kind of research, text and talk often play a subordinate role. Furthermore, with its attention to social practices, ethnography is occasionally set in deliberate contrast to discourse analysis, which, allegedly, produces lopsided research "relegating or even erasing people's experiences and everyday understandings of the phenomena under question" (Megoran 2006: 622). Proponents of discourse analysis, on the other hand, might argue that the problem of methodogenesis in ethnography turns discourses into creatures of the ethnographer's own making instead of reflecting larger social structures. After all, the ethnographic researcher does not merely record or retrieve data, but actively partakes in its creation.

Notwithstanding the seeming incommensurability of ethnography and discourse analysis, I would like to argue that there is added value in combining the two. In particular, ethnography is able to elucidate the workings of discourse in specific contexts. In so doing, it looks at how discourses from the global or national level play out in particular settings that might otherwise be off-limits for other research methods.

> "Attempts to understand the complex relations between the international and everyday demonstrate the importance of ensuring that small, mundane daily practices of everyday life are understood in relation to the reconstructions of the nation and the international" (Dowler and Sharp 2001: 174).

Analysing the mechanisms through which discursive subjectivation becomes powerful is the key advantage of harnessing ethnography for discourse analysis. It examines the power of discourse to structure the social world and make subjects that identify with certain subject positions. By engaging with people instead of systems or states, an ethnographic discourse analysis collapses the distance between the research subjects and the researcher (Bigo and Walker 2007).

Discourse analysis drawing on the work of Laclau and Mouffe is not dogmatic about the choice of methodology. In fact, Howarth (2004: 336) explicitly includes ethnographic methods such as qualitative interviewing and participant observation in the discourse analytic repertoire and cautions against "linguistic reductionism". Of course, employing such reactive methods of data collection demands an adequate problematisation of the research process. Issues of positionality and researcher subjectivity, access and rapport, power asymmetries, or selectivity must not be bracketed in a discourse analysis that relies on ethnographic material. For the present case, a comprehensive treatment of methodological issues can be found in Müller (2009).

I conducted the ethnographic research for this study when I was an exchange student at MGIMO during the academic year 2005/2006, attending lectures and seminars that seemed relevant to my overall interest in geopolitical identities. A professor at MGIMO supervised my research in order to ensure compliance with the tacit local codes governing primary research. During the time at MGIMO, I kept a field diary, audiotaped lectures, and, towards the end of my research time, conducted 39 semi-structured interviews with students of different departments at MGIMO. The following analysis draws on 25 hours of transcribed material from lectures and seminars and 22 hours of transcribed material from interviews with students on Russian foreign policy and Russia's role in world politics. Insofar as the interviews did not occur naturally, they inevitably reflect the influence of the interviewer to a much greater degree than the lectures.

It is only through *in situ* fieldwork such as ethnography that suitable material for an analysis of discourses at MGIMO can be gathered. One caveat is in order, however: it is not my intention, nor indeed is it possible, to paint a representative picture of the whole student and lecturer body at MGIMO. The verbatim excerpts presented in this article have been chosen to reflect what I have interpreted as the dominant themes in the material and are meant to represent typical cases – to the extent that this is ever possible. Moreover, my position as a German and European researcher is inevitably tightly knit into almost all stages of my research, making the interpretations of great-power visions rendered in this chapter not a somehow external object of inquiry but, to a significant degree, my own creation.

Imagining a strong Russia

The professors and students from my sample largely recite a discourse of Russia as a strong and prospering country on the upswing. While Russia was weak and troubled in the 1990s, afflicted with domestic unrest and engrossed in a search for itself, the inauguration of President Putin and the start of the new millennium – so the story goes – have broken this deadlock. Russia's re-emergence as a strong power is articulated at MGIMO by drawing together elements from a range of different, sometimes even conflicting geopolitical discourses. The notion of a "strong Russia" has such diverse meanings as recuperating Russia's geopolitical influence in world politics and, particularly, in the post-Soviet states, establishing Russia as an independent pole in a multipolar world order, defending Russian national pride and cranking up Russia's economy.

Students' comments on Russia's geopolitical ambitions express the self-confidence of a young generation that has come of age in the rising Russia of the new millennium. Mikhail (Year 3, International Relations, 11/68)[1] observes that Russia has recently progressed from being a state that was more or less ignored in world politics and needed help to sort itself out to one that counts as a key player, as is evident in the Iran conflict or in its membership in the G8. Xenia underscores this point (Year 4, Other Department, 33/3) and claims that Russia is a powerful country that is respected and even feared by other states.

Russia's endeavour to rebuild its geopolitical influence is framed within a narrative of restoring the status of a great power, which it lost in the post-Soviet transformation. It is therefore not a new quality, but one that has always rightfully belonged to Russia. Only few claim that Russia's great-power status vanished irrevocably with the collapse of the Soviet Union and can hardly be regained, whereas the majority is convinced that in one way or another Russia, is either in the process of becoming a great power or has already become one. The conception that Russia's "great powerness" is virtually ingrained in the Russian people, that Russia is destined to be a great power, is seen as very prominent in Russian society. Sergei even claims that being a great power is virtually inescapable for Russia:

> "In fact, if Russia is fated to make a choice at some point, if it wants to exist, then it has to be a great power. To some degree, even our leadership understands this. The phrase that Russia must either be great or not exist at all is attributed to Vladimir Putin. [...] Russia must be, and we believe that it is destined to become, a great power." (Sergei, Year 3, International Relations, 01/71)

The notion of great power is associated with certain attributes and demands that a great power needs to fulfil. At MGIMO, being a great power means that Russia should play a more salient role in the post-Soviet space. There is a

---

[1] Details in parentheses indicate students' progress, subject of study, and the transcript code of the relevant passage.

strong feeling that Russia and the post-Soviet states are still united by a common bond, given their shared history within the Soviet Union. According to this position, one country cannot do without the other:

> "History shows that we live badly without each other, that we are used to being together. [...] That is, the republics of the CIS cannot do without us and, in fact, nor can we do in a meaningful way without them." (Liuba, Year 4, International Relations, 09/47)

Although the notions of dependence and solidarity among post-Soviet states figure prominently in statements at MGIMO, the same students and lecturers also demand Russian independence. A strong Russia is also an independent Russia that does not look to others for orientation or let others dictate Russian actions. Russia is construed as a self-sufficient (*samodostatochnaia*) country that should pursue an independent foreign policy without having to take into account the interests of other states. Once again, integration into a larger alliance of states does not figure prominently in this imagination, as one lecturer elaborates:

> "I want to say that there is no sense in Russia joining the EU, because Russia itself has to become a centre of force. Because all who accede join the EU as a centre of force. But Russia itself has to form something around itself; they should join Russia, this integration in the context of the CIS. That is, Russia should attract others and not the other way round." (Lecture 14/74)

Only if Russia accrues enough strength can it act as an independent centre of force in world politics and work towards establishing a multipolar world order. The vision of a multipolar world is thus invariably tied to Russia's re-emergence as an influential world power.

Only in rare instances does such a great-power vision of Russia's future draw critique. Boris (Year 4, International Journalism, 27/13, 49) is one of the very few students who voices doubts about the usual conceptions of Russia as a great power. Instead, he offers a different idea of what constitutes a great power:

> "For me, a great power is primarily a state that can serve as an epitome of virtue for other states, an example of highly moral, highly cultured political relations with that country. A highly developed society that has a high level of self-awareness, which has its role in the world and which, finally, has good economic indicators. That's what a great power is for me." (Boris, Year 4, International Journalism, 27/49)

Boris therefore does not completely dismiss the great-power concept for Russia. However, he envisions a great power with different, more humanist attributes, but one that is still influential in the world. The emphasis that Boris places on economic indicators is shared by many of his fellow students: Economic success serves to buttress Russia's claim to a leading position in world politics. It not only garners the respect of the world's leading states and perhaps places Russia among them, but it also enables Russia to play the desired preeminent role in the post-Soviet space:

> "[W]ithout economic relations, without economic growth, it is impossible to return these republics to Russia, to tie them closer to Russia just through some political will."
> (Tatiana, Year 4, International Relations, 08/3)

Economic development is thus not an aim in itself, but always constitutive of the larger project of rebuilding a strong Russia.

It is important to emphasise that arguing in favour of Russian strength and independence in such manifold ways does not necessarily imply a hostile or uncooperative stance towards the West. In fact, many students view cooperation with Europe and the US as essential if Russia wants to become a true world leader and be included in the ranks of the most powerful states. For Mila (Year 4, International Relations, 13/81), cooperation is a necessity in a globalised world if states do not want to fall behind. The clarion call in the foreign policy of today's Russia is thought to be cooperation and not, as in the Soviet Union, aggressive conflict. A strong Russia thus maintains constructive relations with the West, all the while safeguarding its sovereignty and independence.

At MGIMO, the vision of Russia as a strong and independent state is linked to a multitude of ideas about Russia's role and place in world politics and its relations to other states. A strong Russia is a sovereign state; it is neither East nor West, but unique in its constitution; it unifies the post-Soviet space; it defends Russian national interests; it enjoys economic prosperity; it upholds national pride; it regains global influence and respect; it cooperates with Western states. The idea of a strong Russia is able to unify the social terrain by providing a comprehensive universal screen onto which all kinds of geopolitical hopes, demands, and aspirations can be projected.

RETHINKING "STRONG RUSSIA" 335

This unifying effect is characteristic for what Laclau (1996: 36) calls *empty signifiers* – signifiers without a signified. Empty signifiers collapse all differences into chains of equivalence. In this process, the idea of a strong Russia becomes essentially amorphous: It does not have any intrinsic meaning, but is defined by the demands inscribed on it. As the meaning of other signifiers becomes partially fixed in relation to the empty signifier, the chain of equivalence begins to structure an ever-greater part of the social. This results in the emergence of a discourse in which the flow of differences is arrested around empty signifiers as privileged discursive centres that institute definite meanings. The presence of empty signifiers is thus the very condition of the emergence of hegemonic discourses (Laclau 1996: 43).

The success of the hegemonic discourse of a strong Russia is predicated on the ability of various forces to claim that they fill the empty signifier of "strong Russia". Given the range of different demands projected onto the idea of a strong Russia, the project seems to be fairly successful as a unifying force. This testifies to the ability of the empty signifier to cancel differences: There is hardly anyone who would reject the project of a strong Russia. It successfully unites elements that are often articulated in separate, even conflicting Russian geopolitical discourses identified by authors like O'Loughlin et al. (2005), Smith (1999), or Tsygankov (2003): The reassertion of Russian influence in the Near Abroad and the unity of Slavic people appeals to demands often ascribed to a Slavophile position; the attempt to make Russia a respected, full-fledged member of the global group of leading states and recoup its great-power status picks up demands voiced from what is typically described as a statist position; the agenda of establishing Russia as an independent centre of power in Eurasia ties in with demands articulated within various Eurasianist geopolitical discourses; and the focus on improving Russia's economic performance fulfils demands that are commonly attributed to a geo-economic discourse. The concept of a strong Russia is thus a hegemonic discourse.

The hegemonic discourse at MGIMO shares many similarities with what Smith (1999), O'Loughlin et al. (2005), and many others have identified as a democratic statist position. Russia is considered a great power that is different from the West, but nevertheless accepts that cooperation with it is necessary in certain issues or plays the role of a political broker to mediate in conflicts with states like Iran. Just like at MGIMO, democratic statism represents the Near Abroad as somehow belonging to one community with Russia and as crucial to

Russian geopolitical interests and its re-assertion as a great power. Both Smith (1999) and O'Loughlin et al. (2005) find that democratic statism is the dominant discourse among Russia's ruling elites and in the Russian population – a dominance that is also evident at MGIMO.

This empirical parallel underscores MGIMO's close involvement in the Russian state apparatus. Its status as an elite school ensures that its graduates occupy high-ranking positions not only in foreign policy, but in the Russian state and the corporate world at large. MGIMO alumni are oligarchs, ministers, heads of state, and top business managers. MGIMO acts as a locus of consecration, bestowing societal distinction on a social group that is elected to become the governing elite (cf. Bourdieu 1996). It fashions a future elite with the authority to perpetuate the hegemonic geopolitical structures.

What prevents a strong Russia from being?

Articulations of a strong Russia at MGIMO do not go uncontested, however. They are accompanied by misgivings about Russia's ability to live up to this image, to realise this identity. Russia is frequently portrayed as "not quite yet a strong Russia", as a strong Russia in the making. Optimistic ideas about what Russia should and could be are contrasted with the stark reality of the present day. Frequently, this divide between reality and aspiration is couched in terms of an unfulfilled potential.

> "This is why I think that if we define the situation of Russia, then Russia has the potential and the ability to play the role of one of the great powers, of one of the first powers on a global level. But at the moment this is not true." (Lecture 14/31)

But what is it that prevents this realisation of a strong Russia right now? At MGIMO, several obstacles to this great-power identity are articulated. Most prominently, Western actions obviate Russia's re-emergence. The "Colour Revolutions" in several post-Soviet states are often associated with Western agency, which aims to weaken Russia by snatching away its former brother states. Just as in Soviet times, the West is seen to be still working against Russia:

> "[L]ook at those botanic revolutions, or at the horticultural revolutions or at the flower revolutions, as they call them. Lemon revolution, saffron revolution. All those revolutions cannot do without Western NGOs. The West, in fact, is at work. It is just that in the

closed Soviet society, we did not know how the West worked against us." (Lecture 62/4)

By the same token, the eastern expansion of the European Union and NATO is perceived as an effort to contain Russia:

> "All ex-republics of the CIS are rushing to follow the West, joining NATO or joining the EU. There is a constant tendency of dissociation from Russia, of diminishing the Russian influence over these states." (Tatiana, Year 4, International Relations, 08/3)

If we recall that close integration with the post-Soviet states is a constitutive moment of the "strong Russia" discourse, perceived attempts at drawing these states away from Russia present an assault on this discursive hegemony. The West is seen as supporting the centrifugal tendencies in the post-Soviet states and is thus negotiated into an antagonistic role vis-à-vis Russia. Both factions are vying for influence; they are "pulling the blanket back and forth between each other" (*peretiagivaiut drug na druga odeialo*) (Yulia, Year 4, Political Science, 25/16). This competition sometimes translates into outright opposition to Russia:

> "Right now, I think that Ukraine and Georgia are like cards that the Western countries, the US among others, play in order to curtail Russia's sphere of influence, overturn its political authority and partly even overturn the country itself. I think that this [NATO membership] is a carrot [*kalach*] with which they entice these countries." (Vasily, Year 4, International Relations, 19/59)

It is not only the perceived threat of losing the post-Soviet states and Western opposition that prevent Russia from becoming the influential power it wants to become. There is also the impression at MGIMO that Russia is excluded from world politics more generally. The global dominance of the US foils all Russian attempts at building a multipolar world that recognises the interests of other powers than the US. It appears that Russia's wish to play a role equal to that of European states does not find recognition. On the contrary, at MGIMO, sometimes the feeling prevails that many in the West would prefer to see Russia revert to imperialist sphere-of-influence thinking and thus confirm the deeply ingrained stereotypes.

"One other thing that I feel sad about is that Russia very often plays the role of a whipping boy [*mal'chik dlia bit'ia*] in international relations, because Russia's prestige, its image in the eyes of other countries is not improving or is only improving very slowly. All of my friends who were in Europe say that Russia is perceived as a monster there. Such negative dispositions! And at all conferences that were especially organised for Russians and Europeans, to jointly study and research certain problems, Russia serves as an example of all the anti-democratic vices you can possibly think of in this world." (Natalia, Year 3, Political Science, 29/5)

Rather than being taken seriously as an equal partner, Russia is looked down upon as backward and underdeveloped.

"We can do what we want: we stay unreliable partners. Here, again, it is tried to create such a negative image of Russia." (Aleksandr, Year 3, International Relations, 14/57)

Russia's willingness to cooperate with the West, as expressed in imaginations of a strong Russia in the previous section, is thus thwarted by the imputed reluctance of the West to recognise Russia as a serious partner. This lack of recognition is a persistent and recurring topos in descriptions of Russia's relations with Western states.

The motif of exclusion points to the tight conceptual coupling of antagonism and dislocation emphasised by Laclau (1990: 5-41). The West acts as an (external) antagonist and threat to Russia's great-power project, whereas the lack of recognition and lament of Russia's unfulfilled potential present a (internal) dislocation. Both antagonism and dislocation prevent the full constitution of a strong Russia and therefore need to be countered if Russia wants to become strong. The favoured strategy at MGIMO for countering these blockages consists in reaffirming the hegemonic discourse of a strong Russia: in order to withstand outside threats and overcome exclusion, Russia must become stronger.

"We should learn our lessons from all this and gather our strength in order to then solve our tasks. We don't feel hurt that others will play give-away with us [*igrat' v poddavki*], that they want to settle their accounts with us. As long as we are not strong, nobody is obliged to us in any way." (Alexander, Year 3, International Relations, 14/50)

Russia must develop its potential if it wants to garner recognition in the international arena and put an end to exclusion. Marina invokes the example of the USSR as a great power that nobody dared to ridicule or ignore:

"If we just take the USSR. It was a great power [*velikaia derzhava*]. Nobody would have said this [such derogatory things] about it. There were a lot of bad things, but still it was a great power." (Marina, Year 4, Other Department, 34/62)

Only if Russia gains in power will it have a chance to counter exclusion and opposition and work towards the aim of realising the identity of a strong Russia. The possibility of a weak Russia that gives in to outside forces must be ruled out.

The majority opinion of students at MGIMO holds that on its path towards becoming a great power, Russia is required first of all to increase its economic leverage. Most students preferred realising Russian economic interests over Russian political interests, when asked directly. This primacy of the economy is often justified as a new pragmatism that has supposedly replaced the ideological baggage of the Soviet Union.

> "I think that Russia's position now is pragmatic and ideologically we do not look to anyone specifically. Even economically. In my opinion, the engine of history now is the economy and not ideology, religion or something else. We are pragmatic and develop the relations with our partners, with those who are ready." (Ivan, Year 4, International Journalism, 05/9)

Viktor (Year 4, Political Science, 18/5) similarly judges that political confrontation is "too costly: we don't have money for all that nonsense". Foresighted economic policy guarantees stability and improves the welfare of Russian citizens. Only in the case of societal prosperity can a state conduct a successful domestic and foreign policy, students believe:

> "I think that right now, realising Russian economic interests is more important, because political interests follow them. If economic interests are more or less satisfied, then politics follows them anyway. This is inevitable. They always go together. But primarily it will be economic ones, because if people are hungry in your country, they won't support those politicians that will realise the government of the state." (Oleg, Year 4, International Relations, 26/9)

> "Generally speaking, politics – that's words, and economy – that's business [*delo*]. It's more important to see something in practice and that's what the economy is all about." (Vitaly, Year 4, International Relations, 28/9)

For Tatiana, the neglect of the economy was one of the primary reasons for the demise of the USSR:

> "What is the reason for the disintegration of the Soviet Union? It is because the leaders of the Soviet Union did not understand that when the economy is starting to stall, when it stops working, then one has to direct all attention not towards extending one's sphere of influence, but towards the economy. Because a strong economy means a strong politics, as Marx already said. Now we no longer believe in Marx, but this postulate remains and it is a correct statement." (Tatiana, Year 4, International Relations, 08/11)

Post-Soviet Russia is seen as having learned from this experience and following the correct order: first the economy, then politics. In the competition with other states, garnering their recognition is an important element:

> "Improving our economic situation, we become more important in the world arena and the big countries will turn their attention to us. [...] I think that we first have to develop the economy as it is necessary, and then they will already address us in a completely different way." (Galia, Year 4, International Relations, 23/10)

Recovering its economic potential will allow Russia to turn from an object into a subject of international relations and shape international political processes more actively. It will allow it to shake off and withstand the antagonistic forces:

> "When we have completely gotten back on our feet, when we have acquired that economic power, only then can we dictate our terms." (Larissa, Year 4, International Relations, 15/11)

"Great powerness" is thus primarily associated with the soft power of the economy and not with the hard power of military clout. This prominence of the economy seems all the more plausible when looking at students' socialisation and life trajectories. In a time when the Russian economy was booming and companies were scouring the Russian labour market for new graduates, the attention of highly qualified students at MGIMO was increasingly attracted by private business. A similar thing may be said about lecturers, who also experienced first-hand the economic upturn in Russia and the new possibilities it opens up in the international arena.

With Laclau (1990), the strategy of making Russia still stronger to defeat the antagonistic forces blocking its identity is founded on the illusion that upon defeating the antagonist, the subject will be able to complete its identity. Antagonism, however, not only blocks the realisation of Russia's geopolitical identity, but at the same time is the condition of its very possibility.

> "I cannot destroy a context without destroying at the same time the identity of the particular subject who carries out the destruction. It is a very well known historical fact that an oppositionist force whose identity is constructed within a certain system of power is ambiguous vis-à-vis that system, because the latter is what prevents the constitution of identity and it is, at the same time, its condition of existence. And any victory against the system also destabilizes the identity of the victorious force." (Laclau 1996: 27)

The blockages described in this section are thus paradoxically subversive and constitutive of Russian geopolitical identity. They are subversive because they threaten or block the emergence of a strong Russia: Due to their presence, Russia cannot become what it aspires to be. The Western influence in the post-Soviet space, the expansion of NATO and the EU, the disregard for Russia – all this is interpreted as creating the imminent possibility of a weak Russia and needs to be done away with if Russia ever wants to become strong. At the same time, these forces are constitutive of Russian geopolitical identity, because it is only in their presence that a strong Russia can be thought. Russia must be strong, Russia must rebuild its economy in order to resist and overcome outside threats and marginalisation, in order to annihilate the antagonistic forces.

Making the geopolitical subject

We have seen that the discourse of a strong Russia at MGIMO features the qualities necessary to make it hegemonic: It successfully unifies a wide range of political demands and thus is able to assert its objectivity and structure the social field. Whether it is Russian cultural uniqueness, Russian independence and sovereignty in international relations, the concept of multipolarity, the defence of Russian national interests, Russian economic prosperity, or Russian influence in the post-Soviet states – all of those come together in a chain of equivalence around the empty signifier of a "strong Russia".

This empty signifier, however, does not refer to a high density of meaning, but rather expresses an absent fullness. The material from MGIMO demonstrates that the geopolitical discourse of a strong Russia does not refer to a fully constituted identity, but to an unachieved wholeness. The identity of a strong Russia is blocked. Russia is not a strong country, but rather an emerging strong country, a strong country in the making. However, a multiplicity of antagonistic forces always prevents the full realisation of a "strong Russia" identity. By threatening to foil the subject of a "strong Russia", by threatening to leave Russia weak and enfeebled, these antagonistic forces elicit a re-affirmation of this very hegemonic project: In order to counter the threats emanating from the antagonistic forces, Russia must become even stronger.

The geopolitical subject at MGIMO arises from the identification with the hegemonic project of a "strong Russia" that is, however, always faced with antagonistic forces that prevent it from being. Because of the presence of antagonistic forces, the hegemony of the identification with a strong Russia can never be complete. According to Laclau, every hegemonic project always contains in itself the possibility of its negation and subversion: "the incomplete and contingent nature of the totality would spring not only from the fact that no hegemonic system can be fully imposed, but also from the intrinsic ambiguities of the project itself." (Laclau 1990: 28) Hegemonic projects are thus always unstable and constantly challenged by what they exclude.

Being the condition of both the possibility and the impossibility of a strong Russia, a weak Russia is always present as a permanent lack in articulations of a strong Russia. In the discourse theory of Laclau, this corresponds to the constitution of the subject as

> "the subject of the signifier. It strives to inscribe itself as a signifier in the symbolic order, but cannot find a signifier which represents it. The subject is therefore penetrated by a constitutive lack. The subject is this lack, and the subjectivation of the subject through the identification with different subject positions is merely an attempt to fill it." (Torfing 1999: 57)

The subject has a failed structural identity. It is compelled to act in the attempt to fill this structural lack through identification with different subject positions and recreate an imaginary wholeness.

Revising our understanding of a strong Russia

By the end of the Putin presidency, identification as a great power seems to have imparted a measure of stability to Russia. As the hegemonic discourse, it has achieved a broad social consensus around the empty signifier of a "strong Russia" – a consensus that is also reflected at MGIMO. By now, there is a wealth of material examining Russia's ambition to become a great power. However, looking at the discourse of a strong Russia through the lens of Laclau and Mouffe's poststructuralist discourse theory refines our understanding of this project in two respects.

First, it highlights the inherent ambiguity of the project of a strong Russia: this ambiguity is evident throughout MGIMO in the split between what Russia would like to be and what it currently is, between aspiration and reality. This makes for often rather contradictory positions where students and lecturers boast Russia's military and economic power, but lament its marginalisation and exclusion from world politics at the same time. At MGIMO, imaginations of a strong Russia are coupled with imaginations of the impending possibility of a weak Russia. This co-presence of a weak Russia as the opposite of a strong Russia is constitutive of the production of Russian great-power identity. A strong Russia is always predicated on what it claims not to be. Every study of Russian great-power identity therefore also needs to be attentive to the articulation of the blockage that underpins this identity.

Second, Russian identity as articulated at MGIMO is structured around what Laclau calls a constitutive lack. The subject has a failed structural identity, i.e., an identity that is never complete, and comes to act through the need to fill the lack in the discursive structure. Rather than claiming that subjects at MGIMO identify with a Russia that already has a great-power identity, it would be more adequate to say that they identify with a Russia that strives to realise a great-power identity. This difference is not trivial. It means that for a strong Russia to become a hegemonic identification, it needs an antagonist that blocks this very identity. A strong Russia is then articulated as the solution to overcome this blockage. From a discourse theoretical perspective, Western moves directed at opposing or isolating a strong Russia are thus likely to only reinforce the antagonistic divide and buttress Russian strong-power identity instead of assuaging it. Such policy might lead to the emergence of a forceful chain of equivalence in which a reinforced "strong Russia" faces a Western antagonist.

Bibliography

Allison, R. 2008. "Russia resurgent? Moscow's campaign to 'coerce Georgia to peace'". *International Affairs* 84, 6. 1145-1171.

Baer, R. 2008. "The Russian empire strikes back". *Time* 12 August. http://www.time.com/time/specials/packages/article/0,28804,1832294_1832295_1831857,00.html [accessed 28 August 2009]

Bigo, D. and R. Walker. 2007. "International, Political, Sociology". *International Political Sociology* 1, 1. 1-5.

Bourdieu, P. 1996 (1989). *The State Nobility: elite schools in the field of power.* Stanford: Stanford University Press.

Campbell, D. 1992. *Writing Security: United States foreign policy and the politics of identity.* Minneapolis: University of Minnesota Press.

Denzin, N. 1997. *Interpretive Ethnography: ethnographic practices for the 21st century.* Thousand Oaks, CA: Sage.

Derrida, J. 1976. *Of Grammatology.* Baltimore: Johns Hopkins University Press.

Dibb, P. 2008. "The bear is back". *The Australian* 18 August. http://www.theaustralian.news.com.au/story/0,25197,24196162-7583,00.html [accessed 28 August 2009].

Die Zeit 2008. "Die russische Gefahr". *Die Zeit* 14 August. 1.

Dodds, K. 2001. "Political Geography III: critical geopolitics after 10 years". *Progress in Human Geography* 25, 3. 469-484.

Dowler, L. and J. Sharp. 2001. "A Feminist Geopolitics?". *Space & Polity* 5, 3. 165-176.

Edkins, J. 1999. *Poststructuralism and International Relations: bringing the political back in.* London: Lynne Rienner.

George, J. 1994. *Discourses of Global Politics: a critical (re)introduction to international relations.* Boulder: Lynne Rienner.

Howarth, D. 2004. "Applying Discourse Theory: the method of articulation". In *Discourse Theory in European Politics: identity, policy and governance*, edited by D. Howarth and J. Torfing, 316-349. Basingstoke: Palgrave Macmillan.

King, C. 2008. "The Five-Day War". *Foreign Affairs* 87, 6. 2-11.

Kleine-Brockhoff, T. 2008. Russland will nicht mehr nach Westen. *Süddeutsche Zeitung.* 25 August. 2.

Kuus, M. 2007. "Ubiquitous Identities, Elusive Subjects: puzzles from Central Europe". *Transactions of the Institute of British Geographers* 32, 1. 90-101.

Laclau, E. 1990. *New Reflections on the Revolution of our Time.* London: Verso.

―――― 1996. *Emancipation(s).* London: Phronesis.

Laclau, E. and C. Mouffe. 1985. *Hegemony and Socialist Strategy: towards a radical democratic politics.* London: Verso.

Laruelle, M. 2008. *Russian Eurasianism: an ideology of empire.* Baltimore: Johns Hopkins University Press.

Makarychev, A. 2005. "Russia's Discursive Construction of Europe and Herself: towards new spatial imaginary". Paper presented at the conference on "Post-Soviet In/Securities: Theory and Practice", 7-8 October, Mershon Center of the Ohio State University. https://kb.osu.edu/dspace/bitstream/1811/30222/9/MakarychevPaper.pdf [accessed 1 September 2009].

Megoran, N. 2006. "For Ethnography in Political Geography: experiencing and re-imagining Ferghana Valley boundary closures." *Political Geography* 25. 622-640.

Milliken, J. 1999. "The Study of Discourse in International Relations: a critique of research and methods". *European Journal of International Relations* 5, 2. 225-254.

Müller, M. 2009. *Making Great Power Identities in Russia: an ethnographic discourse analysis of education at a Russian elite university.* Zürich: LIT.

Neumann, I. 2002. "Returning Practice to the Linguistic Turn: the case of diplomacy". *Millennium: Journal of International Studies* 31, 3. 627-651.

―――― 2008. "Russia as a Great Power, 1815-2007". *Journal of International Relations and Development* 11, 2. 128-151.

Ó Tuathail, G. 1996. *Critical Geopolitics: the politics of writing global space.* Minneapolis: University of Minnesota Press.

O'Loughlin, J., G. Ó Tuathail, and V. Kolossov. 2005. "Russian Geopolitical Culture and Public Opinion: the masks of Proteus revisited". *Transactions of the Institute of British Geographers* 30, 3. 322-335.

Prozorov, S. 2008. "Belonging and Inclusion in European-Russian Relations: Alain Badiou and the truth of Europe". *Journal of International Relations and Development* 11, 2. 181-207.

Rangsimaporn, P. 2006. "Interpretations of Eurasianism: justifying Russia's role in East Asia". *Europe-Asia Studies* 58, 3. 371-390.

Smith, G. 1999. "The Masks of Proteus: Russia, geopolitical shift and the new Eurasianism". *Transactions of the Institute of British Geographers* 24, 4. 481-494.

Taylor, S. 2001. "Locating and Conducting Discourse Analytic Research". In *Discourse as Data: a guide for analysis*, edited by M. Wetherell, S. Taylor, and S. J. Yates, 5-48. London: Sage.

Torfing, J. 1999. *New Theories of Discourse: Laclau, Mouffe, and Žižek*. Oxford: Blackwell.

Trenin, D. (2006). "Russia Leaves the West". *Foreign Affairs* 85, 4. 87-96.

―――― 2007. "Russia Redefines Itself and Its Relations With the West". *Washington Quarterly* 30, 2. 95-105.

Tsygankov, A. 2003. "Mastering Space in Eurasia: Russia's geopolitical thinking after the Soviet break-up". *Communist and Post-Communist Studies* 36, 1. 101-127.

Zekri, Sonia 2008. "Der Sieg als Niederlage". *Süddeutsche Zeitung* 16/17 August 2008. 4.

V Outside Perspectives

The View from Elsewhere: Western Mediation of Potential Sources of Russian Dislocation in the 1990s

Felicitas Macgilchrist

This chapter compares "Western" news media coverage of two hostage sieges in Russia (Budënnovsk in 1995 and Beslan in 2004). It analyses the resonance of each siege in the West and the representation in each case of Islamic symbols, fanaticism and international terrorism. Although the two crises shared many features, they received dramatically different news coverage in the West. In 1995, the hostage-taking was interpreted as a localised Russian issue; in 2004, the siege was seen as a global threat. The chapter thus draws attention to the central role of Western political priorities and expectations (or hegemonic discourses) in structuring Western understandings of – or neglect of – potential sources of dislocation in Russia. It suggests that an event is only represented as a radical dislocation if it does not radically dislocate current political imaginaries.

On 1 September 2004, around 30 armed masked men and women stormed a school in the small town of Beslan in North Ossetia, taking over 1,000 people hostage (including children, relatives, and teachers). Over 330 civilians died, of whom 186 were children. The hostage-takers employed symbols that signalled their Islamic faith and stated publicly that they were willing to die for their faith. This was widely reported as a dramatic new development for international terrorists, who were now not only willing to die, but also to target the most innocent of victims, children (cf. Macgilchrist 2008).

Turning back to 1995, however, a very similar attack occurred in a different small town in southern Russia. On 14 June 1995, around 200 militants took over 1,800 people hostage in a hospital in Budënnovsk (including children, pregnant women, and other patients). Here, 147 people were killed; more than 400 were wounded. The hostage-takers employed symbols that signalled their Islamic faith and stated publicly that they were willing to die for their faith. This attack received minimal attention in the West at the time.

Beslan and Budënnosk were two similar events, yet there are significant differences in Western news coverage of the two events. "A universal nightmare seemingly beyond scripting or imagining", writes Peter Preston in The Guardian with regard to the Beslan tragedy. Preston emphasises the limitations of previous analyses of events in Russia and Chechnya. It is no longer sufficient, he writes, to link the hostage-taking in the southern Russian school to Boris Yeltsin's mistakes in Chechnya or to blame Vladimir Putin and Russian troops for their brutal actions in the region. The school siege has brought to the foreground the dislocation of Western notions of stability and security: "These could have been our children."

What was it about the Beslan attack that caused such a crisis for standard representations in the West? Furthermore, why did the Budënnovsk tragedy not meet with a similar response? The following study analyses the extent to which Western news coverage of the Budënnovsk hospital siege in 1995 aids our understanding not only of Russian politics, which these news publications ostensibly covered (for more on Russian politics in the 1990s, see the chapters in this volume by Casula and Malinova), but also, and primarily, of hegemonic formations in the countries were these publications were based.

The 2004 siege in Beslan provides a comparative case in order to draw out similarities and differences in the coverage and hence locate the specifics of Budënnovsk. Were the sieges interpreted in the West as dislocations? Which identities were articulated during the sieges, and how did the media respond to these identities? How do these interpretations and identities tap into hegemonic projects of the time?

To explore these questions, this chapter outlines the notion of dislocation before analysing four aspects of the crises. It describes the resonance that each of the hostage-taking episodes received in the Western media, compares the hostage-takers' use of Muslim symbols, considers how the sieges were represented in the Western media in terms of "fanaticism", and traces the circulation of the notion of "international" or "world terrorism". A concluding section considers the insights gained from these two sieges about dislocation and politics.

The analysis presented here is drawn from a broader study of international media coverage of Russia and Russian-Chechen crises (Macgilchrist 2007, 2008). To enable systematic analysis, extracts in this chapter are based on nine leading newspapers – three each in Germany, the United States, and the United Kingdom (Süddeutsche Zeitung, Frankfurter Allgemeine Zeitung [FAZ], Bild Zeitung; The New York Times, The Wall Street Journal, New York Post; The Guardian, The Daily Telegraph, The Sun).[1]

In keeping with the thematic foci of this book, this chapter sets out to reflect on "Western"[2] discourses on potential sources of Russian dislocation in the 1990s. It thus engages with one of the primary mediators of political analysis in society: journalism.[3] Microanalysis of mediated discourses on Russia and Chechnya during these crises, which pays close attention to fissures and ambiguities in the news coverage, draws attention to the North Caucasus as a feature of the political terrain in the mid-1990s that has frequently been neglected in contemporary Western accounts of Russian politics.[4]

---

[1] A note on methods: In order to include a range of political positions, the choice of publications in each country included one major national and/or agenda-setting newspaper describing itself as "conservative", one "liberal/progressive" paper, and one high-circulation tabloid (based on websites and interviews with journalists and editors). As with many studies in this field, the term "the West" is used somewhat illegitimately in the following as shorthand for these three countries. By way of explanation, previous studies have shown that other countries commonly called "Western" show similar tendencies (Wolff 1994; van Hout and Macgilchrist forthcoming). The corpus was created using two news databases, *Factiva* and *LexisNexis*. Parameters were set to the first week of coverage in the nine named newspapers. The keywords "Russia, Russian, Chechnya, Chechen, siege, hostage-taking, hostage-taker, terrorism" (with plurals and variant spellings) and specific terms (e.g., "school, hospital, Beslan") were searched for each event. Irrelevant texts (i.e., relating to other Russian schools/hospitals) were removed to finalise the corpus for analysis.

[2] In using the term "West", I borrow here from Stuart Hall's argument that "[w]e have to use short-hand generalizations, like 'West' and 'Western', but we need to remember that they represent very complex ideas and have no simple or single meaning" and that they were produced by historical processes operating in particular and contingent historical circumstances (1992: 276f.). The same applies to the use of the terms "the Middle East" and "Islam", as used below.

[3] "Journalism" refers here to hard news stories, editorials, opinions pieces, features, and letters (Zelizer 2004: 6). A similar analysis of scholarly accounts of Russia and Chechnya has been offered elsewhere (Macgilchrist 2008).

[4] Of course, scholars with a particular focus on the North Caucasus have paid, and still pay, extensive attention to the region (e.g., Halbach 2001; 2004; Hughes 2001; 2007; Russell 2005).

Dislocation

Before turning to the microanalysis, my use of the term "dislocation" should be clarified. Ernesto Laclau discusses the term at the ontological level in *New Reflections on the Revolution of our Time*, defining it as a central category in the understanding of the social. He emphasises its contradictory effects, arguing that no one single response corresponds to any given dislocation. As capitalism emerged, for instance, dislocatory effects included brutal and exhausting factory work, low wages, insecurity, and the destruction of communities. At the same time, however, "the workers' response to the dislocation of their lives by capitalism was not to submit passively, but to break machines, organise trade unions, and go on strike". Thus, dislocation simultaneously threatens identities and provides a foundation for the construction of new identities. For Laclau, "every identity is dislocated insofar as it depends on an outside which both denies that identity and provides its conditions of possibility at the same time" (Laclau 1990: 39, 65).

I adopt here Aletta Norval's suggestion (in this volume) that we analyse dislocation at the ontic level, i.e., in particular political conjunctures, rather than primarily at the ontological level. Norval understands it as an experience that makes the "ultimate contingency of all forms of identification" visible (Norval 1996: 13). Tracing such moments, in which existing identities and certainties are shattered, has proved useful to understand, inter alia, apartheid in South Africa (Norval 1996), local governance (Hansen and Sørensen 2005), Green ideology (Stavrakakis 2000), and the modern welfare state (Torfing 1999). Since the effects of dislocation cannot be predetermined, central questions guiding these studies include which social/political imaginaries were hegemonic (in the Gramscian sense) prior to dislocation; whether dislocations are re-articulated through already hegemonic discourses or articulated as novel identities; which particular issues and meanings are being contested, i.e., are available for various hegemonic projects; which, if any, project manages to win the struggle for hegemony and achieve partial closure of the discursive terrain.

The concept of dislocation has proven useful for filling a gap in constructionist arguments by elaborating how the need for new constructions of reality arises. The general answer has been that this need arises from some kind of shock or crisis (e.g., Berger and Luckmann 1967: 39), which can be extended in (at least) two ways. On the one hand, as Yannis Stavrakakis argues, this shock can be "conceived as an encounter with the real in the Lacanian sense of the word" (1999: 68), i.e., with a radical exteriority to the social world, something that cannot be represented within current constructions. On the other hand, perhaps we should ask whether it is also interiority. Is it not also precisely because it (and this "it" is deliberately left vague) is represented as unrepresentable (or, to return to Preston, that which is "seemingly beyond scripting or imagining") that a seemingly well-ordered social world is dislocated?[5] The following sections will draw on empirical material to explore this latter interpretation.

Based on this investigation, I intend to recall that dislocation is not an inherent feature of a particular event, action, or political context, but is instead dependent on the ways in which events, etc., are signified (represented). Thus, finally, I propose what may seem to be a contradiction: that an occurrence is only signified as a radical dislocation if it does not radically dislocate the political imaginary. As I will elaborate below, rather than being "beyond scripting or imagining", elements of new configurations, identifications, and imaginaries must already be hovering on the horizon in order for an event to be understood in terms of a dramatic rupture compared to current political and social realities.

Resonance

The school siege in Beslan received extensive media coverage in Germany, the US, and the UK. In the first week of reporting, from 2 to 9 September 2004, 409 news items covered the story in the nine newspapers.

In 1995, there was far less resonance for the hospital siege in Budënnovsk, in which almost twice as many hostages were taken (approximately 1800). In the first week of coverage, from 15 to 22 June 1995, 94 news items covered the events.

What could lead to such disparate media responses to these two crises? One hypothesis, mapping onto traditional news values, is that journalists, editors, news production teams, etc. must understand an event and/or cover it as consonant with existing stories, and meaningful in a culturally proximate and relevant way (Galtung and Ruge 1965; Harcup and O'Neill 2001). One set of understandings in the post-9/11 world makes Islam and/or international (fundamentalist Islamist) terrorism relevant. These signifiers have been increasingly yoked to a threat or danger that is seen to pervade everyday life. They provide a

---

5   Norval (this volume) argues that seemingly new articulations in contemporary political imaginaries were not previously in a radical "outside", but rather had not managed to cross the "threshold of visibility" (see also Norval 2007: 141ff.).

common theme that makes it possible to join various global news occurrences into a single related chain of events. Anthrax spores sent through the US postal service in late 2001, killing five, for instance, were interpreted within the Islamist terrorism discourse, although when the case was closed in 2008, the FBI named a US Army researcher as the sole culprit; he had no known connection to Islam.

Western news coverage of the Beslan siege included extensive debate on potential links to global Islamist fundamentalism. Elsewhere, I have analysed the arguments made by some commentators that "Islamic jihadism" was a cause of the (global/civilisational) conflict in Chechnya, and arguments made by other commentators that it was a consequence of the (local/political) conflict in Chechnya (Macgilchrist 2008: 135-163). At Budënnovsk, there was no such debate. The 1995 siege was reported as the outcome of regional political issues: the Chechen desire for independence from Moscow and the ensuing war between Russia and Chechnya that had started six months previously.

It has been argued that the hostage-takers in 1995 were not primarily signified as Islamist terrorists because they quite simply were not Islamist terrorists. In the 1990s, according to this argument, the conflict between Russia and Chechnya was a political war of independence. Only after the brutalisation of the first war (1994-1996) did "Islamisation" expand in Chechnya. The second Russian-Chechen war (beginning in 1999) was then fought under the banner of Islam (cf. Hughes 2007; Sakwa 2005: 8f.).

This argument is not undisputed. First, some argue that Islam played a role early on in the first Russian-Chechen conflict. For instance, then Chechen President Dzhokhar Dudayev claimed before the war started that Chechnya could mobilise one million mujahedin (cf. Hahn 2007: 30ff.). The Budënnovsk raid was known at the time as "Operation Jihad" (Dolnik 2007: 105; Murphy 2004: 21). Russian observers described the conflict as part of a Western struggle against a common Islamic enemy (cf. Lieven 1998: 357). Second, others argue that the second war was also a political war of independence and part of the struggle to free Chechnya from Russia, i.e., not primarily a religious war (e.g., Hassel 2003; Wood 2007). Islamisation, in this view, is primarily a consequence of Russian socio-political-cultural domination of the region and of the disproportionate violence against Chechens during the first conflict (de Waal 2005).

Third, a discourse-theoretical perspective argues that since interpretations of conflict are dependent on the contemporary discourses available, it is impossible to ascertain the single true essence of the conflict. Various interpretations will inevitably struggle to become the hegemonic interpretation, i.e., to be understood as the most valid interpretation of that particular political/religious/social configuration. Scholarly, political, and media arguments over the "correct" meaning of the Russian-Chechen conflict(s) are a vivid example of this.

This third argument is supported by three signifiers employed during the two sieges mentioned above: (i) Islam, (ii) fanaticism, and (iii) international terrorism. Although emphasised at Beslan, each remained firmly in the background of news reports during Budënnovsk.

Islam

The signifiers "Islam/Islamism" played a significant role in constructing the identity of the hostage-takers during the Beslan siege in 2004. Photos were published showing Arabic script on female hostage-takers' head coverings; hostage-takers were quoted as stating their devotion to Islam and their desire for martyrdom; the fighters were linked to al-Qaida, Afghanistan, Osama bin Laden, the so-called "War on Terror", the 11 September 2001 attacks in the US, and/or other attacks that had previously been interpreted as international terrorism (e.g., Bali 2002, Madrid 2004). These images and words are consonant with a post-9/11 division of the world into an antagonistic *us – them* relation, in which *we* are defined in the Beslan news coverage as, for example, "democratic and secular nations" (Moitra 2004, in The Guardian), "Western civilisation" (Wehner 2004, in FAZ) or "civilization itself" (Wall Street Journal editorial 2004); *they* are defined as, for example, "Muslim terrorists" (Sun editorial 2004a), "international terrorism" (Wehner, Bannas, and Leithäuser 2004 in FAZ) or "Islamic savagery" (Melloan 2004, in The Wall Street Journal).

In 1995, no such empty signifiers were available to weave a common thread among global news stories of the time, such as the Yugoslav war, the O.J. Simpson trial, the Oklahoma City bombing, and a plane hijacking in Japan. Indeed, of the 94 Budënnovsk news items, few explicitly identify the hostage-takers as "Muslim(s)", "Moslem(s)", or "Islam(ic)". The examples in Fig. 1 constitute all 12 references from the Budënnovsk corpus.[6] They stem from ten news items, i.e., 11 percent of the total. In contrast, 25 percent of news items reporting

---

6   This analysis draws on corpus linguistics, where "key word in context" concordance lines are used to analyse patterns of language use leading to, for instance, conventional phrases, associations, or semantic prosody (attitudes/evaluations) (cf. Hunston 2007; Sinclair 2003). Coniam (2004) and Ghadessy et al. (2001) discuss the value of using small corpora as a body of evidence for observing situated language use.

THE VIEW FROM ELSEWHERE   355

the Beslan siege – over 100 separate news items – explicitly locate the hostage-takers in the field of Muslims/Moslems/Islam.

Figure 1: Explicit religious identification during Budënnovsk: "Muslims", "Moslems", "Islamic"

```
1     nications equipment and training come from fellow  Muslims  -- perhaps deniably, via "gray wolves" in Turkey.
2     it, factions in Turkey are quietly helping fellow  Muslims  in both Chechnya and Bosnia assert their sovereig
3     wjetunion 1991 hatten 90 Prozent der überwiegend   muslimischen Tschetschenen eine Unabhängigkeitserklärung der
4     rund der Offensive im Raum Sarajewo, die bosnisch- muslimische Truppen am 15. Juni begonnen hatten. Sie wollten

5     nen-General Schamil Bassayew (30). Der fanatische  Moslem droht: „Ich sprenge das Krankenhaus in die Luft!"
6     einen olivfarbenen Kampfanzug, grünes Stirnband (  Moslem-Zeichen), dunklen Vollbart, Granaten im Gürtel, e
7     agen. Die Führung in Moskau, dass das rebellische  Moslemvolk durch militärische Übermacht in die Knie zwinge
8     mit weiteren Racheaktionen gerechnet werden. Als   Moslems sind die Tschetschenen unerschrockene Kämpfer, d

9     heiligen Kriegern gebildet, die den Dschihad, den  islamischen Verteidigungskrieg, gegen die Truppen zunaechst Z
10    Gott." Das ist der erste Teil der Schahada, des    islamische Glaubensbekenntnis. Bassajew gilt als unversö
11    ers with handkerchiefs masking their faces, green  Islamic head bands on their foreheads and Kalashnikovs in
12    ew, stets mit grüner Stirnbinde der todesmutigen   islamischen Kämpfer und dichtem schwarzem Bart zu sehen, kä
```

News reports on terrorism today are in stark contrasts to these extracts. Of these 12 Budënnovsk examples, "Moslem" is only collocated three times with terms denoting violence: with "fanatic" in line (5), with "fearless fighters" (*unerschrockene Kämpfer*) in line (8), and with "undaunted by death" (*todesmutig*) in line (12). Other references are less violent, e.g., equipment and training (line 1), Chechen demographics (line 3), traditional images of Chechens as "rebellious Muslim peoples" (line 7), definitions of *jihad* as an "Islamic defence war" (*Verteidigungskrieg*; line 9) and the *shahada* as the Muslim "declaration of belief" (*Glaubensbekenntnis*; line 10). Geographic links are established with Turkey (lines 1 and 2) and Bosnia (lines 2 and 4). The latter, it should be noted, was supported by the West in its conflict with Serbia at the time, and this period was therefore not marked by a straightforward conceptualisation of Muslim regions as the West's *constitutive outside* (cf. Laclau 1990: 17).

A further example of ways in which hegemonic discourses affect understandings of conflict is hinted at in Fig. 1 in lines (6), (11), and (12), which refer to "green headbands" as a Muslim-symbol, a symbol of Islam, or a symbol of *todesmutige* Islamic fighters. Two further news items from this first week of reporting the siege also signify the green headband.

"Mr. Basayev, wearing a green ribbon that identifies him as a Chechen suicide fighter along with about as much ammunition as can fit on a man, said he would release all the children being held as a good-will gesture." (Specter 1995, in New York Times; emphasis added in all extracts)

"One of his supporters, the failed actor Vyacheslav Marychev, appeared in parliament in the guise of a Chechen terrorist, wearing a green headband and brandishing a toy gun. In what he claimed was a mark of honour for those killed in the Budyonnovsk hostage crisis, he wore a Megadeth pop T-shirt over his shirt and tie." (Philps 1995, in The Daily Telegraph)

In each of these extracts, the explicitly religious symbol selected by the Chechen fighters is described as a coloured piece of cloth with no further elaboration of its meaning potential.

Crucially, none of these extracts relate the green headbands or the incident's Islamic character to the West. Indeed, nowhere in the coverage of Budënnovsk is the attack described as impinging on the West. It is not interpreted as a nightmare beyond imagination; it does not dislocate a Western sense of security, in hospitals or elsewhere. The hostage-taking is signified as a particular Russian incident, rather than being expanded to the perception of a global threat as in the case of the attack in Beslan.

Fanaticism

One way in which the Beslan siege is made directly relevant to the West is through demands for Western political action. In a New York Post story, "exquisite sacrifice" will be required of soldiers "in the worldwide struggle against Islamic fanaticism" in order to "stand between America and another 9/11, or a Madrid, or a Bali, or – God forbid – a Beslan" (New York Post editorial 2004b). The Sun explicitly marks 9/11 as "a turning point for the US" after which it transformed its ways of dealing with "suspected terrorists". Rather than following suit, "the attitude to West-hating zealots is still alarmingly liberal [in the rest of the world]" (Moore 2004, in The Sun). An opinion piece in the Süddeutsche Zeitung warns that "placation [*Nachgiebigkeit*] will lead to even more terror", and praises the effectiveness of "vigilance [*Wachsamkeit*] and the work of the police and intelligence agencies. A change will only be noticeable when fanaticism has disappeared and terror is also seriously ostracised [*geächtet*] in Muslim societies" (Kornelius 2004).

What is notable in these three examples is the linking of demands for action (a tightening of security or increase in military engagement, and a corresponding move away from liberalism) to the highly evaluative lexis "fanatic" and "zealot". In the Beslan corpus, the root term fanat* (i.e., the terms "fanatic", "fanatics", "fanatical", "fanaticism" and "fanatised") appears 31 times; the root term extremis* ("extremism", "extremist") 51 times, and zealot* ("zealot", "zealots") four times. Each of these terms co-occurs primarily with terms from a discourse of Islamic terrorism, e.g., "West-hating zealots", "Islamist extremists", or "Islamic extremists". Of the 51 instances of extremist/extremism, over one third (18) co-occur with such lexis. Fig. 2 illustrates the 12 lines in the Beslan corpus that link fanaticism in a chain of equivalence with "Islamic", "jihadi movement" (*Dschihadisten-Bewegung*), "Islamism" (*Islamismus*), "Muslim" (*muslimischen*), "religious" (*religiöser*), "Omar Bakri", "al Qaeda", "the Middle East", and "Arabs".

Figure 2: Discourse of fanatical (Islamic) terrorism during Beslan

```
1     an, and in the worldwide struggle against Islamic fanaticism, will require exquisite sacrifice by the few - on
2     school, told Britain's Sky News that the Islamic fanatics, who wore long hair and beards, made the hostages
3     aus dem Umfeld der Dschihadisten-Bewegung weiter fanatisiert. Und der Islamismus verband sich mit den ohnehin
4     SICK ZEALOT REMAIN IN BRITAIN? BODY:          MUSLIM fanatic Omar Bakri has outraged readers with his comments
5     eränderung wird nur dann zu spüren sein, wenn der Fanatismus schwindet und Terror auch in muslimischen Gesells
6     anz - im Islam dagegen rohe Gewalt und religiöser Fanatismus. Aber das stimmt so nicht. Das Verhalten der radi
7     nanosecond?    This week, Syrian-born religious fanatic Omar Bakri said of Beslan: "If an Iraqi Muslim ca
8     lking about the bloody siege in Beslan, religious fanatic Omar Bakri said: "If an Iraqi Muslim carried out
9     ain about the likes of Bakri, but when these evil fanatics threaten people what do they expect?     CLAIRE
10    fferent, even more depraved level."    Chechen fanatics are now working hand-in-glove with al Qaeda terro
11    o far more harm than good when it comes to ending fanaticism in the Middle East. But the president is certainl
12    hildren streamed out of the burning school as the fanatics -who included at least ten Arabs - mercilessly sh
```

That over one third of the instances of "fanaticism", "fanatics", and "fanatised" (*fanatisiert*) in the coverage on Beslan are articulated in a discourse of Islamic, Middle Eastern, or Arab terrorism indicates the active iteration of a hegemonic formation. "Fanaticism", in its meaning potential of "irrational excess", is seen to share interests with Islam and the Middle East. Since contemporary discourses generally take fanaticism to be the binary opposite of rationality (cf. Sprinzak 2000), the extracts fix the meaning potential of the hostage-taking within the realm of irrationality. Not only is the other thereby constructed as irrational; its opposite (the We which in this case includes Russia) is therefore, by implication, the rational, reasonable or just.

In the coverage of Budënnovsk, this discourse was far less apparent. The single example of "extremism" is attributed to Dudayev, who is quoted in the FAZ as saying that this is the action of "an unorganised group of desperate extremists" who have discredited the Chechen people's fight for liberation (Bacia 1995). The single instance of "fanatical" is, as above, linked to Islam.

"5000 patients, pregnant women and children are quivering! They are still in the hands of Chechen General Shamil Basayev (30). The fanatical Moslem threatens: 'I'll blow the hospital up!' More than 50 people have already been murdered by Basayev and his men – most of them with a shot in the neck. He says: 'For me, this is about freedom or death.'" (Bild, 17 June 1995: 1; see also Fig. 1, line 5)

In addition, this extract associates fanaticism with excess and suicidal desire ("murder", "shot in the neck", "freedom or death"). This is, however, the only instance during Budënnovsk in which a discourse of irrational fanaticism is explicitly articulated.

The extract thus indicates a fissure in the discursive horizon against which this attack was primarily interpreted in these newspapers. More generally, the attack enabled a positively valued rationality to be attached to the attack and the attackers. Basayev, for instance, was described as "the most talented and ruthless of the Chechen commanders" who had won "audacious victories over [his] Russian foes"; this "well-planned act of revenge" "succeeded in outwitting the Russian security forces" (Philps 1995; Warren 1995; Philps 1995, all in Daily/Sunday Telegraph). The Süddeutsche Zeitung described the hostage-takers as "resistance fighters" (*Widerstandskämpfer*; Neubert 1995). These descriptions would seem anomalous at the time of the Beslan siege, and were indeed not found in that corpus.

Thus in 1995, hegemonic discourses were not disturbed by descriptions of the hostage-takers in terms of social approval. Simultaneously, the hostage crisis was located almost entirely at the local, regional, Russian level, with no relevance to Western politics. In 2004, it did not seem unusual to strongly associate the hostage-takers with fanaticism, and to associate fanaticism in turn with religion. Simultaneously, it had become possible (thinkable, printable, newsworthy, commonsensical) to articulate the crisis with demands for a transformation in Western political action.

We should recall, however, that the discourse of fanatical Muslims was already in circulation in 1995 (as shown above), albeit rare in the West. Given the use of Muslim symbols by Basayev and his fighters and the availability of this discourse, its relative absence from Western media indicates the double role of the media. They report what is being said and done in Russia, while simultaneously co-constructing a discursive horizon which constrains the reporting of certain words or actions.

International terrorism

After 2001, "international terrorism" became a prevalent term in political discourse to make sense of how Western politics should respond or relate to the 11 September attacks. Scholars, for instance, have described 9/11 as a crisis that "forced us to change our conceptual understanding of world politics and to look for new analytical methods and tools to gain a better understanding of its transforming nature" (Aras and Toktaş 2007: 1035). "The international terror attacks on Istanbul, Madrid, London and Sharm al-Sheikh, among others, [...] will engender serious consequences for both the countries under attack and for international security" (ibid.: 1033). "International terror(ism)" thus became a central signifier in reading (giving meaning to) the dislocation created by attacks after 11 September.

In the Beslan corpus, the phrase "international terror(ism)" appears 32 times. In almost all instances, Putin is criticised for trying to link the Chechen war to international terrorism, and thereby ruling out talks with Chechen leaders. In these cases, the newspapers distance themselves from the phrase by attributing it to Putin. In other cases, newspapers directly aver the phrase in their own voice, thus presupposing its truth effects and articulating the phrase as a credible means of making sense of events (on averral and attribution, cf. Bednarek 2006; Hunston 1999). An FAZ story, for instance, writes: "Just like the attack on the World Trade Center back then. International terrorism finds its international public" (Thomann 2004). The Süddeutsche Zeitung notes that: "[t]he Chechen rebels' connections to international terrorism are alarming" (Zekri 2004).

Looking beyond the specific term "international terror(ism)", both The Sun and the New York Post ran stories headlined "Russia's 9/11" (New York Post editorial 2004a; Sun double page spread 2004b). A Bild editorial (2004) writes that "[t]he terror is devouring all values and all borders! A world that cannot protect its children is a horror-world". The Süddeutsche Zeitung's "Topic of the Day" on 2 September is "The Internationale of Terror" (*Die Internationale des Terrors*): "Nairobi, New York, Madrid, Moscow – no one and nothing is safe from terrorism any longer. Osama bin Laden and his network al Qaeda have paved the way for ever more excessive terror." The Guardian reports that "[f]or many politicians and commentators, the massacre served to reinforce international alliance and extend battle lines in the war against terrorism" (Bowcottt 2004).

In the Budënnovsk corpus, "international terrorism" appears three times, and "world terrorism" four times. All seven examples attribute the phrase to a particular speaker, with none averring it directly in their own voice. Six of these seven examples refer to the G7 meeting in Halifax at which "Mr Yeltsin told the cameras in Canada: 'Chechenia [sic] is the centre of world terrorism.'" (Hearst 1995, in The Guardian).

The seventh example appears in the FAZ's (1995) "Voices of the Others" (*Stimmen der Anderen*) section, which reprints selected extracts from other newspapers: "[t]he actions of the Chechens in Budënnovsk were no more international terrorism than those of the Russian troops in Samashki or Grozny." In this example, the Russian daily, Moskovskii Komsomolets, negates the proposal that the actions of the Chechens in Budënnovsk constitute international terrorism. Since "the negative carries with it the positive" (White 2001: 3), i.e., since it always also includes the presence of that which is negated, this extract articulates the suggestion made by others that the actions do indeed constitute international terrorism.

Such fissures in the Western reporting enable a glimpse of contemporary Russian discourses, which have not yet received extended scholarly attention. Yeltsin's statement, for instance, indicates that a discourse of international terrorism was already circulating in Russia in 1995. The Moskovskii Komsomolets text is part of a public debate about the applicability of the term, which in itself illustrates the discursive struggle between at least two discourses, one articulating global implications and networks of terror and one articulating a regional political conflict and Russian military brutality.

The Russian discourse of the internationality of terrorism did not, however, resonate widely in the West in the mid-1990s. Yeltsin's statement was, for instance, delegitimised in a New York Times editorial (1995) by linking it with the then Russian president's instability and agitation: "Adding to his history of unbalanced public performances, an agitated Mr. Yeltsin called Chechnya the 'center of world terrorism'". Crucially, as noted above, in 1995, these news media did not discuss whether or how the West should respond to the hostage-taking. The problem was seen as a distant issue; there was no dislocation, no "crisis in which we experience the limits of our meaning structures" (Stavrakakis 1999: 67).

Conclusion

I do not argue here that the hostage-taking in Budënnovsk was part of international Islam-inspired terrorism. The point is to shed light on the different conditions within which the meaning of a remarkably similar set of signifiers can be fixed as a localised Russian issue or as a global threat dislocating normal social relations. In this sense, attending to the micro-level processes of fixing such floating signifiers illustrates the everyday production of hegemonic discourses in the reporting countries. It also, however, gives an indication of the discursive terrain in mid-1990s Russia, where the construction of "world terrorism" and an "Islamist threat" may have prepared the ground for Putin's appointment as prime minister in 1999 and his election as president in 2000.

Three conclusions can be drawn at this stage. First, social disruptions and dislocations are not inherent properties of an event. Very similar verbal and non-verbal processes unfolded during the sieges in Budënnovsk and Beslan. Only in the latter case, however, were these processes symbolised in the Western media as a fundamental dislocation of the social terrain. Only in the latter case was the particular event – now a dislocatory event – given meaning within a discursive space structured around what was interpreted as a (fanatical) international/Islamist terrorist threat. Budënnovsk, on the other hand, did not disturb the well-ordered social world. This earlier siege was read within contemporary meaning structures as a localised political conflict between Russia and the separatist republic of Chechnya.

Drawing on discourse theoretical lexis, we could say that in 1995, these religious signifiers had not yet become established *nodal points* – that is, privileged signs that "quilt" the social fabric – providing the means by which a wide range of issues, events, and demands are fixed into (new) configurations of meaning (cf. Laclau and Mouffe 1985: 112).

Thus, secondly, it is important to remember that an event is only signified as dislocation if elements necessary to create these new nodal points are already available in the discursive terrain, albeit perhaps on the margins or in the fissures of hegemonic discourses. For something to dislocate the structure, i.e., to rupture existing norms, expectations, imaginaries, etc., it must already be possible to integrate it into these norms, expectations, and imaginaries. It cannot constitute a complete breach vis-à-vis that which already exists. As Laclau argues, a discourse will not be accepted "if its proposals clash with the basic principles informing the organisation of a group" (1990: 66). Slavoj Zizek develops a similar argument in Lacanian terms, turning to the 11 September attacks to make his point.

> "When we hear how the attacks were a totally unexpected shock, how the unimaginable Impossible happened, we should remember the other defining catastrophe from the beginning of the twentieth century, that of the *Titanic*: this, also, was a shock, but the space for it had already been prepared in ideological fantasising, since the *Titanic* was the symbol of the might of the nineteenth-century industrial civilisation. Does not the same hold for these attacks? Not only were the media bombarding us all the time with talk about the terrorist threat; this threat was also obviously libidinally invested – just recall the series of movies from *Escape from New York* to *Independence Day*. That is the rationale behind the often-mentioned association of the attacks with Hollywood disaster movies: the unthinkable which happened was the object of fantasy, so in a way, America got what it had fantasised about – and that was the greatest surprise." (Zizek 2002: 231)

The unimaginable, therefore, is only experienced as unimaginable if it is not entirely unimaginable. In a circular process, Beslan could only be articulated as an unthinkable nightmare and a turning point demanding new political actions if its possibility and the accompanying demands (tighter security, less liberalism) already constituted an object of fantasy, or had already informed the organisation of the discursive community in question. At the same time, the reporting on Beslan is part of the mundane, everyday constitution of this discursive community; the reporting itself participates in forming readers' identities, in shifting the horizons of intelligibility, and in establishing new discursive limits.

In concluding this chapter, I would like to present a final thought framed as a question. Since the Budënnovsk siege did not dislocate the sense of social order for the Western media, it was not reported as a potential dislocation to a Russian sense of social order. The question now is to what extent the signifiers analysed here – Islam, fanaticism, international terrorism – were articulated in Russia as a response to a fundamental dislocation in the summer of 1995. The answer will involve exploring the extent to which the Budënnovsk attack not only threatened identities, but also provided a foundation for constructing new identifications and new demands. Analysis could then investigate the extent to which these identifications and demands remained unfulfilled during Yeltsin's presidency. If they were then satisfied during Putin's tenure – and his consistently high population figures suggest that they were – how was this achieved?

If one follows the fissures of "Western" discourse, as this analysis has done, the suggestion arises that although these signifiers were backgrounded by Western news, they may indeed have been more firmly established within hegemonic projects in mid-1990s Russia. If so, this means that a restructuring of society began to be re-articulated around these nodal points years before they appeared on the Western radar. Indeed, a final hope for this chapter is that it will encourage others to explore the questions it has raised. This line of inquiry could prove fruitful to gain an increased understanding of political developments not only under Yeltsin, but also throughout Putin's presidency.

Bibliography

Aras, B. and Ş. Toktaş. 2007. "Al-Qaida, 'War on Terror' and Turkey". *Third World Quarterly* 28, 5. 1033-1050.

Bacia, H. 1995. "Das Feuer im Kaukasus erfasst Russland". *Frankfurter Allgemeine Zeitung* 16 June. 7.

Bednarek, M. 2006. "Epistemological Positioning and Evidentiality In English News Discourse: A text-driven approach". *Text & Talk* 26, 6. 635-660.

Berger, P. and T. Luckmann. 1967. *The Social Construction of Reality*. Harmondsworth: Penguin.

Bild Zeitung. 1995. "Das Geisel-Krankenhaus: Tschetschenen-General: Ich sprenge alles in die Luft". 17 June. 1.

―――― 2004. "Der Terror verschlingt alle Werte". 4 September. 2.

Bowcott, O. 2004. "Dutch provoke diplomatic row by questioning siege tactics". *The Guardian* 6 September. 4.

Casula, P. In this volume.

Coniam, D. 2004. "Concordancing Oneself: Constructing individual textual profiles". *International Journal of Corpus Linguistics* 9, 2. 271-298.

De Waal, T. 2005. "Chechnya: The breaking point". In *Chechnya: From past to future*, edited by R. Sakwa, 181-197. London: Anthem.

Dolnik, A. 2007. *Understanding Terrorist Innovation: Technology, tactics and global trends*. London: Routledge.

Frankfurter Allgemeine Zeitung. 1995. "Zwei Verbrechen". 21 June. 2.

Galtung, J. and M. Ruge. 1965. "The Structure of Foreign News: The presentation of the Congo, Cuba and Cyprus crisis in four Norwegian newspapers". *Journal of Peace Studies* 2. 64-91.

Ghadessy, M., A. Henry, and R. Roseberry. 2001. *Small Corpus Studies and ELT: Theory and Practice*. Amsterdam: John Benjamins.

Hahn, G. 2007. *Russia's Islamic Threat*. New Haven: Yale University Press.

Halbach, U. 2001. "Zehn Jahre danach: Postsowjetische Konfliktlandschaften des Kaukasus". *Osteuropa* 9. 1087-1109.

────── 2004. *Gewalt in Tschetschenien: Ein gemiedenes Problem internationaler Politik*. Berlin: Stiftung Wissenschaft und Politik.

Hall, S. 1992. "The West and the Rest: Discourse and power". In *Formations of Modernity*, edited by S. Hall and B. Gieben, 275-320. Cambridge: Polity Press.

Hansen, A. and E. Sørensen. 2005. "Polity as Politics: Studying the shaping and effects of discursive politics". In *Discourse Theory in European Politics: Identity, Policy and Governance*, edited by D. Howarth and J. Torfing, 93-116. Basingstoke: Palgrave Macmillan.

Harcup, T. and D. O'Neill. 2001. "What is News? Galtung and Ruge revisited". *Journalism Studies* 2, 2. 261-280.

Hassel, F. 2003. *Der Krieg im Schatten. Russland und Tschetschenien*. Frankfurt: Suhrkamp.

Hearst, D. 1995. "Russian PM calls halt to Chechen war in hostage deal". *The Guardian* 19 June. 3.

Hughes, J. 2001. "Chechnya: The Causes of a Protracted Post-Soviet Conflict". Civil Wars 4, 4. 11-48.

―――― 2007. *Chechnya: From Nationalism to Jihad*. Philadelphia: University of Pennsylvania Press.

Hunston, S. 1999. "Evaluation and the Planes of Discourse". In *Evaluation in Text: Authorial Stance and the Construction of Discourse*, edited by S. Hunston and G. Thompson, 176-207. Oxford: Oxford University Press.

―――― 2007. "Semantic Prosody Revisited". *International Journal of Corpus Linguistics* 12, 2. 249-268.

Kornelius, S. 2004. "Der entfesselte Terror". *Süddeutsche Zeitung* 2 September. 4.

Laclau, E. 1990. *New Reflections on the Revolution of our Time*. London: Verso.

Laclau, E. and C. Mouffe. 1985. *Hegemony and Socialist Strategy: Towards a Radical Politics*. London: Verso.

Lieven, A. 1998. *Chechnya: Tombstone of Russian Power*. New Haven & London: Yale University Press.

Macgilchrist, F. 2007. "Metaphorical Politics: Is Russia Western?". In *Nation in Formation: Inclusion and Exclusion in Central and Eastern Europe*, edited by C. Baker, C. Gerry, B. Madaj, E. Mellish, and J. Nahodilova, 73-90. London: Studies in Russia and Eastern Europe.

――― 2008. Imagining Russia: A cultural discourse analysis of news coverage in the international media. PhD diss., European University Viadrina, Frankfurt/Oder.

Melloan, G. 2004. "Beslan's Message: Terrorists Don't Have Souls". *The Wall Street Journal* 7 September. 21.

Moitra, S. 2004. "Beslan's Warnings to the West". Letter to the editor. *The Guardian* 6 September. 17.

Moore, J. 2004. "We Must Root out the Terror Sympathisers". *The Sun* 8 September. 11.

Murphy, P. 2004. *The Wolves of Islam: Russia and the faces of Chechen terror.* Dulles: Brassey's.

Neubert, M. 1995. "Rußland: Folgt dem Geiseldrama von Budjonnowsk das Ende des Kriegs in Tschetschenien?" *Süddeutsche Zeitung* 19 June. 3.

The New York Post. 2004a. "Russia's 9/11". 8 September. 28.

――― 2004b. "1,000". 9 September. 34.

The New York Times. 1995. "A Way Out of Chechnya". 20 June. 14.

Norval, A. 1996. *Deconstructing Apartheid Discourse.* London: Verso.

Philps, A. 1995a. "Russia Bows to Gunmen as Hostages are Released". *The Daily Telegraph* 20 June. 15.

――― 1995b. "Failed Actor Turns Russian Parliament Into Circus". *The Daily Telegraph.* 22 June. 10.

――― 1995c. "Troops Flood Moscow to Deter Rebels". *The Daily Telegraph* 22 June. 10.

Preston, P. 2004. "Writing the Script for Terror: Media-makers must defuse these weapons of mass hysteria". *The Guardian* 6 September. 15.

Russell, J. 2005. "Terrorists, Bandits, Spooks and Thieves: Russian demonisation of the Chechens before and since 9/11". *Third World Quarterly* 26, 1. 101-116.

Sakwa, R. 2005. "Introduction: Why Chechnya?". In his *Chechnya: From past to future*, 1-20. London: Anthem.

Sinclair, J. 2003. *Reading Concordances: An introduction*. Harlow: Longman.

Specter, M. 1995. "Chechen Rebels Said to Kill Hostages at Russian Hospital". *The New York Times* 16 June. 1.

Sprinzak, E. 2000. "Rational Fanatics". *Foreign Policy* September/ October. 66-73.

Stavrakakis, Y. 1999. *Lacan and the Political*. London: Routledge.

────── 2000. "On the Emergence of Green Ideology: The dislocation factor in Green politics". In *Discourse Theory and Political Analysis: Identities, hegemonies and social change*, edited by D. Howarth, A. Norval, and Y. Stavrakakis, 100-118. Manchester: Manchester University Press.

The Sun. 2004a. "Guilty Ones". 6 September. 8.

────── 2004b. "Russia's 9/11 is Caught on Film". 8 September. 4f.

Thomann, J. 2004. "Der Radioreporter weiß es als erster". *Frankfurter Allgemeine Zeitung* 4 September. 41.

Torfing, J. 1999. *New Theories of Discourse: Laclau, Mouffe, Žižek*. Oxford: Blackwell.

Van Hout, T. and F. Macgilchrist. Forthcoming. "Framing the News: An ethnographic view of business newswriting". *Text & Talk*.

The Wall Street Journal. 2004. "Innocents Abroad". 2 September. 12.

Warren, M. 1995. "Men of Destiny". *The Sunday Telegraph* 18 June. 24.

Wehner, M. 2004. "Schwarze Tage". *Frankfurter Allgemeine Zeitung* 6 September. 1.

Wehner, M., G. Bannas, and J. Leithäuser. 2004. "Rußland kündigt Präventivschläge gegen Terrorismus in aller Welt an". *Frankfurter Allgemeine Zeitung* 9 September. 1.

White, P. 2001. *Engagement and Dialogistic Positioning.* http://www.grammatics.com/appraisal/ [Accessed 21 March 2005].

Wolff, L. 1994. *Inventing Eastern Europe: The map of civilization on the mind of the Enlightenment.* Stanford: Stanford University Press.

Wood, T. 2007. *Chechnya: The Case for Independence.* London: Verso.

Zekri, S. 2004. "Schule des Terrors, Kinder des Krieges". *Süddeutsche Zeitung* 8 September. 11.

Zelizer, B. 2004. *Taking Journalism Seriously: News and the Academy.* Thousand Oaks: Sage.

Zizek, S. 2002. *Revolution at the Gates: Žižek on Lenin, the 1917 Writings.* London: Verso.

"Europe" and "Russia" in Ukraine's Narratives on National Identity: Historical and Cultural Myths[1]

Svitlana Kobzar

This chapter applies elements of discourse theory to the case study of Ukraine to analyse articulations of the concepts of "Europe" and "Russia" in post-Soviet historiography. It focuses on the role of intellectuals and government officials and their attempts to partially fix meaning(s) of the Soviet past shared by Ukraine and Russia and the consequences resulting from the divergent historical narratives. The chapter also examines how the myth of Europe is articulated within the discourse on national identity and sovereignty. The approach of this study departs from the transition paradigm traditionally used for analysing post-Soviet democratisation processes. History-writing in the post-Soviet region has been challenging, but nonetheless integral to nation-building and identity politics. Ukraine's historical narratives are constructed to support its central national narrative, which has been at odds with the Russian national narrative. Analysing Ukraine's historiography thus highlights the tensions inherent in its relations with Russia and explains its pro-European policy declarations.

> "Throughout European history, my country, Ukraine, has been badly misunderstood in Western capitals. Until the middle of the past century, it was referred to as 'the Okraina,' literally the borderlands between European civilisation and a distant unfathomable Russia. There are perhaps many in Europe who still see us that way, but in fact things have changed in Ukraine, to an extent that surprises even those of us who played a part in bringing about those changes." (Viktor Yanukovych, Prime Minister of Ukraine, 2006)

After many years of interdependence, it is not surprising that the Russian post-Communist identity has been closely linked to that of Ukraine. However, even though Ukraine and Russia share some historical myths, including Cold War memories of the antagonisms articulated as the "West", these two post-Soviet countries ended up with different historiographies. While the Ukrainian discourse

---
1 The author thanks Khadidjah Mattar for helping to revise this chapter.

has been constructed using different *other(s)* from the ones articulated within the Russian discourse, analysing the case of Ukraine fits well with the aims of this volume, which departs from the traditional transition paradigm used for studying post-Soviet "democratisation" movements.

According to the transition paradigm, in the early years of its independence, Ukraine was confronted with multiple "transitions". In addition to the "dual transition" inherent in the post-Communist Eastern European democratisation process, which included the need to implement political and economic reforms, Ukraine was also faced with the challenge of simultaneously pursuing state-building and nation-building (see D'Anieri et al. 1999: 6). Several scholars questioned the very possibility of pursuing such a "quadruple transition" in parallel (i.e., state-building, nation-building, political and economic reforms), since some of these reforms appeared incompatible with one another (D'Anieri et al. 1999: 6; Kuzio 1997: 227; Riabchuk 2001: 107).

While the transition paradigm helps in understanding the state-building challenges of Ukraine, discourse theory allows for a deeper analysis of identity issues that have been closely interconnected with "hard issues" traditionally considered by rational-choice theorists. History-writing and foreign-policy declarations – issues that have been usually relegated to identity politics – have been articulated in the same chain of equivalences with the politicised economic disputes, most notably the recent gas row between Ukraine and Russia.

This chapter focuses on the role of intellectuals and government officials and their attempts to partially fix meaning(s) of the Soviet past shared by Ukraine and Russia and the consequences resulting from the divergent historical narratives. The chapter also examines how the myth of "Europe" was articulated within the discourse on national identity and sovereignty.

Historical myths in identity politics

Historical narratives and definitions of the term "Ukraine" and its place on the map of Europe have been transformed over centuries. The understanding of the "European frontier" has been rather fluid. Mikkeli, for instance, notes: "[T]he frontier between East and West is not just a line on a map or even a geographical border [...] it is a constantly shifting frontier moulded in the course of history by changing political conditions and cultural identities" (Mikkeli 1998). After the fall of the Soviet Union, The New York Times reported on Ukraine's vote for independence, highlighting the divisions inherent in the history of Ukraine by stating:

"Literally, Ukraine means borderland, which is appropriate given its position straddling Europe's two halves, its split between two relations – Eastern Orthodox and Greek Catholic – and a history that has repeatedly put Ukrainians at the mercy of other peoples' territorial ambitions – Mongols, Lithuanians, Poles, Austro-Hungarians, but mostly Russians, first under the czars and then the Communists." (Bohlen 1991: 1)

The concept of what "Europe" means, and, more importantly, where it ends, has had a profound influence on Ukraine's national movement. Whether or not Ukraine is a European state has been contested in discourses of history, geography, and literature. The concept of the "modern nation" has been the central component of national movements in both Europe and Russia. The articulation of national ideas can be traced back to the French Revolution and German Romanticism, when discourse was focused on ideas of sovereignty and self-determination (see Plokhy 2005). Ukraine's national movement has also begun to articulate these notions (Yekelchyk 2007: 7).

Historical myths construct the debate on Ukraine's identity and foreign policy. As many scholars have recognised, history-writing and nation-building are ultimately very much interconnected and complex (see Kuzio 2005f, 2006b, 2008; Plokhy 2001, 2005, 2007; Yekelchyk 2007). Kuzio argues: "Where contestation is high, as in the Ukrainian-Russian relationship since the disintegration of the USSR, the writing and interpretation of history also impact upon their domestic and foreign policies and, most notably, their inter-state relations" (2006b: 407). Historical narratives are constructed to support the central national narrative that has become the cornerstone of the Ukrainian government discourse. In fact, history discourse articulates the meaning of national identity. However, these narratives are articulated from existing story lines based on the context of discourses that existed prior to a dislocation. As Yekelchyk points out, "Ukrainian scholars were not writing from scratch. They could take on the interpretations developed by pre-Soviet patriotic historians of the so-called national school and kept alive among Ukrainian émigrés in the West" (2007: 13). Wilson further states that "historical memory is a secondary phenomenon shaped by how the past is constantly being reinterpreted in the present" (1995: 265). History-writing is inevitably selective in the facts it chooses to highlight.

For Ukraine, history has been a focal point in its national and foreign policy discourse, providing many points of contestation in its relations with Russia. As Freeland commented when reporting on a statement by President Yushchenko during his visit to Canada, "history may matter more to you if it has been rough, as Ukraine's has" (2008: 1). According to Kuzio, there are four main historical discourses that claim the history of the inception of Russian, Ukrainian, and Belarusian nations: the Russophile, Sovietophile, Eastern Slavic, and Ukrainophile discourses (2006b: 407).[2] The main goal for Ukraine's national historians and government officials has been to ensure a Ukrainian national discourse, which claims that Ukraine's national roots go back to the inception of Kyivan Rus', thus separating its ethnic identity from that of Russia. This has been a dilemma, since many Russian officials are still reluctant to agree with such claims and publicly question the existence of a separate Ukrainian nationality. For instance, Roy Medvedev, a Russian historian, writes: "A sovereign and independent Ukraine only appeared on world and European maps fairly recently, after the disintegration of the Soviet Union" (2007: 1). Vladimir Putin has publicly expressed his nostalgic feelings toward "Slavic unity" and bemoaned the collapse of the Soviet empire by referring to it as "the greatest geopolitical catastrophe of the century" (quoted in The Washington Times 2005a: 1). This creates difficulties for Ukrainian politicians as they pursue the policy of nation-building. Leonid Kuchma, Ukraine's former president, argues in his book that in addition to difficulties inherent in post-Communist transition, Ukraine has had to confront "existential fear" (Kuchma 2003: 210).

Discourse theory suits this case study particularly well. The concept of "Europe" has been integrated into the post-Soviet discourse of Ukraine's historiography. Several authors noted the importance of analysing both structural factors and matters relating to agency (i.e., the role of individuals and groups, including politicians and business alliances as well as think-tanks and government institutions). Discourse theory fits such a holistic approach. The approach is especially suited for analysing how and why the ruling elite has articulated the concept of Ukrainian identity as one linked to "Europe" and contrasted against "Russia".

---

2   The Russophile historiography emerged in the Tsarist Empire and re-emerged in post-Soviet Russia. It also established a dominant position amongst Western historians of Russia. Sovietophile historiography existed primarily in the Soviet era, although allegiance to it has continued among radical left political parties (in both Ukraine and Russia). Eastern Slavic and Ukrainophile schools are dominant in Ukraine.

Discourse theory

Discourse theory, particularly the approach developed by Ernesto Laclau and Chantal Mouffe (see Laclau 1990, 1993, 2005; and Laclau and Mouffe 1982, 1987, 2001) offers a poststructuralist approach to the classical debates on democratisation, hegemony, nationalism, and identity. While basing their theory on the Marxist and structuralist tradition, where "the whole social field is understood as a web of processes in which meaning is created" (Jørgensen and Louise 2004: 25), Laclau and Mouffe's approach differs substantially in the way that it argues that meaning "cannot be fixed so unambiguously and definitely" as scholars from the structuralist tradition contend (ibid.). Analysing the *attempts* to fix the meaning, however, is crucial to discourse analysis in general and Laclau and Mouffe's theory in particular. By applying discourse analysis to empirical work, researchers focus on the *process* of fixing meaning while also unpacking the consequences resulting from this process.[3]

As has been mentioned, the central supposition of the strand of discourse theory adopted here is that "all objects and actions are meaningful, and that their meaning is conferred by historically specific systems of rules" (Howarth and Stavrakakis 2000: 2). These meanings are attached within pre-established discourses (Torfing 2005: 14). However, unlike the notion of structure, defined here as "the closure of a topography, a construction, or an architecture, whose internal order is determined by a privileged centre" (Torfing 1999: 85), discourse is not a complete totality and not governed by a fixed centre (Laclau and Mouffe 2001: 11). Torfing elaborates on this core assumption of the theory, stating that "our cognition and speech-acts only become meaningful within certain pre-established discourses, which have different structurations that change over time" (Torfing 1999: 85). By articulating national history, actors attach meanings to *nodal points* – their national conception, which in turn reveals power struggles among various groups and individuals as they attempt to articulate meanings favourable to their subject positions. For example, in contested discourse on national history, one person's national hero may be articulated by another as their enemy. As Howarth and Stavrakakis (2000: 3) conclude, "meaning depends on the orders of discourse that constitute its identity and significance".

In line with this neo-Gramscian approach, this chapter adopts the assumption that all objects and human actions are objects of discourse. They are mean-

---
3 For a fine analysis of this theory as well its empirical use, see Howarth and Stavrakakis 2000; Jørgensen and Louise 2004; Torfing 1999, 2005.

ingful, in the sense that through interaction, at both the material and the discursive levels, human agency develops structures of meaning, outside of which reality could not be conceived. Antonio Gramsci's concept of "organic intellectuals" whose main role is to "organize the masses" is still relevant for analysing political processes (Torfing 1999: 110). In his *Prison Notebooks* (1929-1935), Gramsci attached particular importance to the role of intellectuals, who, as Simon points out, "are not only thinkers, writers and artists but also organisers such as civil servants and political leaders" (1990: 93). Thus, even though the relationship between structure and agency is fairly complex, by using such concepts as "organic intellectuals" and "dislocation",[4] this chapter adopts Laclau and Mouffe's theory of discourse for analysing Ukraine's post-Communist identity. This, in turn, helps in understanding how, after the major dislocation caused by the collapse of the Soviet Union, political leaders who traditionally identified with the Communist Party rearticulated their role as national leaders of newly independent states and retained hegemonic subject positions.

It is in the nature of politics, or *the Political,* that the competition for power takes the shape of attempts to hegemonise the content of the realm of policy. Hegemonic struggles take place by means of articulation, defined as a "practice that establishes a relation among discursive elements" (Torfing 2005: 15). As Laclau puts it: "The field of the social could thus be regarded as a trench war in which different political projects strive to articulate a greater number of social signifiers around themselves" (1990: 28). Despite the possibility of certain discourses becoming dominant, there is always a limit to their articulation, since there are alternative meanings within the constitutive outside that may challenge the hegemony. A dominant discourse fosters its identity through the conflict with alternative articulations, or "the Other" (Howarth and Stavrakakis 2000: 9).

Hegemonic discourse pushes alternative discourses into a "constitutive outside" comprised of social antagonisms (Torfing 1999: 124). This applies particularly to cases in which structural dislocation occurs. The collapse of the Soviet Union, for example, has challenged the Communist discourse and Soviet historiography. Dislocations present decisive opportunities for social and political agencies to reconstruct their identities by articulating different solutions to the crisis (see Norval and Howarth's chapter in this volume). Such articulations take the form of myths, which if accepted turn into social imaginaries. It is important

---

4   Dislocation is defined as "the process by which the contingency of discursive structures is made visible" (Torfing 1999: 13).

to distinguish between these two concepts. Myths provide an initial interpretation to the solution of the crisis. Myths that become deeply ingrained into hegemonic discourse and are "successful in neutralising social dislocations" are referred to as social imaginaries (Howarth and Stavrakakis 2000: 15f.). The discourse of foreign policy may integrate different myths of national identity, globalisation, and economic and political reforms into attempts to achieve hegemony. In the process of competing for hegemony, some myths become social imaginaries, while influencing the boundaries for possible policy articulations.

Ukraine's "Organic Intellectuals": threats to Soviet hegemony

Even prior to the collapse of the Soviet Union, many dissidents and other political activists with strong nationalistic feelings reignited some of the meanings attached to the concept of a Ukrainian nation that had been articulated by the intellectual movement of the 1920s and 1930s. While promoting Ukraine's independence, the nationalist discourse was guided by the "creative intelligentsia", composed of many writers, journalists, and cultural activists (Nastysh 2003: 310). The discourse was able to compete for hegemony following a dislocation created by the 1986 Chernobyl explosion. Because the ruling elite did not inform the general public about the explosion immediately after it took place, many fatalities ensued. The growing social discontent resulting from the nuclear disaster, as well as economic difficulties, made it difficult for the ruling elite to maintain the Communist hegemony. The Chernobyl catastrophe was perceived as a major mistake of the Communist regime.

The political dissidents, many of whom were released in the late 1980s, attempted to define Ukraine, its statehood, and its nationhood, by taking recourse to ethno-cultural and national historic discourses. In 1989, for example, the Popular Movement for Perestroika in Ukraine (Rukh) was created, which created a logic of equivalence among various groups and individuals with different political backgrounds and wide-ranging views on reform united by the search for change.[5] Within the dissident discourse, the nationalists attempted to use the concept of Europe as a consolidating tool by defining the Ukrainian nation and determining the direction of state-building reforms. "Europe" provided both domestic policy direction, as a nation-building instrument, and foreign policy direction, captured in the slogan of the "return to Europe".

---

5   For a discussion of the dissident movement and Ukraine's ruling elite of the late 1980s, see Nastych (2003), Subtelny (1994), and Wolczuk (2001), among others.

However, this discourse was not able to achieve hegemony. As Wolczuk notes, "because of the tight cultural and political integration, anti-Moscow fervour was not an automatic response to the opening of public space initiated by Mikhail Gorbachev" (2001: 65). Many dissidents were sidelined and "barely tolerated" by Ukraine's Soviet ruling elite (ibid.). Nevertheless, as the Soviet discourse began to disintegrate and was unable to signify the changes that were rapidly unfolding, Ukraine's Communist officials emerged as split subjects and identified quickly with the nationalist cause.

Despite cooperation between the former Communist ruling elite and the nationalists, the proclamation of Ukraine's independence did not bring many dissidents into the government ranks, as was the case in its Western neighbours, where independence caused many to return from exile and from political prisons to lead their countries in the new direction. Nevertheless, the fact that Ukraine had a much more interdependent relationship with Russia than the Central Eastern European countries (CEECs) meant that the dissolution of the USSR created a massive dislocation in the country's political terrain, which had to redefine its internal and external policies almost from scratch.

Ukraine's sovereignty: from myth to imaginary

Having attained independence, Ukraine's ruling elites articulated their visions of "statehood", "sovereignty", "independence", and "nation", all of which became floating signifiers without solidified meanings. "Independent Ukraine" became a nodal point around which these moments were attached to new meanings.

The "return to Europe" was one of the myths to which the concept of Ukrainian nationhood was linked. As Torfing states, "[t]he homogenisation and substantialisation of the national space will take the form of a number of predicative statements defining what the nation is" (1999: 193). The myth of Europe was articulated within the discourse on national identity and sovereignty. "'Europe' was portrayed as a symbol of political stability and harmony, economic prosperity and national unity, 'an unattainable ideal'" (Prykhoda 2008: 40).

However, the myth of the "return to Europe" in Ukrainian post-Communist discourses differed substantially from that in the CEECs. Wolczuk, for instance, highlights one of the important differences:

"Ukrainian independence could not be equated with a break from the past and the 'restoration of normality' through a 'return to Europe', the metaphor which encapsulated the transformation embarked on in East-Central Europe, including the Baltic states [...]. There could be no 'restorative revolution' in Ukraine in 1991, because of the paucity of collective historical memories which treasured a vision of a 'golden past' and the template of a 'normal' social and political order." (Wolczuk 2001: 93)

In the case of Ukraine, "Europe" was articulated within the discourse of a cultural and political heritage rather than as politics and foreign policy, at least in the early 1990s. Ukrainian politicians did list the goal of European integration among other aims to be pursued (in contrast to some Russian democratic strands); however, it was a myth[6] that did not come to dominate the discourse on foreign policy. Nevertheless, elites drafting the "Declaration of Independence" (1990) proclaimed Ukraine's plan to become part of the European integration process. This point was reiterated on 25 December 1990, when Ukrainian policy-makers adopted the "Declaration on Ukraine's Sovereignty and Foreign Policy". Leonid Kravchuk, the first president of post-Communist Ukraine, was especially instrumental in creating the logic of equivalence linking the nodal point of the Ukrainian nation to the concept of "Europe", which in turn became a floating signifier.

"Post-Orange" articulations: Russia, Ukraine, and the shadows of post-Soviet history(ies)

Since the "Orange Revolution" in 2004, Ukraine's pro-Western rhetoric has led to many disagreements with Russia about the interpretation of the two countries' shared past. The history discourse, the core premise of which is that Ukraine is a European nation in a cultural and historical (rather than political and economic) sense, has become hegemonic in Ukraine's foreign policy. During the Kuchma presidency (1994-2004), the dominant government historiographic discourse was Eastern Slavic (Kuzio 2006b: 407). The Kuchma government articulated its support for the discursive myth that Ukrainians, Russians, and Belarusians belong to the Slavic peoples that have their roots in Kyivan Rus', established in the 9th century and destroyed by Mongols in the 13th century (see Yekelchuk, 2007). According to this discourse, Ukrainian Cossacks managed to create an independent state in the 16th and 17th centuries.

---

6 According to Laclau (1990: 61-65), myths can take variety of forms, thus making it difficult to distinguish between a well-articulated and accepted myth and a social imaginary.

After the "Orange Revolution", the Yushchenko government adopted the Ukrainophile historiography, which stresses Ukraine's difference from the *Russkii* nation. The interpretation of the Treaty of Pereiaslav[7] has been greatly debated. Ukrainian historians argue that the treaty did not entail Ukraine's submission to Russia's authority. Russian historians disagree. Thus, the current policy debates are about whether to consider this treaty a "reunification" (Plokhy 2001: 493).

There are substantial differences between Ukrainian and Russian historians when it comes to the perception of Hetman Bohdan Khmelnytsky, who on behalf of the Ukrainian Cossack state decided to seek the protection of Moscow by agreeing to the treaty. Most Russian historians and politicians perceive Khmelnytsky as "a great man, as he had not only united Russia and Ukraine but also conceived of a larger East European federation" (Plokhy 2001: 489). In Ukraine, on the other hand, the hero status that Khmelnytsky enjoyed during the Soviet era and maintained even after independence (at least according to the articulations during Kuchma's presidencies) has been seriously questioned. His role in bringing about the Russo-Ukrainian agreement at Pereiaslav has become a subject of post-Soviet historical debates that help fuel foreign-policy discourses. Serhii Plokhy, the Harvard-based historian, concludes:

> "It may be said that in Ukraine official historiographical discourse has followed the major turns of state-sponsored ideology, gradually shifting focus from state-building to nation-building elements of the national historical narrative. In the post-independence years one of the main characteristics of the Ukrainian nation-building project has been the restoration and reinvention of the national tradition, while orienting the nation's culture toward the West and stressing its distinctiveness from Russian culture and tradition." (2001: 502)

In contrast to Ukraine's historiographical discourse, which focuses on its European heritage, Russia's discussion of Ukraine has placed emphasis on the idea that it is a vital part of the Slavic and Orthodox unity that also includes Russia and Belarus (Plokhy 2001: 502). Moreover, Russian history textbooks have further exacerbated these contentions. Putin's beliefs regarding historiography were highlighted when he asserted that even though "Russian history did contain some problematic pages […] we [Russians] can't allow anyone to impose a

---

7   Hetman Bohdan Khmelnytsky entered into the Treaty of Pereiaslav with Moscow in 1654 to protect Ukraine from Poland.

sense of guilt on us" (*Economist* 2007: 1). A new history manual, entitled "A Modern History of Russia: 1945-2006: A Manual for History Teachers", justifies Stalin's actions as a response to "a cold war started by America against the Soviet Union" (ibid.). Stalin's actions were appropriate for the post-World War II period and the aims of the Soviet Union, according to the Manual. Ends justify the means, and unity of the country is of paramount importance, thus making Stalin's actions "understandable" (BBC 2008b: 1).

Russian historiographic discourse is in sharp contrast to Ukraine's interpretation of Stalin's actions.[8] President Yushchenko argues that there is a wealth of historical material detailing the specific features of Stalin's forced collectivisation and terror famine policies against Ukraine. The Holodomor (the Famine of 1932-33) has been highly contested in Russia. Ukraine's government has been lobbying world capitals to recognise it as an act of genocide. In 2007, Yushchenko's article in The Wall Street Journal stated:

> "Seventy-five years ago the Ukrainian people fell victim to a crime of unimaginable horror. Usually referred to in the west as the Great Famine or the Terror famine, it is known to Ukrainians as the Holodomor. It was a state-organized program of mass starvation that in 1932-33 killed an estimated seven to ten million Ukrainians, including up to a third of the nation's children [...]. The specifically national motive behind Stalin's treatment of Ukraine was also evident in the terror campaign that targeted the institutions and individuals that sustained the cultural and public life of the Ukrainian nation [...]. This was a systematic campaign against the Ukrainian nation, its history, culture, language and way of life." (2007: 1)

The distinct contrast between Ukrainian and Russian historical paradigms has had a profound effect on many foreign-policy issues. Yushchenko's staunch support for Euro-Atlantic integration has re-opened the issue of the Crimea and the Black Sea Fleet. For the Russians, the Crimea is an issue of strategic importance as well as one of identity.[9] Russia holds a lease on the naval base until

---

8   Russian historiographic discourse is also contested within Russia, as is the Ukrainian interpretation within Ukraine. In Russia, there are various groups, who may be described as "organic intellectuals", who also dispute the view of history that articulates Stalin's actions in a positive light. The main focus of this paper, however, is on the discourses within Ukraine and articulations of "Europe" and "Russia" within the historiographic discourse.
9   For Russia, the Crimea is of geostrategic importance, since it provides access to the Black Sea. Many Russian officials consider the Crimea to be historically part of Russia. The Crimea was annexed by Empress Catherine II in 1783. It has been under Ukraine's

2017, although since the "Orange Revolution", Ukrainian politicians have made clear that they would like the lease to end after it expires (Korenovska 2008: 1). The dispute even led to some Russians politicians becoming *personae non gratae*: Yury Luzhkov, the mayor of Moscow, has been banned from Ukraine for publicly stating that Sevastopol should not be considered part of Ukraine (Gee 2008: 2). Luzhkov has also successfully lobbied the State Duma to adopt a resolution that supported Russia's abrogation of the 1997 treaty if Ukraine joins NATO (Oxford Analytica 2008: 1). Some Russian politicians interpret Ukraine's wish to join NATO as a Western conspiracy that also fuelled the "Orange Revolution" (ibid.).

The historiographic discourses have also been prevalent in the religious discussion. In fact, Ukraine's Orthodox Church has been an active promoter of Ukraine's pro-European foreign policy. Patriarch Filaret, who heads the Ukrainian Orthodox Church, has argued that "there is only one way for Ukraine, and this way is to Europe" (BBC Ukrainian 2008a: 1). On the other hand, the late Patriarch Alexy II of Moscow held a ceremonial procession in Kiev, praying that Ukraine would not be accepted into NATO (Pravda 2008: 1). The rift between the Russian and Ukrainian Orthodox churches has been part of the nationalist discourse of both countries. While the Russian Church promotes a message of unity between the Ukrainian and Russian peoples, the Ukrainian Church stresses the distinct nature of Ukraine's national identity (The Washington Times 2005). The Ukrainian government's discourse of nationality is consistent with one of geography, which is that Ukraine is distinct from Russia and belongs to Europe not only historically and culturally, but also geographically.

However, given the large Russian-speaking minority[10] and the East-West split in the electorate within Ukraine, its politicians have changed their official rhetoric and references to "Europe" and "Ukraine" before elections. The 2004 presidential elections showed that Ukraine's voting pattern split the country in half: the Orange bloc, which is mainly associated with Yulia Tymoshenko and Viktor Yushchenko; and the anti-Orange bloc, which includes the Party of Regions and the Communist Party. Analysing a poll taken in 2005, psephologist

---

political control since 1954, when Soviet Premier Nikita Khrushchev transferred it from Russia on the grounds that it had better economic and transport links with Ukraine.

10 The study conducted by the Razumkov Centre in Kyiv demonstrates that about 57 percent of Russian-speaking citizens wish for Russian to be a second state language, with a quarter wanting to see Russian as "an official language in some regions of the country" (Yakymenko 2008).

Arel pointed out: "What these numbers suggest is that the 2006 election will be extremely close. The Party of Regions and their natural ally, the Communist Party, would combine for 44.8% of the seats, while the two Orange blocs (Tymoshenko and Yushchenko) are currently at 44.5%" (Arel 2006). In terms of regional dimension, the poll showed that "anti-Orange" parties were popular in the east (receiving 78.4 percent) while the "Orange" parties were popular in the west (receiving 74.2 percent)[11] (ibid.). Moreover, the study shows evidence of nostalgia for the USSR among some members of the Ukrainian population, especially pensioners, who were among Yanukovych's core supporters during the 2004 presidential campaign (Khmelko 2005). About one-third of Russian-speakers identify closely with Soviet culture (as opposed to 6 percent who identify with European culture). At the same time, about one-third of Russian-speakers "identify themselves as bearers of the Ukrainian cultural tradition" (see Yakymenko 2008).

Considering the Ukrainian electorate and the cultural differences between East and West, it is not surprising that its politicians articulate their myths to appeal to their electorate. Nevertheless, the "East vs. West" paradigm that divides Ukraine's parties into either pro-Russian or pro-Western ones is simplistic. As Solonenko noted, "the situation in Ukraine is very patchy with different competing interests being present and having an impact" (Solonenko 2007: 1). After being elected, most Ukrainian politicians have made general references to Ukraine's place in Europe. However, the meaning of "Europe" has been articulated differently, from the romanticised myth of "Europe" as Ukraine's national beacon to a pragmatic concept where "Europe" was equated with high living standards and the rule of law. Moreover, in the course of Ukraine's democratisation, the roles of political activists who are not part of the government, but in some instances have some influence on it, such as members of the business, think-tanks, and, in some instances, academic communities, have also been transformed, thus strengthening the links among pro-European "organic intellectuals".

The relationship with Russia, on the other hand, has remained strained. Identity politics have been mixed with "hard issues", particularly gas disputes.

---

11 Further scrutiny shows that in the south of Ukraine, "Orange" parties received 22.0 percent and "anti-Orange" parties won 54.9 percent of votes cast, while in the central region, the figures stood at "Orange" 57.0 percent and anti-Orange at 18.3 percent (Arel 2006: 3).

For Russia, European gas sales were a crucial source of essential revenue. Ukraine, however, struggled to pay for gas but had no way (and in some cases, no desire) of replacing its energy sources. A cycle of problems between Russia and Ukraine persisted through the 1990s and escalated in the 2000s. What would seem to be an economic problem was articulated as a foreign-policy issue, thus constructing this dispute within the East vs. West historiographic myth.

Conclusion

Following the collapse of the Soviet Union, neither Ukraine nor Russia experienced a "true revolution". Instead, there was an "evolutionary rather than revolutionary change", with gradual readjustment of the Soviet elite leading to the breakaway of the Ukrainian republic from the Union (D'Anieri 2001: 26ff.). Prizel notes, "Ukraine appeared to be one of the republics least likely to assert its independence and undertake democratisation" (1997: 331). Unlike other CEECs, primarily Poland, Hungary, Romania, and the Baltic states, Ukraine lacked a strong national identity. Being more firmly entrenched into the Russian political structure, Ukraine experienced a deeper cultural, political, and economic assimilation than other Soviet republics. This point was noted as early as the 1920s by Ivan Rudnycky, the Ukrainian émigré scholar, who highlighted the lack of a consolidated Ukrainian elite with a sense of independent statehood that was present in other CEECs (Prizel 1997: 331). Subsequent post-Soviet identities of both Russia and Ukraine have been closely interlinked with the foreign policies of these two states.

After Ukraine became independent, the historiographic myth of the "return to Europe" was one of the discourses competing for hegemony. The myth articulated the concept of a Ukrainian nation at the heart of the government policy of European integration. The myth of Europe was articulated within the discourse on national identity and sovereignty. "Europe" was portrayed as a symbol of political stability and harmony, economic prosperity, and national unity, "an unattainable ideal" (Prykhoda 2008: 40). The *other* was the Soviet historiography, which articulated Ukraine as part of the Slavic heritage.

Ukraine's "European choice" became the nodal point of the pro-reform discourse. The term "European" was attached to multiple meanings. When Kuchma was in power, the "Orange" discourse was unified within the logic of equivalence linking the "return to Europe" to Ukraine's national project, which was articulated as a pro-democracy and pro-reform movement. This discursive myth was difficult for any political group to oppose, even for those that also identified with articulations of the Soviet historiography. Nevertheless, the discourse of Ukraine's historiography that stresses its "Europeanness" and separateness from Russia's national identity is still contested, particularly at times of dislocations caused by economic and political upheavals as well as increased pressure from Russia, thus demonstrating that identity is also closely linked to economic pressures. Discourse theory is particularly useful for analysing various both "hard" and "soft" issues that construct identity, thus allowing the incorporation of various forms of policy analysis.

Bibliography

Arel, D. 2006. "Three Months Before the 2006 Parliamentary Elections: The Latest KIIS Survey Yanukovych and the Orangists Head to Head, Regional Factor as Strong as Ever". In *Kiev International Institute of Sociology*. http://www.kiis.com.ua/index.php?id=4&sp=1&num=5&lng=eng [accessed 31 August 2009].

BBC Ukrainian. 2008a. "Patriarkh Filaret: Doroha u nas odna – v lev-ropu". August.
http://www.bbc.co.uk/ukrainian/domestic/story/2008/07/080719_church_filaret_is.shtml [accessed 2 September 2009].

BBC Ukrainian. 2008b. "Istoryk Miller pro amoral'ni pidruchnyky istoriï Rosiï". August.
http://www.bbc.co.uk/ukrainian/indepth/story/2008/08/080828_miller_rus_oh.shtml [accessed 2 September 2009]

Bohlen, C. 1991. "The World: A 'Borderland' Whose History Reflects That Troubled Role". *The New York Times*, 1 December. http://www.nytimes.com/1991/12/01/weekinreview/the-world-a-borderland-whose-history-reflects-that-troubled-role.html [accessed 31 August 2009].

Economist. 2007. "The rewriting of history". 8 November. http://www. economist.com/world/europe/displaystory.cfm?story_id=E1_TDTDNJNT [accessed 31 August 2009].

Freeland, C. 2008. "Ukraine Rifles its History for Heroes". *Financial Times* 13 June. http://www.ft.com/cms/s/0/50364f76-3955-11dd-90d7-0000779fd2ac.html?nclick_check=1 [accessed 31 August 2009].

Gee, A. 2008. "Is Ukraine's Crimea the Next Flash Point With Russia?". *U.S. News & World Report* 1 September. http://www.usnews.com/articles/news/world/2008/08/26/is-ukraines-crimea-the-next-flash-point-with-russia.html [accessed 31 August 2009].

Howarth, D. 2000a. "The Difficult Emergence of a Democratic Imaginary: Black Consciousness and non-racial democratic in South Africa". In *Discourse theory and political analysis: Identities, hegemonies and social change*, edited by D. Howarth, A.J. Norval, and Y. Stavrakakis, 168-192. Manchester & New York: Manchester University Press.

—— 2000b. *Discourse*. Buckingham & Philadelphia: Open University Press.

—— 2005. "Applying Discourse Theory: The Method of Articulation". In *Discourse Theory in European Politics: Identity, policy and governance*, edited by D. Howarth and J. Torfing, 316-349. New York: Palgrave Macmillan.

Howarth, D. and Y. Stavrakakis. 2000. "Introducing Discourse Theory and Political Analysis". In *Discourse Theory and Political Analysis: Identities, hegemonies and social change*, edited by D. Howarth, A.J. Norval, and Y. Stavrakakis, 1-23. Manchester & New York: Manchester University Press.

Jørgensen, M. and L. Phillips. 2004. *Discourse Analysis as Theory and Method*. London, Thousand Oaks, & New Delhi: SAGE Publications.

Khmel'ko, V. 2005. "Dinamika Reitingov i sotsial'nyi sostav elektoratov V. Yushchenko i V. Yanukovycha v isbiratel'noi kampanii 2004 goda". In Kiev International Institute of Sociology. http://www.kiis.com.ua/txt/doc/16022006/KHMELKO-R.pdf [accessed 2 September 2009].

Korenovska, S. 2008. "Crimea's Port Dispute". *The Washington Times* 31 July. http://www.washingtontimes.com/news/2008/jul/31/crimeas-port-dispute [accessed 31 August 2009].

Kuchma, L. 2003. *Ukraina - ne Rosiia*. Moskva: Vremia.

Kuzio, T. 2005. "Nation Building, History Writing and Competition over the Legacy of Kyiv Rus in Ukraine". *Nationalities Papers* 33, 1. 29-58.

────── 2006. "National Identity and History Writing in Ukraine." *Nationalities Papers* 34, 4. 407-427.

────── 2008. "Russian-Ukrainian Relations Reveal Deeper Problems". *The Jamestown Foundation*, 17 June. http://www.jamestown.org/single/?no_cache=1&tx_ttnews[tt_news]=33725 [accessed 1 September 2009].

Laclau, E. 1990. *New Reflections on The Revolution of Our Time*. Lon-don and New York: Verso.

────── 2007. *Emancipation(s)*. 2nd edition. London & New York: Verso.

Laclau, E. and C. Mouffe. 1987. "Post-Marxism without apologies". *New Left Review* 166. 79-106.

────── 1990. "Post-Marxism without Apologies". In *New Reflections on The Revolution of Our Time*, edited by E. Laclau, 97-132. London & New York: Verso.

────── 2001. *Hegemony and Socialist Strategy: Towards a Radical Democratic Politics*. 2nd edition. London: Verso.

Medvedev, R. 2007. "A Splintered Ukraine". *Russia in Global Affairs* 2, July-September. http://eng.globalaffairs.ru/numbers/20/1139.html [accessed 31 August 2009].

Mikkeli, H. 1998. *Europe as an Idea and an Identity*. New York: St. Martin's Press.

Nastych, A. 2003. "Elites and Masses in the Political Process in Ukraine since 1991". *Perspectives on European Politics and Society* 4, 2. 300-330.

Oxford Analytica. 2008. "Russia/Ukraine: Black Sea Fleet dispute intensifies." Global Strategic Analysis, 26 June. www.taraskuzio.net/media21_files/40.pdf [accessed 1 September 2009].

Plokhy, S. 2001. "The Ghosts of Pereyaslav: Russo-Ukrainian Historical Debates in the Post-Soviet Era". *Europe-Asia Studies* 53, 3. 489-505.

—— 2005. *Unmaking Imperial Russia: Mykhailo Hrushevsky and the writing of Ukrainian history*. Toronto, Buffalo, & London: University of Toronto Press.

—— 2006. *The Origins of the Slavic Nations: Premodern identities in Russia, Ukraine, and Belarus*. Cambridge & New York: Cambridge University Press.

—— 2007. *Ukraine's Quest for Europe: Borders, cultures, identities*. Saskatoon: Heritage Press, University of Saskatchewan.

Pravda. 2008. "Russian and Ukrainian Christians fight over orthodox baptism celebrations". 24 July. http://english.pravda.ru/news/society/24-07-2008/105869-russia-ukraine-0 [accessed 31 August 2009].

Prykhoda, I. 2008. "Kontsept Ievropa v Ukraiins'kii Publitsistytsi: Kognityvno-linhvistychni aspekty". Electronic Catalogue of Dissertations Defended in Ukraine. Dissertation Report [Submitted in 2004, defended in 2005, posted online in 2008]. Faculty of Journalism. Lviv: Lviv National University im. Ivana Franka. 10 January. http://www.lib.ua-ru.net/inode/4097.html [accessed 2 September 2009].

Rettman, A. 2007. "Ukraine takes EU to task for weak words on new treaty". *EUobserver*. http://euobserver.com/?aid=23317 [accessed 31 August 2009].

Solonenko, I. 2007. "Ukraine's 2007 parliamentary elections: implications for the foreign policy and international perception". *International Renaissance Foundation*. 1-8. www.ispionline.it/it/documents/PB_133_2009.pdf [accessed 2 September 2009].

Simon, R. 1990. *Gramsci's Political Thought: An Introduction*. London: Lawrence & Wishart.

Subtelny, O. 2000. *Ukraine: A History*. 2nd edition. Toronto, Buffalo, & London: University of Toronto Press.

Washington Times. 2005. "Ukrainians threaten Orthodox split". 16 July. http://www.washingtontimes.com/news/2005/jul/16/20050716-112835-2270r/ [accessed 31 August 2009].

——— 2005a. "Putin calls collapse of Soviet Union 'catastrophe'". 26 April. http://www.washtimes.com/news/2005/apr/26/20050426-120658-5687r/ [accessed 31 August 2009].

Torfing, J. 1999. *New Theories of Discourse: Laclau, Mouffe, and Žižek*. Oxford & Malden: Blackwell.

——— 2002. "Discourse Analysis and the Post-Structuralism of Laclau and Mouffe". *European Political Science (EPS)*. Symposium: Discourse Analysis & Political Science. http://www.essex.ac.uk/ECpR/publications/ eps/onlineissues/autumn2002/research/torfing.htm [accessed 2 September 2009].

——— 2005. "Discourse Theory: Achievements, Arguments, and Challenges". In *Discourse Theory in European Politics*, edited by D. Howarth and J. Torfing. 1-32. Basingstoke: Palgrave Macmillan.

Wilson, A. 1995. "The Donbas between Ukraine and Russia: The Use of History in Political Disputes". *Journal of Contemporary History* 30, 2. 265-289.

Wolczuk, K. 2001a. "EU Justice and Home Affairs in the Context of Enlargement". European University Institute. The Robert Schuman Centre for Advanced Studies. Report of the Working Group on the Eastern Enlargement of the European Union. *EUI Policy Paper* RSC 01/4. 16 November. http://www.eui.eu/RSCAS/WP-Texts/02_04p.pdf [accessed 2 September 2009].

—— 2001b. *The Moulding of Ukraine: The Constitutional Politics of State Formation*. Budapest: Central European University Press.

—— 2004. "Integration without Europeanisation: Ukraine and its Policy towards the European Union". European University Institute. The Robert Schuman Centre for Advanced Studies. *EUI Working Paper* RSCAS 2004/15. http://www.eui.eu/RSCAS/WP-Texts/04_15.pdf [accessed 2 September 2009].

—— 2008. "A Dislocated and Mistranslated EU-Ukraine Summit". *ISS Opinion*, European Union Institute for Security Studies, October. http://www.iss.europa.eu/uploads/media/EU-Ukraine_Summit.pdf [accessed 2 September 2009].

—— 2003. *Ukraine's Foreign and Security Policy 1991-2000*. London & New York: RoutledgeCurzon.

Yakymenko, Iu. 2008. "Russian-Speaking Citizens of Ukraine: 'Imaginary Society' as it is". *Razumkov Centre*. http://razumkov.org.ua/eng/article.php?news_id=676 [accessed 31 August 2009].

Yanukovych, V. 2006. "Ukraine's Choice: Toward Europe". *The Washington Post* 5 October. http://www.washingtonpost.com/wp-dyn/content/article/2006/10/04/AR2006100401541.html [accessed 1 September 2009].

Yekelchyk, S. 2007. *Ukraine: Birth of a Modern Nation*. Oxford & New York: Oxford University Press.

Yushchenko, V. 2007. "Holodomor". *The Wall Street Journal* 27 November. http://www.mfa.gov.ua/usa/en/publication/content/20664.htm [accessed 2 September 2009].

Constructing or Deconstructing Democracy? The Geopolitical Context of Ukraine's Democratic Choice

Sergii Glebov

Ukraine presents an interesting case of democratic transformation within the post-Soviet space. Located between Europe and Russia, Ukraine's democratisation is to be seen in the context of a geopolitical choice between two different models: Western-style liberal democracy and Russia's version of "sovereign democracy". Given the Russian dominance in the region, Russia may well succeed in hampering Ukraine's efforts as regards the European orientation of the country's democratic trajectory.

Ukraine's democratisation trajectory since the collapse of the Soviet Union in 1991 can only be understood if international factors are taken into account as well. In many ways, the Ukrainian experience reflected the developments in other former Soviet republics. At the same time, it was also conditioned by these developments, namely as regards Ukraine's most important neighbour: Russia.

Sharing a long history and close ethnic relations, Russia remains one of the most powerful actors to influence Ukraine's state-building. Russia's involvement must be seen against the larger background of geopolitical rivalry with the West over spheres of influence in the post-Soviet space. Democracy as a discourse thus has an important political connotation. To put it simply: If Ukraine accepts Russia's version of democracy, it will at least implicitly also accept the geopolitical predominance of Russia over the West. The domestic debate on democracy cannot but take the geopolitical context into account.

This chapter will thus put particular emphasis on the geopolitical context for understanding Ukraine's democratic choice, which is one between Europe, or "the West", and Russia. However, the outcome of this choice may well represent something entirely different: the Ukrainian version of democracy.

Democracy and geopolitics

The signifier of democracy has always drawn a demarcation line between *us* and *them*. During the Cold War, ideological concepts such as "the free world" vs. "tyranny" (US rhetoric) or "the imperialist and antidemocratic camp" vs. "the anti-imperialist and democratic camp" (USSR rhetoric) were used as rhetorical means to rally allies behind a "just" cause and thereby justify geopolitical expansion. The situation today is not very different. In fact, we will argue in the following that democracy is part of a larger political game, in which it acts as an instrument in international relations.

The "correct" interpretation of democracy determines who is a friend and who is a foe. The West, primarily the United States, does not cease to criticise Russia for its lack of democratic reforms, while Moscow, in turn, tries to defend Russia's "sovereign path" to democracy and freedom and attacks the United States for alleged "double standards".

The report "Russia's Wrong Direction: What the United States Can and Should Do" by the Council on Foreign Relations (2006) is an example of such an attempt to judge Russia through a Western conception of democracy. The authors were concerned by the trend of "de-democratization" and called for increased efforts to "democratize" Russia. As it turned out, the US criticism triggered just the opposite reaction from Russia. In 2007, Russian President Vladimir Putin drastically changed his tone, became more self-assertive, and called for "open cards" in talking to the US and her allies. Among the issues that Putin mentioned were democracy, nuclear weapons – and Ukraine.

In his February 2007 speech at the Munich Conference on Security Policy (Putin 2007a) and in an interview with TIME magazine in December 2007 (Putin 2007b), he accused the US of threatening the unity of Ukraine by interfering with its internal affairs and openly supporting the pro-US political elite against the pro-Russian one.

The examples above illustrate the similarities between the new global competition between Russia and the US and the Cold War, even though there are clear differences. At the moment, there is no risk of direct military confrontation. The conflict between Washington and Moscow is a collision of interests concerning issues such as the next round of NATO's eastern expansion or the stationing of an anti-missile shield and radar systems in Eastern Europe. The conditions for engaging in a full-fledged version of a new Cold War are no longer given – Russia is not in a position to challenge the US militarily, nor has the regime subscribed to an ideology that is in essence hostile towards Western values (in fact, Russia has subscribed to democratic values in her constitution); it might in practice not adhere to the principles of free market and an open society, yet it does not officially reject these principles, either.

Given the lack of an essential ideological gap, the confrontation in the realm of ideology is not over democracy and human rights as key values, but rather over the exact *meaning* of democracy. It is in this realm that Russia as well as the US and other Western countries are trying to defend their fixations of the signifier "democracy".

In an interview with the Indian Broadcasting Corporation Doordarshan on 4 December 2008, Russian President Dmitry Medvedev (Prezident Rossii 2008) was asked: "[A]re we moving towards a new version, a new 'edition' of the Cold War?" He responded as follows:

> "I don't think that we are on the verge of some new version of the Cold War. At least I would hate it. Indeed, we have found ourselves in a situation when a number of our partners made harsh statements, when we heard talks of some restrictive measures. But in my view, first of all, all these talks led to nothing and could not lead to anything because in the present-day world any attempts to isolate a country – especially such country as Russia – are undoubtedly doomed to failure. And since it is so, there is no sense and no use in talking about any new 'Cold War' and another iron curtain. Moreover, I can say that there is no ideological ground for that. In the past it was at least ideologically substantiated: two worlds, two systems and competition between them. Today we share the same values. It is only necessary to ensure that these values are understood in the same way. And that is the most difficult thing."

From Russia's official point of view, the contest with the West is thus not over values, but how these values are interpreted. Western criticism of Russian democracy is portrayed as an attempt by the West to extend its own model of democracy, and thereby its geopolitical influence, into the former Soviet space. From a Western perspective, this is perceived as a poor justification of a Russian attempt to maintain its claim to dominance over the former Soviet republics and hush up the fact that Russia has been abandoning the core values of democracy.

Russia's "sovereign democracy" and Ukraine's dilemma of choice

Ukraine is literally in the middle of this Western-Russian contest over interpreting values. Like so many times before in its troubled past as a border country between West and East, Ukraine is at an important threshold in its history. The author believes that the country would be well advised to orient itself clearly towards those countries where democratic traditions are strong, meaning the West. The most important reason for this turn westwards is related to security. It is an established truth that democracies are very unlikely to engage in warfare against each other. Moving towards the Western model of democracy and engaging with other democracies thus enhances Ukraine's own security.

One may argue that by choosing the Western model, Ukraine is challenging Russia, thus eventually provoking a reaction that might even lead to military confrontation. However, Ukraine's choice to move further on the way of democracy is not directed against Russia, and it is important that Ukraine's politicians make this clear. It is rather to be hoped that a strong Ukrainian democracy will mean an end to the domestic political upheavals that the country has experienced in its recent past. By embracing democracy and human rights, Ukraine also takes upon itself the obligation to protect all of its citizens, guarantee minority rights, and ensure that all strata of its population are represented politically through free and fair elections. Stabilising the domestic situation essentially means that stability and security also move closer towards Russia's own borders.

Ukraine's democratisation path was and remains bumpy. Like Russia, the country in 1991 adopted democratic principles and enshrined these in its constitution. The result, though, was a mixture of Soviet traditions, Western democratic "imports", and Russian influence. The most interesting aspect in this context is the Russian factor. The question here is whether the Russian version of democracy is at all applicable to Ukraine.

Democracy is usually defined in opposition to authoritarian and totalitarian regimes as a form of government in which a constitution guarantees basic civil and political rights, fair and free elections, and independent courts of law. Among the basic principles are: human rights; separation of powers; freedom of speech and the media; religious liberty; and the general and equal right to vote. Unlike authoritarian governments, which are usually not chosen by the public in free and fair elections, a democratically elected government is thus expected to rule in the interest of a majority of the people. Its actions are controlled not only by the separation of powers, but also by a free media, and it is thus also expected to be less corrupt.

Is Russia a democracy? In the common Western opinion, which is also based on the assessments of the various democratic indices (such as the one by Freedom House), it is not. The press is not free, there are no real opposition parties, and there is no effective separation of the executive, legislative, and judiciary branches. Does this mean, however, that the Russian population is not free?

Compared to the Soviet era, Russians today clearly enjoy many more liberties. They are allowed to travel, to consume, to open their own businesses, and they are in a position to gather information via other channels than the state-controlled media – for example, through the internet or some of the newspapers. Thus, the state is largely absent from their private sphere. Politically, however, the Russian citizens are not free, as there remain obstacles to the formation of political opposition parties or independent media. The state also does not allow large anti-government demonstrations. The combination of limited political rights with freedom for the individual has thus led Western observers to qualify Russian democracy as "defective", "semi-", or "quasi-democracy" (see also the chapter by Nicolas Hayoz in this book).

Not coincidentally, the West does not cease to criticise Russia for the weakening of democratic processes. During his presidency, Putin often defended Russia's "particular path" to democracy and freedom in response to Western criticism. A good example is the following statement made on 26 September 2003 at Columbia University in response to criticism of the abridgement of freedom of speech in Russia:

> "[W]e have never had free speech in Russia, so I don't quite understand what there is to be infringed upon. As you know, we had a totalitarian state for a hundred years and before that tsarism was infringing upon everything. We had no parliamentary activities; we formed a parliament and then dissolved it and so on". (Putin 2003)

This is the classical official way of justifying the state of democracy in Russia when addressing a Western audience. Putin says that Russia has in fact embraced democracy, but due to a long anti-democratic tradition, the country will need time in order to put the democratic values it has embraced into practice.

What the West pessimistically perceives as the "half empty glass" of Russian democracy is treated in Russia as "half full". This may be a signal from the Russian authorities to democratic countries. In addition, in mid-September 2007, during a meeting with Western reporters at his Bocharov Creek residence, Putin called on the West "to stop lecturing Russia on democracy" (Prezident Rossii 2007). The construction of democracy in Russia is taking place, but it is adapted to national "circumstances". At the same time, Russian authorities do not explain what the essence of this "special way" is. They only refer to Russian history. The direction in which it is moving – diametrically opposed to the Western model – is not reassuring.

Thus, according to a survey conducted by the Levada Center in summer of 2007, the percentage of Russians that reject Western values in recent years has increased significantly. Support for the "special way of Russia" has increased in six years from 53 percent to 74 percent. According to Russian experts, this is "evidence of growing national isolationism in Russia" (Gazeta.ru 2007).

How democracy is interpreted has thus become a key attribute of political identification. Is there any conceptual difference between the (post-) Soviet experience of Russia and the (post-) Soviet experience of Ukraine in elaborating democracy? For the Ukrainian state, located on the Western boundary of Russia, it is imperative that a democratic process within the country should not be developed as an alternative model to the European understanding of democracy. The Ukrainian constitution thus proclaims a democratic state without adding any further attributes.

Ukraine currently finds itself at a difficult stage in the process of implementing a public system of democratic institutions. The country is caught in the crossfire of the debate between Russia and the West over the basic principles of democracy. It can choose to "please" Russia and establish its own "quasi-" or "semi-" democracy, or it can go ahead and embrace democracy as practiced in Western states.

It is likely, however, that Russia will try to influence Ukraine's domestic choice. Moscow fears that any free and fair elections might bring anti-Russian forces to power. It is thus in Russia's interest that the country should adapt a Russian-style version of democracy, which will guarantee continued Russian influence through Ukraine's corrupt political system. To be sure, there are strong political and economic interest groups in Ukraine that favour close ties to Russia;

these interest groups can only survive as long as the political system remains corrupt. The clearest example of this is the highly opaque area of Russian-Ukrainian energy relations.

The Ukrainian political situation is developing in slow motion, with the essence of current political crises remaining unchanged since 2004 and without any prospect of amelioration until at least the 2009 presidential elections. What outsiders perceive as a "crisis" is perceived by Ukrainians as the *courant normal*.

Not surprisingly, post-stabilisation Russia counterposes its stability and model of "managed democracy" which "saved" Russia from the chaos of the 1990s, to the Ukrainian "state of crisis". "Sovereign" democracy and "order" seem to be *nodal points* in Russian official discourse, which must embrace democracy while simultaneously distancing itself from the chaos of the 1990s as well as, to some lesser extent, from the permanent Ukrainian "crisis".

Russian rhetoric illustrates this. After President Medvedev had stated that in Ukraine, "there is another state-governmental crisis" (see Medvedev 2008a), one of the speakers of Putin's regime, Head of the Council of the Federation Sergei Mironov, added:

> "Events in Ukraine only confirm that for countries like Russia and Ukraine, a parliamentary republic is premature [...]. The third election in the last three years – is too much. It is good that Russia did not go the way of a parliamentary republic." (Korrespondent.net 2008a)

Washington had a different view on Ukraine's decision to conduct early elections. The US Department of State was sure that this was "Ukrainian democracy in action" (Korrespondent.net 2008b). The shadowboxing between the Kremlin and the White House, which instrumentalised the case of Ukraine, was continued. The Department of State, expressing the position of the US president, said that "democracy is not always calm, but always the best form of polity." In this case, the US was in favour of identifying Ukraine as democratic.

When reading Russian statements about Ukraine, one should not forget the special meaning that Russia attaches to Ukraine as its "Slavic brother" and historical partner. Moscow considers any deviation of Ukraine from what Russia considers her key national interests to be not just a mere nuisance, but an affront.

In this regard, Putin's statement expressing his disappointment with Ukraine's democratic transformation, which he interprets as a retreat from the Russian understanding of democracy, is interesting: "That was the only hope for the people from Ukraine, but they just completely discredited themselves, they are on the way to continuous tyranny" (Prezident Rossii 2007).

Ukraine: retreating from Russian "democracy" to European "tyranny"?

Where is Ukraine headed in its democratic development? The European Union should criticise the slow democratic reforms in Ukraine. The EU is interested in further democratisation as that would make the country a more predictable partner, both in political and in economic terms.

As long as the level of democracy is so low, Ukraine is unlikely to be integrated into the EU any time soon. At the same time, Ukraine's instable development makes it susceptible to Russian influence – a situation not to the liking of the West. As experience has shown in the Balkans, the prospect of EU integration or of further rapprochement with the EU was and is an important tool for the Balkan countries to speed up political and economic reforms in order to make themselves attractive partners for Europe. The same could happen in Ukraine if the political class wishes to engage on the path of rapprochement with the EU.

In any case, the path to Europe, and towards achieving the high European standards of democracy, is long and thorny. Any political and economic reform will fail if the "rule of corruption" continues to prevail over the rule of law in the political and legal system of Ukraine. Ukraine currently still lacks respect for private property; the political process is not transparent; and the law is often bent to satisfy certain interest groups and is subjected to political considerations.

The fight against corruption is thus one of the most important activities and lies at the core of post-Soviet democratisation. In Russia, President Medvedev declared the struggle against corruption one of his top priorities upon taking office in May 2008. He signed a decree to set up a presidential anti-corruption council only two weeks after his inauguration (RIA Novosti 2008a). Not accidentally, the topic of corruption is also part of the Russian-US discourse on democracy. Nevertheless, it is symptomatic that the Russian side is interpreting US calls for democracy, accompanied by a call to fight corruption, as attempts to interfere with the domestic affairs of Russia. Referring again to the example of the Council on Foreign Relations document mentioned above, Vladimir Frolov, director of the National Laboratory for Foreign Policy, interpreted anti-corruption calls from Washington as one of the instruments by which the US sought to bring about regime change in Russia (see Frolov 2006).

Russian power is highly concerned with the global discourse on democracy and Russia's place in it – and this is why the Kremlin reacts in an aggressive manner to any outside criticism. It is telling that in his first address to the Federal Assembly on 5 November 2008, Medvedev stressed democracy as the main "development goal" of society, clearly in response to outside criticism (Medvedev 2008b):

> "The free development of individuals and their social protection will always be the priorities of public policy. This will be our main concern. It will be our society's development goal. Dear friends! We live in a free and modern country. And we have managed to do much. We have a positive experience in establishing a democratic state. And more than success, we have real victories. And together we are moving forward to find answers to difficult questions. To succeed again. And to win again."

How did the regime respond the "difficult questions" of moving towards democracy? It decided, with the approval of the parliament, to change the Russian constitution and extend the president's term in office from four to six years. What Western observers saw as a further curbing of democracy, Russia portrayed as a strengthening. According to presidential advisor Veniamin Yakovlev, for example, this initiative is aimed at strengthening the rule of the people and enhancing its control over state bodies in Russia (Korrespondent.net 2008c).

This discourse provokes the question: If this is indeed a strengthening of societal control over the state, why was the proposal to change the Russian constitution and prolong the president's term in office not a bottom up initiative rooted in civil society? It does not matter much whether or not Putin will indeed attempt to return to the presidential office after 2012, when Medvedev has served his term, or whether Medvedev decides to stay. These two politicians have consolidated their hold on power for the foreseeable future. Also, it is doubtful whether Medvedev is more liberal than Putin. He does not seem to be in a rush to improve his image compared to that of Putin in 2007 and 2008. CBS News reporter Alexei Kuznetsov believes that some observers have changed their view of Medvedev:

"Appearances can be deceiving. Six months ago, when Dmitry Medvedev was inaugurated as Russia's new president, many hoped there would be a thaw in U.S.-Russia relations. The soft-spoken lawyer has never worked for the KGB. His reputation as a liberal seemed to contrast sharply with his predecessor, Vladimir Putin. However, for the past six months it seems that President Medvedev has been working hard to dismantle his liberal image and revive memories of the Cold War." (Kuznetsov 2008)

Conclusion: Ukraine's choice

What does this all mean for Ukraine? Western observers, as well as the press and politicians, tend to portray Ukraine in a more positive light than Russia with regard to democratic progress. Thus, according to Zbigniew Brzezinski (2007),

"Ukraine, in a way, offers not only a lesson, but a hopeful avenue for Russia, and an avenue that all of us in the West should hope that Russia will pursue. Because it would be in the interest of the larger West if Russia, in time, became more closely and more genuinely associated with the West."

Does this black-and-white picture reflect the real situation in Ukraine? It could be argued that descriptions such as Brzezinski's are manifestations of selective perception. If Putin declares that he loves Russia and thinks that Russia is unique, he is a nationalist, retreating from Western democratic achievements. If the president of Ukraine, Viktor Yushchenko, declares his devotion to Ukraine, he is a patriot and fighting for a just cause – the independence of Ukraine from Russia and the establishment of democracy. Russia's image as the "enemy" reinforces the image of Ukraine as a democratic country, as standing up against Russian imperialism, and as differing from "Russian democracy".

The perception in Russia is quite different. From the Russian perspective, if Putin loves Russia, he is a patriot; if Yushchenko loves Ukraine, he is a betrayer of Slavic brotherhood with Russia (and Belarus) and a nationalist who hates Russians. "If Putin acts tough towards Western counterparts he is defending the national interests of Russia, but if Yushchenko speaks hard to Russia he is working for the West"; "If Putin speaks to Bush – he is restoring cooperation, if Yushchenko speaks to Bush – they conspire against Russia" (Kuhner 2008).

Again, we see that Russia and the West are not actually talking about Ukraine and are not really analysing the domestic situation or the state of the country's democracy; Ukraine is merely one element in a larger geopolitical game. In contrast to Russia, however, the EU and the US do not question Ukrainian territorial integrity, independence, and sovereignty, or its right to develop towards democracy, while Russia questions the status of Ukraine as a sovereign and independent actor capable of developing democracy. Does Russia see Ukraine as an object of its influence? The answer to this question is obvious to some in the West, who are ready to "antagonize" Russia against "democratic" Ukraine (Kuhner 2008).

Ukraine, being stuck between the West and Russia, is faced with the necessity of taking sides in the discourse on democracy. The choice would be easy if all centres of power shared the same approaches to democracy. Instead, Ukraine wavers between Western and Russian approaches to democracy. It has embraced democratic values in theory, but in practice it still struggles when it comes to their application. Ukraine is, at best, still a very weak democracy based on a highly corrupt political system and malfunctioning economy.

Ukraine cannot engage on a separate path of democracy, as Russia has done, because it lacks the material, economic, political, and ideological requirements for such a path. Russia does not consider itself part of any larger geopolitical unity because it sees itself as a great power and a pole of attraction for other parts. Thus, Ukraine may be theoretically part of a democratic Europe and a democratic world, while Russia will always consider itself a unique global pole, and claim the right to uphold its own interpretation of democracy.

Thus, in the discussion of the conflicting blueprints for democracy, the geopolitical context, global positions, foreign policy agendas, and international relations are of great importance. The gap between the Russian Federation and Ukraine in terms of potential, status, and resources dictates the different theoretical backgrounds and strategic paradigms of development that shape the trajectories of both countries towards democracy.

Will Ukraine orient itself Westwards or Eastwards? The question is difficult to answer, since Ukraine is only now trying to reassess its national interests and conceptual values while constructing democracy. Ukraine is, however, unlikely to return to anything resembling a totalitarian regime. Ukrainian society passed the "point of no return" after the "Orange Revolution" of 2004/2005, when the Ukrainian people manifested itself as a single (though still diverse) political nation, which should prevent any backsliding to a non-democratic system.

Also, Ukraine is still much more polycentric than Russia, as shown in the discussion on the characteristics of the Ukrainian democratic "chaos" and "state of crisis" (contrary to the "Russian order"). Both the "chaos" and the "state of crisis" in Ukraine were products of a struggle for power permanently involving at least three major political parties. We believe that the mere existence of political competition itself will automatically bring more democracy to Ukrainian society, which only recently emerged from a one-party totalitarian state system.

In this whole process, however, the West, and especially Europe, will have a crucial role to play. At this difficult moment of historical choice, it is essential that Europe stand by Ukraine and give the country a perspective of closer economic and possibly, at a later stage, political integration. It should be clear that this process would not be directed against Russia, and both Europe and Ukraine must communicate this message unmistakeably – not only rhetorically, but also by strengthening their ties with Russia at the same time.

Bibliography

Brzezinski, Z. 2007. "Ukraine Should Not Hesitate to Say to Its Younger brother, Russia, That It Should Learn Ukrainian Political Culture." *Ukrayinska Pravda* [internet] 14 November. http://www.pravda.com.ua/en/news/2007/11/14/9433.htm [accessed 6 September 2009].

Council on Foreign Relations. 2006. *Independent Task Force Report # 57. Russia's Wrong Direction: What the United States Can and Should do.* Overview. http://www.cfr.org/publication/9997/ [accessed 6 September 2009].

Frolov, V. 2006. "Kreml' popriderzhal doklad". *Nezavisimaia gazeta* 21 September. http://www.ng.ru/world/2006-09-21/9_kremlin.html [accessed 6 September 2009].

Gazeta.ru. 2007. "Ot redaktsii: Gosudarstvo-osobist". 13 August. http://www.gazeta.ru/comments/2007/08/13_e_2035912.shtml [accessed 1 September 2009].

Korrespondent.net. 2008a. "Sovet Federatsii RF: Krizis v Ukraine obuslovlen ee konstitutsiei." 13 October. http://korrespondent.net/russia/613952 [accessed 1 September 2009].

—— 2008b. "Gosdep USA: Rospusk Verkhovnoi Radi – eto demokratiia v deistvii". 9 October. http://korrespondent.net/ukraine/politics/610371 [accessed 1 September 2009].

—— 2008c. "V Rossii schitaiut, chto predlozheniia Medvedeva ukrepliaiut demokratiiu". 6 November http://korrespondent.net/russia/638654 [accessed 1 September 2009].

Kuhner, J.T. 2008. "Will Russia-Ukraine be Europe's next war?". *Washington Times* 12 October. http://www.washtimes.com/news/2008/oct/12/europes-next-war [accessed 6 September 2009].

Kuznetsov, A. 2008. "Russia's Medvedev's Tough Guy Act". *CBS News* 24 November. http://www.cbsnews.com/stories/2008/11/24/world/main 4631526.shtml?source=mostpop_story [accessed 26 November 2008].

Medvedev, D. 2008a. "V Ukraine – gosudarstvenno-pravitelstvennii krizis". *Korrespondent.net* 10 October. http://korrespondent.net/russia/611255 [accessed 6 September 2009].

—— 2008b. Address to the Federal Assembly of the Russian Federation. Grand Kremlin Palace, Moscow, 5 November. http://www.kremlin.ru/eng/speeches/2008/11/05/2144_type70029type82917type127286_208836.shtml [accessed 6 September 2009].

Prezident Rossii. 2007. "Interview with mass-media journalists from the member-countries of the 'G-8'". 4 June. http://www.kremlin.ru/text/appears/2007/06/132615.shtml [accessed 6 September 2009].

—— 2008. "Dmitry Medvedev's Interview with Indian Broadcasting Corporation Doordarshan, The Kremlin, Moscow". 4 December.

http://www.kremlin.ru/eng/speeches/2008/12/04/0928_type82916_210105.shtml [accessed 6 September 2009].

Putin, V. 2003. Speech and Answers to Questions at Columbia University, New York. 26 September. http://www.kremlin.ru/eng/speeches/2003/09/26/0100_type82914type82917type84779_52868.shtml [accessed 6 September 2009].

——— 2007a. Speech at the 43rd Munich Conference on Security Policy, February 10. http://www.securityconference.de/konferenzen/rede.php?sprache=en&id=179 [accessed 6 September 2009].

——— 2007b. "Q&A: Full Transcript". *Time* 18 December http://www.time.com/time/specials/2007/personoftheyear/article/0,28804,1690753_1690757_1695787,00.html [accessed 6 September 2009].

RIA Novosti. 2008a. "Russia's corruption rate in law enforcement up 35%". 6 November. http://en.rian.ru/russia/20081106/118154843.html [accessed 6 September 2009].

——— 2008b. "Russia to deploy Iskander missiles near Polish border – Medvedev". 5 November. http://en.rian.ru/russia/20081105/118136001.html [accessed 6 September 2009].

Index

A

antagonism 39, 42, 43, 111, 135, 136, 141, 212, 230, 237, 260, 270, 280, 338

B

Bakhtin 308, 309
Belarus 48, 56, 184, 273, 378, 399
Berezovsky 110, 271, 317

C

capitalism 41, 47, 50, 55, 112, 117, 129, 136, 137, 152, 263, 351
Chechnya 21, 53, 71, 219, 292, 293, 317, 349, 350, 353, 360, 361
Communism 20, 22, 51, 57, 113, 126, 127, 136, 149, 154, 161, 165, 204, 291, 295, 310
constitutive outside 26, 27, 51, 203, 289, 296, 310, 355, 374
corruption 20, 55, 58, 77, 79, 83, 127, 191, 315, 397

D

demands 27, 33, 34, 35, 36, 37, 43, 45, 46, 47, 48, 51, 54, 55, 58, 59, 60, 62, 63, 133, 180, 182, 194, 252, 254, 257, 258, 260, 262, 263, 284, 287, 290, 292, 294, 297, 330, 332, 334, 335, 341, 356, 358, 361, 362
discourse theory 19, 20, 26, 27, 31, 47, 51, 107, 296, 327, 329, 342, 343, 369, 370, 373
dislocation 27, 28, 37, 39, 40, 41, 42, 43, 44, 45, 107, 108, 115, 121, 136, 199, 203, 211, 212, 225, 226, 234, 237, 269, 285, 286, 287, 298, 300, 302, 338, 348, 349, 351, 352, 359, 360, 361, 362, 371, 374, 375, 376

E

empty signifier 25, 33, 34, 37, 51, 62, 116, 199, 252, 253, 254, 256, 257, 262, 263, 321, 335, 341, 342, 343, 354
Eurasia 60, 335
European Union 98, 102, 103, 105, 153, 173, 211, 337, 397

F

floating signifier 34, 51, 108, 115, 199, 262, 263, 271, 286, 290, 292, 361, 376, 377
foreign policy 54, 61, 71, 151, 193, 211, 213, 217, 218, 223, 224, 229, 231, 236, 295, 327, 328, 331, 333, 334, 336, 339, 371, 372, 375, 377, 380, 400

G

Gorbachev 39, 51, 52, 54, 59, 68, 96, 151, 153, 155, 156, 158, 164, 272, 273, 277, 291, 376
Gramsci 40, 49, 194, 215, 218, 374

H

hegemony 25, 27, 33, 34, 36, 48, 99, 107, 110, 121, 129, 130, 134, 144, 194, 196, 203, 206, 218, 230, 232, 234, 236, 248, 253, 256, 257, 258, 260, 264, 265, 309, 337, 342, 351, 373, 374, 375, 376, 382

I

ideology 20, 27, 28, 32, 50, 71, 110, 112, 114, 125, 127, 128, 133, 139, 150, 153, 159, 176, 182, 183, 191, 197, 213, 214, 216, 218, 229, 236, 237, 250, 270, 290, 316, 329, 339, 351, 378, 392
international relations 26, 33, 213, 328, 329, 338, 340, 341, 391, 400

K

Khodorkovsky 138, 317, 322
Kozyrev 50, 52, 57, 60, 117

L

Laclau 20, 25, 26, 31, 32, 33, 34, 35, 36, 37, 39, 40, 41, 42, 43, 44, 45, 46, 48, 62, 94, 107, 108, 111, 130, 135, 194, 195, 199, 203, 218, 230, 234, 235, 236, 248, 249, 251, 252, 253, 254, 255, 257, 260, 261, 262, 264, 269, 270, 271, 280, 285, 286, 287, 289, 296, 297, 298, 301, 308, 327, 328, 330, 335, 338, 341, 342, 343, 351, 355, 361, 373, 374, 377
Lefort 140, 141, 145
Lenin 69, 272, 280, 316
Luzhkov 110, 278, 320, 380

M

Marxism 113, 114, 290
Medvedev 143, 191, 192, 214, 233, 274, 277, 280, 303, 306, 307, 372, 392, 396, 397, 398, 399
Mouffe 20, 25, 26, 33, 48, 62, 94, 107, 108, 111, 130, 141, 194, 218, 230, 236, 269, 270, 271, 280, 285, 286, 296, 301, 327, 329, 330, 343, 361, 373, 374
myth 28, 284, 285, 286, 287, 288, 289, 290, 291, 292, 293, 294, 295, 297, 298, 300, 301, 302, 303, 369, 370, 376, 377, 381, 382, 383

N

national identity 19, 27, 28, 36, 47, 48, 49, 51, 52, 54, 55, 56, 59, 62, 71, 113, 159, 162, 163, 164, 165, 172, 176, 182, 195, 219, 220, 236, 269, 270, 277, 280, 284, 285, 298, 302, 303, 307, 314, 369, 370, 371, 375, 376, 380, 382, 383
nationalism 27, 48, 113, 114, 148, 149, 150, 151, 152, 153, 154, 156, 158, 159, 161, 162, 164, 165, 171, 179, 180, 181, 182, 226, 227, 232, 237, 250, 291, 312, 373
NATO 52, 53, 60, 61, 103, 185, 201, 233, 297, 337, 341, 380, 391

nodal point 28, 59, 220, 272, 286, 288, 292, 298, 300, 302, 361, 363, 373, 376, 377, 382, 396

O

official discourse 23, 27, 28, 36, 47, 51, 62, 115, 121, 141, 236, 237, 285, 288, 291, 292, 295, 296, 298, 299, 300, 301, 302, 303, 309, 396
oligarchs 19, 20, 37, 58, 222, 301, 336

P

political discourse 53, 55, 61, 108, 111, 115, 116, 121, 125, 129, 130, 141, 198, 221, 236, 259, 264, 265, 269, 285, 295, 297, 323, 359
political identity 20, 22, 23, 27, 37, 47, 52, 58, 62, 107, 111, 193, 217, 253, 264, 265
populism 27, 31, 32, 33, 34, 35, 36, 37, 44, 45, 62, 141, 191, 248, 251, 253, 257, 260, 263
Primakov 57, 58, 59, 60, 61, 62

R

racism 54, 119, 179, 180

S

Serbia 53, 159, 355
sovereign democracy 24, 27, 28, 62, 125, 126, 127, 128, 129, 130, 131, 132, 133, 137, 139, 142, 143, 144, 189, 190, 192, 193, 194, 195, 196, 197, 198, 199, 200, 201, 202, 203, 204, 205, 206, 211, 212, 214, 216, 218, 222, 227, 234, 237, 309, 390
stability 19, 20, 22, 23, 24, 25, 26, 31, 33, 48, 62, 75, 96, 98, 111, 125, 127, 129, 132, 133, 135, 142, 190, 206, 221, 226, 237, 248, 249, 288, 302, 303, 322, 328, 339, 343, 349, 376, 382, 393, 396
Stalin 220, 271, 272, 276, 277, 278, 279, 280, 289, 291, 379
Surkov 24, 115, 192, 193, 195, 196, 197, 198, 200, 202, 204, 214, 217, 226, 227, 228, 233, 237

T

terrorism 21, 24, 78, 154, 174, 177, 203, 219, 293, 296, 297, 299, 301, 348, 349, 350, 352, 354, 355, 357, 359, 360, 361, 362

U

Ukraine 28, 56, 128, 148, 173, 184, 189, 192, 201, 277, 297, 298, 337, 369, 370, 371, 372, 374, 375, 376, 377, 378, 379, 380, 381, 382, 383, 390, 391, 393, 395, 396, 397, 399, 400, 401
US 54, 57, 59, 60, 102, 134, 143, 160, 172, 173, 185, 217, 223, 229, 231, 233, 234, 295, 322, 334, 337, 352, 353, 354, 356, 391, 392, 396, 397, 400

Y

Yeltsin 20, 21, 22, 42, 47, 50, 52, 53, 54, 57, 67, 71, 72, 96, 100, 107, 108, 111, 112, 114, 115, 121, 142, 155, 158, 173, 174, 203, 216, 219, 221, 269, 270, 272, 273, 292, 293, 301, 349, 360, 362, 363
Yugoslavia 53, 61, 149, 152, 154, 155, 159

Z

Zizek 35, 133, 308, 318, 321, 361, 362
Zyuganov 76, 100, 114, 118, 219, 273, 300

SOVIET AND POST-SOVIET POLITICS AND SOCIETY

Edited by Dr. Andreas Umland

ISSN 1614-3515

1   Андреас Умланд (ред.)
    Воплощение Европейской
    конвенции по правам человека в
    России
    Философские, юридические и
    эмпирические исследования
    ISBN 3-89821-387-0

2   Christian Wipperfürth
    Russland – ein vertrauenswürdiger
    Partner?
    Grundlagen, Hintergründe und Praxis
    gegenwärtiger russischer Außenpolitik
    Mit einem Vorwort von Heinz Timmermann
    ISBN 3-89821-401-X

3   Manja Hussner
    Die Übernahme internationalen Rechts
    in die russische und deutsche
    Rechtsordnung
    Eine vergleichende Analyse zur
    Völkerrechtsfreundlichkeit der Verfassungen
    der Russländischen Föderation und der
    Bundesrepublik Deutschland
    Mit einem Vorwort von Rainer Arnold
    ISBN 3-89821-438-9

4   Matthew Tejada
    Bulgaria's Democratic Consolidation
    and the Kozloduy Nuclear Power Plant
    (KNPP)
    The Unattainability of Closure
    With a foreword by Richard J. Crampton
    ISBN 3-89821-439-7

5   Марк Григорьевич Меерович
    Квадратные метры, определяющие
    сознание
    Государственная жилищная политика в
    СССР. 1921 – 1941 гг
    ISBN 3-89821-474-5

6   Andrei P. Tsygankov, Pavel
    A.Tsygankov (Eds.)
    New Directions in Russian
    International Studies
    ISBN 3-89821-422-2

7   Марк Григорьевич Меерович
    Как власть народ к труду приучала
    Жилище в СССР – средство управления
    людьми. 1917 – 1941 гг.
    С предисловием Елены Осокиной
    ISBN 3-89821-495-8

8   David J. Galbreath
    Nation-Building and Minority Politics
    in Post-Socialist States
    Interests, Influence and Identities in Estonia
    and Latvia
    With a foreword by David J. Smith
    ISBN 3-89821-467-2

9   Алексей Юрьевич Безугольный
    Народы Кавказа в Вооруженных
    силах СССР в годы Великой
    Отечественной войны 1941-1945 гг.
    С предисловием Николая Бугая
    ISBN 3-89821-475-3

10 Вячеслав Лихачев и Владимир
    Прибыловский (ред.)
    Русское Национальное Единство,
    1990-2000. В 2-х томах
    ISBN 3-89821-523-7

11 Николай Бугай (ред.)
    Народы стран Балтии в условиях
    сталинизма (1940-е – 1950-е годы)
    Документированная история
    ISBN 3-89821-525-3

12 Ingmar Bredies (Hrsg.)
    Zur Anatomie der Orange Revolution
    in der Ukraine
    Wechsel des Elitenregimes oder Triumph des
    Parlamentarismus?
    ISBN 3-89821-524-5

13 Anastasia V. Mitrofanova
    The Politicization of Russian
    Orthodoxy
    Actors and Ideas
    With a foreword by William C. Gay
    ISBN 3-89821-481-8

14   Nathan D. Larson
      Alexander Solzhenitsyn and the
      Russo-Jewish Question
      ISBN 3-89821-483-4

15   *Guido Houben*
      Kulturpolitik und Ethnizität
      Staatliche Kunstförderung im Russland der
      neunziger Jahre
      Mit einem Vorwort von Gert Weisskirchen
      ISBN 3-89821-542-3

16   *Leonid Luks*
      Der russische „Sonderweg"?
      Aufsätze zur neuesten Geschichte Russlands
      im europäischen Kontext
      ISBN 3-89821-496-6

17   *Евгений Мороз*
      История «Мёртвой воды» – от
      страшной сказки к большой
      политике
      Политическое неоязычество в
      постсоветской России
      ISBN 3-89821-551-2

18   *Александр Верховский и Галина
      Кожевникова (ред.)*
      Этническая и религиозная
      интолерантность в российских СМИ
      Результаты мониторинга 2001-2004 гг.
      ISBN 3-89821-569-5

19   *Christian Ganzer*
      Sowjetisches Erbe und ukrainische
      Nation
      Das Museum der Geschichte des Zaporoger
      Kosakentums auf der Insel Chortycja
      Mit einem Vorwort von Frank Golczewski
      ISBN 3-89821-504-0

20   *Эльза-Баир Гучинова*
      Помнить нельзя забыть
      Антропология депортационной травмы
      калмыков
      С предисловием Кэролайн Хамфри
      ISBN 3-89821-506-7

21   *Юлия Лидерман*
      Мотивы «проверки» и «испытания»
      в постсоветской культуре
      Советское прошлое в российском
      кинематографе 1990-х годов
      С предисловием Евгения Марголита
      ISBN 3-89821-511-3

22   *Tanya Lokshina, Ray Thomas, Mary
      Mayer (Eds.)*
      The Imposition of a Fake Political
      Settlement in the Northern Caucasus
      The 2003 Chechen Presidential Election
      ISBN 3-89821-436-2

23   *Timothy McCajor Hall, Rosie Read
      (Eds.)*
      Changes in the Heart of Europe
      Recent Ethnographies of Czechs, Slovaks,
      Roma, and Sorbs
      With an afterword by Zdeněk Salzmann
      ISBN 3-89821-606-3

24   *Christian Autengruber*
      Die politischen Parteien in Bulgarien
      und Rumänien
      Eine vergleichende Analyse seit Beginn der
      90er Jahre
      Mit einem Vorwort von Dorothée de Nève
      ISBN 3-89821-476-1

25   *Annette Freyberg-Inan with Radu
      Cristescu*
      The Ghosts in Our Classrooms, or:
      John Dewey Meets Ceauşescu
      The Promise and the Failures of Civic
      Education in Romania
      ISBN 3-89821-416-8

26   *John B. Dunlop*
      The 2002 Dubrovka and 2004 Beslan
      Hostage Crises
      A Critique of Russian Counter-Terrorism
      With a foreword by Donald N. Jensen
      ISBN 3-89821-608-X

27   *Peter Koller*
      Das touristische Potenzial von
      Kam''janec'–Podil's'kyj
      Eine fremdenverkehrsgeographische
      Untersuchung der Zukunftsperspektiven und
      Maßnahmenplanung zur
      Destinationsentwicklung des „ukrainischen
      Rothenburg"
      Mit einem Vorwort von Kristiane Klemm
      ISBN 3-89821-640-3

28   *Françoise Daucé, Elisabeth Sieca-
      Kozlowski (Eds.)*
      Dedovshchina in the Post-Soviet
      Military
      Hazing of Russian Army Conscripts in a
      Comparative Perspective
      With a foreword by Dale Herspring
      ISBN 3-89821-616-0

29 *Florian Strasser*
Zivilgesellschaftliche Einflüsse auf die Orange Revolution
Die gewaltlose Massenbewegung und die ukrainische Wahlkrise 2004
Mit einem Vorwort von Egbert Jahn
ISBN 3-89821-648-9

30 *Rebecca S. Katz*
The Georgian Regime Crisis of 2003-2004
A Case Study in Post-Soviet Media Representation of Politics, Crime and Corruption
ISBN 3-89821-413-3

31 *Vladimir Kantor*
Willkür oder Freiheit
Beiträge zur russischen Geschichtsphilosophie
Ediert von Dagmar Herrmann sowie mit einem Vorwort versehen von Leonid Luks
ISBN 3-89821-589-X

32 *Laura A. Victoir*
The Russian Land Estate Today
A Case Study of Cultural Politics in Post-Soviet Russia
With a foreword by Priscilla Roosevelt
ISBN 3-89821-426-5

33 *Ivan Katchanovski*
Cleft Countries
Regional Political Divisions and Cultures in Post-Soviet Ukraine and Moldova
With a foreword by Francis Fukuyama
ISBN 3-89821-558-X

34 *Florian Mühlfried*
Postsowjetische Feiern
Das Georgische Bankett im Wandel
Mit einem Vorwort von Kevin Tuite
ISBN 3-89821-601-2

35 *Roger Griffin, Werner Loh, Andreas Umland (Eds.)*
Fascism Past and Present, West and East
An International Debate on Concepts and Cases in the Comparative Study of the Extreme Right
With an afterword by Walter Laqueur
ISBN 3-89821-674-8

36 *Sebastian Schlegel*
Der „Weiße Archipel"
Sowjetische Atomstädte 1945-1991
Mit einem Geleitwort von Thomas Bohn
ISBN 3-89821-679-9

37 *Vyacheslav Likhachev*
Political Anti-Semitism in Post-Soviet Russia
Actors and Ideas in 1991-2003
Edited and translated from Russian by Eugene Veklerov
ISBN 3-89821-529-6

38 *Josette Baer (Ed.)*
Preparing Liberty in Central Europe
Political Texts from the Spring of Nations 1848 to the Spring of Prague 1968
With a foreword by Zdeněk V. David
ISBN 3-89821-546-6

39 Михаил Лукьянов
Российский консерватизм и реформа, 1907-1914
С предисловием Марка Д. Стейнберга
ISBN 3-89821-503-2

40 *Nicola Melloni*
Market Without Economy
The 1998 Russian Financial Crisis
With a foreword by Eiji Furukawa
ISBN 3-89821-407-9

41 *Dmitrij Chmelnizki*
Die Architektur Stalins
Bd. 1: Studien zu Ideologie und Stil
Bd. 2: Bilddokumentation
Mit einem Vorwort von Bruno Flierl
ISBN 3-89821-515-6

42 *Katja Yafimava*
Post-Soviet Russian-Belarussian Relationships
The Role of Gas Transit Pipelines
With a foreword by Jonathan P. Stern
ISBN 3-89821-655-1

43 *Boris Chavkin*
Verflechtungen der deutschen und russischen Zeitgeschichte
Aufsätze und Archivfunde zu den Beziehungen Deutschlands und der Sowjetunion von 1917 bis 1991
Ediert von Markus Edlinger sowie mit einem Vorwort versehen von Leonid Luks
ISBN 3-89821-756-6

44 *Anastasija Grynenko in Zusammenarbeit mit Claudia Dathe*
Die Terminologie des Gerichtswesens der Ukraine und Deutschlands im Vergleich
Eine übersetzungswissenschaftliche Analyse juristischer Fachbegriffe im Deutschen, Ukrainischen und Russischen
Mit einem Vorwort von Ulrich Hartmann
ISBN 3-89821-691-8

45 *Anton Burkov*
The Impact of the European Convention on Human Rights on Russian Law
Legislation and Application in 1996-2006
With a foreword by Françoise Hampson
ISBN 978-3-89821-639-5

46 *Stina Torjesen, Indra Overland (Eds.)*
International Election Observers in Post-Soviet Azerbaijan
Geopolitical Pawns or Agents of Change?
ISBN 978-3-89821-743-9

47 *Taras Kuzio*
Ukraine – Crimea – Russia
Triangle of Conflict
ISBN 978-3-89821-761-3

48 *Claudia Šabić*
"Ich erinnere mich nicht, aber L'viv!"
Zur Funktion kultureller Faktoren für die Institutionalisierung und Entwicklung einer ukrainischen Region
Mit einem Vorwort von Melanie Tatur
ISBN 978-3-89821-752-1

49 *Marlies Bilz*
Tatarstan in der Transformation
Nationaler Diskurs und Politische Praxis 1988-1994
Mit einem Vorwort von Frank Golczewski
ISBN 978-3-89821-722-4

50 *Марлен Ларюэль (ред.)*
Современные интерпретации русского национализма
ISBN 978-3-89821-795-8

51 *Sonja Schüler*
Die ethnische Dimension der Armut
Roma im postsozialistischen Rumänien
Mit einem Vorwort von Anton Sterbling
ISBN 978-3-89821-776-7

52 *Галина Кожевникова*
Радикальный национализм в России и противодействие ему
Сборник докладов Центра «Сова» за 2004-2007 гг.
С предисловием Александра Верховского
ISBN 978-3-89821-721-7

53 *Галина Кожевникова и Владимир Прибыловский*
Российская власть в биографиях I
Высшие должностные лица РФ в 2004 г.
ISBN 978-3-89821-796-5

54 *Галина Кожевникова и Владимир Прибыловский*
Российская власть в биографиях II
Члены Правительства РФ в 2004 г.
ISBN 978-3-89821-797-2

55 *Галина Кожевникова и Владимир Прибыловский*
Российская власть в биографиях III
Руководители федеральных служб и агентств РФ в 2004 г.
ISBN 978-3-89821-798-9

56 *Ileana Petroniu*
Privatisierung in Transformationsökonomien
Determinanten der Restrukturierungs-Bereitschaft am Beispiel Polens, Rumäniens und der Ukraine
Mit einem Vorwort von Rainer W. Schäfer
ISBN 978-3-89821-790-3

57 *Christian Wipperfürth*
Russland und seine GUS-Nachbarn
Hintergründe, aktuelle Entwicklungen und Konflikte in einer ressourcenreichen Region
ISBN 978-3-89821-801-6

58 *Togzhan Kassenova*
From Antagonism to Partnership
The Uneasy Path of the U.S.-Russian Cooperative Threat Reduction
With a foreword by Christoph Bluth
ISBN 978-3-89821-707-1

59 *Alexander Höllwerth*
Das sakrale eurasische Imperium des Aleksandr Dugin
Eine Diskursanalyse zum postsowjetischen russischen Rechtsextremismus
Mit einem Vorwort von Dirk Uffelmann
ISBN 978-3-89821-813-9

60   Олег Рябов
     «Россия-Матушка»
     Национализм, гендер и война в России XX
     века
     С предисловием Елены Гощило
     ISBN 978-3-89821-487-2

61   *Ivan Maistrenko*
     Borot'bism
     A Chapter in the History of the Ukrainian
     Revolution
     With a new introduction by Chris Ford
     Translated by George S. N. Luckyj with the
     assistance of Ivan L. Rudnytsky
     ISBN 978-3-89821-697-5

62   *Maryna Romanets*
     Anamorphosic Texts and
     Reconfigured Visions
     Improvised Traditions in Contemporary
     Ukrainian and Irish Literature
     ISBN 978-3-89821-576-3

63   *Paul D'Anieri and Taras Kuzio (Eds.)*
     Aspects of the Orange Revolution I
     Democratization and Elections in Post-
     Communist Ukraine
     ISBN 978-3-89821-698-2

64   *Bohdan Harasymiw in collaboration
     with Oleh S. Ilnytzkyj (Eds.)*
     Aspects of the Orange Revolution II
     Information and Manipulation Strategies in
     the 2004 Ukrainian Presidential Elections
     ISBN 978-3-89821-699-9

65   *Ingmar Bredies, Andreas Umland and
     Valentin Yakushik (Eds.)*
     Aspects of the Orange Revolution III
     The Context and Dynamics of the 2004
     Ukrainian Presidential Elections
     ISBN 978-3-89821-803-0

66   *Ingmar Bredies, Andreas Umland and
     Valentin Yakushik (Eds.)*
     Aspects of the Orange Revolution IV
     Foreign Assistance and Civic Action in the
     2004 Ukrainian Presidential Elections
     ISBN 978-3-89821-808-5

67   *Ingmar Bredies, Andreas Umland and
     Valentin Yakushik (Eds.)*
     Aspects of the Orange Revolution V
     Institutional Observation Reports on the 2004
     Ukrainian Presidential Elections
     ISBN 978-3-89821-809-2

68   *Taras Kuzio (Ed.)*
     Aspects of the Orange Revolution VI
     Post-Communist Democratic Revolutions in
     Comparative Perspective
     ISBN 978-3-89821-820-7

69   *Tim Bohse*
     Autoritarismus statt Selbstverwaltung
     Die Transformation der kommunalen Politik
     in der Stadt Kaliningrad 1990-2005
     Mit einem Geleitwort von Stefan Troebst
     ISBN 978-3-89821-782-8

70   *David Rupp*
     Die Rußländische Föderation und die
     russischsprachige Minderheit in
     Lettland
     Eine Fallstudie zur Anwaltspolitik Moskaus
     gegenüber den russophonen Minderheiten im
     „Nahen Ausland" von 1991 bis 2002
     Mit einem Vorwort von Helmut Wagner
     ISBN 978-3-89821-778-1

71   *Taras Kuzio*
     Theoretical and Comparative
     Perspectives on Nationalism
     New Directions in Cross-Cultural and Post-
     Communist Studies
     With a foreword by Paul Robert Magocsi
     ISBN 978-3-89821-815-3

72   *Christine Teichmann*
     Die Hochschultransformation im
     heutigen Osteuropa
     Kontinuität und Wandel bei der Entwicklung
     des postkommunistischen Universitätswesens
     Mit einem Vorwort von Oskar Anweiler
     ISBN 978-3-89821-842-9

73   *Julia Kusznir*
     Der politische Einfluss von
     Wirtschaftseliten in russischen
     Regionen
     Eine Analyse am Beispiel der Erdöl- und
     Erdgasindustrie, 1992-2005
     Mit einem Vorwort von Wolfgang Eichwede
     ISBN 978-3-89821-821-4

74   *Alena Vysotskaya*
     Russland, Belarus und die EU-
     Osterweiterung
     Zur Minderheitenfrage und zum Problem der
     Freizügigkeit des Personenverkehrs
     Mit einem Vorwort von Katljin Malfliet
     ISBN 978-3-89821-822-1

75 Heiko Pleines (Hrsg.)
Corporate Governance in post-
sozialistischen Volkswirtschaften
ISBN 978-3-89821-766-8

76 Stefan Ihrig
Wer sind die Moldawier?
Rumänismus versus Moldowanismus in
Historiographie und Schulbüchern der
Republik Moldova, 1991-2006
Mit einem Vorwort von Holm Sundhaussen
ISBN 978-3-89821-466-7

77 Galina Kozhevnikova in collaboration
with Alexander Verkhovsky and
Eugene Veklerov
Ultra-Nationalism and Hate Crimes in
Contemporary Russia
The 2004-2006 Annual Reports of Moscow's
SOVA Center
With a foreword by Stephen D. Shenfield
ISBN 978-3-89821-868-9

78 Florian Küchler
The Role of the European Union in
Moldova's Transnistria Conflict
With a foreword by Christopher Hill
ISBN 978-3-89821-850-4

79 Bernd Rechel
The Long Way Back to Europe
Minority Protection in Bulgaria
With a foreword by Richard Crampton
ISBN 978-3-89821-863-4

80 Peter W. Rodgers
Nation, Region and History in Post-
Communist Transitions
Identity Politics in Ukraine, 1991-2006
With a foreword by Vera Tolz
ISBN 978-3-89821-903-7

81 Stephanie Solywoda
The Life and Work of
Semen L. Frank
A Study of Russian Religious Philosophy
With a foreword by Philip Walters
ISBN 978-3-89821-457-5

82 Vera Sokolova
Cultural Politics of Ethnicity
Discourses on Roma in Communist
Czechoslovakia
ISBN 978-3-89821-864-1

83 Natalya Shevchik Ketenci
Kazakhstani Enterprises in Transition
The Role of Historical Regional Development
in Kazakhstan's Post-Soviet Economic
Transformation
ISBN 978-3-89821-831-3

84 Martin Malek, Anna Schor-
Tschudnowskaja (Hrsg.)
Europa im Tschetschenienkrieg
Zwischen politischer Ohnmacht und
Gleichgültigkeit
Mit einem Vorwort von Lipchan Basajewa
ISBN 978-3-89821-676-0

85 Stefan Meister
Das postsowjetische Universitätswesen
zwischen nationalem und
internationalem Wandel
Die Entwicklung der regionalen Hochschule
in Russland als Gradmesser der
Systemtransformation
Mit einem Vorwort von Joan DeBardeleben
ISBN 978-3-89821-891-7

86 Konstantin Sheiko in collaboration
with Stephen Brown
Nationalist Imaginings of the
Russian Past
Anatolii Fomenko and the Rise of Alternative
History in Post-Communist Russia
With a foreword by Donald Ostrowski
ISBN 978-3-89821-915-0

87 Sabine Jenni
Wie stark ist das „Einige Russland"?
Zur Parteibindung der Eliten und zum
Wahlerfolg der Machtpartei
im Dezember 2007
Mit einem Vorwort von Klaus Armingeon
ISBN 978-3-89821-961-7

88 Thomas Borén
Meeting-Places of Transformation
Urban Identity, Spatial Representations and
Local Politics in Post-Soviet St Petersburg
ISBN 978-3-89821-739-2

89 Aygul Ashirova
Stalinismus und Stalin-Kult in
Zentralasien
Turkmenistan 1924-1953
Mit einem Vorwort von Leonid Luks
ISBN 978-3-89821-987-7

90 Leonid Luks
    Freiheit oder imperiale Größe?
    Essays zu einem russischen Dilemma
    ISBN 978-3-8382-0011-8

91 Christopher Gilley
    The 'Change of Signposts' in the
    Ukrainian Emigration
    A Contribution to the History of
    Sovietophilism in the 1920s
    With a foreword by Frank Golczewski
    ISBN 978-3-89821-965-5

92 Philipp Casula, Jeronim Perovic
    (Eds.)
    Identities and Politics
    During the Putin Presidency
    The Discursive Foundations of Russia's
    Stability
    With a foreword by Heiko Haumann
    ISBN 978-3-8382-0015-6

Quotes from reviews of SPPS volumes:

On vol. 1 – *The Implementation of the ECHR in Russia*: "Full of examples, experiences and valuable observations which could provide the basis for new strategies."
Diana Schmidt, *Neprikosnovennyi zapas*

On vol. 2 – *Putins Russland*: "Wipperfürth draws attention to little known facts. For instance, the Russians have still more positive feelings towards Germany than to any other non-Slavic country."
Oldag Kaspar, *Süddeutsche Zeitung*

On vol. 3 – *Die Übernahme internationalen Rechts in die russische Rechtsordnung*: "Hussner's is an interesting, detailed and, at the same time, focused study which deals with all relevant aspects and contains insights into contemporary Russian legal thought."
Herbert Küpper, *Jahrbuch für Ostrecht*

On vol. 5 – *Квадратные метры, определяющие сознание*: "Meerovich provides a study that will be of considerable value to housing specialists and policy analysts."
Christina Varga-Harris, *Slavic Review*

On vol. 6 – *New Directions in Russian International Studies*: "A helpful step in the direction of an overdue dialogue between Western and Russian IR scholarly communities."
Diana Schmidt, *Europe-Asia Studies*

On vol. 8 – *Nation-Building and Minority Politics in Post-Socialist States*: "Galbreath's book is an admirable and craftsmanlike piece of work, and should be read by all specialists interested in the Baltic area."
Andrejs Plakans, *Slavic Review*

On vol. 9 – *Народы Кавказа в Вооружённых силах СССР*: "In this superb new book, Bezugolnyi skillfully fashions an accurate and candid record of how and why the Soviet Union mobilized and employed the various ethnic groups in the Caucasus region in the Red Army's World War II effort."
David J. Glantz, *Journal of Slavic Military Studies*

On vol. 10 – *Русское Национальное Единство*: "A work that is likely to remain the definitive study of the Russian National Unity for a very long time."
Mischa Gabowitsch, *e-Extreme*

On vol. 14 – *Aleksandr Solzhenitsyn and the Modern Russo-Jewish Question*: "Larson has written a well-balanced survey of Solzhenitsyn's writings on Russian-Jewish relations."
Nikolai Butkevich, *e-Extreme*

On vol. 16 – *Der russische "Sonderweg"?*: "Luks's remarkable knowledge of the history of this wide territory from the Elbe to the Pacific Ocean and his life experience give his observations a particular sharpness and his judgements an exceptional weight."

Peter Krupnikow, *Mitteilungen aus dem baltischen Leben*

On vol. 17 – *История «Мёртвой воды»*: "Moroz provides one of the best available surveys of Russian neo-paganism."

Mischa Gabowitsch, *e-Extreme*

On vol. 18 – *Этническая и религиозная интолерантность в российских СМИ*: "A constructive contribution to a crucial debate about media-endorsed intolerance which has once again flared up in Russia."

Mischa Gabowitsch, *e-Extreme*

On vol. 25 – *The Ghosts in Our Classroom*: "Inan-Freyberg's well-researched and incisive monograph, balanced and informed about Romanian education in general, should be required reading for those Eurocrats who have shaped Romanian spending priorities since 2000."

Tom Gallagher, *Slavic Review*

On vol. 26 – *The 2002 Dubrovka and 2004 Beslan Hostage Crises:* "Dunlop's analysis will help to draw Western attention to the plight of those who have suffered by these terrorist acts, and the importance, for all Russians, of uncovering the truth of about what happened."

Amy Knight, *Times Literary Supplement*

On vol. 29 – *Zivilgesellschaftliche Einflüsse auf die Orange Revolution*: "Strasser's study constitutes an outstanding empirical analysis and well-grounded location of the subject within theory."

Heiko Pleines, *Osteuropa*

On vol. 33 – *Cleft Countries*: "Katchanovski succeeds in crafting a convincing and well-supported set of arguments and his research certainly constitutes a step forward in dealing with the notoriously thorny concept of political culture."

Thomas E. Rotnem, *Political Studies Review*

On vol. 34 – *Postsowjetische Feiern*: "Mühlfried's book contains not only a solid ethnographic study, but also points at some problems emerging from Georgia's prevalent understanding of culture."

Godula Kosack, *Anthropos*

On vol. 35 – *Fascism Past and Present, West and East*: "Committed students will find much of interest in these sometimes barbed exchanges."
Robert Paxton, *Journal of Global History*

On vol. 37 – *Political Anti-Semitism in Post-Soviet Russia*: "Likhachev's book serves as a reliable compendium and a good starting point for future research on post-Soviet xenophobia and ultra-nationalist politics, with their accompanying anti-Semitism."
Kathleen Mikkelson, *Demokratizatsiya*

On vol. 39 – *Российский консерватизм и реформа 1907-1914*: "Luk'ianov's work is a well-researched, informative and valuable addition, and enhances our understanding of politics in late imperial Russia."
Matthew Rendle, *Revolutionary Russia*

On vol. 43 – *Verflechtungen der deutschen und russischen Zeitgeschichte:* "Khavkin's book should be of interest to everybody studying German-Soviet relations and highlights new aspects in that field."
Wiebke Bachmann, *Osteuropa*

On vol. 50 – *Современные интерпретации русского национализма*: "This thought-provoking and enlightening set of works offers valuable insights for anyone interested in understanding existing expressions and interpretations of Russian nationalism."
Andrew Konitzer, *The Russian Review*

On vol. 57 – *Russland und seine GUS-Nachbarn*: "Wipperfürth's enlightening and objective analysis documents detailed background knowledge and understanding of complex relationships. "
Julia Schatte, *Eurasisches Magazin*

On vol. 59 – *Das sakrale eurasische Imperium des Aleksandr Dugin*: "Höllwerth's outstanding 700-page dissertation is certainly the, so far, most ambitious attempt to decipher Dugin's body of thought."
Tanja Fichtner, *Osteuropa*

On vol. 80 – *Nation, Region and History in Post-Communist Transition*: "Rodgers provides with his analysis an important contribution to a specific view on Ukraine."
Marinke Gindullis, *Zeitschrift für Politikwissenschaft*

Series Subscription

Please enter my subscription to the series *Soviet and Post-Soviet Politics and Society*, ISSN 1614-3515, as follows:

❏ complete series   OR   ❏ English-language titles
                                    ❏ German-language titles
                                    ❏ Russian-language titles
starting with
❏ volume # 1
❏ volume # ___
    ❏ please also include the following volumes: #___, ___, ___, ___, ___, ___, ___
❏ the next volume being published
    ❏ please also include the following volumes: #___, ___, ___, ___, ___, ___, ___

❏ 1 copy per volume   OR   ❏ ___ copies per volume

Subscription within Germany:
You will receive every volume at 1st publication at the regular bookseller's price – incl. s & h and VAT.
Payment:
❏ Please bill me for every volume.
❏ Lastschriftverfahren: Ich/wir ermächtige(n) Sie hiermit widerruflich, den Rechnungsbetrag je Band von meinem/unserem folgendem Konto einzuziehen.

Kontoinhaber: _____ Kreditinstitut: _____
Kontonummer: _____ Bankleitzahl: _____

International Subscription:
Payment (incl. s & h and VAT) in advance for
❏ 10 volumes/copies (€ 319.80)   ❏ 20 volumes/copies (€ 599.80)
❏ 40 volumes/copies (€ 1,099.80)
Please send my books to:

NAME _____ DEPARTMENT _____
ADDRESS _____
POST/ZIP CODE _____ COUNTRY _____
TELEPHONE _____ EMAIL _____

date/signature _____

A hint for librarians in the former Soviet Union: Your academic library might be eligible to receive free-of-cost scholarly literature from Germany via the German Research Foundation. For Russian-language information on this program, see
http://www.dfg.de/forschungsfoerderung/formulare/download/12_54.pdf.

Please fax to: **0511 / 262 2201 (+49 511 262 2201)**
or mail to: *ibidem*-Verlag, Julius-Leber-Weg 11, D-30457 Hannover, Germany
or send an e-mail: ibidem@ibidem-verlag.de

ibidem-Verlag
Melchiorstr. 15
D-70439 Stuttgart
info@ibidem-verlag.de

www.ibidem-verlag.de
www.ibidem.eu
www.edition-noema.de
www.autorenbetreuung.de